WARS

OF THE

IRISH KINGS

ALSO BY
DAVID WILLIS McCULLOUGH

FICTION
Think on Death
Point No-Point

NONFICTION
People, Books & Book People
Brooklyn . . . and How It Got That Way

ANTHOLOGIES
Great Detectives
American Childhoods
City Sleuths and Tough Guys
Chronicles of the Barbarians

WARS
OF THE
IRISH KINGS

A THOUSAND YEARS OF STRUGGLE
FROM THE AGE OF MYTH THROUGH THE
REIGN OF QUEEN ELIZABETH I

EDITED BY
DAVID WILLIS McCULLOUGH

Crown Publishers
New York

The endpaper art depicts Kinsale in 1601: the Spanish-held village near Cork is besieged by the English, who in turn are attacked by the combined forces of Hugh O'Neill and Hugh O'Donnell. The disastrous result was a turning point in Irish history. This picture-map is a detail of the bottom right corner of a massive wall-hung painting, currently located outside the Henry Jones room in the National Library of Ireland.

Copyright © 2000 by David Willis McCullough

Published by Crown Publishers, New York, New York
Member of the Crown Publishing Group
Random House, Inc. New York, Toronto, London, Sydney, Auckland
www.randomhouse.com

Published simultaneously with the History Book Club, New York.

CROWN is a trademark and the Crown colophon is a registered trademark of Random House, Inc.

Design by Felicia Telsey-MacKinnon

Printed in the United States of America

Library of Congress Cataloging-in-Publication Data is available upon request.

ISBN 0-8129-3233-1

10 9 8 7 6 5 4 3 2 1

First Crown Edition

*For Meghan Elizabeth Sheridan
and Darian O'Brien Cork*

ACKNOWLEDGMENTS

Three people played key roles in the creation of this book. In the beginning there was Leslie Pockell, and at the end there were Kathleen Kiernan and Benjamin Hallman. I am also most appreciative of the thoughtful advice of Katharine Simms, professor of medieval history at Trinity College, Dublin, and of Catherine McKenna, professor of medieval studies at the New York University Graduate Program. Their kind generosity, of course, should not be thought to include their imprimatur. Finally there are the libraries. This book could not have existed without them: the New York Public Library, the Hastings-on-Hudson Library, and the Westchester County Library System in the United States, and the National Library of Ireland, the Royal Irish Academy, and the Royal Antiquarian Society, all in Dublin. And before them, there were all those people whose names we don't know or have barely heard, who for one reason or another chose to write down or preserve what they believed—or hoped—was the history of their land.

—D.W.McC.

CONTENTS

CONTENTS

Illustrations follow pages 64, 160, and 256.

A BATTLE BEGINS

The battalions then made a stout, furious, barbarous, smashing onset on each other. But, alas! these were the faces of foes in battle-field, and not the faces of friends at a feast. And each party of them remembered their ancient animosities towards each other, and each party of them attacked the other. And it will be one of the wonders of the day of judgment to relate the description of this tremendous onset. And there arose a wild, impetuous, precipitate, furious, dark, frightful, voracious, merciless, combative, contentious vulture, screaming and fluttering over their heads. And there arose also the satyrs, and the idiots, and the maniacs of the valleys, and the witches, and the goblins, and the ancient birds, and the destroying demons of the air and of the firmament, and the feeble demoniac phantom host; and they were screaming and comparing the valour and combat of both parties.

—From *The War of the Gaedhil with the Gaill,*
twelfth century

INTRODUCTION
NOTHING BUT TROUBLE

L OOKING BACK ACROSS THE thousand or so years between the mythical legends of Ireland's origins and the disastrous battle at Kinsale
in 1601, it seems downright shortsighted that people pick out a few
years in the twentieth century and call them "The Troubles." Offhand, it
looks as though there was nothing but trouble from the very beginning.

It all began—so we're told in *Lebor Gabala* (*The Book of Invasions*)—
during the lifetime of the biblical Abraham, 310 years after Noah's flood.
Ireland had been peacefully invaded by a leader named Partholon. The
rivers and lakes had been created. The first natural death and burial had
taken place, and the first incident of adultery was just about to happen,
when Ireland witnessed its first battle. Partholon's men took on the
Fomoire (who may have been monsters from the sea) on a field near
Dublin Bay. *The Book of Invasions* tells us that the enemy was men with
"single noble legs and single full hands," that there were three hundred of
them, that their leader's mother had four eyes on her back, and that they
were "cut down in a week." But, unfortunately, the book doesn't tell how
an army of one-armed, one-legged men actually fought. It must have
involved a good deal of hopping around.

The Partholonians were the first of a series of invaders, each of which
brought something to the island (everyone's favorite conqueror seems to
be the Tuatha De Danann, from the Greek isles, who brought magic and
the arts), and each is defeated in turn until the arrival of Miles Hispaniae
(his name means "the soldier from Spain") and his followers, who are the
forebears of the Irish. Or so the story goes.

One of the remarkable things about Ireland is that very early in its history decisions were made in monasteries all over the island to record stories like these about its history and what was thought to be its history.
Later, in the twelfth century, these earlier records and memories of the oral
tradition of storytelling were used to create books meant to be read—and
this is both unusual and important—by laymen as well as monks and

priests. These early scribe-historians created a literature shaped by political propaganda, family pride, a bit (but not much) of religiosity, and the love of a good story that glorified, romanticized, or simply recorded the past. At the very beginning of Irish history, it would seem, there was already nostalgia for an earlier time. There was a strong sense that current events could be justified—or explained—by knowledge of past events.

Another wave of historical interest came in the seventeenth century, and in the nineteenth century, amid an awakened sense of nationalism, those ancient documents—still amazingly preserved—were rediscovered and translated into English.

The earliest tales, although not the first written, were about the mythical conquests that created Ireland. They combined references to events in the Old Testament and Greek mythology with ancient Irish gods and heroes (who seem cut from the same cloth), and actual historical events. Take, for instance, two battles fought during the De Danann conquest on different parts of the plain—called Moytura (Mag Tured)—outside Sligo. The first battle was probably based on a historical event. The second, which we are told took place at the time of the Trojan War, probably was not. Gods stroll around quite casually, and one of them—known for his gluttony and love of porridge—is used for comic relief. There is a hero who cannot be voted king because he lost an arm in battle and kings must be physically intact, but then a magical craftsman makes him a silver arm, which, not surprisingly, turns into a real arm. And that may be a way of explaining through myth how one ancient, maimed chieftain got around the rules of kingship.

Long after the waves of invasions covered in *Lebor Gabala*, two great figures emerge in early literature: Cuchulain and Finn MacCool. Cuchulain is the hero of Ulster, who has two fathers, the king of Cooley and the god Lug. The entire Ulster Cycle of stories is built around him, the most famous being the *Tain Bo Cuailnge* (*The Cattle Raid of Cooley*), which is usually pointed out as the finest example of early Irish literature. In spite of his great deeds (the Irish Hercules is an overused phrase), there is often a tinge of sadness about Cuchulain, and his frequent rages make him appear to be more than a little insane.

Finn MacCool (Fionn mac Cuimhaill) appears later in Irish mythical history, and with his loyal knights, the Fenians (the legends about him are called the Fenian Cycle), he often resembles an Irish King Arthur. Finn and his entire court became extremely popular with artists and composers in the nineteenth century. It seems likely that Sir William Wilde, a society eye surgeon in Dublin as well as an amateur archaeologist, and his wife, who wrote romantically nationalist poems under the name Speranza, probably named their younger son after Finn's brave and handsome grandson with the decidedly un-Irish-sounding name of Oscar.

The "real" history during this time was being recorded by annalists, monks who compiled year-by-year records of what they thought to be important, including the death of kings, local battles, rumors of trouble elsewhere, ecclesiastical appointments, weather reports, and amazing happenings such as a mermaid washing ashore. The earliest histories were based on these annals as have most medieval histories of Ireland ever since. Later, compilations of annals, from individual monasteries were made to create annals of provinces and the country as a whole. The most important of these was a mammoth work called *Annals of the Four Masters,* compiled in the early seventeenth century by a group of Donegal Franciscans.

The earliest histories, such as the one written in Irish by Geoffrey Keating at the beginning of the seventeenth century, were a liberal mixture of the annals and material from the myths presented as fact. Keating, for example, includes Partholon's first battle but never says how many limbs the Fomoire had. As Irish history progresses from local squabbles, through the real invasions of Vikings, English, and Scots, to the rise of truly national leaders such as Brian Boru (an upstart king from nowhere) and Hugh O'Neill (who had the most distinguished name in Ireland), more and more hands became involved in the writing of history. But two themes persist. One is the coming and going of kings. The other is war.

⚜

The saints aside, Ireland's earliest visitors from abroad were military men who seemed to be confused by the number of kings they encountered and by the curious way the Irish fought their battles. The two oddities were, in fact, connected.

From its earliest days Ireland was divided into four tidy quarters, the provinces—moving clockwise—of Ulster, Leinster, Munster, and Connacht. There was a single high king (*ard ri*) of all Ireland who ruled from the sacred hill of Tara, sacred to both pagans and Christians, but more often than not it was an empty title. A few high kings such as Rory O'Connor (Ruaidri O'Conchobhair), who ruled at the time of the English invasion in 1170, were powerful leaders, but the *ard ri*'s influence was more mystical, even religious, than political or military. In time the title would become just another glittering adornment of the O'Neill family. Below the high king, each province had its king, and below each of them were dozens of lesser kings. As the Norman author of the *Song of Dermot and the Earl* observes, there were as many kings in Ireland as there were counts in other lands. It is partly a semantic problem—the word *ri* does not in fact mean "king"—but king was what they were called, and between the fifth and twelfth centuries there could have been as many as 150 of them, great and small, ruling at a time.

And none of them, great or small, inherited his crown outright.

Each Irish king was chosen or approved by the nobles of his kingdom. *Elected* is probably too democratic a word for it, and as a matter of practice sons did tend to follow their fathers onto the throne. But it did not have to be that way. Any man who was a son, grandson, or great-grandson of a king could become king if he had the support of the men—frequently his relatives—who were his rivals for office. This constant search for a constituency was the primary cause of most of the small Irish wars, not, as was traditionally the case in Europe, a king's desire for more land to rule. Besides battles, other ways of winning support included bribery and marriage, which partially explains the elaborate medieval rituals of gift giving and the fact that so many Irish battles seem to have been between sons and fathers-in-law or brother-in-law against brother-in-law. By its very nature it was an unstable system that discouraged central government.

In fact, land in pre-twelfth-century Ireland had little political value. Although there were rich plains, it was not a farming culture but a decentralized grazing one in which wealth was measured in cattle. There were no cities, and the kingdoms, which rarely had roads or clearly defined boundaries, were separated by dense forests and bogs, which were more of a deterrent to travel (or easy military movement) than the mountains. A reading of the sometimes-cryptic early annals suggests an endless series of battles and cattle raids. To be glib, early medieval Ireland sounds like a somewhat crazed Wisconsin, in which every dairy farm is an armed camp at perpetual war with its neighbors, and every farmer claims he is a king.

Ireland was also seriously underpopulated. Scholars have estimated that there were only about half a million people on the entire island. Military activity was costly both in actual expense and in time taken away from earning a living. For in spite of what sounds like constant combat, there was no military class in Ireland, no standing armies always at the ready. When a king needed an army, he called up a "hosting," a temporary draft, during which his subjects dropped what they were doing and turned out armed and ready to fight or threaten. It was a system that discouraged long military campaigns in favor of single—often indecisive—battles.

Just as there were hints of democracy in the selection of kings, there was a suggestion of a citizen army here that was unknown in feudal Europe. Although these conscripts were not paid until the late sixteenth century (unlike the hired mercenaries brought over from Scotland), host-ings were so expensive they rarely lasted for more than a few months. Unfortunately, one way of saving money and time was to not fight an enemy's army directly but to try to weaken him by pillaging his land, burning the homes and barns of his people, kidnapping their daughters and young men of fighting age, and making off with the cattle, if only to hold the cows hostage for ransom.

Which brings us to the Irish fighting style, a style that seemed to change little in the six hundred years after the first millennium. Mobility was the key. They never wore armor (except leather vests) even after it had been introduced to the island by the Vikings and the English. They carried small, round shields, swords, spears, and sharp, deadly darts. Horses, when they used them, were small and fast, unlike the massive warhorses of Europe.

Their tactics confused outsiders as much as the American colonists' tactics later confused the English and later still the Vietcong the Americans. The Tudor poet Edmund Spenser, an Englishman who parlayed a bureau-cratic government job in Dublin into an Irish estate (and a loathing of the Irish), wrote the following in his *A View of the State of Ireland* (1633):

> It is well known that [the Irishman] is a flying enemy, hiding himself in woods and bogs from whence he will not draw forth [except] into some straight passage and perilous ford, where he knows the army must need pass, there will he lie in wait, and, if he find advantage fit, will dangerously hazard the troubled soldier. Therefore, to seek him out that still flitteth and follow him that can hardly be found [would be] vain and bootless; but I would divide my men in garrison upon his country in such places as I think must most annoy him.

Which pretty much sums up the English policy in Ireland for hundreds of years.

According to Katharine Simms, an Irish medievalist, two quotations epitomize the situation. The first is from the fourteenth-century French writer Jean Froissart: "It is hard to find a way of making war on the Irish effectively for, unless they choose, there is no one there to fight and there are no towns to be found." The second is a paraphrase of something an Irish king says in the fourteenth-century Scottish poem "The Bruce" by John Barbour: "Our custom is to pursue and fight and fight when retreat-ing, and not to stand in hand-to-hand conflict until the other side is defeated."

Yet, in spite of what Froissart thought, many people did manage to "war on the Irish effectively." Beginning in the ninth century, Ireland experienced a new wave of invaders, and this time there was nothing mythical about them. The Viking raids began as just that: quick looting expeditions in which a ship or two would put ashore only long enough for its warriors to take what they could carry away. Later entire fleets came, but rather than leaving established settlements, they would pillage and go. It has been said that the Vikings' great gifts to Ireland were red heads and cities. The gift of red hair may be debatable, but there were no cities in Ireland until Viking winter camps and trading posts alongside harbors all around the island grew and became known by names such as Dublin, Wexford, Waterford, Cork, and Limerick.

As the years went by after the first raids, the Vikings—most of whom came from present-day Norway and Denmark—played greater social and commercial roles in Irish life. In occupied areas, Viking men were quartered in Irish homes. Viking armies took sides in local wars. And in the eleventh century, an obscure king from the west named Brian Boru grew in power and influence and became known—at least in retrospect—as the man who defeated the Vikings.

There are two great expulsion myths in early Irish history. One was that St. Patrick drove out the snakes in the fifth century, the other that Brian Boru drove out the Vikings in the eleventh. Of course there were no snakes to begin with and the Vikings never left, but both men—one in religion, one in government—became Ireland's first national leaders. Brian challenged the traditional role of minor Irish kings by seeking control of more and more land and more and more kingdoms until much of the island (the very north excepted) was his to command. He forced the high king—an O'Neill, of course—to step aside and had himself crowned in his place, not at Tara, as tradition would have it, but on another sacred hill. This one, Cashel, was in the south. He was killed at Clontarf on Dublin Bay in 1014, defeating a combined army of rebellious Irish and Vikings from both Dublin and abroad. Afterward, in a pattern that would become familiar in Irish history, things went back pretty much to the way they were before. Only now, Brian's family clan, who once called themselves the Dal Cais, would be known as the O'Briens, and they would do all they could to keep alive the memory of their family hero.

The next invasion came a century and a half later, and it would change Ireland forever. It used to be popular to call it the Norman invasion, although the invaders did not come from Normandy. Many call it the English invasion, although few of the invaders were actually English. Welsh nationalists have been heard to call it the Welsh Conquest of

Ireland, since the invaders—Normans whose families had settled in southern Wales after 1066—did indeed sail from there. But whatever its name, the little army that landed on the coast between Waterford and Wexford in 1170, and began its first battle against the Irish by driving a herd of captured cattle toward them, brought English rule to Ireland.

The situation, of course, was not as simple as it seemed. The Welsh-Normans (let's call them that) had been invited over by an Irish king to fight with him against the high king, lured with promises of land and—in one case—marriage to the king's daughter. They invaded without the permission of the English king, who, as it happened, had the blessing of the pope to make just such a move. The Irish, so Pope Adrian IV wrote King Henry II, had strayed from St. Patrick's example. But Henry had other problems to worry about, the French in particular. As for the pope, who believed the sinful ways of the Irish needed to be straightened out by a firm hand from abroad, he was English, the only Englishman ever to be pope.

Led by an earl called Strongbow (his name was actually Richard de Clare), the invaders moved without too much trouble from Waterford to Dublin, and although there were a few sallies into the west, English power more or less centered on that broad corridor. King Henry rushed over belatedly to put the crown's stamp on the earl's upstart Irish enterprise and accept the allegiance of the Irish kings. Then the English got down to business making money in Dublin, while new Norman landowners got to work building castles on their new estates in the south and southeast. The Irish kings, for the most part, found themselves ignored and stronger than ever. It's unclear whether the general moral tone of the land was changed one way or the other.

Next came the Scots in an invasion history has largely forgotten about, perhaps because there has always been a strong Scottish presence on the island. The strait between the east coast of Ulster and the west coast of Scotland is only about twenty miles wide, and as early as the third century a Celtic clan called the Dal Riada spanned the divide and in time introduced both Gaelic and Christianity eastward into Scotland. The Viking raids broke the clan in two, but a close relationship continued. In the twelfth century, the Irish kings began hiring Scots mercenaries called gallowglass (and later redshanks, because of their bare legs) to fight in their wars.

The gallowglass were not common foot soldiers (or kerns), but minor knights for hire, who, unlike the Irish, wore distinctive light armor, chain-mail jerkins, and pointed metal helmets that can still be easily spotted in medieval tombstone carvings. Their favorite weapon was a pole ax with a foot-long head; according to the military historian G. A. Hayes-McCoy, a contemporary described it as "resembling double bladed hatchets, almost

A gallowglass soldier.

sharper than razors, fixed on shafts of more than ordinary length, which when they strike they inflict a dreadful wound." Most gallowglass came attended by two young squires, one carrying weapons (which also included javelins and darts), the other, provisions. By the fifteenth century entire families of gallowglass had settled in northern Ireland, the MacDonalds and the MacSwineys being among the best known. Unlike their neighbors, they were still paid to fight, only now they lived locally.

In 1315, a year after Robert Bruce defeated the English at Bannockburn in Scotland and became king of the Scots, his brother Edward led a huge army across the strait to Larne in Ulster and declared himself king of the Irish. There has always been debate over what the Bruces were up to. They may have just been putting another thorn in the side of the hated English. Or they may have honestly been trying to inspire their Gaelic brothers from across the sea to rise up and fight for a nation of their own. (A similar plan was in the works for Wales.) Perhaps Edward simply wanted a kingdom like his older brother's. Whatever the motive, the Bruces had the support of a few Irish leaders in the north and clearly hoped their presence would inspire a general uprising against the English. One of the Scots' allies was Donal O'Neill (Donnall Ua Neill), a local king who had been having his own problems with the English. In 1317 he sent Pope John XXII his "Remonstrance of the Irish Princes," which, with its list of outrages committed by a foreign king and its justification for rebellion, bears a sometimes striking resemblance to the American Declaration of Independence written four and a half centuries later:

> [In] order to shake off the harsh and insupportable yoke of servitude to them [the English] and to recover our native freedom, which for the time being we have lost through them, we are compelled to enter a deadly war against the aforementioned, preferring . . . to face the dangers of war like men in defense of our right rather than to go on bearing their cruel outrages like women.
>
> And in order to achieve our aim more swiftly and more fully in this matter we call to our help and assistance the illustrious Edward de Bruce, earl of Carrick and brother of the Lord Robert by grace of God the most illustrious king of Scots, and sprung from our noblest ancestors.

O'Neill, of course, was not choosing independence but an allegiance to a new monarch whom he saw, interestingly enough, as having a common ancestry with the Irish.

But an uprising of support never came. And in the three years before Edward was killed in battle not far from where his troops had originally landed, his forays around northern Ireland produced nothing but devastation and famine. Ireland returned to its old ways with the English pretty much keeping within what was called the English Pale, the area around Dublin that included what are now the counties of Meath, Louth, and Kildare, while elsewhere the kings continued their traditional rivalries. The area within the Pale (which at one time had actually been marked off with an earthen dike or pale) was called "The Land of Peace." The "unprotected" rest of Ireland was "The Land of War."

The next great struggle—the one that put an end to the notion that there were kings of Ireland or that there were parts of the island that were not under English domination—was triggered not by an invasion but by an edict from London. In 1536, Henry VIII, as part of his break with Rome, declared himself head of the church in England and Ireland. The churches, from country chapels to the two great cathedrals in Dublin, became Protestant, the monasteries were dissolved, and the Irish people had a new term of identity. The buildings may have converted, but most of the people did not. They were now not only Irish but Catholic as well. What followed was a series of revolts that culminated in Hugh O'Neill's rebellion, which is often called the Nine Years War.

Under Henry VIII and his daughter Elizabeth, English policy was to no longer stay within the Pale but to control—or try to—the whole land. Confronted by O'Neill, who was the earl of Tyrone and a master of the Irish art of hit-and-run warfare, the English were baffled, at least until he changed his tactics. In 1601, O'Neill's new ally, His Most Catholic Majesty Philip III of Spain, ordered a small army to Ireland to help the rebels. They landed in the south and took the walled city of Kinsale, near Cork. The English laid siege, and O'Neill, his fellow rebel Hugh O'Donnell, and their men rushed to aid the Spaniards. The traditional, and terribly brief, European-style battle that followed was a disaster that many came to believe blighted the cause of Irish independence for generations to come. There were—and still are—recriminations and bouts of what-if second-guessing, but no one, any longer, talked of Irish kings unless telling stories from the past.

This collection, however, is nothing but stories from the past about how, over the course of about a thousand years, a few kings from generations of kings in a country on the edge of the known world fought their battles. It does not attempt to be a detailed history of early Ireland. Every effort has been made to find source material that was written as closely as possible to the time of the events it describes. None of the texts is more recent than the seventeenth century, and even that material is based on earlier sources. This choice was made not because older material was thought to be more accurate. As most police officers understand, no one's story is more untrustworthy than that of an eyewitness, unless it's the story of someone an eyewitness told his story to. What the early sources do is create a vivid feeling for the times in which the original events took place and a sense of the biases and thought processes that combine with fact to create what we call history.

Henry Ford once got into a lot of trouble for calling history "more or less bunk." It is unclear what he meant by *bunk*, but it is clear that in spite of our love of facts and tidy accuracy, history is more or less what the historians and storytellers down the ages have said it is. This collection is a compendium of lies, distortions, myths, dreams, facts, and amazing insights, and the best we can hope from it is a raw and perhaps astonishing appreciation of a time we can never fully understand. In its way, the collection is a history of how Irish history has come to be written.

The material includes the annals of medieval monks, the diary of a siege, unabashed political propaganda for one family or another, honest attempts at accurate history, and the record of early myths and tales. An Irish historian who looked at a proposed table of contents advised—vigorously—that readers must be warned that not all the entries should be treated with the same level of credulity. The introduction and notes in each chapter are intended to guide the reader toward a reasonable level of skepticism. The editor's advice is to believe nothing outright, then enjoy everything for its sheer exuberance.

Reading much of this book should be like looking at a primitive painting. The genius is in the small details. Look, for example, at the version of the fourteenth-century battle fought outside Athenry in Raphael Holinshed's *Chronicles of Ireland*. It was a terrible slaughter, and the author dutifully lists the names of some of the celebrity casualties, but the story he tells in detail is about a young soldier. He is sent back onto the field after the battle is over to see if his officer's enemy is indeed dead. The enemy—his name is O'Kelley—appears and, in effect, offers the young soldier a job. As a result there is more bloodshed. It is a curious tale, but the details bring the battle statistics alive. In *The Book of Howth* some soldiers cannot believe that their officer, a Scot, probably a gallowglass, is indeed dead, so they bring by a woman and then some food to see if he will revive, and in the end they still cannot bear to bury him.

Of course some of the writing here is highly sophisticated. *The Tain* (*The Cattle Raid of Cooley*) is one of the masterpieces of medieval literature, although it is a work that probably evolved over centuries, while *Buile Suibne* (*The Frenzy of Sweeney*) seems certain to have been consciously written as a work of literature. Gerald of Wales probably wrote of the conquest of Ireland with a politically influential London audience in mind, while three hundred years later, an archdeacon from Aberdeen wrote an epic poem that included the Scottish invasion to glorify the Bruce family back home. And in the seventeenth century, Philip O'Sullivan Beare could write about the Nine Years War in Latin and make it sound like pages torn from *The Lives of the Saints*.

If one theme seems to run through the book, it is what a divided history Ireland has had. One of the most popular Irish patriotic songs has a impassioned refrain that goes, "A nation once again, A nation once again!" Again? The sad question that comes to mind is: When was it ever one nation? Among the earliest stories of the kings is how Conn of the Hundred Battles, from the north, and Owen the Great, from the south, draw a line across the center of Ireland—just about where the road today goes from Dublin to Galway—to divide the island between Conn's half and Owen's half. It was a line that was referred to for centuries to come. Centuries later in their annals, the Four Masters list, along with the reports of death of kings, the landing of Vikings, and damage done by high winds, the news that in year 808 a band of O'Neills from the north met a party of O'Neills from the south, but that "through the miracles of God . . . they separated from each other at that time without slaughter or one of them spilling a drop of the other's blood." The fact that nothing happened was worth recording for the ages.

The accounts in this collection are almost always the stories of noblemen and their families. The stories of the common people (or even the kings' wives) are of limited interest to those keeping track of history. There are exceptions. We hear of Alice of Abervenny, a widow, who after the first battle of the Norman invasion was called in to do some grim work, and of the harp player whose head was mistakenly sent to the king of England after the Battle of Faughart, and of the unnamed soldier who discovered the dangers of gunpowder at the Battle of Yellow Ford. Their appearances are so rare they are memorable. More often than not, this is the story of kings and their sons.

Yet the great destruction and violence that are so common in these tales were often felt by the poorest, who always remain nameless. In fact, they were frequently the targets when it was too expensive or too time consuming to attack those wearing the crowns. There were refugees even then, and it is worth remembering this rare, brief, glimpse we get of them in *The Annals of Connacht*. The year is 1225. The place is in what is now County Mayo. One faction of the O'Connor clan is warring against another and its foreign allies:

> They plundered Coolcarney and wrought destruction of its cattle and folk on that day, for as many of them [the fleeing people] as reached the level plain without being drowned [in the river] were plundered and slain; A pitiful thing: all who went to Ballycong were drowned and the weirs [dams] were found to have their wattles full of drowned children. Some of the refugees of Clonn Tomalhaig who evaded the Galls and escaped drowning went into Tirawhey, where O'Dubda fell on upon them and left them without a single cow.

—D.W.McC.

WARS
OF THE
IRISH KINGS

EDITOR'S NOTE

Cuchulainn, Cu Cnulaind, Cuchulain, and Cuculan are all different ways of writing the same name. Malachy and Mael Sechnaill are the same eleventh-century high king. The O'Neills are sometimes the Ui Neills. When it comes to early Irish proper names, there is little uniformity of spelling. Names are sometimes kept in their original Irish form, sometimes not. One writer's Suibne may well be another's Sweeney. Each generation might have its own version. Each writer—or translator—might have a preferred spelling all his own.

Since this is a collection of early writing with nothing more recent than the seventeenth century, idiosyncratic spellings of names have been retained to respect the spirit and feeling of the individual texts. The variations are usually as obvious as those in the case of Cuchulain, but introductions and notes throughout the book make it clear, when necessary, just who in fact is indeed who.

I.

MYTHICAL WARS

AND

WARRIORS

INTRODUCTION

AS MONKS IN THE MONASTERIES of medieval Ireland compiled their yearly records of what was happening (or what was said to be happening) in their land, they were also collecting ingenious stories about the past, a long and complex catalog of tales about gods and goddesses, wars and warriors.

No one presumed that Adam and Eve had dwelled in Ireland, but beginning with the remaking of the world after Noah's flood, the Irish envisioned a series of fantastical invaders conquering Ireland and each other. Wave after wave of them arrived. After Noah's granddaughter was sent to Ireland to escape the flood, the Partholonians fought and won the first battle in Ireland against an army of one-legged, one-armed monsters, only to be wiped out by a plague. Then came the Nemedians, the dark Fir Bolgs, the mystical Tuatha De Danann, and finally came the western European Milesians, the supposed ancestors of the Irish. All of this was collected into the twelfth-century *Lebor Gabala* (*The Book of Invasions*), with its allusions to the Old and New Testaments of the Bible, Greek mythology, and local gods. Some of these stories were indeed based on historical incidents, most made use of actual geographic locations, and all of them may reflect a very real fear of Viking invaders.

The tales about Ireland's first great hero, Cuchulain, date from the seventh and eighth centuries and are probably older than the invasion accounts. The stories are set in Ulster—the general term for them all is the Ulster Cycle—and Cuchulain is usually presented as having two fathers, an earthly one (Sualdam, king of Cuailgne or Cooley) and an otherworldly one (Lug, often described as the Celtic sun god). Cuchulain's name was originally Setania, but as a boy—while training with the knights at Emain Macha (now called Navan Fort, near Armagh)—he killed the dog of a blacksmith named Culann. To make amends, he took a name that meant "hound of Culann." Throughout the tales he is affectionately called "hound" or "little hound," perhaps because he is described as being short, an unusual quality in a mythic hero. But he has another unusual quality. He can write. In *The Cattle Raid of Cooley*, the epic account of his defense of the champion bull of Ulster, he is depicted leaving written warning messages on stone for the cattle raiders from Connacht. He is often a terrifying figure of towering rages who usually fights alone, armed only with a spear and a sword.

The Fenian Cycle—stories about Finn MacCool (Fionn mac Cuimhaill), the other major mythic hero—is not quite as old as the Ulster Cycle. And most of the stories are set in a medieval Ireland that has been converted to Christianity by St. Patrick. Some folklorists have argued that Cuchulain and Finn are two versions of the same mythic figure, but they are actually very different men. Cuchulain is a northerner. Finn's adventures take place in the south or southwest, in Leinster or Munster. Cuchulain is often alone. Finn (his name means "fair" or "light") is usually surrounded by a royal court worthy of King Arthur. Moreover, Finn has a son and grandson to carry on his line and play major roles in the cycle.

The fourth genre to come out of this period of mythmaking is called the Historical Cycle, which can be seen as a precursor of the modern historical novel. Fictional tales built around an actual historical figure or event proved to be a popular form of writing in Ireland for years to come. Often it was done for political purposes to advance the reputation of one family or to defame another. But one of the earliest examples, *The Frenzy of Suibne*, the story of Sweeney, a seventh-century king who went mad, seems to have been written solely as literature, not propaganda. As such, it is probably the most lyrical writing to come out of early Ireland.

THE SECOND BATTLE
OF MOYTURA

The two battles of Moytura (Mag Tured)—the first between the Tuatha De Danann and the Fir Bolgs and the second between the De Danann and the Fomoire—were first described in The Book of Invasions *and then later retold in greater detail. This version, based on earlier Old Irish versions, dates from a vellum manuscript that seems to have been written (or copied) in the first half of the sixteenth century by a scribe named Gilla Riabhach O'Cleirigh.*

The name Mag Tured can be translated as "the plain of towers" or "the plain of weeping," and the mythic battles—the first may have been based on an actual battle—occurred in two different places. Oscar Wilde's father, Sir William Wilde, a distinguished amateur archaeologist who named his family's summer home Moytura, believed the first battle to have taken place south of Sligo near Cong and Lough Corrib. Most historians accept a plain near Lough Arrow, north of Sligo, as the supposed site of the second. In any case, the De Danann, a clan well steeped in the arts and in magic, won both battles. After the first, the sinister Fir Bolgs fled to the Aran Islands in Galway Bay, where they are credited, in legend at least, with having built many of the stone forts there. The Fomoire, defeated in the second battle, were a Scandinavian seagoing tribe who—at one point—are said to have invaded Ireland on a bridge of ships.

Gods and mortals mix freely in Irish mythology. Lug Lamfhota ("the long armed"), the Irish god of sun and light, first appears in this account as "a handsome, well-built young warrior" who seeks admission to Tara's banqueting hall. Unrecognized by the doorkeepers, he undergoes a long cross-examination that ends with a game of chess or fidchell. Later, he becomes commander of the De Danann forces. As for that game, a medieval scribe added a primly pedantic parenthesis to the text: "(But if fidchell was invented at the time of the Trojan war, it had not reached Ireland yet, for the battle of Mag Tured and the destruction of Troy occurred at the same time.)" Other gods who appear in the tale include a rather comic Dagda (who combines quali-

ties of Zeus, Jupiter, and Odin and in some accounts is called the "father of all") and Ogma (Dagda's son, a poet, orator, and inventor of writing).

The account, which ends with prophecy and song, also makes clear how dangerous it was to be an Irish king. One king is killed in battle, another is removed from his throne because the loss of an arm makes him ineligible, and a third is driven off because he is inept.

THE TÚATHA DÉ DANANN were in the northern islands of the world [Greece], studying occult lore and sorcery, druidic arts and witchcraft and magical skill, until they surpassed the sages of the pagan arts. . . .

[They] came with a great fleet to Ireland to take it by force from the Fir Bolg. Upon reaching the territory of Corcu Belgatan (which is Conmaicne Mara today), they at once burned their boats so that they would not think of fleeing to them. The smoke and the mist which came from the ships filled the land and the air which was near them. For that reason it has been thought that they arrived in clouds of mist.

The [first] battle of Mag Tured was fought between them and the Fir Bolg. The Fir Bolg were defeated, and 100,000 of them were killed including the king, Eochaid mac Eirc.

[King] Núadu's hand was cut off in that battle—Sreng mac Sengainn struck it from him. So with Crédne the brazier helping him, Dían Cécht the physician put on him a silver hand that moved as well as any other hand. . . .

Then those of the Fir Bolg who escaped from the battle fled to the Fomoire, and they settled in Arran and in Islay and in Man and in Rathlin.

There was contention regarding the sovereignty of the men of Ireland between the Túatha Dé and their wives, since Núadu was not eligible for kingship after his hand had been cut off. They said that it would be appropriate for them to give the kingship to Bres the [illegitimate] son of Elatha, to their own adopted son, and that giving him the kingship would knit the Fomorians' alliance with them, since his father Elatha mac Delbaith was king of the Fomoire.

Now the conception of Bres came about in this way.

One day one of their women, Ériu the daughter of Delbáeth, was looking at the sea and the land from the house of Máeth Scéni; and she saw the sea as perfectly calm as if it were a level board. After that, while she was there, she saw something: a vessel of silver appeared to her on the sea. Its size seemed great to her, but its shape did not appear clearly to her; and the current of the sea carried it to the land.

Then she saw that it was a man of fairest appearance. He had golden-yellow hair down to his shoulders, and a cloak with bands of gold thread around it. His shirt had embroidery of gold thread. On his breast was a brooch of gold with the lustre of a precious stone in it. Two shining silver spears and in them two smooth riveted shafts of bronze. Five circlets of gold around his neck. A gold-hilted sword with inlayings of silver and studs of gold.

The man said to her, "Shall I have an hour of lovemaking with you?"

"I certainly have not made a tryst with you," she said.

"Come without the trysting!" said he.

Then they stretched themselves out together. The woman wept when the man got up again.

"Why are you crying?" he asked.

"I have two things that I should lament," said the woman, "separating from you, however we have met. The young men of the Túatha Dé Danann have been entreating me in vain—and you possess me as you do."

"Your anxiety about those two things will be removed," he said. He drew his gold ring from his middle finger and put it into her hand, and told her that she should not part with it, either by sale or by gift, except to someone whose finger it would fit.

"Another matter troubles me," said the woman, "that I do not know who has come to me."

"You will not remain ignorant of that," he said. "Elatha mac Delbaith, king of the Fomoire, has come to you. You will bear a son as a result of our meeting, and let no name be given to him but Eochu Bres (that is, Eochu the Beautiful), because every beautiful thing that is seen in Ireland—both plain and fortress, ale and candle, woman and man and horse—will be judged in relation to that boy, so that people will then say of it, 'It is a Bres.'". . .

But after Bres had assumed the sovereignty, three Fomorian kings (Indech mac Dé Domnann, Elatha mac Delbaith, and Tethra) imposed their tribute upon Ireland—and there was not a smoke from a house in Ireland which was not under their tribute. In addition, the warriors of Ireland were reduced to serving him: Ogma beneath a bundle of firewood and the Dagda as a rampart-builder, and he constructed the earthwork around Bres's fort. . . .

Now Núadu was being treated, and Dían Cécht put a silver hand on him which had the movement of any other hand. But his son Miach did not like that. He went to the hand and said "joint to joint of it, and sinew to sinew"; and he healed it in nine days and nights. The first three days he carried it against his side, and it became covered with skin. The second three days he carried it against his chest. The third three days he would cast white wisps of black bulrushes after they had been blackened in a fire. . . .

At that time, Bres held the sovereignty as it had been granted to him. There was great murmuring against him among his maternal kinsmen the Túatha Dé, for their knives were not greased by him. However frequently they might come, their breaths did not smell of ale; and they did not see their poets nor their bards nor their satirists nor their harpers nor their pipers nor their horn-blowers nor their jugglers nor their fools entertaining them in the household. They did not go to contests of those pre-eminent in the arts, nor did they see their warriors proving their skill at arms before the king. . . .

Now after that the Túatha Dé went together to talk with their adopted son Bres mac Elathan, and they asked him for their sureties. He gave them restoration of the kingship, and they did not regard him as properly qualified to rule from that time on. He asked [them to wait] for seven years. "You will have that," the same assembly agreed, "provided that the safeguarding of every payment that has been assigned to you—including house and land, gold and silver, cattle and food—is supported by the same securities, and that we have freedom of tribute and payment until then."

"You will have what you ask," Bres said.

This is why they were asked for the delay: that he might gather the warriors of the *síd*, the Fomoire, to take possession of the Túatha by force provided he might gain an overwhelming advantage. He was unwilling to be driven from his kingship.

Then he went to his mother and asked her where his family was. "I am certain about that," she said, and went onto the hill from which she had seen the silver vessel in the sea. She then went onto the shore. His mother gave him the ring which had been left with her, and he put it around his middle finger, and it fitted him. She had not given it up for anyone, either by sale or gift. Until that day, there was none of them whom it would fit.

Then [Bres] went forward until they reached the land of the Fomoire. They came to a great plain with many assemblies upon it, and they reached the finest of these assemblies. Inside, people sought information from them. They answered that they were of the men of Ireland. Then they were asked whether they had dogs, for at that time it was the custom, when a group of men visited another assembly, to challenge them to a friendly contest. "We have dogs," said Bres. Then the dogs raced, and those of the Túatha Dé were faster than those of the Fomoire. Then they were asked whether they had horses to race. "We have," and they were faster than the horses of the Fomoire.

Then they were asked whether they had anyone who was good at sword-play, and no one was found among them except Bres. But when he lifted the hand with the sword, his father recognized the ring on his finger and asked who the warrior was. His mother answered on his behalf and told the king that Bres was his son. She related to him the whole story as we have recounted it.

His father was sad about him, and asked, "What force brought you out of the land you ruled?"

Bres answered, "Nothing brought me except my own injustice and arrogance. I deprived them of their valuables and possessions and their own food. Neither tribute nor payment was ever taken from them until now."

"That is bad," said his father. "Better their prosperity than their kingship. Better their requests than their curses. Why then have you come?" asked his father.

"I have come to ask you for warriors," he said. "I intend to take that land [of the Dé Danann] by force."

"You ought not to gain it by injustice if you do not gain it by justice," he said.

"I have a question then: what advice do you have for me?" said Bres.

After that he sent him to the champion Balor, grandson of Nét, the king of the Hebrides, and to Indech mac Dé Domnann, the king of the Fomoire; and these gathered all the forces from Lochlainn [Scandinavia] westwards to Ireland, to impose their tribute and their rule upon them by force, and they made a single bridge of ships from the Hebrides to Ireland.

No host ever came to Ireland which was more terrifying or dreadful than that host of the Fomoire. There was rivalry between the men from Scythia of Lochlainn and the men out of the Hebrides concerning that expedition.

As for the Túatha Dé, however, that is discussed here.

After Bres [departed], Núadu was once more in the kingship over the Túatha Dé; and at that time he held a great feast for the Túatha Dé in Tara. Now there was a certain warrior whose name was Samildánach on his way to Tara. At that time there were doorkeepers at Tara named Gamal mac Figail and Camall mac Ríagail. While the latter was on duty, he saw the strange company coming toward him. A handsome, well-built young warrior with a king's diadem was at the front of the band.

They told the doorkeeper to announce their arrival in Tara. The doorkeeper asked, "Who is there?"

"Lug Lonnansclech is here, the son of Cían son of Dían Cécht and of Ethne daughter of Balor. He is the foster son of Tailtiu the daughter of Magmór, the king of Spain, and of Eochaid Garb mac Dúach."

The doorkeeper then asked of Samildánach, "What art do you practice? For no one without an art enters Tara."

"Question me," he said, "I am a builder."

The doorkeeper answered, "We do not need you. We have a builder already, Luchta mac Lúachada."

He said, "Question me, doorkeeper: I am a smith."

The doorkeeper answered him, "We have a smith already, Colum Cúaléinech of the three new techniques."

He said, "Question me: I am a champion."

The doorkeeper answered, "We do not need you. We have a champion already, Ogma mac Ethlend."

He said again, "Question me." "I am a harper," he said.

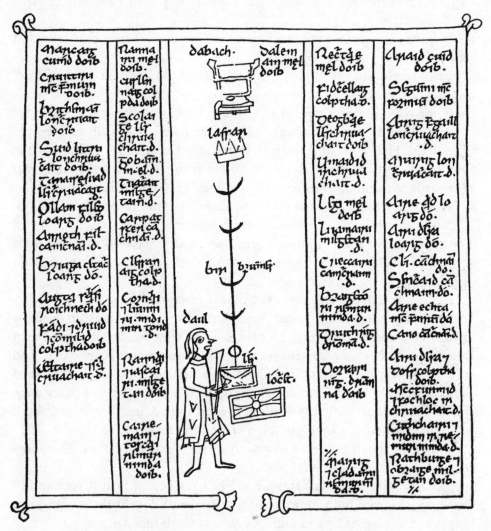

Seating plan of the Banquet Hall of Tara, from The Book of Leinster.

"We do not need you. We have a harper already, Abcán mac Bicelmois, whom the men of the three gods chose in the *síd*-mounds."

He said, "Question me: I am a warrior."

The doorkeeper answered, "We do not need you. We have a warrior already, Bresal Etarlam mac Echdach Báethláim."

Then he said, "Question me, doorkeeper. I am a poet and a historian."

"We do not need you. We already have a poet and historian, Én mac Ethamain."

He said, "Question me. I am a sorcerer."

"We do not need you. We have sorcerers already. Our druids and our people of power are numerous."

He said, "Question me. I am a physician."

"We do not need you. We have Dían Cécht as a physician."

"Question me," he said. "I am a cupbearer."

"We do not need you. We have cupbearers already: Delt and Drúcht and Daithe, Tae and Talom and Trog, Glé and Glan and Glésse."

He said, "Question me: I am a good brazier."

"We do not need you. We have a brazier already, Crédne Cerd."

He said, "Ask the king whether he has one man who possesses all these arts: if he has I will not be able to enter Tara."

Then the doorkeeper went into the royal hall and told everything to the king. "A warrior has come before the court," he said, "named Samildánach; and all the arts which help your people, he practices them all, so that he is the man of each and every art."

Then he said that they should bring him the *fidchell* [chess] boards of Tara, and he won all the stakes. (But if *fidchell* was invented at the time of the Trojan war, it had not reached Ireland yet, for the battle of Mag Tured and the destruction of Troy occurred at the same time.)

Then that was related to Núadu. "Let him into the court," said Núadu, "for a man like that has never before come into this fortress."

Then the doorkeeper let him past, and he went into the fortress, and he sat in the seat of the sage, because he was a sage in every art.

Then Ogma threw the flagstone, which required fourscore yoke of oxen to move it, through the side of the hall so that it lay outside against Tara. That was to challenge Lug, who tossed the stone back so that it lay in the centre of the royal hall; and he threw the piece which it had carried away back into the side of the royal hall so that it was whole again.

"Let a harp be played for us," said the hosts. Then the warrior played sleep music for the hosts and for the king on the first night, putting them to sleep from that hour to the same time the next day. He played sorrowful music so that they were crying and lamenting. He played joyful music so that they were merry and rejoicing.

Then Núadu, when he had seen the warrior's many powers, considered whether he could release them from the bondage they suffered at the hands of the Fomoire. So they held a council concerning the warrior, and the decision which Núadu reached was to exchange seats with the warrior. So Samildánach went to the king's seat, and the king arose before him until thirteen days had passed.

The next day he and the two brothers, Dagda and Ogma, conversed together on Grellach Dollaid; and his two kinsmen Goibniu and Dían Cécht were summoned to them.

They spent a full year in that secret conference, so that Grellach Dollaid is called the *Amrún* of the Men of the Goddess.

Then the druids of Ireland were summoned to them, together with their physicians and their charioteers and their smiths and their wealthy landowners and their lawyers. They conversed together secretly.

Then he asked the sorcerer, whose name was Mathgen, what power he wielded. He answered that he would shake the mountains of Ireland beneath the Fomoire so that their summits would fall to the ground. And it would seem to them that the twelve chief mountains of the land of Ireland would be fighting on behalf of the Túatha Dé Danann: Slieve League, and Denda Ulad, and the Mourne Mountains, and Brí Erigi and Slieve Bloom and Slieve Snaght, Slemish and Blaíslíab and Nephin Mountain and Slíab Maccu Belgodon and the Curlieu hills and Croagh Patrick.

Then he asked the cupbearer what power he wielded. He answered that he would bring the twelve chief lochs or Ireland into the presence of the Fomoire and they would not find water in them, however thirsty they were. These are the lochs: Lough Derg, Lough Luimnig, Lough Corrib, Lough Ree, Lough Mask, Strangford Lough, Belfast Lough, Lough Neagh, Lough Foyle, Lough Gara, Loughrea, Márloch. They would proceed to the twelve chief rivers of Ireland—the Bush, the Boyne, the Bann, the Blackwater, the Lee, the Shannon, the Moy, the Sligo, the Erne, the Finn, the Liffey, the Suir—and they would all be hidden from the Fomoire so they would not find a drop in them. But drink will be provided for the men of Ireland even if they remain in battle for seven years.

Then Figol mac Mámois, their druid, said, "Three showers of fire will be rained upon the faces of the Fomorian host, and I will take out of them two-thirds of their courage and their skill at arms and their strength, and I will bind their urine in their own bodies and in the bodies of their horses. Every breath that the men of Ireland will exhale will increase their courage and skill at arms and strength. Even if they remain in battle for seven years, they will not be weary at all.

The Dagda said, "The power which you boast, I will wield it all myself."

"You are the Dagda ['the Good God']!" said everyone; and "Dagda" stuck to him from that time on.

Then they disbanded the council to meet that day three years later. . . .

The men of Ireland came together the day before All Hallows. Their number was six times thirty hundred, that is, each third consisted of twice thirty hundred.

Then Lug sent the Dagda to spy on the Fomoire and to delay them until the men of Ireland came to the battle.

Then the Dagda went to the Fomorian camp and asked them for a truce of battle. This was granted to him as he asked. The Fomoire made porridge for him to mock him, because his love of porridge was great. They filled for him the king's cauldron, which was five fists deep, and poured four score gallons of new milk and the same quantity of meal and fat into it. They put goats and sheep and swine into it, and boiled them all together with the porridge. Then they poured it into a hole in the ground, and Indech said to him that he would be killed unless he consumed it all; he should eat his fill so that he might not satirize the Fomoire.

Then the Dagda took his ladle, and it was big enough for a man and a woman to lie in the middle of it. These were the bits that were in it: halves of salted swine and a quarter of lard.

Then the Dagda said, "This is good food if its broth is equal to its taste." But when he would put the full ladle into his mouth he said, "'Its poor bits do not spoil it,' says the wise old man."

Then at the end he scraped his bent finger over the bottom of the hole among mould and gravel. He fell asleep then after eating his porridge. His belly was as big as a house cauldron, and the Fomoire laughed at it.

Then he went away from them to Tráigh Eabha. It was not easy for the warrior to move along on account of the size of his belly. His appearance was unsightly: he had a cape to the hollow of his elbows, and a gray-brown tunic around him as far as the swelling of his rump. He trailed behind him a wheeled fork which was the work of eight men to move, and its track was enough for the boundary ditch of a province. It is called "The Track of the Dagda's Club" for that reason. His long penis was uncovered. He had on two shoes of horsehide with the hair outside. . . .

The Fomoire advanced until their tenths were in Scétne. The men of Ireland were in Mag Aurfolaig. At this point these two hosts were threatening battle.

"Do the men of Ireland undertake to give battle to us?" said Bres mac

Elathan to Indech mac Dé Domnann.

"I will give the same," said Indech, "so that their bones will be small if they do not pay their tribute."

In order to protect him, the men of Ireland had agreed to keep Lug from the battle. . . . They feared an early death for the warrior because of the great number of his arts. For that reason they did not let him go to the battle.

Then the men of rank among the Túatha Dé were assembled around Lug. He asked his smith, Goibniu, what power he wielded for them.

"Not hard to say," he said. "Even if the men of Ireland continue the battle for seven years, for every spear that separates from its shaft or sword that will break in battle, I will provide a new weapon in its place. No spearpoint which my hand forges will make a missing cast. No skin which it pierces will taste life afterward. Dolb, the Fomorian smith, cannot do that. I am now concerned with my preparation for the battle of Mag Tured."

"And you, Dían Cécht," said Lug, "what power do you wield?"

"Not hard to say," he said. "Any man who will be wounded there, unless his head is cut off, or the membrane of his brain or his spinal cord is severed, I will make him perfectly whole in the battle on the next day."

"And you, Crédne," Lug said to his brazier, "what is your power in the battle?"

"Not hard to answer," said Crédne. "I will supply them all with rivets for their spears and hilts for their swords and bosses and rims for their shields."

"And you, Luchta," Lug said to his carpenter, "what power would you attain in the battle?"

"Not hard to answer," said Luchta. "I will supply them all with whatever shields and spearshafts they need.

"And you, Ogma," said Lug to his champion, "what is your power in the battle?"

"Not hard to say," he said. "Being a match for the king and holding my own against twenty-seven of his friends, while winning a third of the battle for the men of Ireland."

"And you, Morrígan," said Lug, "what power?"

"Not hard to say," she said. "I have stood fast; I shall pursue what was watched; I will be able to kill; I will be able to destroy those who might be subdued."

"And you, sorcerers," said Lug, "what power?"

"Not hard to say," said the sorcerers. "Their white soles will be visible after they have been overthrown by our craft, so that they can easily be killed; and we will take two-thirds of their strength from them, and prevent them from urinating."

"And you, cupbearers," said Lug, "what power?"

"Not hard to say," said the cupbearers. "We will bring a great thirst upon them, and they will not find drink to quench it."

"And you, druids," said Lug, "what power?"

"Not hard to say," said the druids. "We will bring showers of fire upon the faces of the Fomoire so that they cannot look up, and the warriors contending with them can use their force to kill them."

"And you, Coirpre mac Étaine," said Lug to his poet, "what can you do in the battle?"

"Not hard to say," said Coirpre. "I will satirize them and shame them so that through the spell of my art they will offer no resistance to warriors."

"And you, Bé Chuille and Díanann," said Lug to his two witches, "what can you do in the battle?"

"Not hard to say," they said. "We will enchant the trees and the stones and the sods of the earth so that they will be a host under arms against them; and they will scatter in flight terrified and trembling."

"And you, Dagda," said Lug, "what power can you wield against the Fomorian host in the battle?"

"Not hard to say," said the Dagda. "I will fight for the men of Ireland with mutual smiting and destruction and wizardry. Their bones under my club will soon be as many as hailstones under the feet of herds of horses, where the double enemy meets on the battlefield of Mag Tured."

Then in this way Lug addressed each of them in turn concerning their arts, strengthening them and addressing them in such a way that every man had the courage of a king or great lord. . . .

Now when the time came for the great battle, the Fomoire marched out of their encampment and formed themselves into strong indestructible battalions. There was not a chief nor a skilled warrior among them without armor against his skin, a helmet on his head, a broad . . . spear in his right hand, a heavy sharp sword on his belt, a strong shield on his shoulder. To attack the Fomorian host that day was "striking a head against a cliff," was "a hand in a serpent's nest," was "a face brought close to fire."

These were the kings and leaders who were encouraging the Fomorian host: Balor son of Dot son of Nét, Bres mac Elathan, Tuire Tortbuillech mac Lobois, Goll and Irgoll, Loscennlomm mac Lommglúinigh, Indech mac Dé Domnann, king of the Fomoire, Ochtríallach mac Indich, Omna and Bagna, Elatha mac Delbaíth.

On the other side, the Túatha Dé Danann arose and left his nine companions guarding Lug, and went to join the battle. But when the battle ensued, Lug escaped from the guard set over him, as a chariot-fighter, and it was he who was in front of the battalion of the Túatha Dé. Then a keen and cruel battle was fought between the race of the Fomoire and the men of Ireland.

Lug was urging the men of Ireland to fight the battle fiercely so they should not be in bondage any longer, because it was better for them to find death while protecting their fatherland than to be in bondage and under tribute as they had been. Then Lug chanted the spell which follows, going around the men of Ireland on one foot and with one eye closed. . . .

The hosts gave a great shout as they went into battle. Then they came together, and each of them began to strike the other.

Many beautiful men fell there in the stall of death. Great was the slaughter and the grave-lying which took place there. Pride and shame were there side by side. There was anger and indignation. Abundant was the stream of blood over the white skin of young warriors mangled by the hands of bold men while rushing into danger for shame. Harsh was the noise made by the multitude of warriors and champions protecting their swords and shields and bodies while others were striking them with spears and swords. Harsh too the tumult all over the battlefield—the shouting of the warriors and the clashing of bright shields, the swish of swords and ivory-hilted blades, the clatter and rattling of the quivers, the hum and whirr of spears and javelins, the crashing strokes of weapons.

As they hacked at each other their fingertips and their feet almost met; and because of the slipperiness of the blood under the warriors' feet, they kept falling down, and their heads were cut off them as they sat. A gory, wound-inflicting, sharp, bloody battle was upheaved, and spearshafts were reddened in the hands of foes.

Then Núadu Silverhand and Macha the daughter of Ernmas fell at the hands of Balor grandson of Nét. Casmáel fell at the hands of Ochtríallach son of Indech. Lug and Balor of the piercing eye met in the battle. The latter had a destructive eye which was never opened except on a battlefield. Four men would raise the lid of the eye by a polished ring in its lid. The host which looked at that eye, even if they were many thousands in number, would offer no resistance to warriors. It had that poisonous power for this reason: once his father's druids were brewing magic. He came and looked over the window, and the fumes of the concoction affected the eye and the venomous power of the brew settled in it. Then he and Lug met. . . .

"Lift up me eyelid, lad," said Balor, "so I may see the talkative fellow who is conversing with me."

The lid was raised from Balor's eye. Then Lug cast a sling stone at him which carried the eye through his head, and it was his own host that looked at it. He fell on top of the Fomorian host so that twenty-seven of them died under his side; and the crown of his head struck against the breast of Indech mac Dé Domnann so that a gush of blood spouted over his lips. . . .

Then the Morrígan the daughter of Ernmas came, and she was strengthening the Túatha Dé to fight the battle resolutely and fiercely. She then chanted the following poem:

"Kings arise to the battle! . . ."

Immediately afterwards the battle broke, and the Fomoire were driven to the sea. The champion Ogma son of Elatha and Indech mac Dé Domnann fell together in single combat. . . .

"A question: what is the number of the slain?" Lug said to Lóch.

"I do not know the number of peasants and rabble. As to the number of Fomorian lords and nobles and champions and over-kings, I do know: 3 + 3 x 20 + 50 x 100 men + 20 x 100 + 3 x 50 + 9 x 5 + 4 x 20 x 1000 + 8 + 8 x 20 + 7 + 4 x 20 + 6 + 4 x 20 + 5 + 8 x 20 + 2 + 40, including the grandson of Nét with 90 men. That is the number of the slain of the Fomorian over-kings and high nobles who fell in the battle.

"But regarding the number of peasants and common people and rabble and people of every art who came in company with the great host—for every warrior and every high noble and every over-king of the Fomoire came to the battle with his personal followers, so that all fell there, both their free men and their unfree servants—I count only a few of the over-kings' servants. This then is the number of those I counted as I watched: 7 + 7 x 20 x 20 x 100 x 100 + 90 including Sab Úanchennach son of Coirpre Colc, the son of a servant of Indech mac Dé Domnann (that is, the son of a servant of the Fomorian king).

"As for the men who fought in pairs and the spearmen, warriors who did not reach the heart of the battle who also fell there—until the stars of heaven can be counted, and the sands of the sea, and flakes of snow, and dew on a lawn, and hailstones, and grass beneath the feet of horses, and the horses of the son of Lir in a sea storm—they will not be counted at all."

Immediately afterward they found an opportunity to kill Bres mac Elathan. He said, "It is better to spare me than to kill me."

"What then will follow from that?" said Lug.

"The cows of Ireland will always be in milk," said Bres, "if I am spared."

"I will tell that to our wise men," said Lug.

So Lug went to Máeltne Mórbrethach and said to him, "Shall Bres be spared for giving constant milk to the cows of Ireland?"

"He shall not be spared," said Máeltne. "He has no power over their age or their calving, even if he controls their milk as long as they are alive."

Lug said to Bres, "That does not save you; you have no power over their age or their calving, even if you control their milk."

Bres said, "Máeltne has given bitter alarms!"

"Is there anything else which will save you, Bres?" said Lug.

"There is indeed. Tell your lawyer they will reap a harvest every quarter in return for sparing me."

Lug said to Máeltne, "Shall Bres be spared for giving the men of Ireland a harvest of grain every quarter?"

"This has suited us," said Máeltne. "Spring for plowing and sowing, and the beginning of summer for maturing the strength of the grain, and the beginning of autumn for the full ripeness of the grain, and for reaping it. Winter for consuming it."

"That does not save you," said Lug to Bres.

"Máeltne has given bitter alarms," said he.

"Less rescues you," said Lug.

"What?" asked Bres.

"How shall the men of Ireland plow? How shall they sow? How shall they reap? If you make known these things, you will be saved."

"Say to them, on Tuesday their plowing; on Tuesday their sowing seed in the field; on Tuesday their reaping."

So through that device Bres was released.

Now in that battle Ogma the champion found Orna, the sword of Tethra, king of the Fomoire. Ogma unsheathed the sword and cleaned it. Then the sword told what had been done by it, because it was the habit of swords at that time to recount the deeds that had been done by them whenever they were unsheathed. And for that reason swords are entitled to the tribute of cleaning after they have been unsheathed. Moreover spells have been kept in swords from that time on. Now the reason why demons used to speak from weapons then is that weapons used to be worshipped by men and were among the sureties of that time. . . .

Then Lug and the Dagda and Ogma went after the Fomoire, because they had taken the Dagda's harper, Úaithne. Eventually they reached the banqueting hall where Bres mac Elathan and Elatha mac Delbaith were. There was the harp on the wall. That is the harp in which the Dagda had bound the melodies so that they did not make a sound until he summoned them, saying,

"Come Daur Dá Bláo,
Come Cóir Cetharchair,
Come summer, come winter,
Mouths of harps and bags and pipes!"

(Now that harp had two names, Daur Dá Bláo and Cóir Cetharchair.)

Then the harp came away from the wall, and it killed nine men and came to the Dagda; and he played for them the three things by which a harper is known: sleep music, joyful music, and sorrowful music. He played sorrowful music for them so that their tearful women wept. He played joyful music for them so that their women and boys laughed. He played sleep music for them so that the hosts slept. So the three of them escaped from them unharmed—although they wanted to kill them.

The Dagda brought with him the cattle taken by the Fomoire through the lowing of the heifer which had been given him for his work; because when she called her calf, all the cattle of Ireland which the Fomoire had taken as their tribute began to graze.

Then after the battle was won and the slaughter had been cleaned away, the Morrígan, the daughter of Ernmas, proceeded to announce the battle and the great victory which had occurred there to the royal heights of Ireland and to its *síd*-hosts, to its chief waters and to its rivermouths. And that is the reason Badb still relates great deeds. "Have you any news?" everyone asked her then.

"Peace up to heaven.
Heaven down to earth.
Earth beneath heaven,
Strength in each,
A cup very full,
Full of honey;
Mead in abundance.
Summer in winter. . . .
Peace up to heaven . . ."

THE CATTLE RAID OF COOLEY

CUCHULAIN

The Cattle Raid of Cooley (Tain Bo Cuailnge) *is usually cited as the greatest work of classical Irish literature. It begins with a bedroom squabble between Medb, the queen of Connacht, and her husband, Ailill, over which of them is richer. Its climax—after a long-running battle between Connacht and Ulster across the entire north of Ireland— is a fight between two bulls, one white and one brown. At the outset, Medb concedes defeat in the bedroom: her husband's white bull is indeed more valuable than anything she owns. But the queen intends to change that. Medb summons her army and the armies of her allies throughout the island to set out for Ulster to capture the most valuable bull in all of Ireland, the brown bull of Cooley. Stealing the bull, however, requires her to confront Cuchulain, the son of the king of Cooley and Ulster's greatest hero.*

In the episode that follows, Cuchulain, exhausted and seriously wounded after single-handedly battling the invaders for weeks, is talked into taking a nap by the god Lug, his divine father. The result is disastrous, but Cuchulain's heroic rage is awesome, and the detailed descriptions of his clothes, weapons, tactics, and chariot (including the charioteer) seem historically inspired.

The earliest versions of the The Tain—*containing sections in both prose and verse—date from the seventh and eighth centuries, with later versions appearing in* The Book of the Dun Cow *(c. 1100),* The Book of Leinster *(c. 1160), and* The Yellow Book of Lecan *(c. 1390). The modern Irish poet Thomas Kinsella made this translation.*

THE FOUR PROVINCES OF Ireland settled down and camped on Murtheimne Plain, at Breslech Mór (the place of their great carnage). They sent their shares of cattle and plunder southward ahead of them to Clithar Bó Ulad, the Cattle-Shelter of Ulster. Cuchulain took his place near them at the gravemound in Lerga. At nightfall his charioteer Laeg mac Riangabra kindled a fire for him. And he saw in the distance over the heads of the four provinces of Ireland the fiery flickering of gold weapons in the evening sunset clouds. Rage and fury seized him at the sight of that army, at the great forces of his foes, the immensity of his enemies. He grasped his two spears, his shield and his sword and he shook the shield and rattled the spears and flourished the sword and gave the warrior's scream from his throat, so that demons and devils and goblins of the glen and fiends of the air replied, so hideous was the call he uttered on high. Then the Nemain stirred the armies to confusion. The weapons and spear-points of the four armed provinces of Ireland shook with panic. One hundred warriors fell dead of fright and terror that night in the heart of the guarded camp.

Laeg stood in his place and saw a solitary man crossing between the camp of the men of Ireland straight toward him out of the northeast.

"There is a man coming toward us alone, Little Hound," Laeg said.

"What kind of man is he?" Cuchulain said.

"It is soon told: a tall, broad, fair-seeming man. His close-crossed hair is blond and curled. A green cloak is wrapped about him, held at his breast by a bright silver brooch. He wears a knee-length tunic of kingly silk, red-embroidered in red gold, girded against his white skin. There is a knob of light gold on his black shield. He carries a five-pointed spear in his hand and a forked javelin. His feats and graceful displays are astonishing, yet no one is taking any notice of him and he heeds no one: it is as though they couldn't see him."

"They can't, my young friend," Cuchulain said. "This is some friendly one of the *síde* [the other world] that has taken pity on me. They know my great distress now on the Táin Bó Cuailnge, alone against all four provinces of Ireland."

Cuchulain was right. When the warrior came up to him he said in pity:

"This is a manly stand, Cuchulain."

"It isn't very much," Cuchulain said.

"I am going to help you now,' the warrior said.

"Who are you?" Cuchulain said.

"I am Lug mac Ethnenn, your father from the *síde*."

"My wounds are heavy. It is time they were let heal."

"Sleep a while, then, Cuchulain," the warrior said, "a heavy sleep of three days and three nights by the gravemound at Lerga. I'll stand against the armies for that time."

He sang to Cuchulain, as men sing to men, until he slept. Then he examined each wound and cleaned it. Lug made this chant:

"Rise son of mighty Ulster
    with your wounds made whole
a fair man faces your foes
    in the long night over the ford
rest in his human care
    everywhere hosts hewn down
succour has come from the *síde*
    to save you in this place
your vigil on the hound fords
    a boy left on lonely guard
defending cattle and doom
    kill phantoms while I kill
they have none to match your span
    of force or fiery wrath
your force with the deadly foe
    when chariots travel the valleys
then arise arise my son."

Cuchulain slept three days and three nights, and well he might; for if his sleep was deep so was his weariness. From the Monday after the feast of Samain at summer's end to the Wednesday after the feast of Imbolc at spring's beginning, Cuchulain never slept—unless against his spear for an instant after the middle of the day, with head on fist and fist on spear and the spear against his knee—for hacking and hewing and smiting and slaughtering the four great provinces of Ireland.

Then the warrior from the *síde* dropped wholesome healing herbs and grasses into Cuchulain's aching wounds and several sores, so that he began to recover in his sleep without knowing it.

The boy-troop in Ulster spoke among themselves at this time.

"It is terrible," they said, "that our friend Cuchulain must do without help."

"Let us choose a company to help him," Fiachna Fuilech, the Bloodspiller, said—a brother of Fiacha Fialdána mac Fir Febe.

Then the boy-troop came down from Emain Macha in the north carrying their hurling-sticks, three times fifty sons of Ulster kings—a third of their whole troop—led by Follamain, Conchobor's son. The army saw them coming over the plain.

"There is a great number crossing the plain toward us," Ailill said.

Fergus went to look.

"These are some of the boy-troop of Ulster coming to help Cuchulain," he said.

"Send out a company against them," Ailill said, "before Cuchulain sees them. If they join up with him you'll never stand against them."

Three times fifty warriors went out to meet them, and they all fell at one another's hands at Lia Toll, the Pierced Standing-Stone. Not a soul came out alive of all those choice children except Follomain mac Conchoboir. Follamain swore he would never go back to Emain while he drew breath, unless he took Ailill's [the husband of Queen Medb] head with him, with the gold crown on top. But that was no easy thing to swear; the two sons of Bethe mac Báin, sons of Ailill's foster-mother and foster-father, went out and attacked him, and he died at their hands.

"Make haste," Ailill said, "and ask Cuchulain to let you move on from here. There will be no forcing past him once his hero-halo springs up."

Cuchulain, meanwhile, was sunk in his sleep of three days and nights by the gravemound at Lerga. When it was done he rose up and passed his hand over his face and turned crimson from head to foot with whirling excitement. His spirit was strong in him; he felt fit for a festival, or for marching or mating, or for an ale-house or the mightiest assembly in Ireland.

"Warrior!" Cuchulain said. "How long have I been in this sleep?"

"Three days and three nights," the warrior said.

"Alas for that!" Cuchulain said.

"Why?" the warrior said.

"Because their armies were free from attack all that time," Cuchulain said.

"They were not," the warrior said.

"Tell me what happened," Cuchulain said.

"The boy-troop came south from Emain Macha, three times fifty sons of Ulster kings, led by Follamain, Conchobor's son, and they fought three battles with the armies in the three days and nights you slept, and they slew three times their own number. All the boy-troop perished except Follamain mac Conchoboir. Follamain swore to take home Ailill's head, but that was no easy thing, and he too was killed."

"Shame," Cuchulain said, "that I hadn't my strength for this! If I had, the boy-troop wouldn't have perished as they did and Follamain mac Conchoboir wouldn't have fallen."

"Onward, Little Hound; there is no stain on your good name, no slight on your courage."

"Stay with us tonight," Cuchulain said, "and we'll avenge the boy-troop together."

"I will not stay," the warrior said. "No matter what deeds of craft or courage a man does in your company the glory and fame and name go to you, not to him. So I will not stay. Go bravely against the army by your-self. They have no power over your life at this time."

"The sickle chariot, friend Laeg," Cuchulain said, "can you yoke it? Have you everything needed? If you have, get it ready. If you haven't, leave it be."

The charioteer rose up then and donned his charioteer's war-harness. This war-harness that he wore was: a skin-soft tunic of stitched deer's leather, light as a breath, kneaded supple and smooth not to hinder his free arm movements. He put on over this his feathery outer mantle, made (some say) by Simon Magus for Darius king of the Romans, and given by Darius to Conchobor, and by Conchobor to Cuchulain, and by Cuchulain to his charioteer. Then the charioteer set down on his shoulders his plated, four-pointed, crested battle-cap, rich in colour and shape; it suited him well and was no burden. To set him apart from his master, he placed the charioteer's sign on his brow with his hand: a circle of deep yellow like a single red-gold strip of burning gold shaped on an anvil's edge. He took the long horse-spancel and the ornamental goad in his right hand. In his left hand he grasped the steed-ruling reins that give the charioteer control. Then he threw the decorated iron armour-plate over the horses, covering them from head to foot with spears and spit-points, blades and barbs. Every inch of the chariot bristled. Every angle and corner, front and rear, was a tearing-place.

He cast a protecting spell on his horses and his companion-in-arms and made them obscure to all in the camp, while everything remained clear to themselves. It was well he cast such a spell, for he was to need his three greatest charioteering skills that day: leaping a gap, straight steering and the use of the goad.

Then the high hero Cuchulain, Sualdam's son, builder of the [battle goddess] Badb's fold with walls of human bodies, seized his warrior's battle-harness. This was the warlike battle-harness he wore: twenty-seven tunics of waxed skin, plated and pressed together, and fastened with strings and cords and straps against his clear skin, so that his senses or his brain wouldn't burst their bonds at the onset of his fury. Over them he put on his heroic deep battle-belt of stiff, tough, tanned leather from the choicest parts of the hides of seven yearlings, covering him from his narrow waist to the thickness of his armpit; this he wore to repel spears or spikes, javelins, lances or arrows—they fell from it as though dashed at stone or horn or hard rock. Then he drew his silk-smooth apron, with its light-gold speckled border, up to the softness of his belly. Over this silky skin-like apron he put on a dark apron of well-softened black leather from the choicest parts of the hides of four yearlings, with a battle-belt of cowhide to hold it. Then the kingly champion gripped his warlike battle-weapons. These were the warlike weapons he chose: eight short swords with his flashing, ivory-hilted sword; eight small spears with his five-pronged spear, and a quiver also; eight light javelins with his ivory javelin; eight small darts with his feat-playing dart, the *del chliss*; eight feat-playing shields with his dark-red curved shield that could hold a prize boar in its hollow, its whole rim so razor sharp it could sever a single hair against the stream. When Cuchulain did the feat of the shield-rim he could shear with his shield as sharply as spear or sword. He placed on his head his warlike, crested battle-helmet, from whose every nook and cranny his longdrawn scream re-echoed like the screams of a hundred warriors; so it was that the demons and devils and goblins of the glen and fiends of the air cried out from that helmet, before him, above him and around him, whenever he went out to spill the blood of warriors and heroes. His concealing cloak was spread about him, made of cloth from Tír Tairngire, the Land of Promise [an otherworldly paradise]. It was given to him by his magical foster-father [Lug].

The first warp-spasm seized Cuchulain, and made him into a monstrous thing, hideous and shapeless, unheard of. His shanks and his joints, every knuckle and angle and organ from head to foot, shook like a tree in the flood or a reed in the stream. His body made a furious twist inside his skin, so that his feet and shins and knees switched to the rear and his heels and calves switched to the front. The ballad sinews of his calves switched to the front of his shins, each big knot the size of a warrior's bunched fist. On his head the temple-sinews stretched to the nape of his neck, each mighty, immense, measureless knob as big as the head of a month-old child. His face and features became a red bowl: he sucked one eye so deep into his head that a wild crane couldn't probe it onto his cheek out of the depths of his skull; the other eye fell out along his cheek. His mouth weirdly distorted: his cheek peeled back from his jaws until the gullet appeared, his lungs and liver flapped in his mouth and throat, his lower jaw struck the upper a lion-killing blow, and fiery flakes large as a ram's fleece reached his mouth from his throat. His heart boomed loud in his breast like the baying of a watch-dog at its feed or the sound of a lion among bears. Malignant mists and spurts of fire—the torches of the Badb—flickered red in the vaporous clouds that rose boiling above his head, so fierce was his fury. The hair of his head twisted like the tangle of a red thornbush stuck in a gap; if a royal apple tree with all its kingly fruit were shaken above him, scarce an apple would reach the ground but each would be spiked on a bristle of his hair as it stood up on his scalp with rage. The hero-halo rose out of his brow, long and broad as a warrior's whetstone, long as a snout, and he went mad rattling his shields, urging on his charioteer and harassing the hosts. Then, tall and thick, steady and strong, high as the mast of a noble ship, rose up from the dead centre of his skull a straight spout of black blood darkly and magically smoking like the smoke from a royal hostel when a king is coming to be cared for at the close of a winter day.

When that spasm had run through the high hero Cuchulain he stepped into his sickle war-chariot that bristled with points of iron and narrow blades, with hooks and hard prongs and heroic frontal spikes, with ripping instruments and tearing nails on its shafts and straps and loops and cords. The body of the chariot was spare and slight and erect, fitted for the feats of a champion, with space for a lordly warrior's eight weapons, speedy as the wind or as a swallow or a deer darting over the level plain. The chariot was settled down on two fast steeds, wild and wicked, neat-headed and narrow-bodied, with slender quarters and roan breast, firm in hoof and harness—a notable sight in the trim chariot-shafts. One horse was lithe and swift-leaping, high-arched and powerful, long-bodied and with great hooves. The other flowing-maned and shining, slight and slender in hoof and heel.

In that style, then, he drove out to find his enemies and did his thunder-feat and killed a hundred, then two hundred, then three hundred, then four hundred, then five hundred, where he stopped—he didn't think it too many to kill in that first attack, his first full battle with the provinces of Ireland. Then he circled the outer lines of [the armies of] the four great provinces of Ireland in his chariot and he attacked them in hatred. He had the chariot driven so heavily that its iron wheels sank into the earth. So deeply the chariot-wheels sank in the earth that clods and boulders were torn up, with rocks and flagstones and the gravel of the ground, in a dyke as high as the iron wheels, enough for a fortress-wall. He threw up this circle of the Badb round about the four great provinces of Ireland to stop them fleeing and scattering from him, and corner them where he could wreak vengeance for the boy-troop. He went into the middle of them and beyond, and mowed down great ramparts of his enemies' corpses, circling completely around the armies three times, attacking them in hatred. They fell sole to sole and neck to headless neck, so dense was that destruction. He circled them three times more in the same way, and left a bed of them six deep in a great circuit, the soles of three to the necks of three in a ring around the camp. This slaughter on the Táin was given the name Seisrech Bresligi, the Sixfold Slaughter. It is one of the three uncountable slaughters on the Táin: Seisrech Bresligi, Imslige Glennamnach—the mutual slaughter at Glenn Domain—and the Great Battle at Gáirech and

Irgairech (though this time it was horses and dogs as well as men.) Any count or estimate of the number of the rabble who fell there is unknown, and unknowable. Only the chiefs have been counted. The following are the names of these nobles and chiefs: two called Cruaid, two named Calad, two named Cír, two named Cíar, two named Ecell, three named Crom, three named Caur, three named Combirge, four named Feochar, four named Furechar, four named Cass, four named Fota, five named Aurith, five named Cerman, five named Cobthach, six named Saxan, six named Dach, six named Dáire, seven named Rochad, seven named Ronan, seven named Rurthech, eight named Rochlad, eight named Rochtad, eight named Rinnach, eight named Coirpre, eight named Mulach, nine named Daithi, nine more named Dáire, nine named Damach, ten named Fiac, ten named Fiacha and ten named Feidlimid.

In this great Carnage on Murtheimne Plain Cuchulain slew one hundred and thirty kings, as well as an uncountable horde of dogs and horses, women and boys and children and rabble of all kinds. Not one man in three escaped without his thighbone or his head or his eye being smashed, or without some blemish for the rest of his life. And when the battle was over Cuchulain left without a scratch or a stain on himself, his helper or either of his horses.

THE PALACE OF THE QUICKEN TREES

FINN MacCOOL

Finn MacCool (Fionn mac Cuimhaill), perhaps the most popular of the Irish mythical heroes, has appeared over the centuries in many guises. As a giant, he is given credit for building the Giant's Causeway, a natural rock formation on the Antrim coast, and for cutting many mountain passes in both Ireland and Scotland with his sword. In the Old Irish version of "Tristan and Isolde" ("The Pursuit of Dermat and Grania"), he is a bumbling old fool. Geoffrey Keating, the seventeenth-century historian, claimed he was a historical figure who died in A.D. 283. But in most of the tales he appears as an Arthurian ruler—a descendant of Nuadu, the silver-armed king of the De Danann—who is surrounded by a band of followers, Fenians, who are not unlike the knights of the roundtable. Among them are his son, the poetic Oisin, and his grandson, the heroic Oscar, both of whom became especially popular during the nineteenth-century Celtic revival.

The quicken trees in the title are European mountain ash, often thought to have magical powers. Although this tale includes many magical elements, it also has its realistic aspects, such as the Viking threat, the presence of high-born hostages in royal courts, and the fact that most medieval skirmishes did indeed take place near fords across streams or rivers. The King of the World in the story may be a reference to the Holy Roman emperor Charlemagne.

The Palace of the Quicken Trees (Bruidhean Chaorthainn) came out of the eighth- and ninth-century oral tradition and seems to have been first written down in the tenth century.

COLGA, KING OF LOCHLANN, INVADES ERIN, AND IS SLAIN

A NOBLE, WARLIKE KING ruled over Lochlann [home of the Danes], whose name was Colga of the Hard Weapons. On a certain occasion, this king held a meeting of his chief people, on the broad, green plain before his palace of Berva. And when they were all gathered together, he spoke to them in a loud, clear voice, from where he sat high on his throne; and he asked them whether they found any fault with the manner in which he ruled them, and whether they knew of anything deserving of blame in him as their sovereign lord and king. They replied, as if with the voice of one man, that they found no fault of any kind.

Then the king spoke again and said, "You see not as I see. Do you not know that I am called King of the Four Tribes of Lochlann, and of the Islands of the Sea? And yet there is one island which acknowledges not my rule."

And when they had asked which of the islands he meant, he said—

"That island is Erin of the green hills. My forefathers, indeed, held sway over it, and many of our brave warriors died there in fight. But though our hosts at last subdued the land and laid it under tribute, yet they held it not long; for the men of Erin arose and expelled our army, regaining their ancient freedom.

"And now it is my desire that we once more sail to Erin with a fleet and an army, to bring it under my power, and take, either by consent or by force, the tributes that are due to me by right. And we shall thereafter hold the island in subjection till the end of the world."

The chiefs approved the counsel of the king, and the meeting broke up.

Then the king made proclamation, and sent his swift scouts and couriers all over the land, to muster his fighting men, till he had assembled a mighty army in one place.

And when they had made ready their curve-sided, white-sailed ships, and their strong, swift-gliding boats, the army embarked. And they raised their sails and plied their oars; and they cleft the billowy, briny sea; and the clear, cold winds whistled through their sails; and they made neither stop nor stay, till they landed on the shore of the province of Ulad [Ulster].

The King of Ireland at that time was Cormac Mac Art, the grandson of Conn the Hundred-fighter. And when Cormac heard that a great fleet had come to Erin, and landed an army of foreigners, he straightway sent tidings of the invasion to Allen [in Kildare], where lived Finn, and the noble Fena of the Gaels.

When the king's messengers had told their tale, Finn despatched his swift-footed couriers to every part of Erin where he knew the Fena dwelt; and he bade them to say that all should meet him at a certain place, near that part of the coast where the Lochlann army lay encamped. And he himself led the Fena of Leinster northwards to join the muster.

They attacked the foreigners, and the foreigners were not slow to meet their onset; and the Fena were sore pressed in that battle, so that at one time the Lochlanns were like to prevail.

Oscar, the son of Oisin [Finn's son], when he saw his friends falling all round him, was grieved to the heart; and he rested for a space to gather his wrath and his strength. Then, renewing the fight, he rushed with fury towards the standard of Colga, the Lochlann king, dealing havoc and slaughter among those foreigners that stood in his track. The king saw Oscar approach, and met him; and they fought a deadly battle hand-to-hand. Soon their shields were rent, their hard helmets were dinted with sword-blows, their armour was pierced in many places, and their flesh was torn with deep wounds. And the end of the fight was, that the king of the foreigners was slain by Oscar, the son of Oisin.

When the Lochlanns saw their king fall, they lost heart, and the battle went against them. But they fought on nevertheless, till evening, when their army entirely gave way, and fled from the field. And of all the nobles and princes and mighty chiefs who sailed to Erin on that expedition, not one was left alive, except the youngest son of the king, whose name was Midac. Him Finn spared on account of his youth; with intent to bring him up in his own household.

After the Fena had rested for a time, and buried their dead, they turned their faces southward, and marched slowly towards Allen, bringing their sick and wounded companions. And Finn placed Midac among the household of Allen, treating him honourably, and giving him servants and tutors. Moreover, he enlisted him in the Fena, and gave him a high post as befitted a prince.

MIDAC, THE SON OF COLGA, MEDITATES REVENGE

After this things went on as before, while Midac grew up towards manhood, and hunted and feasted with the Fena, and fought with them when they fought. But he never lost an opportunity of making himself acquainted with all their haunts and hunting-grounds, their palaces and fortresses, and in particular with their manner of carrying on war.

It happened one day that Finn and some of his leading chiefs were in council, considering sundry matters, especially the state and condition of the Fena; and each chief was commanded by Finn to speak, and give his opinion or advice on anything that he deemed weighty enough to be debated by the meeting.

And after many had spoken, Conan Mail, the son of Morna, stood up and said—

"It seems to me, O king, that you and I and the Fena in general are now in great danger. For you have in your house, and mixing with your people, a young man who has good cause of enmity towards you; that is to say, Midac, the son of the king of Lochlann. For was it not by you that his father and brothers and many of his friends were slain? Now I notice that this young prince is silent and distant, and talks little to those around him. Moreover, I see that day after day he takes much pains to know all matters relating to the Fena; and as he has friends in Lochlann, mighty men with armies and ships, I fear me the day may come when this prince will use his knowledge to our destruction."

Finn said that all this was quite true, and he asked Conan to give his opinion as to what should be done.

"What I advise in the matter is this," said Conan, "that Midac be not allowed to abide any longer in the palace of Allen. But as it is meet that he should be treated in a manner becoming a prince, let him be given a tract of land for himself in some other part of Erin, with a home and a household of his own. Then shall we be freed from his presence, and he can no longer listen to our counsels, and learn all our secrets and all our plans."

This speech seemed to Finn and the other chiefs reasonable and prudent, and they agreed to follow the advice of Conan Mail.

Accordingly Finn sent for the prince, and said to him—

"Thou knowest, Midac, that thou hast been brought up from boyhood in my household, and that thou hast been dealt with in every way as becomes a prince. Now thou art a man, and standest in no further need of instruction, for thou hast learned everything needful for a prince and for a champion of the Fena; and it is not meet that thou shouldst abide longer in the house of another. Choose, therefore, the two cantreds that please thee best in all Erin, and they shall be given to thee and to thy descendants for ever as a patrimony. There thou shalt build houses and a homestead for thyself, and I will help thee with men and with cattle and with all things else necessary."

Midac listened in silence; and when the king had done speaking, he replied in a cold and distant manner and in few words, that the proposal was reasonable and proper, and pleased him well. And thereupon he chose the rich cantred of Kenri on the Shannon, and the cantred of the Islands lying next to it on the north, at the other side of the river [near Limerick].

Now Midac had good reasons for choosing these two territories beyond all others in Erin. For the river opens out between them like a great sea, in which are many islands and sheltered harbours, where ships might anchor in safety; and he hoped to bring a fleet and an army into Erin some day, to avenge on Finn and the Fena the defeats they had inflicted on his countrymen, and above all, the death of his father and brothers. And being bent on treachery, he could not have chosen in all Erin a territory better suited for carrying out his secret designs.

So these two cantreds were bestowed on Midac. Finn gave him also much cattle and wealth of all kinds; so that when his houses were built, and when he was settled in his new territory, with his servants and his cattle and his wealth all round him, there was no brugaid [local ruler] in Erin richer or more prosperous than he.

For fourteen years Midac lived in his new home, growing richer every year. But the Fena knew nothing of his way of life, for he kept himself apart, and none of his old acquaintances visited him. And though he was enrolled in the ranks of the Fena, he never, during all that time, invited one of them to his house, or offered them food or drink or entertainment of any kind.

One day, Finn and the Fena went to hunt in the district of Fermorc, and over the plains of Hy Conall Gavra. And when all was arranged and the chase about to begin, Finn himself, and a few of his companions, went to the top of the hill of Knockfierna [near Limerick] to see the sport; while the main body of the Fena scattered themselves over the plain with their dogs and attendants, to start the deer and the wild boars and all the other game of the forest.

Then Finn's people pitched their tents, and made soft couches of rushes and heather, and dug cooking-places; for they intended the hill to be the resting-place of all who chose to rest, till the chase was ended.

After Finn and his companions had sat for some time on the hill, they saw a tall warrior coming towards them, armed in full battle array. He wore a splendid coat of mail of Lochlann workmanship, and over it a mantle of fine satin dyed in divers colours. A broad shield hung on his left shoulder, and his helmet glittered in the morning sun like polished silver. At his left side hung a long sword, with golden hilt and enamelled sheath; and he held in his right hand his two long, polished, death-dealing spears. His figure and gait were wonderfully majestic, and as he came near, he saluted the king in stately and courteous words.

Finn returned the salutation, and spoke with him for a while; and at length he asked him whence he had come, and if he had brought any tidings.

"As to the place I came from," he answered, "that need not be spoken of; and for news, I have nothing to tell except that I am a ferdana [poet], and that I have come to thee, O king of the Fena, with a poem."

"Methinks, indeed," replied Finn, "that conflict and battle are the poetry you profess; for never have I seen a hero noble in mien and feature."

"I am a ferdana nevertheless," answered the stranger, "and if thou dost not forbid me, I will prove it by reciting a poem I have brought for thee."

"A mountain-top is not the place for poetry," said Finn; "and moreover, there is now no opportunity either for reciting or listening. For I and these few companions of mine have come to sit here that we may view the chase, and listen to the eager shouts of the men, and the sweet cry of the hounds.

"But if you are, as you say," continued Finn, "a ferdana, remain here with us till the chase is ended; and then you shall come with me to one of our palaces, where I shall listen to your poem, and bestow on you such gifts as are meet for a poet of your rank."

But the strange champion answered, "It is not my wish to go to your palace; and I now put you under gesa [solemn vow], which true heroes do not decline, that you listen to my poem, and that you find out and explain its meaning."

"Well then," said Finn, "let there be no further delay; repeat your poem."

So the hero recited a verse that began—

> I saw a house by a river's shore,
> Famed through Erin in days of yore,

"I can explain that poem," said Finn. "The mansion you saw is Bruga of the Boyne, the palace of Angus, son of the Dagda, which is open to all who wish to partake of its feasts and its enjoyments. It cannot be burned by fire, or drowned by water, or spoiled by robbers, on account of the great power of its lord and master; for there is not now, and there never was, and there never shall be, in Erin, a man more skilled in magic arts than Angus of the Bruga."

"That is the sense of my poem," said the stranger; "and now listen to this other, and explain it to me if thou canst." It began—

> I saw to the south a bright-faced queen,
> With couch of crystal and robe of green;

"I understand the sense of that poem also," said Finn. "The queen you saw is the river Boyne, which flows by the south side of the palace of Bruga. Her couch of crystal is the sandy bed of the river; and her robe of green the grassy plain of Bregia, through which it flows. Her children, which you can see through her skin, are the speckled salmon, the lively, pretty trout, and all the other fish that swim in the clear water of the river. The river flows slowly indeed; but its waters traverse the whole world in seven years, which is more than the swiftest steed can do."

"These are my poems," said the champion; "and thou hast truly explained their meaning."

"And now," said Finn, "as I have listened to thy poetry and explained it, tell us, I pray thee, who thou art and whence thou hast come; for I marvel much that so noble a champion should live in any of the five provinces of Erin without being known to me and my companions."

Then Conan Mail spoke. "Thou art, O king, the wisest and most far-seeing of the Fena, and thou hast unravelled and explained the hard poetical puzzles of this champion. Yet, on the present occasion, thou knowest not a friend from a foe; for this man is Midac, whom thou didst bring up with much honour in thine own house, and afterwards made rich, but who is now thy bitter enemy, and the enemy of all the Fena. Here he has lived for fourteen years, without fellowship or communication with his former companions. And though he is enrolled in the order of the Fena, he has never, during all that time, invited thee to a banquet, or come to see any of his old friends, or given food or entertainment to any of the Fena, either master or man."

Midac answered, "If Finn and the Fena have not feasted with me, that is none of my fault; for my house has never been without a banquet fit for either king or chief; but you never came to partake of it. I did not, indeed, send you an invitation; but that you should not have waited for, seeing that I was one of the Fena, and that I was brought up in your own household. Howbeit, let that pass. I have now a feast ready, in all respects worthy of a king; and I put you under gesa that you and the chiefs that are here with you, come this night to partake of it. I have two palaces, and in each there is a banquet. One is the Palace of the Island, which stands on the sea; and the other is the Palace of the Quicken Trees, which is a little way off from this hill; and it is to this that I wish you to come."

Finn consented; and Midac, after he had pointed out the way to the Palace of the Quicken Trees, left them, saying he would go before, that he might have things in readiness when they should arrive.

FINN IS ENTRAPPED BY MIDAC, AND HELD BY ENCHANTMENT IN THE PALACE OF THE QUICKEN TREES

Finn now held council with his companions, and they agreed that the king's son, Oisin, and five other chiefs, with their followers, should tarry on the hill till the hunting party returned, while Finn went to the palace with the rest.

And it was arranged that Finn should send back word immediately to the party on the hill, how he fared; and that Oisin and the others were to follow him to the palace when the hunting party had returned.

Those that remained with Oisin were Dermat O'Dyna; Fatha Conan, the son of the son of Conn; Kylta Mac Ronan; Ficna, the son of Finn; and Innsa, the son of Swena Selga.

And of those who went with Finn to the Palace of the Quicken Trees, the chief were Gaul Mac Morna; Dathkeen the Strong-limbed; Mac Luga of the Red Hand; Glas Mac Encarda from Beara; the two sons of Aed the Lesser, son of Finn; Racad and Dalgus, the two kings of Leinster; Angus Mac Bresal Bola; and the two leaders of the Connaught Fena, namely, Macna-Corra and Corr the Swift-footed.

As Finn and his party came nigh to the palace, they were amazed at its size and splendour; and they wondered greatly that they had never seen it before. It stood on a level green, which was surrounded by a light plantation of quicken trees, all covered with clusters of scarlet berries. At one side of the little plain, very near the palace, was a broad river, with a rocky bank at the near side, and a steep pathway leading down to a ford.

But what surprised them most was that all was lonely and silent—not a living soul could they see in any direction; and Finn, fearing some foul play, would have turned back, only that he bethought him of his gesa and his promise. The great door was wide open, and Conan went in before the others; and after viewing the banqueting hall, he came out quite enraptured with what he had seen. He praised the beauty and perfect arrangement of everything, and told his companions that no other king or chief in all Erin had a banqueting hall to match the hall of Midac, the son of Colga. They all now entered, but they found no one—neither host nor guests nor attendants.

As they gazed around, they thought they had never seen a banquet hall so splendid. A great fire burned brightly in the middle, without any smoke, and sent forth a sweet perfume, which filled the whole room with fragrance, and cheered and delighted the heroes. Couches were placed all round, with rich coverlets and rugs, and soft, glossy furs. The curved walls were of wood, close-jointed and polished like ivory; and each board was painted differently from those above and below; so that the sides of the room, from floor to roof, were all radiant with a wonderful variety of colours.

Still seeing no one, they seated themselves on the couches and rugs. Presently a door opened, and Midac walked into the room. He stood for a few moments before the heroes, and looked at them one after another, but never spoke one word; then, turning round, he went out and shut the great door behind him.

Finn and his friends were much surprised at this; however, they said nothing, but remained resting as they were for some time, expecting Midac's return. Still no one came, and at length Finn spoke—

"We have been invited here, my friends, to a banquet; and it seems to me very strange that we should be left so long without attendance, and without either food or drink. Perhaps, indeed, Midac's attendants have made some mistake, and that the feast intended for this palace has been prepared in the Palace of the Island. But I wonder greatly that such a thing should have happened."

"I see something more wonderful than that," said Gaul Mac Morna; "for lo, the fire, which was clear and smokeless when we first saw it, and which smelled more sweetly than the flowers of the plain, now fills the hall with a foul stench, and sends up a great cloud of black, sooty smoke!"

"I see something more wonderful than that," said Glas Mac Encarda; "for the boards in the walls of this banquet hall, which were smooth and close-jointed and glorious all over with bright colours when we came, are now nothing but rough planks, clumsily fastened together with tough quicken tree withes, and as rude and unshapen as if they had been hacked and hewed with a blunt axe!"

I see something more wonderful than that," said Foilan, the son of Aed the Lesser; "for this palace, which had seven great doors when we came in, all wide open, and looking pleasantly towards the sunshine, has now only one small, narrow door, close fastened, and facing straight to the north!"

"I see something more wonderful than that," said Conan Mail; "for the rich rugs and furs and the soft couches, which were under us when we sat here first, are all gone, not as much as a fragment or a thread remaining; and we are now sitting on the bare, damp earth, which feels as cold as the snow of one night!"

Then Finn again spoke. "You know, my friends, that I never tarry in a house having only one door. Let one of you then, arise, and break open that narrow door, so that we may go forth from this foul, smoky den!"

"That shall be done," cried Conan; and, so saying, he seized his long spear, and, planting it on the floor, point downwards, he attempted to spring to his feet. But he found that he was not able to move, and turning to his companions, he cried out with a groan of anguish—

"Alas, my friends! I see now something more wonderful than all; for I am firmly fixed by some druidical spell to the cold clay floor of the Palace of the Quicken Trees!"

And immediately all the others found themselves, in like manner, fixed where they sat. And they were silent for a time, being quite confounded and overwhelmed with fear and anguish.

At length Gaul spoke, and said, "It seems clear, O king, that Midac has planned this treachery, and that danger lies before us. I wish, then, that you would place your thumb under your tooth of knowledge, and let us know the truth; so that we may at once consider as to the best means of escaping from this strait."

Whereupon Finn placed his thumb under his tooth of knowledge, and mused for a little while. Then suddenly withdrawing his thumb, he sank back in his seat and groaned aloud.

"May it be the will of the gods," said Gaul, "that it is the pain of thy thumb that has caused thee to utter that groan!"

"Alas! not so," replied Finn. "I grieve that my death is near, and the death of these dear companions! For fourteen years has Midac, the son of the king of Lochlann, been plotting against us; and now at last he has caught us in this treacherous snare, from which I can see no escape.

"For in the Palace of the Island there is, at this moment, an army of foreigners, whom Midac has brought hither for our destruction. Chief over all is Sinsar of the Battles, from Greece, the Monarch of the World, who has under his command sixteen warlike princes, with many others of lesser note. Next to Sinsar is his son, Borba the Haughty, who commands also a number of fierce and hardy knights.

"There are, besides, the three kings of the Island of the Torrent, large-bodied and bloodthirsty, like three furious dragons, who have never yet yielded to an enemy on the field of battle. It is these who, by their sorcery, have fixed us here; for this cold clay that we sit on is part of the soil of the enchanted Island of the Torrent, which they brought hither, and placed here with foul spells. Moreover, the enchantment that binds us to this floor can never be broken unless the blood of these kings be sprinkled on the clay. And very soon some of Sinsar's warriors will come over from the Palace of the Island, to slay us all, while we are fixed here helpless, and unable to raise a hand in our own defence."

Full of alarm and anguish were the heroes when they heard these tidings. And some began to shed bitter tears in silence, and some lamented aloud. But Finn again spoke and said—

"It becomes us not, my friends, being heroes, to weep and wail like women, even though we are in danger of death; for tears and lamentations will avail us nothing. Let us rather sound the Dord-Fian [war cry], sweetly and plaintively, according to our wont, that it may be a comfort to us before we die."

So they ceased weeping, and, joining all together, they sounded the Dord-Fian in a slow, sad strain.

INNSA, FINN'S FOSTER SON, DEFENDS THE FORD LEADING TO THE PALACE OF THE QUICKEN TREES

Now let us speak of Oisin, and the party who tarried with him on the hill of Knockfierna. When he found that his father Finn had not sent back a messenger as he had promised, though the night was now drawing nigh, he began to fear that something was wrong; and he said to his companions—

"I marvel much that we have got no news from the king, how he and his companions have fared in the Palace of the Quicken Trees. It is clear to me that he would have fulfilled his promise to send us word, if he had not been hindered by some unforeseen difficulty. Now, therefore, I wish to know who will go to the palace and bring me back tidings."

Ficna, the son of Finn, stood forth and offered to go; and Finn's foster son, Innsa, the son of Swena Selga, said he would go with him.

They both set out at once, and as they travelled with speed, they soon reached the plain on which stood the Palace of the Quicken Trees; and now the night was darkening around them. As they came near to the palace, they marvelled to hear the loud, slow strains of the Dord-Fian; and Innsa exclaimed joyfully—

"Things go well with our friends, seeing that they are amusing themselves with the Dord-Fian!"

But Ficna, who guessed more truly how things really stood, replied—

"It is my opinion, friend, that matters are not so pleasant with them as you think; for it is only in time of trouble or danger that Finn is wont to have the Dord-Fian sounded in a manner so slow and sad."

While they talked in this wise, it chanced that the Dord-Fian ceased for a little space; and Finn hearing the low hum of conversation outside, asked was that the voice of Ficna. And when Ficna answered, "Yes," Finn said to him—

"Come not nearer, my son; for this place teems with dangerous spells. We have been decoyed hither by Midac, and we are all held here by the foul sorcery of the three kings of the Island of the Torrent."

And thereupon Finn told him the whole story of the treachery that had been wrought on them, from beginning to end; and he told him also that nothing could free them but the blood of those three kings sprinkled on the clay.

Then he asked who the second man was whom he had heard conversing with Ficna; and when he was told that it was Innsa, the son of Swena Selga, he addressed Ficna earnestly—

"Fly, my son, from this fatal place! Fly, and save my foster child from the treacherous swords of the foreigners; for they are already on their way hither!"

But Innsa quickly answered, "That I will never do. It would, indeed, be an ungrateful return to a kind foster father, to leave thee now in deadly strait, and seek my own safety."

And Ficna spoke in a like strain.

Then Finn said, "Be it so, my sons; but a sore trial awaits you. Those who come hither from the Palace of the Island must needs pass the ford under the shadow of these walls. Now this ford is rugged and hard to be crossed; and one good man, standing in the steep, narrow entrance at the hither side, might dispute the passage for a time against many. Go now, and defend this ford; and haply some help may come in time."

So both went to the ford. And when they had viewed it carefully, Ficna, seeing that one man might defend it for a short time almost as well as two, said to Innsa—

"Stay thou here to guard the ford for a little time, while I go to the Palace of the Island to see how the foreigners might be attacked. Haply, too, I may meet with the party coming hither, and decoy them on some other track."

And Innsa consented; and Ficna set out straightway for the Palace of the Island.

Now as to the Palace of the Island. When Midac returned in the morning, and told how Finn and his people were held safe in the Palace of the Quicken Trees, the foreigners were in great joy. And they feasted and drank and were merry till evening; when an Irla [earl] of the King of the World spoke in secret to his brother, and said—

"I will go now to the Palace of the Quicken Trees, and I will bring hither the head of Finn the son of Cumal; and I shall gain thereby much renown, and shall be honoured by the King of the World."

So he went, bringing with him a goodly number of his own knights; and nothing is told of what befell them till they arrived at the brink of the ford under the Palace of the Quicken Trees. Looking across through the darkness, the Irla thought he saw a warrior standing at the other brink; and he called aloud to ask who was there.

And when Innsa answered that he belonged to the household of Finn, the son of Cumal, the Irla said—

"Lo, we are going to the Palace of the Quicken Trees, to bring Finn's head to the King of the World; and thou shalt come with us and lead us to the door."

"That, indeed," replied Innsa, "would be a strange way for a champion to act who has been sent hither by Finn to guard this ford. I will not allow any foe to pass—of that be sure; and I warn you that you come not to my side of the ford!"

At this the Irla said to his knights, "Force the ford: then shall we see if yonder hero can fight as well as he threatens."

And at the word, they rushed through the water, as many as could find room. But only one or two at a time could attack; and the young champion struck them down right and left as fast as they came up, till the ford became encumbered with their bodies.

And when the conflict had lasted for a long time, and when they found that they could not dislodge him, the few that remained retired across the ford; and Innsa was fain to rest after his long combat.

But the Irla, seeing so many of his knights slain, was mad with wrath; and, snatching up his sword and shield, he attacked Innsa; and they fought a long and bloody fight.

Now the Irla was fresh and strong, while Innsa was weary and sore wounded; and at length the young hero fell in the ford, and the Irla beheaded him, and, exulting in his victory, brought the head away.

Finn and his companions, as they sat in miserable plight in the Palace of the Quicken Trees, heard the clash of arms at the ford, and the shouts and groans of warriors; and after a time all was still again; and they knew not how the fight had ended.

And now the Irla, thinking over the matter, deemed it unsafe to go to the Palace of the Quicken Trees without a larger body of knights; so he returned towards the Palace of the Island, intending to bring Innsa's head to the King of the World. When he had come within a little distance of the palace, he met Ficna, who was then on his way back to the ford; and seeing that he was coming from the Palace of the Island, he deemed that he was one of the knights of the King of the World.

Ficna spoke to him, and asked whither he had come.

"I come," replied the Irla, "from the ford of the Palace of the Quicken Trees. There, indeed, on our way to the palace, to slay Finn the son of Cumal, we were met by a young champion, who defended the ford and slew my knights. But he fell at length beneath my sword; and, lo, I have brought his head for a triumph to the King of the World!"

Ficna took the head tenderly, and kissed the cheek thrice, and said, sorrowing—

"Alas, dear youth! only this morning I saw the light of valour in those dim eyes, and the bloom of youth on that faded cheek!"

Then turning wrathfully to the Irla, he asked—

"Knowest thou to whom thou hast given the young warrior's head?"

And the Irla replied, "Hast thou not come from the Palace of the Island, and dost thou not belong to the host of the King of the World?"

"I am not one of his knights," answered Ficna; "and neither shalt thou be, after this hour!"

Whereupon they drew their swords, and fought where they stood; and the foreign Irla fell by the avenging sword of Ficna, the son of Finn. Ficna beheaded him and returned to the ford, bringing the head, and also the head of Innsa. And when he had come to the ford, he made a grave of green sods on the bank, in which he laid the body and the head of Innsa, sometimes grieving for the youth, and sometimes rejoicing that his death had been avenged.

Then he went on to the Palace of the Quicken Trees, bringing the Irla's head; and when he had come nigh the door, he called aloud to Finn, who, impatient and full of anxious thoughts, asked—

"Tell us, Ficna, who fought the battle at the ford, and how it has ended."

"Thine own foster son, Innsa, defended the ford against many foes, whose bodies now encumber the stream."

"And how is it now with my foster son?" asked Finn.

"He died where he fought," replied Ficna; "for at the end, when he was weary and sore wounded, the foreign Irla attacked him, and slew him."

"And thou, my son, didst thou stand by and see my nursling slain?"

"Truly I did not," answered Ficna. "Would that I had been there, and I would have defended and saved him! And even now he is well avenged; for I met the Irla soon after, and lo, I have brought thee his head. Moreover, I buried thy nursling tenderly in a grave of green sods by the ford."

And Finn wept and said, "Victory and blessings be with thee, my son! Never were children better than mine. Before I saw them, few were my possessions and small my consideration in Erin; but since they have grown up around me, I have been great and prosperous, till I fell by treachery into this evil plight. And now, Ficna, return and guard the ford, and peradventure our friends may send help in time."

So Ficna went and sat on the brink of the ford.

FICNA, THE SON OF FINN, DEFENDS THE FORD

Now at the Palace of the Island, another Irla, whose name was Kironn, brother to him who had been slain by Ficna, spoke to some of his own followers—

"It is long since my brother left for the Palace of the Quicken Trees; I fear me that he and his people have fared ill in their quest. And now I will go to seek for them."

And he went, bringing a company of knights well armed; and when they had come to the ford, they saw Ficna at the far side. Kironn called out and asked who he was, and asked also who had made such a slaughter in the ford.

Ficna answered, "I am one of the household champions of Finn the son of Cumal, and he has sent me here to guard this ford. As to the slaughter of yonder knights, your question stirs my mind to wrath, and I warn you, if you come to this side of the ford, you will get a reply, not in words, but in deeds."

Then Kironn and his men rushed through the water, blind with rage, and struck wildly at Ficna. But the young hero watchfully parried their strokes and thrusts; and one after another they fell beneath his blows, till only a single man was left, who ran back with all speed to the Palace of the Island to tell the tale. And Ficna sat down on the brink, covered all over with wounds, and weary from the toil of battle.

When these tidings were brought to the palace, Midac was very wroth, and he said, "These men should not have gone to force the ford without my knowledge; for they were far too few in number, and neither were they bold and hardy enough to meet Finn's valiant champions. I know these Fena well, and it is not to me a matter of surprise that the Irla and his people fell by them.

"But I will now go with a choice party of my own brave men; and I will cross the ford despite their guards, and slay Finn and all his companions in the Palace of the Quicken Trees.

"Moreover, there is one man among them, namely, Conan Mail, who of all the men of Erin has the largest appetite, and is fondest of choice eating and drinking. To him will I bring savoury food and delicious drink, not, indeed, to delight him with eating and drinking, but that I may torment him with the sight and smell of what he cannot taste."

So, having got the food, he set out with a chosen band; and when he had arrived at the ford, he saw a warrior at the far side. He asked who he was, and finding that it was Ficna, he spoke guilefully to him.

"Dear art thou to me, Ficna, dearer even than all the rest of Finn's household; for during the time I lived among the Fena, you never used me ill, or lifted a hand to either man or dog belonging to me."

But Ficna spurned his smooth words, and replied, "While you lived among the Fena, there was not a man among them that had less to do with you than I. But this I know, that you were treated kindly by all, especially by my father Finn, and you have repaid him by ingratitude and treachery."

When Midac heard this speech he was filled with wrath, and no longer hiding his evil mind, he ordered Ficna with threats to leave the ford. But Ficna laughed with scorn, and replied—

"The task is easy, friend Midac, to dislodge a single champion; and surely it is a small matter to you whether I stand in this narrow pass or abandon my post. Come forward, then, you and your knights; but here I will remain to receive you. I only regret you did not come sooner, while my blood was hot, and before my wounds grew stiff, when you would have got a better welcome!"

Then Midac ordered forward his knights, and they ran eagerly across the ford. But Ficna overthrew them with a mighty onset, like a hawk among a flight of small birds, or like a wolf among a flock of sheep. When Midac saw this, he buckled on his shield and took his sword. Then, treading warily over the rough rocks, and over the dead bodies of his knights, he confronted Ficna, and they attacked each other with deadly hate and fury.

We shall now speak of those who remained on Knockfierna. When Oisin found that the two heroes did not return as soon as he expected, he thus addressed his companions—

"It seems to me a long time, my friends, since Ficna and Innsa went to the Palace of the Quicken Trees; methinks if they have sped successfully they should have long since come back with tidings of Finn and the others."

And one of his companions answered, "It is plain that they have gone to partake of the feast, and it fares so well with them that they are in no haste to leave the palace."

But Dermat O'Dyna of the Bright Face spoke and said, "It may be as you say, friend, but I should like to know the truth of the matter. And now I will go and find out why they tarry, for my mind misgives me that some evil thing has happened."

And Fatha Conan said he would go with him.

So the two heroes set out for the Palace of the Quicken Trees; and when they were yet a good way off from the ford they heard the clash of arms. They paused for a moment, breathless, to listen, and then Dermat exclaimed—

"It is the sound of single combat, the combat of mighty heroes; it is Ficna fighting with the foreigners, for I know his war-shout. I hear the clash of swords and the groans of warriors; I hear the shrieks of the ravens, and the howls of the wild men of the glens! Hasten, Fatha, hasten, for Ficna is in sore strait, and his shout is a shout for help!"

And so they ran like the wind till they reached the hill-brow over the river; and, looking across in the dim moonlight, they saw the whole ford heaped with the bodies of the slain, and the two heroes fighting to the death at the far side. And at the first glance they observed that Ficna, being sore wounded, was yielding and sheltering behind his shield, and scarce able to ward off the blows of Midac.

Then Fatha cried out, "Fly, Dermat, fly! Save our dear companion! Save the king's son from death."

And Dermat, pausing for a moment, said, as if communing with himself—

"This is surely an evil plight: for if I run to the other side, the foreigner, being the more enraged for seeing me, will strike with greater fury, and I may not overtake the prince alive; and if I cast my spear, I may strike the wrong man!"

But Fatha, overhearing him, said, "Fear not, Dermat, for you never yet threw an erring cast of a spear!"

Then Dermat, putting his finger in the silken loop of his spear, threw a deadly cast with unerring aim, and struck Midac, so that the iron spearhead went right through his body, and the length of a warrior's hand beyond.

"Woe to the man," exclaimed Midac—"woe to him whom that spear reaches: for it is the spear of Dermat O'Dyna!"

And now his wrath increased, and he struck at Ficna more fiercely than before.

Dermat shouted to him to hold his hand and not slay the king's son; and as he spoke he rushed down the slope and across the ford, to save the young hero. But Midac, still pressing on with unabated strength and fury, replied—

"Had you wished to save the prince's life, you should have spared mine: now that I have been wounded to death by your spear, Finn shall never see his son alive!"

Even as he spoke, he raised his sword for a mighty blow; and just as Dermat, shouting earnestly, was closing on them, he struck the prince lifeless to the earth, but fell down himself immediately after.

Dermat came up on the instant, and looked sadly at his friend lying dead. Then, addressing Midac, he said—

"If I had found thee dead, I would have passed thee untouched; but now that I have overtaken thee alive, I must needs behead thee, for thy head will be to Finn a worthy eric [a fine paid as compensation] for his son."

And so saying, he struck off Midac's head with one sweep of his heavy sword.

Dermat now repaired to the Palace of the Quicken Trees, leaving Fatha to watch the ford till his return. And when he had come near, he called aloud and struck the door with his heavy spear, for his wrath had not yet left him; but the door yielded not.

Finn knew the voice, and called out impatiently, "Do not try to enter here, Dermat, for this place is full of foul spells. But tell us first, I pray thee, who fought that long and bitter fight; for we heard the clash of arms and the shouts of warriors, but we know nothing more."

"Thy noble son, Ficna," returned Dermat, "fought single-handed against the foreigners."

"And how fares it with my son after that battle?"

"He is dead," answered Dermat; "first sore wounded by many foes whom he slaughtered, and afterwards slain by Midac, the son of Colga. But thy son is avenged; for though I came to the ford indeed too late to save him, I have slain Midac, and here I have brought thee his head as an eric."

And for a long time Dermat heard no more.

At last Finn spoke again and said—

"Victory and blessings be with you, Dermat, for often before did you relieve the Fena from sore straits. But never have we been in such plight as this. For here we sit spell-bound, and only one thing can release us, the blood of the three fierce kings of the Island of the Torrent sprinkled on this clay. Meantime, unless the ford be well defended, the foreigners will come and slay us. In you, Dermat, we trust, and unless you aid us well and faithfully now, we shall of a certainty perish. Guard the ford till the rising of the sun, for then I know the Fena will come to aid you."

"I and Fatha will of a certainty keep the enemy at bay," replied Dermat; and he bade them farewell for a time, and was about to return to the ford: but Conan Mail, with a groan, said—

"Miserable was the hour when I came to this palace, and cold and comfortless is the clay on which I sit—the clay of the Island of the Torrent. But worst of all to be without food and drink so long. And while I sit here, tormented with hunger and thirst, there is great plenty of ale and wine and of rich, savoury food yonder in the Palace of the Island. I am not able to bear this any longer; and now, Dermat, I beseech you to bring me from the palace as much food as I can eat and a drinking-horn of wine."

"Cursed be the tongue that spoke these selfish words!" said Dermat. "A host of foreigners are now seeking to compass your death, with only Fatha and myself to defend you. Surely this is work enough for two good men! And now it seems I must abandon my post, and undertake a task of much danger, to get food for the gluttonous Conan Mail!"

"Alas, Dermat-na-man!" replied Conan, "if it were a lovely maiden, with bright eyes and golden hair, who made this little request, quickly and eagerly you would fly to please her, little recking of danger or trouble. But now you refuse me, and the reason is not hard to see. For you formerly crossed me four times in my courtships; and now it likes you well to see me die of hunger in this dungeon!"

"Well, then," said Dermat, "cease your upbraiding, and I will try to bring you food; for it is better to face danger than suffer the revilings of your foul tongue."

So saying, he went back to the ford to Fatha, where he stood watching; and after he had told him how matters stood, he said to him—

"I must needs go to the Palace of the Island, to get food for Conan Mail; and you shall guard the ford till I return."

But Fatha told him that there was food and drink enough at the other side of the ford, which Midac had brought from the palace, and urged him to bring a good meal of this to Conan.

"Not so," said Dermat. "He would taunt me with bringing him food taken from the hands of dead men; and though one may recover from his blow, it is not so easy to recover from the venom of his tongue."

So he left Fatha at the ford, and repaired to the Palace of the Island.

As he drew nigh, he heard the noise of feasting and revelry, and the loud talk and laughter of men deep in drink. Walking tiptoe, he peered warily through the open door, and saw the chiefs and the knights sitting at the tables; with Sinsar of the Battles and his son Borba high seated over all. He saw also many attendants serving them with food and drink, each holding in his hand a large ornamented drinking-horn, filled with wine.

Dermat entered the outer door softly, and stood in a dark part of the passage near the door, silent and stern, with sword drawn, watching his opportunity. And after a time one of the attendants, unsuspecting, passed close to him; when Dermat, with a swift, sure blow, struck off his head. And he snatched the drinking-horn from the man's hand before he fell, so that not a drop of the wine was spilled.

Then, laying the drinking-horn aside for a moment, he walked straight into the hall, and taking up one of the dishes near where the king sat, he went out through the open door, bringing with him both dish and drinking-horn. And amidst the great crowd, and the drinking, and the noise, no one took the least notice of him, so that he got off without hindrance or harm of any kind.

When he reached the ford, he found Fatha lying fast asleep on the bank. He wondered very much that he could sleep in the midst of such a slaughter; but knowing that the young warrior was worn out with watching and toil, he left him lying asleep, and went to the Palace of the Quicken Trees with the food for Conan.

When he had come to the door, he called aloud to Conan and said—

"I have here a goodly meal of choice food: how am I to give it to thee?"

Conan said, "Throw it towards me through yonder little opening."

Dermat did so; and as fast as he threw the food, Conan caught it in his large hands, and ate it up ravenously. And when it was all gone, Dermat said—

"I have here a large drinking-horn of good wine: how am I to give it to thee?"

47

Conan answered, "There is a place behind the palace where, from a rock, you may reach the lower parapet with a light, airy bound. Come from that straight over me, and break a hole in the roof with your spear, through which you can pour the wine down to me."

Dermat did so; and as he poured down the wine, Conan, with upturned face, opened his great mouth and caught it, and swallowed it every drop.

After this Dermat came down and returned to the ford, where he found Fatha still asleep; and he sat beside him, but did not awaken him.

DERMAT O'DYNA SLAYS THE THREE KINGS OF THE ISLAND OF THE TORRENT, BREAKS THE SPELL WITH THEIR BLOOD, AND FREES FINN

Tidings were brought to the Palace of the Island that Midac and all whom he led were slain at the ford; and the three kings of the Island of the Torrent said—

"The young king of Lochlann did wrong to make this attempt without asking our counsel; and had we known of the thing we would have hindered him. For to us belongs the right to behead Finn and his companions, since it is the spell-venom of the clay which we brought from the Island of the Torrent that holds them bound in the Palace of the Quicken Trees. And now, indeed, we will go and slay them all."

So they set out with a strong party, and soon reached the ford. Looking across in the dim light, they saw Dermat, and called aloud to ask who he was.

"I am Dermat O'Dyna," he replied, "one of Finn's champions. He has sent me to guard this ford, and whoever you are, I warn you not to cross!"

Then they sought to beguile Dermat, and to win him over by smooth words; and they replied—

"It is a pleasure to us to meet you, Dermat; for we are old friends of yours. We are the three kings of the Island of the Torrent, your fellow-pupils in valour and all heroic feats. For you and we lived with the same tutors from the beginning; and you never learned a feat of arms that we did not learn in like manner. Leave the ford, then, that we may pass on to the Palace of the Quicken Trees."

But Dermat answered in few words, "Finn and his companions are under my protection till morning; and I will defend the ford as long as I am alive!"

And he stood up straight and tall like a pillar, and scowled across the ford.

A number of the foreigners now rushed towards Dermat, and raging in a confused crowd, assailed him. But the strong hero met them as a rock meets the waves, and slew them with ease as they came within the range of his sword. Yet still they pressed on, others succeeding those that fell; and in the midst of the rage of battle, Fatha started up from his sleep, awakened by the crashing of weapons and the riving of shields.

He gazed for a moment, bewildered, at the combatants, and, seeing how matters stood, he was wroth with Dermat for not awakening him; so that he ran at him fiercely with drawn sword. But Dermat stepped aside, and, being angry, thus addressed him—

"Slake thy vengeance on our foes for the present: for me, the swords of the foreigners are enough, methinks, without thine to aid them!"

Then Fatha turned and attacked the foe, and his onset was even more deadly than that of Dermat; so that they fell before him to the right and left on the ford.

And now at last the three kings, seeing so many of their men falling, advanced slowly towards Dermat; and Dermat, unterrified, stood in his place to meet them. And their weapons clashed and tore through their shields, and the fight was long and furious; till at last the champion-pride and the battle-fury of Dermat arose, so that the three dragon-like kings fell slain one by one before him, on that ford of red slaughter.

And now, though smarting with wounds, and breathless, and weary, Dermat and Fatha remembered Finn and the Fena; and Dermat called to mind what Finn had told him as to how the spell was to be broken. So he struck off the heads of the three kings, and, followed by Fatha, he ran with them, all gory as they were, to the Palace of the Quicken Trees.

As they drew nigh to the door, Finn, knowing their voices and their footsteps, called aloud anxiously to ask how it fared with the combatants at the ford; "For," said he, "the crashing and the din of that battle exceeded all we have yet heard, and we know not how it has ended."

Dermat answered, "King of the Fena, Fatha and I have slain the three kings of the Island of the Torrent; and lo, here we have their heads all bloody; but how am I to bring them to thee?"

"Victory and blessings be with you, Dermat; you and Fatha have fought a valiant fight, worthy of the Fena of Erin! Now sprinkle the door with the blood."

Dermat did so, and in a moment the door flew wide open with a crash. And inside they saw the heroes in sore plight, all pale and faint, seated on the cold clay round the wall. Dermat and Fatha, holding the gory heads by the hair, sprinkled the earth under each with the blood, beginning with Finn, and freed them one by one; and the heroes, as they found the spell broken, sprang to their feet with exulting cries. And they thanked the gods for having relieved them from that perilous strait, and they and the two heroes joyfully embraced each other.

But danger still threatened, and they now took counsel what they should do; and Finn, addressing Dermat and Fatha, said—

"The venom of these foul spells has withered our strength, so that we are not able to fight; but at sunrise they will lose their power, and we shall be strong again. It is necessary, therefore, that you still guard the ford, and at the rising of the sun we shall relieve you."

So the two heroes went to the ford, and Fatha returned with food and drink for Finn and the others.

After the last battle at the ford, a few who had escaped brought back tidings to the King of the World and his people, that the three kings of the Island of the Torrent had fallen by the hands of Dermat and Fatha. But they knew not that Finn and the others had been released.

Then arose the king's son, Borba the Haughty, who, next to the king himself, was mightiest in battle of all the foreign host. And he said—

"Feeble warriors were they who tried to cross this ford. I will go now and avenge the death of our people on these Fena, and I will bring hither the head of Finn the son of Cumal, and place it at my father's feet."

So he marched forth without delay, with a large body of chosen warriors, till he reached the edge of the ford. And although Dermat and Fatha never trembled before a foe, yet when they saw the dark mass drawing nigh, and heard the heavy tread and clank of arms, they dreaded that they might be dislodged and overpowered by repeated attacks, leaving Finn and the rest helpless and unprotected. And each in his heart longed for the dawn of morning.

No parley was held this time, but the foreigners came straight across the ford—as many abreast as could find footing. And as they drew near, Dermat spoke to Fatha—

"Fight warily, my friend: ward the blows of the foremost, and be not too eager to slay, but rather look to thy own safety. It behoves us to nurse our strength and prolong the fight, for the day is dawning, and sunrise is not far off!"

The foreigners came on, many abreast; but their numbers availed them naught, for the pass was narrow; and the two heroes, one taking the advancing party to the right, and the other to the left, sometimes parried and sometimes slew, but never yielded an inch from where they stood.

And now at last the sun rose up over the broad plain of Kenri; and suddenly the withering spell went forth from the bones and sinews of the heroes who sat at the Palace of the Quicken Trees, listening with anxious hearts to the clash of battle at the ford. Joyfully they started to their feet, and, snatching up their arms, hastened down to the ford with Finn at their head; but one they sent, the swiftest among them, to Knockfierna, to take the news to Oisin.

Dermat and Fatha, fighting eagerly, heeded not that the sun had risen, though it was now indeed glittering before their eyes on the helmets and arms of their foes. But as they fought, there rose a great shout behind them; and Finn and Gaul and the rest ran down the slope to attack the foreigners.

The foreigners, not in the least dismayed, answered the attack; and the fight went on, till Gaul Mac Morna and Borba the Haughty met face to face in the middle of the ford, and they fought a hard and deadly combat. The battle-fury of Gaul at length arose, so that nothing could stand before him, and, with one mighty blow, he cleft the head from the body of Borba.

And now the foreigners began to yield: but they still continued to fight, till a swift messenger sped to the Palace of the Island, and told the great king, Sinsar of the Battles, that his son was dead, slain by Gaul; and that his army was sore pressed by the Fena, with Finn at their head.

When the people heard these tidings, they raised a long and sorrowful cry of lamentation for the king's son; but the king himself, though sorrow filled his heart, showed it not. And he arose and summoned his whole host; and, having arranged them in their battalions and in their companies under their princes and chiefs, he marched towards the battle-field, desiring vengeance on the Fena more than the glory of victory.

THE FIGHT AT THE FORD, WITH THE FOREIGN ARMY

All the Fena who had gone to the chase from Knocktierna had returned, and were now with Oisin, the son of Finn. And the messenger came slowly up the hillside, and told them, though with much difficulty, for he was weary and breathless, the whole story from beginning to end, of Finn's enchantment, and of the battles at the ford, and how their companions at that moment stood much in need of aid against the foreigners.

Instantly the whole body marched straight towards the Palace of the Quicken Trees, and arrived on the hill-brow over the ford, just as the King of the World and his army were approaching from the opposite direction.

And now the fight at the ford ceased for a time, while the two armies were put in battle array; and on neither side was there any cowardice or any desire to avoid the combat.

The Fena were divided into four battalions. The active, bright-eyed Clann Baskin marched in front of the first battalion; the fierce, champion-like Clann Morna led the second; the strong, sanguinary Mic-an-Smoil brought up the third; and the fourth was led forward by the fearless, venomous Clann O'Navnan.

And they marched forward, with their silken banners, each banner-staff in the hand of a tall, trusty hero; their helmets glittering with precious gems; their broad, beautiful shields on their left shoulders; with their long, straight, deadly lances in their hands; and their heavy, keen-edged swords hanging at the left side of each. Onward they marched; and woe to those who crossed the path of that host of active, high-minded champions, who never turned their backs on an enemy in battle!

And now at last the fight began with showers of light, venomous missiles; and many a hero fell even before the combatants met face to face. Then they drew their long, broad-bladed swords, and the ranks closed and mingled in deadly strife. It would be vain to attempt a description of that battle, for it was hard to distinguish friend from foe. Many a high-souled hero fell wounded and helpless, and neither sigh nor groan of pain escaped them; but they died, encouraging their friends to vengeance with voice and gesture. And the first thought of each champion was to take the life of his foe rather than to save his own.

The great king Finn himself moved tall and stately from battalion to battalion, now fighting in the foremost ranks, and now encouraging his friends and companions, his mighty voice rising clear over the clash of arms and the shouts of the combatants. And wherever he moved, there the courage of the Fena rose high, and their valour and their daring increased, so that the ranks of their foes fell back thinned and scattered before them.

Oscar, resting for a moment from the toil of battle, looked round, and espied the standard of the King of the World, where he stood guarded by his best warriors, to protect him from the danger of being surrounded and outnumbered by his foes; and the young hero's wrath was kindled when he observed that the Fena were falling back dismayed wherever that standard was borne.

Rushing through the opposing ranks like a lion maddened by dogs, he approached the king; and the king laughed a grim laugh of joy when he saw him, and ordered his guards back; for he was glad in his heart, expecting to revenge his son's death by slaying with his own hand Finn's grandson, who was most loved of all the youthful champions of the Fena. Then these two great heroes fought a deadly battle; and many a warrior stayed his hand to witness this combat. It seemed as if both should fall; for each inflicted on the other many wounds. The king's rage knew no bounds at being so long withstood, for at first sight he despised Oscar for his youth and beauty; and he made an onset that caused Oscar's friends, as they looked on, to tremble; for during this attack the young hero defended himself, and no more. But now, having yielded for a time, he called to mind the actions and the fame of his forefathers, and attacked the king in turn, and, with a blow that no shield or buckler could withstand, he swept the head from the king's body.

Then a great shout went up from the Fena, and the foreigners instantly gave way; and they were pursued and slaughtered on every side. A few threw away their arms and escaped to the shore, where, hastily unmooring their ships, they sailed swiftly away to their own country, with tidings of the death of their king and the slaughter of their army.

The Giant's Causeway, County Antrim, Northern Ireland. Legend has it that these unusual basalt structures were built by Finn MacCool as a pathway to Scotland.

THE FRENZY OF SWEENEY

The Tain *may be the greatest work of classical Irish literature, but* The Frenzy of Suibne *is the most beautiful. According to legend, Sweeney (Suibne) was a pagan king of Dal Araidhe in present-day County Down, who attacked a Christian cleric, was cursed by him, and then went mad at the Battle of Mag Rath (*A.D. *637). He spent most of the rest of his life thinking he was a bird and flying from tree to tree across the face of Ireland. Although* The Frenzy, *written in the twelfth century, contains glimpses of battle and ends with Sweeney's conversion to Christianity, its intent seems to be neither historic nor didactic but poetic. As such, it has appealed to many modern writers who have made use of Sweeney's madness, sometimes comically. Among them have been James Joyce, W. B. Yeats, W. D. Snodgrass, Joseph O'Connor, and Flann O'Brien, whose novel* At Swim-Two-Birds *(named for one of Sweeney's resting places) was, to quote Dylan Thomas, "just the book to give your sister if she's a loud, dirty, boozy girl."*

Whether or not Sweeney was actually a historic figure, the Battle of Mag Rath (Magh Rath or Moira),—a clash between the high king Donnall (Domnall) and Congal Claen, who had the support of a Scottish clan settled in northeast Ireland—is mentioned in a number of chronicles. Sweeney is described in one of them, Cath Maige Ratha:

> *The standard of Suibne, a yellow banner,*
> *the renowned king of Dal Araidhe,*
> *yellow satin over that wild man of hosts,*
> *the white fingered stripling himself in the middle of them.*

AS TO SUIBNE, SON OF Colman Cuar and king of Dal Araidhe, we have already told how he went wandering and flying out of battle. Here are set forth the cause and occasion whereby these symptoms and fits of frenzy and flightiness came upon him beyond all others, likewise what befell him thereafter.

There was a certain noble, distinguished holy patron in Ireland, Ronan

A holy bell once thought to have been St. Patrick's.

Finn, son of Bearach, son of Criodhan, son of Earclugh, son of Ernainne, son of Urene, son of Seachnusach, son of Colum Cúile, son of Mureadhach, son of Laoghaire, son of Niall; a man who fulfilled God's command and bore the yoke of piety, and endured persecutions for the Lord's sake. He was God's own worthy servant, for it was his wont to crucify his body for love of God and to win a reward for his soul. A sheltering shield against evil attacks of the devil and against vices was that gentle, friendly, active man.

On one occasion he was marking out a church named Cell Luinne [Killaney] in Dal Araidhe. (At that time Suibne, son of Colman, of whom we have spoken, was king of Dal Araidhe.) Now, in the place where he was, Suibne heard the sound of Ronan's bell as he was marking out the church, and he asked his people what it was they heard. "It is Ronan Finn, son of Bearach," said they, "who is marking out a church in your territory and land, and it is the sound of his bell you now hear." Suibne was greatly angered and enraged, and he set out with the utmost haste to drive the cleric from the church. His wife Eorann, daughter of Conn of Ciannacht, in order to hold him, seized the wing of the fringed, crimson cloak which was around him. Therewith, leaving his cloak with the queen, he set out stark-naked in his swift career to expel the cleric from the church, until he reached the place where Ronan was.

He found the cleric at the time glorifying the King of heaven and earth by blithely chanting his psalms with his lined, right-beautiful psalter in front of him. Suibne took up the psalter and cast it into the depths of the cold-water lake which was near him, so that it was drowned therein. Then he seized Ronan's hand and dragged him out through the church after him, nor did he let go the cleric's hand until he heard a cry of alarm. It was a serving-man of Congal Claon, son of Scannlan, who uttered that cry; he had come from Congal himself to Suibne in order that he (Suibne) might engage in battle at Magh Rath. When the serving-man reached the place of parley with Suibne, he related the news to him from beginning to end. Suibne then went with the serving-man and left the cleric sad and sorrowful over the loss of his psalter and the contempt and dishonour which had been inflicted on him.

Thereafter, at the end of a day and a night, an otter that was in the lake came to Ronan with the psalter, and neither line nor letter of it was injured. Ronan gave thanks to God for that miracle, and then cursed Suibne, saying: "Be it my will, together with the will of the mighty Lord, that even as he came stark-naked to expel me, may it be thus that he will ever be, naked, wandering and flying throughout the world; may it be death from a spear-point that will carry him off. My curse once more on Suibne, and my blessing on Eorann who strove to hold him; and furthermore, I bequeath to the race of Colman that destruction and extinction may be their lot the day they shall behold this psalter which was cast into the water by Suibne"; and he uttered this lay:

> "Suibne, son of Colman, has outraged me,
> he has dragged me with him by the hand,
> to leave Cell Luinne with him,
> that I should be for a time absent from it.
>
> He came to me in his swift course
> on hearing my bell;
> he brought with him vast, awful wrath
> to drive me out, to banish me. . . .
>
> He let not my hand out of his
> until he heard the loud cry
> which said to him: 'Come to the battle,
> Domnall has reached famous Magh Rath.'
>
> Good has come to me therefrom,
> not to him did I give thanks for it
> when tidings of the battle came
> for him to join the high prince.
>
> From afar he approached the battle
> whereby were deranged his sense and reason,
> he will roam through Erin as a stark madman,
> and it shall be by a spear-point he will die.
>
> He seized my psalter in his hand,
> he cast it into the full lake,
> Christ brought it to me without a blemish,
> so that no worse was the psalter.
>
> A day and a night in the full lake,
> nor was the speckled-white [book] the worse;

through the will of God's Son
an otter gave it to me again.

As for the psalter that he seized in his hand,
I bequeath to the race of Colman
that it will be bad for the race of fair Colman
the day they shall behold the psalter.

Stark-naked he has come here
to wring my heart, to chase me;
on that account God will cause
that Suibne shall ever naked be.

Eorann, daughter of Conn of Ciannacht,
strove to hold him by his cloak;
my blessing on Eorann therefor,
and my curse on Suibne."

Thereupon Ronan came to Magh Rath to make peace between Domnall son of Aodh, and Congal Claon son of Scannlan, but he did not succeed. Howbeit, the cleric used to be taken each day as a guarantee between them that nobody would be slain from the time the fighting was stopped [for the day] until it would be again permitted. Suibne, however, used to violate the cleric's guarantee of protection inasmuch as every peace and truce which Ronan would make Suibne would break, for he used to slay a man before the hour fixed for combat each day, and another each evening when the combat ceased. Then on the day fixed for the great battle Suibne came to battle before the rest.

In this wise did he appear. A filmy shirt of silk was next his white skin, around him was a girdle of royal satin, likewise the tunic which Congal had given him the day he slew Oilill Cedach, king of the Ui Faolain, at Magh Rath; a crimson tunic of one colour was it with a close, well-woven border of beautiful, refined gold set with rows of fair gems of carbuncle from one end to the other of the border, having in it silken loops over beautiful, shining buttons for fastening and opening it, with variegation of pure white silver each way and each path he would go; there was a slender-threaded hard fringe to that tunic. In his hands were two spears very long and (shod) with broad iron, a yellow-speckled, horny shield was on his back, a gold-hilted sword at his left side.

He marched on thus until he encountered Ronan with eight psalmists of his community sprinkling holy water on the hosts, and they sprinkled it on Suibne as they did on the others. Thinking it was to mock him that the water was sprinkled on him, he placed his finger on the string of the riveted spear that was in his hand, and hurling it at one of Ronan's psalmists slew him with that single cast. He made another cast with the edged, sharp-angled dart at the cleric himself, so that it pierced the bell which was on his breast and the shaft sprang off it up in the air, whereupon the cleric said: . . .

> "My curse on Suibne!
> great is his guilt against me,
> his smooth, vigorous dart
> he thrust through my holy bell.
>
> That bell which thou hast wounded
> will send thee among branches,
> so that thou shalt be one with the birds—
> the bell of saints before saints.
>
> Even as in an instant went
> the spear-shaft on high,
> mayst thou go, O Suibne,
> in madness, without respite!
>
> Thou hast slain my foster-child,
> thou hast reddened thy spear in him,
> thou shalt have in return for it
> that with a spear-point thou shalt die. . . .
>
> My blessing on Eorann!
> Eorann fair without decay:
> through suffering without stint
> my curse on Suibne!"

Thereafter, when both battle-hosts had met, the vast army on both sides roared in the manner of a herd of stags so that they raised on high three mighty shouts. Now, when Suibne heard these great cries together with their sounds and reverberations in the clouds of Heaven and in the vault of the firmament, he looked up, whereupon turbulence (?), and darkness, and fury, and giddiness, and frenzy, and flight, unsteadiness, restlessness, and unquiet filled him, likewise disgust with every place in which he used to be and desire for every place which he had not reached. His fingers were palsied, his feet trembled, his heart beat quick, his senses were overcome, his sight was distorted, his weapons fell naked from his hands, so that through Ronan's curse he went, like any bird of the air, in madness and imbecility.

Now, however, when he arrived out of the battle, it was seldom that his feet would touch the ground because of the swiftness of his course, and when he did touch it he would not shake the dew from the top of the grass for the lightness and the nimbleness of his step. He halted not from that headlong course until he left neither plain, nor field, nor bare mountain, nor bog, nor thicket, nor marsh, nor hill, nor hollow, nor dense-sheltering wood in Ireland that he did not travel that day, until he reached Ros Bearaigh, in Glenn Earcain [in County Antrim], where he went into the yew-tree that was in the glen.

Domnall, son of Aedh, won the battle that day. Suibne had a kinsman in the battle, to wit, Aongus the Stout, son of Ardgal, son of Macnia, son of Ninnidh, of the tribes of Ui Ninnedha of Dal Araidhe; he came in flight with a number of his people out of the battle, and the route he took was through Glenn Earcain. Now he and his people were conversing about Suibne (saying) how strange it was that they had not seen him alive or dead after the battle-hosts had met. Howbeit, they felt certain it was because of Ronan's curse that there were no tidings of his fate. Suibne in the yew-tree above them heard what they spoke, and he said:

> "O warriors, come hither,
> O men of Dal Araidhe,
> you will find in the tree in which he is
> the man whom you seek.
>
> God has vouchsafed me here
> life very bare, very narrow,
> without music and without restful sleep,
> without womenfolk, without a woman-tryst.
>
> Here at Ros Bearaigh am I,
> Ronan has put me under disgrace,
> God has severed me from my form,
> know me no more, O warriors."

When the men heard Suibne reciting the verses, they recognized him, and urged him to trust them. He said that he would never do so. Then, as they were closing round the tree, Suibne rose out of it very lightly and nimbly (and went) to Cell Riagain [Kilrean] in Tir Conaill where he perched on the old tree of the church. It chanced that it was at that tree Domnall, son of Aedh, and his army were after the battle, and when they saw the madman going into the tree, a portion of the army came and closed in all round it. Thereupon they began describing aloud the madman; one man would say that it was a woman, another that it was a man, until Domnall himself recognized him, whereupon he said: "It is Suibne, king of Dal Araidhe, whom Ronan cursed the day the battle was fought. Good in sooth is the man who is there," said he, "and if he wished for treasures and wealth he would obtain them from us if only he would trust us. Sad is it to me," said he, "that the remnant of Congal's people are thus, for both good and great were the ties that bound me to Congal. . . . Whereupon Domnall uttered the lay:

> "How is that, O slender Suibne?
> thou wert leader of many hosts;
> the day the iniquitous battle was fought
> at Magh Rath thou wert most comely.
>
> Like crimson or like beautiful gold
> was thy noble countenance after feasting,
> like down or like shavings
> was the faultless hair of thy head.
>
> Like cold snow of a single night
> was the aspect of thy body ever;
> blue-hued was thine eye, like crystal,
> like smooth, beautiful ice.
>
> Delightful the shape of thy feet,
> not powerful methinks was thy chieftainship;
> thy fortunate weapons—they could draw blood—
> were swift in wounding. . . .
>
> Thy body will be a feast for birds of prey,
> ravens will be on thy heavy silence,
> a fierce, black spear shall wound thee,
> and thou shalt be laid on thy back, destitute. . . ."

Now when Suibne heard the shout of the multitude and the tumult of the great army, he ascended from the tree towards the rain-clouds of the firmament, over the summits of every place and over the ridge-pole of every land. For a long time thereafter he was (faring) throughout Ireland, visiting and searching in hard, rocky clefts and in bushy branches of tall ivy-trees, in narrow cavities of stones, from estuary to estuary, from peak to peak, and from glen to glen, till he reached ever-delightful Glen Bolcain [in Antrim]. It is there the madmen of Ireland used to go when their year in madness was complete, that glen being ever a place of great delight for madmen. For it is thus Glen Bolcain is: it has four gaps to the wind, likewise a wood very beautiful, very pleasant, and clean-banked wells and cool springs, and sandy, clear-water streams, and green-topped watercress and brooklime bent and long on their surface. Many likewise are its sorrels, its wood-sorrels, its *lus-bian* and its *biorragan*, its berries, and its wild garlic, its *melle* and its *miodhbhun*, its black sloes and its brown acorns. The madmen moreover used to smite each other for the pick of watercress of that glen and for the choice of its couches.

Suibne also remained for a long time in that glen until he happened one night to be on the top of a tall ivy-clad hawthorn tree which was in the glen. It was hard for him to endure that bed, for at every twist and turn he would give, a shower of thorns off the hawthorn would stick in him, so that they were piercing and rending his side and wounding his skin. Suibne thereupon changed from that bed to another place, where there was a dense thicket of great briars with fine thorns and a single protruding branch of blackthorn growing alone up through the thicket. Suibne settled on the top of that tree, but so slender was it that it bowed and bent under him, so that he fell heavily through the thicket to the ground, and there was not as much as an inch from his sole to the crown of his head that was not wounded and reddened. He then rose up, strengthless and feeble, and came out through the thicket, whereupon he said: "My conscience!" said he, "it is hard to endure this life after a pleasant one, and a year to last night I have been leading this life," whereupon he uttered the lay:

> "A year to last night
> have I been among the gloom of branches,
> between flood and ebb,
> without covering around me.
>
> Without a pillow beneath my head,
> among the fair children of men;
> there is peril to us, O God,
> without sword, without spear.
>
> Without the company of women;
> save brooklime of warrior-bands—
> a pure fresh meal—
> watercress is our desire.
>
> Without a foray with a king,
> I am alone in my home,
> without glorious reavings,
> without friends, without music.

Without sleep, alas!
let the truth be told,
without aid for a long time,
hard is my lot.
Without a house right full,
without the converse of generous men,
without the title of king,
without drink, without food.

Alas that I have been parted here
from my mighty, armed host,
a bitter madman in the glen,
bereft of sense and reason.

Without being on a kingly circuit,
but rushing along every path;
that is the great madness,
O King of Heaven of saints.

Without accomplished musicians,
without the converse of women,
without bestowing treasures;
it has caused my death, O revered Christ.

Though I be as I am to-night,
there was a time
when my strength was not feeble
over a land that was not bad.

On splendid steeds,
in life without sorrow,
in my auspicious kingship
I was a good, great king.

After that, to be as I am
through selling Thee, O revered Christ!
a poor wretch am I, without power,
in the Glen of bright Bolcan.

The hawthorn that is not soft-topped
has subdued me, has pierced me;
the brown thorn-bush
has nigh caused my death.

The battle of Congal with fame,
to us it was doubly piteous;
on Tuesday was the rout;
more numerous were our dead than our living.

A-wandering in truth,
though I was noble and gentle,
I have been sad and wretched
a year to last night."

[After years of random flying around Ireland, Sweeney settles at the monastery of St. Moling in County Carlow, where the monks see that he is fed and cared for. Then, as the curse of St. Ronan foretold, he is killed by a spear, the killer being the cook's husband, who was jealous of the attention the madman was getting. As he converts to Christianity and dies, Sweeney thinks back over his life.]

"There was a time when I deemed more melodious
than the quiet converse of people,
the cooing of the turtle-dove
flitting about a pool.

There was a time when I deemed more melodious
than the sound of a little bell beside me
the warbling of the blackbird to the mountain
and the belling of the stag in a storm.

There was a time when I deemed more melodious
than the voice of a beautiful woman beside me,
to hear at dawn
the cry of the mountain-grouse.

There was a time when I deemed more melodious
the yelping of the wolves
than the voice of a cleric within
a-baaing and a-bleating."

Ireland Before the English Invasion (1170)

Atlantic Ocean

ULSTER

Emain Macha
● Armagh
Faughart ✶
Dundalk

Lough Arrow

CONNACHT

Cong ●
Lough Corrib

Tara ●

LEINSTER

Clontarf ✶

Clonmacnoise ●

Dublin

Inishmore ●

THOMOND

Ferns ●

Limerick ●

Cashel ●

MUNSTER

Wexford ●

Waterford ●

Irish Sea

Atlantic Ocean

The English Invasion

0 Miles   50
0 Kilometers   50

© 2000 Jeffrey L. Ward

Ireland After the English Invasion

Atlantic Ocean

© 2000 Jeffrey L. Ward

DONEGAL

DERRY

ANTRIM

Larne

Yellow ford

TYRONE

Enniskillen

FERMANAGH

ARMAGH

Armagh

DOWN

Sligo

LEITRIM

MONAGHAN

Clontibret

Faughart

SLIGO

CAVAN

LOUTH

Dundalk

MAYO

ROSCOMMON

LONGFORD

MEATH

The English Pale

Knockdoe

WESTMEATH

GALWAY

Atherny

Galway

OFFALY

Kildare

KILDARE

DUBLIN

Howth

Dublin

Dysert O'Day

LEIX

CLARE

WICKLOW

TIPPERARY

CARLOW

Limerick

KILKENNY

WEXFORD

LIMERICK

KERRY

Waterford

WATERFORD

Wexford

CORK

Cork

Kinsale

Atlantic Ocean

Irish Sea

The Bruce Invasion (1315)

0 Miles 50

0 Kilometers 50

II.

KINGS

AND

BATTLES

INTRODUCTION

I T IS IMPOSSIBLE TO LEAF through the early literature of Ireland and stop at a certain place and say, this is where the mythmaking ends and true history begins. When it came time to write about the early kings—sometimes centuries after they lived—fact, memory, current politics, religion, and the love of a good story mixed together in sometimes wildly unequal portions to create a historic tradition.

When Gerald of Wales wrote about the newly invaded Ireland in the twelfth century, he noted, "There are many kings there." Indeed there were and there had been for centuries, as many as 125 at a time, ranging from the kings of tiny local kingdoms to the kings of the four provinces to the high king at Tara. Since none of these kings, great or small, inherited his crown, each had to win—one way or another—the support of his nobles and the recognition of the kings of rival kingdoms. This was done through force, through well-planned marriages, and through an elaborate system of gift giving.

The following accounts of some pre-eleventh-century kings mix legend and fact, but one scene provides some insight on the gift-giving process. Cormac, king of Munster, needs money and asks for gifts. His family and closest allies do not respond, but a distant clan—no doubt seeking closer ties to the ruler—is unexpectedly generous. Usually, however, the giving of gifts was not left to chance and everyone knew exactly what was required. *The Book of Rights* (*Kebor na Cert*), which claims to be from the eleventh century but was probably written later, spells out the gift giving in detail. Here, for example, is a partial list of what was expected from a king of Munster:

- Ten steeds and ten drinking horns and ten swords and ten *scrings* [horse harnesses] and two rings and two chessboards to the king of Gabhran.

- Ten steeds and ten bondmen [slaves] and ten women and ten drinking horns to the king of the Eoghanachta.

- Eight bondmen and eight women and swords and eight horses and eight shields and ten ships to the king of the Deise Momhan.

- Seven hounds and seven steeds and seven drinking horns to the king of Dairbhre.

- Seven women and seven *matals* [cloaks] trimmed in gold and seven drinking horns and seven steeds to the king of Ciarraighe.

Irish knights and their attendants, 1521. The mantles and axes are typically Irish; the swords and armor are not. Drawing by Albrecht Dürer.

BRIEF SKETCHES OF
THREE IRISH KINGS

BY GEOFFREY KEATING

⚶

Geoffrey Keating (c. 1570–1650), a priest born in Tipperary and edu-
cated in Europe, is usually thought of as the first modern Irish historian.
He wrote his history of Ireland from the mythic invasions (which he
accepted more or less at face value) to the Norman invasion (brought
on, he thought, by the sinful ways of the Irish) in Irish rather than
Latin. Although his most enthusiastic admirers call him the Herodotus
of Ireland, Keating is read by students today more for the clarity of his
Irish than for historical fact.

These three selections from his history include a possibly mythic
tale of two second-century kings who divided up Ireland between
themselves, an account of the last battle fought by a tenth-century king
of Munster, and a brief commentary of the Battle of Mag Rath, the battle from which Sweeney was said to flee after he went mad.

There might have been mythical elements in the division of Ireland
between Conn (or Conan) of the Hundred Battles and Eogan Mor
(Owen the Great), between Ulster and Munster, but that line stretch-
ing from present-day Dublin to Galway was fought over for centuries
to come, and for centuries the kings of Munster were chosen from the
Eoganacht clan, who claimed to be descendants of the great Owen.

The account of the last battle of King Cormac has a couple of curious moments. One comes when Cormac, urged on by a priest but
knowing that he will lose the battle and his life, decides to go to war.
Just before the fight begins, one of his officers complains that the "the
ecclesiastics" should fight their own battles. In a history written largely by monks and priests, this is a rare flicker of criticism.

The other moment, after the battle, is the scene involving what was
proposed to be done with Cormac's severed head. A nineteenth-century
editor of the text was so shocked that he added a footnote to his edition saying that he had never before encountered a custom so "horri-
bly distorted and heathenish" and suggesting that if such a thing did
occur it must have had its origins in the East, presumably with the
Mongol hordes. It is also worth noting the many parallels made with

the final hours of Cormac—who was an abbot as well as a king—with
the Last Supper and crucifixion of Christ.

In his brief comments on the Battle of Mag Rath in County Down
in 637, Keating does not discuss tactics or even show much interest in
the outcome. Instead, he writes about flags and insignia. Heraldry had
not been of much interest until the Tudor years, when complex coats
of arms came into fashion. Writing soon after the death of Elizabeth,
Keating shows that even in the seventh century the Irish could field rel-
atively modern-looking armies.

CONN OF THE HUNDRED BATTLES

125 A.D.: Conn Ked-Cathach [of the Hundred Battles] held the sovereignty
of Ireland for twenty years, until, being taken unawares, he was treacherously slain, by the contrivance of Tibradi Tirech, king of Ulster. Fifty warriors, disguised as women, had been sent by Tibradi, for the purpose of
assassinating him; and Emhain Macha was the place whence they set out
upon that treacherous design.

This was that Conn from whom Mogh Nuadath, having vanquished
him in ten battles, wrestled the one half of Ireland.

The contest between these kings originated in the following manner:
The Ernaans had gained supremacy in Munster over the race of Eber Finn;
so that three chieftains of that tribe now held the sovereignty of all
Munster between them. Their names were Lugaidh Ellathach, Dari
Dornmar, and Aengus. But, when Mogh Nuadath saw that the supremacy
of his native principality had been thus usurped by the race of Erimhòn,
he proceeded to Leinster, where he had been fostered by Dari Barrach, and
there he procured from his foster-father a numerous auxiliary force,
wherewith to recover the kingdom of Munster, which was his birth-right.
He then began by marching into Ui Liathain [in County Cork], in the south
of Munster, where that Aengus, above mentioned, had established his
sway. Him Mogh Nuadath vanquished and expelled from that country, so
that he was forced to betake himself straightway to supplicate assistance
from Conn, who gave him five catha (battalions or legions), that is, fifteen
thousand fighting men. With these Aengus marched upon the territory of
Liathan, and there, upon the height of Ard-Nemidh, he was met by Mogh
Nuadath, who routed him a second time with great slaughter of his followers. After this victory, Mogh Nuadath expelled from Munster all of the
Ernanns that refused to do him homage. From these events, a great war
broke out between Conn and the Munster prince, in which the former was
defeated in ten battles, such as the battle of Brosnach, the battle of

Sampait, the battle of Grian, the battle of Ath-luain, the battle of Magh-Atha-Crioch, where Fiacaidh Righ-fada, son of Feidlimidh Rectmar, was slain, the battle of Asal, the battle of Uisnech, &c. This war then lasted ever until Mogh Nuadath had forced Conn to yield up one-half of Ireland to himself. All of Ireland that lies south of Ath-cliath and Galimh (i.e. Dublin and Galway) was ceded to Mogh; and the name which that half got was Leth-Mogha, i.e. Mogh's Half, from Eogan, who was called Mogh. The north half was called Leth-Cuinn, or Conn's Half.

Another reason, also, is given for Eogan's having succeeded in wresting the half of Ireland from Conn. They say that a great famine, which lasted for seven years, came upon Ireland during the reign of Conn, and that, long before the time of scarcity had arrived, one of the druids of Mogh had forewarned him of the calamity that was impending over the whole nation. Eogan, upon hearing it, determined to make preparation to meet the approaching season of want; and, for that purpose, he made use of venison and fish as his principal articles of immediate consumption as food, while he stored up his corn. Besides this, he expended upon corn all the rents and tributes that he received. He thus succeeded in filling up his granaries. Then, when the season of want had come, numbers of the people of Ireland had come to him from all sides, who submitted themselves to Eogan, and covenanted to pay him rents and tributes, as a compensation for their support during the time the famine lasted.

And, furthermore, according to some historians, it was by Conn of the Hundred Battles, who made an attack upon him before dawn, that Eogan Mor was treacherously slain in his bed, as they were on the point of engaging each other in battle upon the plain of Magh-Lèna.

This monarch was called Conn of the Hundred Battles, from the hundreds of battles which he fought against the pentarchs or provincial kings of Ireland.

KING CORMAC'S LAST BATTLE

Cormac, son of Culinan, assumed the sovereignty of Munster about this time [A.D. 896]. And great was the prosperity of Ireland during his reign; for the land became filled with the divine grace, and with worldly prosperity, and with public peace in his days, so that the cattle needed no cowherd, and the flocks no shepherd, as long as he was king. The shrines of the saints were then protected, and many temples and monasteries were built; public schools were established for the purpose of giving instruction in letters, law, and history; many were the tilled fields, numerous were the bees, and plenteous the beehives under his rule; frequent was fasting and prayer, and every other work of piety; many houses of public hospitality were built, and many books written, at his command. And, moreover, whenever he exacted the performance of any good work from others, he was wont to set them the example himself by being the first to practise it, whether it were a deed of alms, or benevolence, or prayer, or attending mass, or any other virtuous deed. It was the good fortune of Ireland during that epoch, that, whilst he was reigning over Munster, the country was abandoned by whatever of the Lochlannaigh [Vikings] had previously infested it for the purposes of plunder.

Upon a certain occasion, when Cormac was staying at Cashel, awaiting the coming of Easter, he sent proclamation to the Eoganacht tribes, requiring of them to send him thither food and treasures for the celebration of that august festival; but they gave him a refusal. Upon hearing this the Dal-g-Cais sent a large supply of food and treasures to the king, so that he felt grateful to them. He again sent word to the clans of the race of Eogan, demanding of them to send him jewels and valuables for the purpose of making presents to strangers, as they had sent him no food. But upon this what the men of the race of Eogan did, was to send him the worst arms and goods that they had then in their possession, and Cormac was very much displeased thereat. The Dal-g-Cais heard this also, whereupon they sent to him the choicest of their weapons and wearing apparel, their jewels and treasures and armor, in order that he might make presents thereof. Thus did Cormac feel again most grateful to that tribe.

When, indeed Cormac, son of Culinan, had spent seven years in peace and happiness as sovereign of Munster, he was instigated by some of his nobles, and more especially by Flathbertach, son of Inmanen, Abbot of Inis Cathaigh, a man of the royal blood, to make a demand of chief-rent from the principality of Leinster, upon the pretext that it formed a portion of Leth Mogha. Thereupon, Cormac convened a general assembly of the men of Munster; and when his nobles had met together thereat, the plan which they adopted, was to march into Leinster for the purpose of levying that chief-rent, in right of the division which had been formerly made between Mogh Nuadath and Conn of the Hundred Battles. Notwithstanding this resolve, it was with great unwillingness that Cormac proceeded upon this expedition, for it had been foreshown to him that he should fall himself therein; but he consented to go upon it nevertheless. Previous to his marching, he made a will, in which he bequeathed certain legacies, which were to be given by Munster to some of the principal churches of Ireland, to wit: An ounce of gold and an ounce of silver, with his accouterments and his steed, to Drum-Abradh, which is called Ard Finnain; a chalice of gold, and a chalice of silver, with a satin vestment, to Lis-mor; a chalice of gold, and a chalice of silver, with four ounces of gold, and five ounces of silver, to Cashel; three ounces of gold and a mass-book, to Imlech Iubair; an ounce of gold and an ounce of silver, to Glenn-da-loch; his wares and clothes, with an ounce of gold and a satin mantle, to Kill-dara; twenty-four ounces of gold and of silver to Ard-Macha; three ounces of gold to Inis Cathaigh; and three ounces of gold and a satin vestment, and his own blessing, to Mungarid.

After this, Cormac, having mustered a large host around himself and around Flathbertach, son of Inmanen, marched into the territory of the Leinstermen, and demanded of them to give him hostages and to pay him tribute as King of Munster, upon the grounds that their country (Leinster) formed part of Leth Mogha [Mogh's Half of Ireland]. Now, when the host of Munster had come together and was all collected into one camp, previous to marching upon the intended expedition, it happened that Flathbertach, son of Inmanen, the abbot of Inis Cathaigh, having mounted upon horseback, rode through the street of the encampment, and that whilst he was thus engaged, his horse fell beneath him into a deep trench. This was esteemed an unlucky omen, and its consequence was that a large portion both of his own people and of the whole army retired from the expedition, having first proposed the adoption of peaceful measures—so unfavorable a prognostic did they deem the sudden fall of the holy abbot when he had mounted his steed.

Then ambassadors arrived from the Leinstermen, and from Kerball, son of Murighen, charged with proposals of peace to king Cormac. These proposals were: first, to have one universal peace maintained throughout Ireland until the following month of May, for it was then the Fortnight of the Harvest, and for that end to place hostages in the hands of Maenach, son of Siadal, abbot of Disert Diarmoda, who was a holy, pious, learned and wise man; and, next, to give a large quantity of jewels and valuables to Cormac himself, and also to Flathbertach, son of Inmanen, as a recompense for having assented to such a peace.

Cormac was most willing to grant their request; whereupon he immediately proceeded to acquaint Flathbertach, that these ambassadors had come to him from the king of Leinster, demanding peace until the ensuing month of May, and offering jewels and valuables to them both from the people of Leinster, provided they would return home in peace to their own country. But when Flathbertach had heard him out, he fell into a violent rage, and he exclaimed, "How easily seen is the weakness of thy mind, and the littleness of thy intellect and thy spirit!" And after this fashion he then addressed much of abusive and contemptuous language to Cormac.

The latter replied to him in the following words, "I know full well what will be the result of all this, to wit, a battle shall be fought with the men of Leinster, in which I shall be slain, and in which it is probable that thou shalt meet thy death likewise."

Having uttered these words, Cormac proceeded, sad and dejected, to his own tent. When he had taken his seat therein, a basket of apples was set before him, which he began to share amongst his attendants, saying, "My dear friends, I shall never more share any apples amongst you, from this hour forth." "Dear lord," said his folk, "thou hast cast us into sadness and grief. Why art thou thus wont to prophesy evil for thyself?" "Believe what I now say, friends of my heart," said Cormac, "for though I am wont to distribute apples amongst you with my own hands, it will be little wonder if somebody else in my stead should share them amongst you henceforth."

Cormac then gave orders to have a guard placed upon his tent, and the pious and learned Maenach sent for, in order that he might confess his sins to that holy man, and make his testament in his presence. He then received the body of Christ from Maenach, before whom he renounced the world, for he was certain that he should be slain in the impending battle, but he did not wish that his warriors should know this.

But, likewise, numbers of the men of Munster had deserted from that expedition without leave, for they had learned that Flann Sinna, son of Maelsechlainn, monarch of Ireland, was in the encampment of Leinster, accompanied by a numerous force, both of cavalry and infantry. It was then that Maenach, son of Siadal, said, "Good people of Munster, it were wise on your part to take the noble hostages, namely, Kerball, King of Leinster, and the son of the king of Osraide, that are offered to you, and either to keep them yourselves, or to place them in the hands of some devout men until May next." Thereupon the whole of the men of Munster replied unanimously, that Flathbertach, son of Inmanen, was the man who had forced them to invade Leinster.

When this complaint was ended, the army of Munster marched eastwards over Sliabh Margi, to the Droiched Leithglinni [the Bridge of Leathglen in Carlow]. Here Tibradi, the comarba [ecclesiastical successor of] of St. Albi, took up his station, accompanied by a numerous array of ecclesiastics, and with him were left the camp followers and the baggage horses. Then the men of Munster sounded their trumpets, and gave the signal for forming into line of battle, and marched onward upon Magh Ailbi, where they took up a strong position in front of a wood, and there awaited the enemy.

The army of Munster was drawn up in three equal divisions. Of these, the first was commanded by Flathbertach, son of Inmanen, and Kellach, son of Kerball, King of Osraide. Cormac, son of Culinan, King of Munster, commanded the second division, and Cormac, son of Molta, King of the Desi, was the leader of the third. And the warriors were disheartened by reason of the multitude of their enemies and of the fewness of their own host, for some authors assert that the army of Leinster was four times more numerous than that of Munster.

Woeful, indeed, was the tumult and clamor of that battle; for there rose the death cry of the men of Munster as they fell, and the shouting of the Leinstermen, exulting in the slaughter of their foes. There were two reasons why the fight went so suddenly against the Munstermen. The first was, because Keilichar, a relative of Kennghegan, a former king of Munster [who had been killed by his own people], jumped hastily upon his steed, and as soon as he found himself mounted, cried out, "Flee, O Free Clans of Munster, flee from this terrible conflict, and let the ecclesiastics fight it out themselves, since they would accept no other condition but that of battle from the people of Leinster." Having thus spoken, he quitted the field of strife, followed by many of the combatants.

The other reason why the men of Munster were routed was because Kellach, son of Kerball, king of Osraide, when he perceived the carnage that was made amongst his people, jumped likewise with haste upon his steed, and thence addressed his host in these words, "Mount your steeds," said he, "and banish these men who stand up against you." But though he used this language, he did not mean to encourage them to drive off their enemies by fighting, but he thus let them know that it was time for themselves to run away. The result of these two causes was that the ranks of the men of Munster were broken, and they were put to sudden and general rout. Alas! great indeed was the carnage that then spread over Magh-n-Ailbi. Neither layman nor ecclesiastic found quarter therein; both were slaughtered indiscriminately, and if any man of either class happened to be spared, he owed his life not to the mercy but to the cupidity of the vanquishers, covetous of his ransom.

Hereupon Cormac rushed toward the van of the first division, but his horse fell beneath into a ditch, and he was himself dashed upon the ground. Some of his people who were running away from the battle saw him in this position, and they came at once to his relief and replaced him upon his steed. It was there that Cormac met one of his own pupils, a freeborn man named Aedh, who was distinguished for his proficiency in wisdom, laws, and history, and in the knowledge of the Latin tongue. To him the royal prelate addressed these words: "Dear son, do not follow me; but betake thyself hence, as well thou mayest, and remember that I had said that I should myself be slain in this battle." Cormac then rode forward, and full of the blood of horses and of men was the way before him. But the slipperiness of that field of carnage soon caused the feet of his horse to glide from under him, and he reared and fell backwards, crushing his rider beneath him. The neck and back of Cormac were broken in that fall, and he died saying, "Into thy hands, O Lord, I commit my spirit!" Then, some wicked folk came up and pierced his body with their javelins and cut off his head.

When the conflict was over, certain folk came into the presence of Flann Sinna, to whom they had brought the head of Cormac, son of Culinan; and they addressed that monarch: "Life and health to thee, O mighty and victorious king! We have brought thee hither the head of Cormac, king of Munster. Take it then, and press it beneath thy thighs; for it has been a custom amongst the kings that have gone before thee, whenever they had slain another king in battle, to cut off his head and to press it beneath their thighs." However, they were disappointed in their expectations; for the sovereign not only returned them no thanks for their present, but he condemned them in severe terms for the evil deed they had committed. And he both said that it was a sad and cruel act, to have cut off the head of that holy bishop, and declared that he would never exult over it. He then took the consecrated head of the pious bishop into his hands and kissed it, and turned round three times therewith. After this, the head was carried with honor to where the body lay.

THE BATTLE OF MAGH RATH

It was Domnall, son of Aedh, son of Anmiri, king of Ireland, that won the battle of Magh Rath, wherein fell Congal Claen, who had been ten years king of Ulidia. And it may be easily learned from the history that is called the Battle of Magh Rath, that the military array in which the Gaelic armies were wont to be drawn up, for the purpose of engaging in the conflict of battle, was exact and well ordered. For it is there read, that the whole host was wont to be placed under the command of one captain-in-chief, and that, under him, each division of his force obeyed its own proper captain; and besides, that every captain of these bore upon his standard his peculiar device or ensign, so that each distinct body of men could be easily distinguished from all others by those shannachies [devices], whose duty it was to attend upon the nobles when about to contend in battle, and that those shannachies might thus have a full view of the achievements of the combatants, so as to be able to give a true account of their particular deeds of valor. It was for such purpose that Domnall, son of Aedh, king of Ireland, was attended by his own shannachie, when he was about to engage in this battle of Magh Rath. And when he was marching against Congal, and when the hosts were in view of each other, we find Domnall, whilst the armies were yet on the opposite banks of a river, making inquiries of his shannachie about each particular one of the standards in the host of his enemy, and the device thereupon; and the shannachie explained them to him, as we read in the duan [epic poem] which begins with this line, "How bravely Congal's host comes on," in which occurs the following verse upon the standard of the king of Uladh himself:

> "A yellow lion upon green satin,
> The standard of the Craebh-Ruadh,
> As borne by noble Concobar,
> Is now by Congal borne aloft."

It was, indeed, long before this time, that the Gaels (that is, the descendants of Gaedal), had adopted the custom of bearing distinctive devices upon their standards, after the example of the Children of Israel, who had already practised this usage in Egypt, and when the children of Israel were marching through the Red Sea, with Moses for their captain-in-chief.

THE ANNALS OF
THE FOUR MASTERS
NINTH- AND TENTH-CENTURY ENTRIES

The men called the Four Masters (although there were probably six of them) were Franciscans led by a lay brother named Michael O'Clereigh or Michael O'Clery (1575–1643), who, after collecting a massive number of monastic annals and other historic records from all over Ireland, set up shop in a friary in Donegal and between 1632 and 1636 produced a monumental history of Ireland from the abeyance of Noah's flood to the beginning of the seventeenth century. Titled Annala Rioghachsa Eireann (Annals of the Kingdom of Ireland) *and usually called* Annals of the Four Masters, *it is a wide-ranging, idiosyncratic, sometimes exasperating compendium of birth and death dates, ecclesiastical appointments, royal advancements, weather reports, local gossip, battles, and miraculous cures. Some events are covered in exacting detail (a mermaid who washed up on shore was 195 feet long with hair 16 feet long and a 7-foot nose), while an entry on the massacre of an entire army can be only a few words long or—more frequently—simply a list of the names of the most distinguished casualties. Yet the lavish wealth of information it contains makes the seven thick volumes of the published version of* The Four Masters *the most consulted work of medieval Irish history. It is the source with which all other sources are compared. Today in the city of Donegal, not far from the ruined friary where the Masters wrote, stands an obelisk in their honor, which must be one of the few civic monuments ever raised for a committee of historians.*

The edited selection from The Four Masters *included here—for the years 799 through 919—presents a vivid picture of both the constant wars among the clans (at one point the Masters think it worth mentioning that two rival branches of the O'Neill family met and did not come to blows) and the first destructive landings of the "foreigners," the Vikings. Some entries may seem to be simply masses of family and place-names, but readers who sail through them without pausing to worry about their identity or present-day locations can gain an intimate feeling for the everyday concerns of that distant time.*

THE AGE OF CHRIST, 799. There happened great wind, thunder, and lightning, on the day before the festival of Patrick of this year, so that one thousand and ten persons were killed in the territory of Corca-Bhaiscinn, and the sea divided the island of Fitha into three parts. . . .

The Age of Christ, 801. The ninth year of [the reign of king] Aedh Oirdnidhe. Congal, son of Maenach, Abbot of Slaine, who was a learned sage and a pure virgin; [and] Loitheach, doctor of Beannchair [Bangor], died. Hi-Coluim-Cille was plundered by foreigners; and great numbers of the laity and clergy were killed by them, namely, sixty-eight. Flaithiusa, son of Cinaedh, lord of Ui-Failghe, was slain at Rath-Imghain. Tir-da-ghlas [Terryglass] was burned. Finnachta, son of Ceallach, King of Leinster, took the government again. Connmhach, Judge of Ui-Briuin, died.

The Age of Christ, 802. . . . The church of Coluim-Cille at Ceanannus was destroyed. Inis-Muireadhaigh was burned by foreigners, and they attacked Ros-Commain. Cormac, son of Donghalach, lord of the North, died. Murchadh Ua Flainn, lord of Ui-Fidhgeinte, died.

The Age of Christ, 803. The eleventh year of Aedh. . . . Finshneachta, son of Ceallach, King of Leinster, died at Cilldara. Cinaedh, son of Conchobhar, was slain at Magh-Cobha, by the Cruithni [of Dal-Araidhe]. A hosting by Muirgheas, son of Tomaltach, with the Connaughtmen about him, to assist Conchobhar, son of Donnchadh, son of Domhnall, to destroy the men of Meath, and they arrived at Tir-an-aenaigh. The king, Aedh, came to protect the men of Meath; and he drove Conchobhar and his forces to flight out of it, as if they were goats and sheep. He afterwards burned that part of the country of Meath which was dearest to Donnchadh.

The Age of Christ, 804. . . . Finbil, Abbess of Cluain-Bronaigh, and Dunchu, Abbot of Tealach-lias, were slain. Cuciarain, Prior of Cluain [-mic-Nois], and Baedan, of Cluain-tuaisceirt, died. A battle by the Ulidians between the two sons of Fiachna, and Cairell defeated Eochaidh. A battle between [two parties of] the Ui-Ceinnsealaigh, in which Ceallach, son of Donnghall, was slain. The plundering of Ulidia by Aedh Oridnidhe, the king, in revenge of the profanation of the shrine of Patrick, against Dunchu. Fire came from heaven, by which persons were killed in Dearthach-Aedhain.

The Age of Christ, 805. . . . Maelfothartaigh, i.e. the scribe, son of Aedhghal, Abbot of Airegal-Dachiarog, died. Anluan, son of Conchobhar, lord of Aidhne, died. Tadhg and Flaithnia, two sons of Muirgheas, son of Tomaltach, were slain by the Luighni; and Luighne [Leyny] was laid waste by Muirgheas, in revenge of them. A hero of the Luighni said:

> Muirgheas slew my son, which very much wounded me;
> It was I that struck the sword into the throat of Tadhg
> afterwards.

The Age of Christ, 818. First year of [the reign of King] Conchobhar. . . . An army was led by Murchadh, son of Maelduin, to Druim-Indech, having the Ui-Neill of the North along with him. Conchobhar, King of Ireland, with the Ui-Neill of the South and the Leinstermen, came from the South, on the other hand; and when they came to one place, it happened, through the miracles of God, that they separated from each other for that time without slaughter, or one of them spilling a drop of the other's blood.

The Age of Christ, 819. . . . The plundering of Edar by the foreigners, who carried off a great prey of women. The plundering of Beg-Eire and Dairinis-Caemhain by them also. An army was led by Conchobhar, son of Donnchadh, to Ardachadh of Sliabh-Fuaid; and all the Airtheara were devastated by him, as far as Eamhain-Macha.

The Age of Christ, 820. . . . An army was led by Murchadh, son of Maelduin, having the men of the North with him, until he arrived at Ard-Breacain. The men of Breagh and the race of Aedh Slaine went over to him, and gave him hostages at Druim-Fearghusa.

The Age of Christ, 826. A battle was gained by Leathlobhar, son of Loingseach, King of Ulidia, over the foreigners. Muireadhach, son of Ruadhrach, King of Leinster, died. Cinaedh, son of Moghron, lord of Ui-Failghe, died. Uada, son of Diarmaid, lord of Teathbha, was slain. . . .

The Age of Christ, 829. The twelfth year of Conchobhar. Airmheadhach, successor of Finnen of Magh-bile, was drowned. Muirenn, Abbess of Cill-dara, died. Ceithearnach, son of Dunchu, scribe, priest, and wise man of Ard-Macha, died.

The Age of Christ, 831. The burning of Tearmann-Chiarain by Feidhlimidh, son of Crimhthann. The plundering of [Dealbhna] Beathra thrice by him also. The plundering of Cilldara by Ceallach, son of Bran. Cinaedh, son of Eochaidh, lord of Dal-Araidhe of the North, was slain. Cinaedh, son of Arthrach, lord of Cualann, and Diarmaid, son of Ruadhrach, lord of Airthear-Life, died. After Conchobhar, son of Donnchadh, had been fourteen years in the monarchy of Ireland, he died, after the victory of penance.

The Age of Christ, 832. The first year of Niall Caille, son of Aedh Oirdnidhe, in sovereignty over Ireland. Reachtabhra, Abbot of Cill-achaidh; and Irghalach, Abbot of Saighir, died. A battle was gained by Niall Caille and Murchadh over the foreigners, at Doire-Chalgaigh, where a slaughter was made of them. The plundering of Cluain-Dolcain by the foreigners. A great number of the family of Cluain-mic-Nois were slain by Feidhlimidh, son of Crumhthan, King of Caiseal; and all their termon [church lands] was burned by him, to the door of the church. In like manner [did he treat] the family of Dearmhach, also to the door of its church. Diarmaid, son of Tomaltach, King of Connaught, died. Cobhthach, son of Maelduin, lord of West Munster, was slain. The plundering of Loch-Bricrenn, against Conghalach, son of Eochaidh, [by the foreigners].

The Age of Christ, 887. The eleventh year of Flann. . . . Maelmordha, son of Gairbhith, lord of Conaille-Muirtheimhne, was beheaded by Ceallach, son of Flannagan. The plundering of Cill-dara and Cluain-Iraird by the foreigners. A slaughter [was made] of the Osraighi by the Deisi, and the killing of Braenan, son of Cearbhall, and also of Suibhne, son of Dunghus, lord of Ui-Fearghusa. A slaughter [was made] of the foreigners by the Ui-Amhalghaidh, in which fell Elair, son of Bairid, one of their chieftains, and others along with him. Maelfabhaill, son of Cleireach, lord of Aidhne, died. . . . A mermaid was cast ashore by the sea in the country of Alba [Scotland]. One hundred and ninety-five feet was her length, eighteen feet was the length of her hair, seven feet was the length of the fingers of her hand, seven feet also was the length of her nose; she was whiter than the swan all over. Conchobhar, son of Flannagan, lord of Ui-Failghe, was destroyed by fire at Cluain-foda-Fini, in the church; and the relics of Finian were violated by the Feara-Tulach, on his way from parleying with Flann, son of Maelseachlainn, King of Ireland.

The Age of Christ, 888. . . . A great wind [occurred] on the festival of St. Martin of this year; and it prostrated many trees, and caused great destruction of the woods of Ireland, and swept oratories and other houses from their respective sites. A battle was gained by Riagan, son of Dunghal, over the foreigners of Port-Lairge, Loch-Carman, and Teach-Moling, in which two hundred heads were left behind. A battle was gained by North Connaught over the foreigners, in which Eloir, son of Barith, was slain. A battle was gained over the Eili by Maelguala and the men of Munster, at Caiseal, in which many noble youths were slain.

The Age of Christ, 919. . . . Foreigners were defeated, a great number of them was slain, but a few of them escaped in the darkness at the very beginning of the night because they were not visible to them [the Irish]. A fleet of foreigners consisting of twenty-two ships at Loch Feabhail . . . and was plundered by them. Fearghal, son of Domhail, Lord of the North, was at strife with them, so that he slew the crew of one of their ships, broke the ship itself and carried off its wealth and goods.

III.

THE

VIKINGS

INTRODUCTION

AN ENTRY FOR THE YEAR 820 in *The Annals of Ulster* reads: "The sea spewed forth floods of foreigners over Erin, so that no haven, no landing-place, no stronghold, no fort, no castle might be found, but it was submerged by waves of vikings and pirates." That is an early mention of the warlike strangers who would come to dominate Irish history for the next two hundred years. The chroniclers called them Norsemen, Danes (no matter where they came from), black gentiles (actual Danes), Gauls, Lochlanns (men from the lakes, probably Norway), land-leapers, Osmen or Ostmen (men from the east), and—most simply and most frequently—the foreigners. And more often than not their sudden appearances were described as natural disasters, storms, tidal waves, or plagues of insects.

The first recorded Viking raid, in 795, was a small affair, a quick looting of an island—Rathlin or Lambay—by men from Norway, but over the next twenty-five years or so the small Norse raiding parties were supplanted by massive well-coordinated fleets of Viking ships manned by Danes. The early marauding bands in their small, fast ships first terrified the Irish with seemingly mindless destruction and then took away what valuables or slaves they could carry. Monasteries were a frequent target because, in the immortal words of the American bank robber Willie Sutton, that's where the money was. Not only were many monasteries wealthy in themselves, but their strong walls and high towers—often more substantial than the neighborhood castle—safeguarded the community's valuables. In a land with no cities and few villages, monasteries were also the population centers. One lasting result of these monastic raids is that the monk-historians represented the "foreigners" in their annals not only as thieves and vandals but also as enemies of God and the true church.

After those first years of hit-and-run pillage—which in fact was not unlike what rival Irish kings were doing to each other—the Vikings came to play a major role in the development of Ireland. They taught the Irish how to live in cities. Before the arrival of the land-leapers and the black gentiles, there was nothing that even resembled a large town. Most of the major cities on the island have Viking roots. Dublin, Wexford, Waterford, Cork, Limerick, and more, all have their origins as Viking trading centers, for although the foreigners arrived as raiders and kidnappers, they later became businessmen who established busy ports (founded as winter camps) both to carry out trade and to provide embarkation points for raids on other lands, notably Scotland and northern Britain.

Nor was it always easy to place the Irish on one side of a battle and Vikings on the other. Almost from the very beginning, Vikings made alliances with Irish leaders—however briefly—and took part in the ongoing skirmishes between and among the Irish kings. (And the Vikings themselves were hardly unified. At one point the Norse and the Danes were battling each other in Ireland, with the Danes claiming the blessing of St. Patrick.) As will become clear in Part IV of this book, even the famous battle at Clontarf in 1014—in which tradition says the Vikings were driven out of Ireland—was actually a fight between one Irish king and another Irish king with his Viking allies.

THE WAR OF THE
GAEDHIL WITH THE GAILL
THE EARLY VIKING RAIDS

*Long after his death, Turgesius (Turgeis) became the Genghis Khan of
the Vikings. His enemies (and their descendants) used him as an example of all that was evil in his people. Geoffrey Keating, in his history,
wrote—invoking the name of another Mongol chieftain—that even
"the great Tamatlane, the scourge of God, could not be compared to
him for cruelty." According to legend, he arrived in northern Ireland at
the end of the ninth century, took command of the Viking forces, ravaged the countryside, captured Armagh, and drove out the bishop and
defiled the sacred relics of St. Patrick. Perhaps even worse was the
story that after he captured the monastery of Clonmacnoise on the
Shannon River, his wife, Ota (or Aud), sat upon the altar and chanted
pagan spells. It is worth noting, however, that* The Annals of
Clonmacoise *recorded only that "Turgesius Prince of the Danes" burned
the monastery in 842 along with "churches and houses of religion" at
Clonfert, Tyrdaglasse, and Lothta.*

*The crimes of Turgesius and other early Viking chiefs are cataloged
in* The War of the Gaedhil with the Gaill (Cogodh Gaedhel re Gallabh),
*a twelfth-century account written to promote the cause of the descen-
dants of Brian Boru and the Dal Cais clan, a book that will be examined in greater detail in Part IV.*

ANOTHER FLEET CAME INTO THE harbour of Luimnech [Limerick, A.D. 834];
and Corco-Baiscinn, and Tradraighe, and Ui Conaill Gabhra were plundered by them. The Ui Conaill defeated them at Senati, under Donnchadh,
son of Scannlan, king of Ui Conaill, and Niall, son of Cennfaeladh, and it
is not known how many of them were there slain.

There came after that [A.D. 839] a great royal fleet into the north of
Erinn, with Turgeis, who assumed the sovereignty of the foreigners of
Erinn; and the north of Erinn was plundered by them, and they spread
themselves over Leth Chuinn. A fleet of them also entered Loch Eathach,

and another fleet entered Lughbudh, and another fleet entered Loch Rai. Moreover, Ard Macha [Armagh] was plundered three times in the same months by them; and Turgeis himself usurped the abbacy of Ard Macha and Farannan, abbot of Ard Macha, and chief comharba [successor] of Patrick, was driven out, and went to Mumhain, and Patrick's shrine with him; and he was four years in Mumhain, while Turgeis was in Ard Macha, and in the sovereignty of the north of Erinn. . . .

There came Turgeis, who [brought] a fleet upon Loch Rai, and from thence plundered Midhe and Connacht; and Cluain Mic Nois [Clonmacnoise] was plundered by him, and Cluain Ferta of Brenann, and Lothra, and Tir-dá-glas, and Inis Celtra [monasteries of Meath and Connaught], and all the churches of Derg-dheirc, in like manner; and the place where Ota, the wife of Turgeis, used to give her audience was upon the altar of Cluain Mic Nois. The Connachtmen, however, gave them battle, in which Maelduin, son of Muirghes, royal heir apparent of Connacht, was slain.

After this came three score and five ships, and landed at Dubhlinn of Athcliath [Dublin] and Laghin [Leinster] was plundered to the sea by them, and Magh Bregh. But the Dal Riada [a clan in Antrim] met them in another battle, in which was slain Eoghan, son of Oengus, king of Dal Riada.

After this there came great sea-cast floods of foreigners into Erinn, so that there was not a point thereof without a fleet. It was by these that Bri-Gobhann [Munster] was plundered, and Tressach, son of Mechill, killed. A fleet came to Ciarraighe Luachra, and all was plundered by them to Cill Ita and Cuil Emhni; and the Martini of Mumhain were plundered by the fleet of Luimnech, who carried off Farannan of Ard Macha, from Cluain Comairdi to Luimneach, and they broke Patrick's shrine.

It was in this year [A.D. 845] Turgeis was taken prisoner by Maelsechlainn; and he was afterwards drowned in Loch Uair, viz., the year before the drowning of Niall Cailli, and the second year before the death of Fedhlimidh, son of Crimhthann; and it was in the time of these two that all these events took place. Now, when Turgeis was killed, Farannan, abbot of Ard Macha, went out of Mumhain [to Ard Macha], and the shrine of Patrick was repaired by him.

Now the same year in which Farannan was taken prisoner, the shrine of Patrick broken, and the churches of Mumhain plundered, [the foreigners] came to Ros Creda [Roscrea, A.D. 845] on the festival of Paul and Peter, when the fair had begun; and they were given battle, and the foreigners were defeated through the grace of Paul and Peter, and countless numbers of them were killed there; and Earl Onphile was struck there with a stone by which he was killed. Much, indeed, of evil and distress did they receive, and much was received from them in those years, which is not recorded at all.

There came after that a fleet of three score ships of the Northmen upon the Boinn [Boyne]; and Bregia and Midhe were plundered by them. [Another] fleet came and settled on Loch Echach, and these plundered all before them to Ard-Macha. Another fleet came and settled on the river of Liffe, and Magh Bregh was plundered by them, both country and churches.

There came after that a very great fleet into the south of Ath-Cliath, and the greater part of Erinn was plundered by them; they plundered, also, Hí of Colum Cille, and Inis Muireoc, and Damhinis, and Glenn dá Locha, and the whole of Laighin, as far as to Achadh Ur, and to Achadh Bó, and to Liath Mocaemhoc, and to Daire-mór, and to Cluain Ferta Molua, and to Ros Cre, and to Lothra, where they broke the shrine of Ruadhan, and they spoiled Cluain Mic Nois, [and as far as Saighir,] and on to Durmhagh. . . .

The [Viking] Earl, Oiter Dubh [Black Otter], came with an hundred ships to Port Lairge, and the east of Mumhain [Waterford] was plundered by him, and its south; and he put all under tribute and service to the foreigners; and he levied his royal rent upon them. The whole of Mumhain [Munster] became filled with immense floods, and countless sea-vomitings of ships, and boats, and fleets, so that there was not a harbour, nor a landing-port, nor a Dún [*dun*, fort], nor a fortress, nor a fastness, in all Mumhain, without fleets of Danes and pirates.

There came there, also, the fleet of Oiberd, and the fleet of Oduinn, and the fleet of Griffin, and the fleet of Snuatgar, and the fleet of Lagmann, and the fleet of Erolf, and the fleet of Sitriuc, and the fleet of Buidnin, and the fleet of Birndin, and the fleet of Liagrislach, and the fleet of Toirberdach, and the fleet of Eoan Barun, and the fleet of Milid Buu, and the fleet of Suimin, and the fleet of Suainin, and lastly the fleet of the Inghen Ruaidh. And assuredly the evil which Erinn had hitherto suffered was as nothing compared to the evil inflicted by these parties. The entire of Mumhain, without distinction, was plundered by them, on all sides, and devastated. And they spread themselves over Mumhain; and they built Dúns, and fortresses, and landing-ports, over all Erinn, so that there was no place in Erinn without numerous fleets of Danes and pirates; so that they made spoil-land, and sword-land, and conquered-land of her, throughout her breadth, and generally; and they ravaged her chieftainries, and her privileged churches, and her sanctuaries; and they rent her shrines, and her reliquaries, and her books. They demolished her beautiful ornamented temples; for neither veneration, nor honour, nor mercy for Termonn, nor protection for church, or for sanctuary, for God, or for

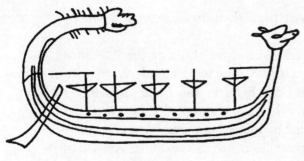

Viking ship

man, was felt by this furious, ferocious, pagan, ruthless, wrathful people. In short, until the sand of the sea, or the grass of the field, or the stars of heaven are counted, it will not be easy to recount, or to enumerate, or to relate what the Gaedhil [Irish] all, without distinction, suffered from them: whether men or women, boys or girls, laics or clerics, freemen or serfs, old or young;—indignity, outrage, injury, and oppression. In a word, they killed the kings and the chieftains, the heirs to the crown, and the royal princess of Erinn. They killed the brave and the valiant; and the stout knights, champions, and soldiers, and young lords, and the greater part of the heroes and warriors of the entire Gaedhil; and they brought them under tribute and servitude; they reduced them to bondage and slavery. Many were the blooming, lively women; and the modest, mild, comely maidens; and the pleasant, noble, stately, blue-eyed young women; and the gentle, well brought up youths, and the intelligent, valiant champions, whom they carried off into oppression and bondage over the broad green sea. Alas! many and frequent were the bright and brilliant eyes that were suffused with tears, and dimmed with grief and despair, at the separation of son from father, and daughter from mother, and brother from brother, and relatives from their race and from their tribe.

THE FREEING OF CELLACHAIN,
KING OF MUNSTER

Cellachain of Cashel was king of Munster from about 940 to the middle of the 950s (the dates are not specific), and although the dramatic battle with the Vikings that ends this account did not actually take place, the explicit details of his election as king, the land battles in which one side is protected by armor and the other is not, and the climactic sea battle of Dundalk are realistic twelfth-century re-creations.

The account is also a lively example of a kind of political propaganda that was popular in Ireland in the twelfth century. The Battles of Cellachain of Cashel (Cathereim Cellachain Chaisil) was probably written around 1130 to enhance the reputation of descendants of men mentioned as heroes of the battle to rescue Cellachain from the Vikings. The usual way of doing this was to take a real battle and people it with ancestors who were not actually there. In this case, an entire historical event was created. Cellachain may never have been tied to the mast of a Viking ship, but the adventure tale is an effective example of how the medieval Irish thought their ancestors struggled with the Scandinavian invaders. It also begins with a rare and accurate description of the investure of an Irish king.

As a work of political propaganda, however, its most important sentence is a seemingly innocuous comment of Cellachain's as a captive. He gives "my benediction to the Dal Cais, as a reward because they have come to my help." The king of the Dal Cais was then Cinneide, father of Brian Boru. This work was translated by Alexander Bugge.

THEN AROSE THE SEVENTEEN TRIBES of the clan Eogan, right readily in order to make Cellachan king of Munster. And they set up his *gairm rig* [i.e. they proclaimed him king] and gave thanks to the true, magnificent God for having found him. The following were the best of those chieftains. The slender, valiant Suilleban before the festive race of Fingin, and the sportive Ribordan before the valorous children of Donngal, and the fierce Caellaidi, and the heroic soldier Laindacan, and the bold Duinechad, and the brave Cuilen, and the battlesome Eigertach, and Ligan of daring deeds. These nobles came to Cellachan and put their hands in his hand and placed the royal diadem round his head, and their spirits were raised at the grand sight of him. For he was a king for great stature, and a brehon [judge] for eloquence, and a learned saga-man for knowledge, and a lion for daring deeds.

Cellachan addressed the clan Eogan and told them to make valiant war with him, and they said they would do it. And they said that they would advance, ten hundred men in number, to [Viking-held] Limerick to burn it. And when they arrived, they sent word to the heroic [Viking] Amlaib to tell them to quickly leave Limerick or to give hostages to them.

When the messengers came to the heroes of Limerick, the Vikings began to deride them, and this is what they expected. And they said that they would give battle.

When the clan Eogan heard this, Suilleban of the noble hosts addressed them, and told them to fight a brave and hardy battle against the Lochlannachs [the Vikings] and valiantly to guard their king in this onslought. And he said to the nobles of the Eoganachts: "Let not the clan of Cormac Cas hear of (any) conditions in your deliberations, let not clan Echach hear of weakness in your princes, but proceed together to the battle, and give your first battle valiantly in defence of your own country against the Danes. If there be defeat and rout of battle before you upon the heroes, it will be all the better for yourselves, and for your prosperity, and your positions. Limerick will be in your hand, and Cashel in your succession, and Munster will be in the possession of your nobles, if yours is the victory in this battle today. . . ."

Then towards the battle arose the descendants of Eogan fiercely, prudently, bravely around their gentle king, around Cellachan. And there was arrayed bravely the heroes ever beautiful, very strong, surrounded by standards, and a solid, very thick palisade of spears, and a strong, princely-ensigned tower of chiefs, and a skilful phalanx of blue blades, and a handsome, strong enclosure of linen cloth around the heroes. For the heroes had neither blue helmets nor shining coats of mail, but only elegant tunics with smooth fringes, and shields, and beautiful, finely wrought collars to protect bodies, and necks, and gentle heads.

Then there was arrayed by the heroes of Lochlann a solid, skilful and firm rampart of strong coats of mail, and a thick, dark stronghold of black iron, and a green-polished, hard-sharp city of battleshields, and a strong enclosure of stout shafts around the heroic Amlaib, and around Lochlann, and Morann, and Magnus. For these were the four battle-heroes of the Lochlann champions, and four hundred accompanied each hero of them.

Then the valorous descendants of Eogan placed themselves at the upper end of the plain in high spirits around their gentle king Cellachan, and they put the hooks of their shields over each another, and they made "champion-knots" by attaching their broad belts to each other, and they arrayed the seventeen brave men who were the most noble of the high lords around their royal prince to protect him well. Great spirit arose in their king, and anger in their champions, and courage in their soldiers, and fury in their heroes, and valour in their gallant men and fierceness in their youths.

However, when their youths, their champions and their proud, haughty folk came to the front of the battle to throw their stones and slender arrows and pointed spears from each side of the heroes, the ground of the plain was left to the soldiers, and the battle-field to the heroes, and the place of slaughter to the veterans. And when the noble warriors of Lochlann and the soldiers of Munster arrived at the place of defence they began to smite their battle-clubs heroically and to strike their swords on each another. However this full encounter was one-sided. For the bodies and skins and hearts of the bright champions of Munster were quickly pierced through the fine linen garments, and their very sharp blades did not take any effect upon the Lochlannachs because of the rough solidity of their blue coats of mail, and their clubs did not maim the heroes, and the swords did not lacerate the heads because of the hardness of the helmets that protected them, and the Lochlannachs made a great havock among the Munstermen during a part of that day.

However when Cellachan perceived that the soldiers were being slain, and that the heroes were being wounded, and that the champions were being maimed, and that Clan Eogan was being slaughtered, then arose his wrath, his rage, and his vigour, and he makes a royal rush, caused by fits of mighty passion, at the nobles of the Lochlannachs, while the noble descendants of the race of Eogan protect him. Cellachan reached the war-like Amlaib and made an attack on the rough mail-coat of the warrior, so that he loosened his helmet under his neck, and split his head with his hard strokes, so that the Lochlannach fell by him.

Then Suilleban with his 150 brave, valiant swordsmen arrived to his defence, and he made a breach of savage ferocity through the centre of the heroic batallion of the Lochlannachs. Then arose the unviolated pillar, and the unsubdued hero, and the lion unconquered until that day, namely the long-haired, high spirited Morann of the fierce people, i.e. the son of the fleet-king of Lewis, with 150 heroes who arose with him. And when the chiefs had met, they smote each another fiercely, like true foes, and with hard strength. Suilleban however planted his spear through the boss of the buckler and beneath the rim of the helmet into the hero, so that it passed quickly into the hero's neck, and placed the head in the power of the battle-soldier. And he beheaded the brave man and brought the head with him to Cellachan to boast of his triumph. And the people of the Lochlannach fell in that fight.

Then Donnchad and brave Magnus met together in the battle. They struck off the points of their broad-grooved swords, and battered their shields into pieces with their full-heavy clubs, and wounded their bodies with their javelins. Magnus however fell by great Donnchad.

Then Lochlann and Riordan engaged in battle before Cellachan, and Lochlann inflicted very sharp, terrible wounds on Riordan. When the hero was wounded, and the champion pierced through, and when he perceived that his arms took no effect upon the veteran who was before him, Riordan made a heroic rush upon Lochlann, and left his sword, and his longbladed spear, and he put in mind his sharp iron-blue mail-coat and laid dexterously hold of the lower part of the cuirass of the Lochlannach with his left hand, and gave the champion a sudden pull, so that he maimed the broad bosom of the hero, and that his bowels and entrails fell out of him. And he beheaded the champion and lifted his head in triumph. Nevertheless there fell these four valiant champions of the Lochlann heroes, and the (other) heroes left their places, and the soldiers were overthrown and made for Limerick to shut themselves quickly up there. And it was through the rear of the Lochlannachs that the nobles of Munster went into the town, so that the Lochlannachs were not able to close the gates, and the champions were killed in the houses and in the towers. They brought their wifes, and children, and people in captivity to the nobles of Munster, and collected the gold, silver and various riches of the town, and brought the heads, trophies, and battle-spoils of the heroes to Cellachan, and the heads of the four who were the most noble of the Lochlannachs were exhibited to him. . . .

Thereupon the heroes collected the spoils, and some of them said that they should stay that night in the town and proceed the next morning to Cashel. Suilleban said to the hosts that they should go that very night to Cork, the place where their hostages and captives were, so that no news or messengers might get there before them. The champions decided on this plan and they came to Cork that night. The Danes and Black Gentiles of the town came out against them to fight with them. The battle was gained on the Danish Black Gentiles, and the town was wrecked by the champions, and they brought away with them their hostages from the captivity in which they were. The men of Munster were that night in Cork consuming their banquets and provisions, and they stayed three days in the city and then made up their mind to proceed to Cashel. . . .

The battle was fought by Donnchad, and it was gained over the Danes, and 300 were slain there by them. They were that night in Cashel, and consumed the feasts and prepared food of the Danes and Dark-Lochlannachs. The next morning they made up their mind, namely to proceed to Port Lairge [Waterford], the place where the women and families of the Lochlannachs were, and to burn the town. And they proceed to the green of Port Lairge. But on the same day Sitric son of [the Viking chief] Turgeis arrived at Port Lairge with a division of six ships and a hundred on each ship of them. But they had not reached the land when the van of the host of Munster arrived at the city. The Danes closed the gates and began to defend the town. However, it was useless for them to engage in combat with the champions; for Cellachan, and gentle Donnchad, and Suilleban, and Ribordan, and the quick, valiant soldiers of Munster leapt into the town. And the Danes were slaughtered in crowds by them, and the Norsemen were cut into pieces. Sitric left the town and went on board his ship, and his wife with him. And only one hundred fugitives of them reached their ships. The race of Eogan burned the town and plundered the district.

[Cellachan and Donnchann, the son of Connetig, are captured by the Danes—not in battle but through trickery—and the men of Munster set off to rescue them. After taking back the Viking-held city of Armagh, they learn that the king and his champion are imprisoned aboard ships at Dundalk, a port north of Dublin.]

They [the men of Munster] went forward in arranged battallions to Dundalk. But the Lochlannachs went away from them in their ships, and they themselves went to the seashore. And the ship that was next to them was the ship of Sitric son of Turgeis, and it was in that ship that Cellachan was. Donnchadh [who should not be confused with Donnchann, the son of Connetig] asked them if they might get Cellachan for a ransom. Sitric pledged his word that he should never be given up, unless they brought back to him all who were slain in the fifteen battles which Cellachan had fought, and all who were slain in the battle of Armagh. When Donnchadh heard this he began to reproach them, and he said that they had not captured Cellachan in battle or open fight, but by lying and open perjury. And he said that after this he would not trust any oath of the Norse. "Give honour to Cellachan in the presence of the men of Munster!" said Sitric, "let him even be bound to the mast! For he shall not be without pain in honour of them." Thus it was done. "The women of Munster will lament this," said Donnchadh, "and your own wife will lament it, O Sitric. And there is not among you a man to carry out that cruelty but has been spared by *his* sword and *his* fight. . . ." [Donnchann, was likewise tied up in the ship of the son of the king of Fuarlochlann.]

Then Cellachan said: "It is not the revenge you will take upon me, that is to be lamented. For I give you my word that I feel more sorry that Cashel is without a successor of the descendants of Eoghan than because I myself am in this torture. And my benediction upon the Dal Cais, as a reward because they have come to my help." After this Cellachan lifted his head and said: "O Donnchadh, has a fleet set out with you?" "It has," said Donnchadh. "I see them," said Cellachan. . . .

Then the Munsterman raised their heads and lifted their nobles eyes, and they saw the harbour being filled with ships and swift barks, the fleet of the men of Munster. Sitric asked who they were, and Donnchadh told their names. "It would be better for us," said Sitric, "if we got to know which of those yonder will undertake to check us in battle to-day, and who are the chiefs of those who are there." Duinechad, son of Fiangus, said that if he got a boat to man and permission to go and to come, that he would go and get knowledge of these news on behalf of Sitric. He got what he asked.

Duinechad went to the place where the fleet was, and asked news of them, and told them news of the men of Munster at Armagh, and he related that Cellachan was in the ship of Sitric, bound to the mast. . . .

"We have given our words," said they, "that if the Munstermen and the Norsemen were joined together, we would not let Cellachan be taken away by them without giving them battle." "If that is so," said Duinechad, "then tell me which of the Lochlann heroes you will choose to match yourselves against? And these are they: Lochlannach of the Blades, and the handsome Lochlannach, and Old Amlaib, the three guardians of Cork." "Let them be given to us," said the three kings of Corcaduibne, namely Flann, and Cobthach, and Edirscel." "For it is to us that they have given cause after coming to Inis Clere, when they carried off our women and youths in captivity. And we have not overtaken them to avenge ourselves upon them, but we shall take them in hand to-day." "Which of you," said Duinechad, "will undertake to fight against Lenn-Turmun of the Journey?" "Let him be left to me," said Dubdaboirenn, the king of Western Ui Echach, "for he has slain a good son of mine." "Which of you," said Duinechad, "will undertake to fight against the three sons of Turgeis, namely Sitric, and Tor and Magnus? And it is in their ship Cellachan is." "Let them be left to us," said Segda, and Failbe, and Congal, "for they went to Scelig Michil and devastated the country. But we shall take them in hand for our share to-day."

"Another reason," said Failbe, "is that we have given our word that there shall not be on sea or on land a place where we see them that we shall not reach to attack them." "Which of you," said Duinechad, "will engage the son of the king of Fair Lochlann?" "Let him be left to me," said Conchubar, king of Ciarraige Luachra, "for he has burned Ard Fothaig Brenaind. But I shall avenge that upon him to-day." "Who will engage in battle with Lenn Turmun na Pers?" said Duinechad. "Let him be left to me," said Diarmaid and Baiscinn, the two kings of Corcobaiscinn. "For they have plundered Inis Cathaig, and we have not overtaken them before to-day." "Who will engage in battle with the king of Cold Lochlann?" said Duinechad. "It is in his ship that Donnchuan is, and he bound fast." "Let him be left to us," said the two kings of Corcamruadh, "for they went to Arann, and it was plundered by them, and we shall avenge it upon them to-day. . . ."

When they saw [their king, Cellachan] bound and fettered to the mast of the Norse ship, the senses, and feelings, and thoughts of the heroes underwent a change, their aspect became troubled, their colour changed, their looks became threatening, and their lips grew pale. And to defend Cellachan there was bravely arranged by the heroes a strong and cunning circle of ships, and a fortified city of helmets, and a firm fold of bows, and a manly, angry, venomous hedge of bright spears.

Then arose those truly heroic, broadweaponed Norsemen and the dark-faced, sullen, terrible Foreigners, and the base, lowborn Danes. . . . There was arranged by them a dense fortress of dark shields, and an immovable oakwood of venomous and strong spears. But, however, when they had reached the warriors in their impetuous and headstrong course, their ships went bravely to the battle so that listening to the noble clans was like listening to the sound, which arises from a seashore full of stones trodden by teams, and herds, and cattle, horses and racing horsemen, and bright cavalry, as the bloody, sharp showers poured down, and their swords and javelins rang forth in cutting up cuirasses and splitting shields, breaking helmets and head-gear and each other's fair bodies around Cellachan.

Then the three fiercely active kings of Ui Luigdech, namely Flann, and Cobthach, and Eiderscel reached the southern angle of the brave hosts. They and the three guardians of Cork, namely Lochlannach of the blades, and the handsome Lochlannach, and Old Amlaib, the senior of the army, went at each other and encountered each other in the battle. However, neither the great size of [the Viking] shields, nor the excessive strength of their spears, nor the whistling shots of their arrows, nor the smiting of swords upon the heroes were of any use to the Norse heroes. For those chiefs leapt into the Norse ships and singled them out under the masts of the galleys till they met in the middle of each ship. And those six fell together along with their hosts. . . .

Then the chief of Ui Echach, namely Dubdaboirenn, and [the Norseman] Lenn-Turmun of the Journey met with their swift barques to fight and to smite each other like two dragons for cunning wounds or like two hawks for eager deeds. The army of the active, and famous clan of Cas leapt into the ships of the Norsemen so that they fell upon the row-benches and strong oars of the mighty ships.

Then the three valiant champions, namely Segda, and Failbe, and Congal came up to the strong fleet of the sons of Turgeis, to Sitric, Tor, and Magnus. The Irishmen quickly flung tough ropes of hemp over the long prows of the Norse ships in order that they might not be separated from each other. The Norsemen then flung rough chains of blue iron over the stately prows of their vessels. There were arranged between the heroes smooth-shafted, sharp-pointed rows of long and stout, most venomous spears. Their helmsmen left off steering, and their crews arose with the oars around the splendid sides of their strong ships, and they raised a barbarous uproar against each other . . .

Then the ship of the heroic Failbe was hurried up and rowed up to the battle-ship of Sitric, and Failbe made a high, and deerlike leap from the broad deck of his ship to the mast of [the ship of] Sitric. The royal champion unsheathed his two brisk, keen-edged blades, and he took one of the swords in his stout right hand encountering the champions of the ship, and the other sword in his heroic left cutting the ropes and fetters that were round Cellachan.

The nobles of Clan Corc [then] arranged an artfully weaponed, hard and keen-edged enclosure round the mast while the hero was cutting the long ropes, so that they left the battle-soldier in the centre of the ship between the champions. Failbe gave one of the two blades into the hand of Cellachan in the hard fight. But Cellachan began to smash the bones of the heroes along the sides of the noble ship, until he leapt into the ship of the heroic Failbe. But there was poured down a vehement and fierce shower of arrows upon the brave Failbe in the dark ship, as many are wont to overpower few.

When the furious Foreigners had slain and stripped that true hero, they struck off the brave man's head and raised it upon the prow of the ship. When the hard, impetuous troops and the sprightly young men of Munster saw that decapitation, the battle became more furious, and the fight closer with the brave hosts. Fiangal arose bravely, though every good hero had become weak, lowspirited and thinking of flight after the fall of his chieftain. He began to lament his lord and pledged his word that Sitric should not get back alive to the Lochlann hosts. For the hero was a fosterbrother of the gentle Failbe. But he was aware that his weapons would take no effect upon the mailclad veteran, and he thought it a pity that his lord should lay in the ship without revenge. . . .

Fiangal then made an eager, falconlike leap into the warship of Sitric and fixed his fair hands in the bosom of the Norseman's coat of mail, and dragged the Fair Lochlannach down into the sea so that they together reached the gravel and the sand of the sea, and rested there.

Then the two other valiant, redarmed chiefs of the same warlike clan, namely Seghda and noble Congal, reached the two strong sons of Turgeis, namely Tor and Magnus. But the looks of the heroes were no faces of friends around ale, nor was it a maiden's love for her mate. But the champions sprang like lions from the massive ships, (or) like the violent indomitable waves over the long sides of the Norse ships. And the heroes left their own ships void and empty, while the Norse ships became full in their hold, and their sides leaned over. For the pouring in of the clan of Corc into their wombs was a terrible addition to the ships, and they [i.e. the ships] were full of Norsemen before; so that the ships did not wait for the fight of the heroes, but burst open to the salt sea, so that every barquee was swamped with its troops. . . .

Then the martial warships of Ciarraige and the furious angry crews of Fair Lochlann met, and they exchanged showers of arrows, and sudden fusilades of hard stones, and sharp showers of javelins, and skilfully directed, very stout spears. And they made a sudden, fierce attack, and a rough, hostile combat. Then Conchubar, the heroic king of Ciarraige, met the slaughtering Ilbrech, son of the king of Fair Lochlann. They fought very hard and eagerly, because the Ciarraige remembered the plundering of their country by the champion. They plied their spears with excessive eagerness, their battle-axes with powerful onslought, their swords with fierce fight, and their knives with furious, sudden assault. For the good ships were close to each another, and their weapons reached each other's breasts and bosoms, so that they fell together on this side and that in their ships. Conchubar however dragged Ilbrec by his head towards him, and struck off the head of the good champion, and exhibited it in triumph. But he fell himself on the neck of the soldier, and thus died. . . .

Then the strong and vigorous descendants of Fergus and the far-plundering descendants of Corc reached the watchful Donnchuan. When they saw the hero as a bound and fettered captive, they ordered that the swift, big ship of Lochlann should be brought up to the one side of the Norse ship and the brownplanked ship of Conchubar to the other side of the high ship. This advice was adopted by the champions, and they leapt over the broad railings of the ship of the Norseman, and untied the hard fetters, and let down the ropes, so that the hero-champion, i.e.

Donnchuan son of Ceinneidigh, was left free in the middle of the ship. But while the chiefs were removing the champion from the mast, the Lochlannachs of the ship slaughtered their people.

The champions became fiercely angry because of this, made a violent attack upon the sullen Lochlannachs, and dealt hard, dangerous blows upon the gloomy Lochlannachs, so that they cleft their shields, and cut their armour into pieces, and tore their targes. And the son of the king of Cold Lochlann fell with the flower of his people. While they were slaying the great Lochlannach, the Lochlannachs of the ship were harassing the rear of the brave champions. They then quickly and suddenly turned round upon the warriors and gave a hard, vehement onslaught on the champions, so that they did not stay in the ship before the heroes, but the champions of the ship leapt over the broad railings into the sea, where they were quickly drowned. But when they found no more Norsemen to slay in the ship, they raised the head of the son of the king of Cold Lochlann in triumph upon the prow of the galley. Conchubar came upon the bow of the ship, and the Norsemen severed their bodies from their souls. . . .

It was ebb-tide when the fleets met, and the broad waves of the flood-tide brought the ships of the Munstermen to land. But when the ships had reached land, the Munstermen went into them to join those who were left of their people. But when the Lochlannachs who were left perceived this, they went away in thirteen ships and left the harbour at once, and carried neither king nor chieftain with them.

Then Cellachan arrived in the ship of Failbe the Fair, but Failbe lay slain in it on his bed of gore. Cellachan was greatly lamenting him and said: "It is a loss to us that this man has fallen, and there will not be found a hero after him who will rescue his lord, as he did, for his sword gave a brave sound as he fought for me in the gallery." And he said, lamenting Failbe:

> "A loss to Munstermen is Failbe the Fair,
> Who gave his life for my sake,
> He sprang to bring it back
> into the ship of Sitric, son of Turgeis.
>
> There was a sword in his right hand,
> And a sword in his nimble left,
> So that he drove them into the sea,
> Where the Norsemen perished.
>
> By him my fetters were cut,
> Though not with the consent of the men.

The sword which was in his left
the heroic king put into my hand.

I myself destroyed with the sword
All that were between me and the side of the ship,

Failbe fought in my rear,
So that I left the ship of the son of Turgeis.

Failbe was not slain alone,
Woe that he should have been in peril!
[He did not fall], until the ship was red of their blood,
[of the blood] of his hosts and [of] the Norse host.

Manly Fiangal leapt away from us
To avenge his lord.
He carried Sitric with him from his ship,
So that the son of the Lagmann's son was drowned.

A blessing upon the soul of Fiangal,
Though he died without fierce wounds,
If Sitric were not under the sea,
The drowning of Fiangal were a loss.

He was the darling of the maidens,
the descendant of Aengus, the fair bright man.
He brought me out of their fetters,
He was the flower of our noble Munstermen. . . ."

The heroic Munstermen assembled their ships from the wide sea, and brought them to land, and Cellachan and Donnchuan were welcomed by the heroes. They began to lament their nobles, their chiefs, and their warriors. . . .

Then the men of Munster set out on their way, and journey, and expedition orderly, bravely, and prudently. They plundered each territory, and burned each fortress and town that they met on their straight way from Dundalk to Ath Cliath. There came a message before them to the royal town, and it was told to the women of the Norsemen that their husbands were slain, and that Cellachan was taken from them by force.

IV.

BRIAN BORU

AND THE

BATTLE OF CLONTARF

INTRODUCTION

I N THE HIERARCHY OF THE Irish kings, Brian Boru (c. 941–1014) began as an outsider and upstart. Boru (or Borumha) was the son of Conneid, king of Thomond, which was a minor kingdom within Munster that corresponded closely with the boundaries of today's County Clare. Romantic legend depicts young Boru as a teenage guerrilla leader defying the Vikings and the nearby Norse community of Limerick, but whatever the case, after the death of his older brother in 976, he became king of Thomond and chief of the Dal Cais, the family clan.

It is impossible to know if Brian had a vision of Ireland as a single nation, as some nationalists later liked to believe, or if he was simply seized with a personal political and military ambition never before seen in Ireland. But beginning with the destruction of Viking Limerick, his shadow moved across the face of the island. He took the crown of Munster from the Eoganacht clan, then moved east to subdue Leinster, then north to confront the powerful O'Neills. Coordinating both land troops and a navy of ships probably captured from the Vikings, Brian demonstrated considerable tactical sophistication at a time when a battle was often simply two lines of troops flailing away at each other. Although he never succeeded in conquering the north, he did intimidate Malachy (or Mael Sechnaill), the high king of Ireland, into handing over the throne to Boru in 997. Dramatically demonstrating that the high kingship was no longer the exclusive property of the O'Neills, Brian had himself crowned not on the traditional Hill of Tara but at the Rock of Cashel, seat of the kings of Munster. Soon afterward, in Armagh, he was called emperor (*imperatoris*) of the Irish, perhaps the only time that word has been used to describe an Irish leader. Under Boru, the title *ard-ri*, high king, was to be no longer hollow or ceremonial.

While the Irish kings struggled with each other, the Vikings—now more often merchants than marauders—still controlled the cities. (Dublin was a virtual city-state with a Norse king all its own.) The complex state of affairs was probably best embodied—quite literally embodied—in Boru's remarkable fourth wife, Gormfhlaith (or Kormlada), daughter of a king of Leinster. He probably married her as a token of his dominance over that province, and they seem to have had no children, but at one time

An imaginary portrait of Brian Boru, high king of Ireland.

or another she was also married to both Olaf Cuaran (king of Dublin) and Boru's adversary, Malachy. Her and Olaf's son, Sitric, was king of Dublin when Boru and Malachy—fighting side by side as allies after Malachy's abdication as high king—tried unsuccessfully to take the city, and her brother was Maelmordha, the king of Leinster, who, with Viking support, rebelled against Boru. The result was the fatal battle at Clontarf.

Clon means "meadow," and Clontarf was a marshy seaside field that ran along a small stream just north of Dublin, close enough to town—according to some accounts—that it could be seen from the city walls. There, during Holy Week in 1014, two armies gathered. On one side was Boru, now in his seventies (although some accounts make him older), his eldest son Murchadh, the men of Munster, the former high king Malachy, and the men of Meath. On the other side was Maelmordha, the men of Leinster, Dublin Vikings, and a Viking fleet from the Orkney Islands. Medieval writers greatly exaggerated the size of the armies, but even modern historians' more modest estimated total of five thousand troops makes it one of the largest battles yet fought in Ireland. At the last minute, Malachy refused to fight, but the battle began without him on Good Friday morning and lasted most of the day.

Today, Brian Boru is best remembered for something he did not do. He did not drive the Vikings out of Ireland at Clontarf, but the battle did mark a turning point in Irish history. Not for centuries, not until the invasion of the Bruces from Scotland in the fourteenth century and the rebellion of Hugh O'Neill at the end of the fifteenth, would anyone again think of Ireland as a whole rather than as a collection of fractious kingdoms.

NJAL'S SAGA
A VIKING ACCOUNT

Njal's Saga is an Icelandic epic ("the mightiest of the Icelandic sagas," says one critic) written by an unknown author sometime around 1280. It is the complex story of Njal Thorgeisson and his family of Bergthorsknoll, in Iceland, most of whom are burned to death in their home by a band of enemies (called the Burners in this translation) led by Flosi Thordason. In the saga's closing pages, Flosi sets sail for Rome to do penance for his sins, and that is where it becomes part of Irish history. Flosi is blown off course and lands in the Orkney Islands, home of an old ally of Njal's, and witnesses some of the planning sessions for a battle against Brian Boru, king of Ireland. Flosi eventually continues on to Rome, while the others head for Clontarf in Dublin Bay. The saga, as is its wont, veers off course to tell the story of the battle from the Viking point of view.

Curiously, Boru—who is technically the enemy—is treated with a good deal more respect than the plotters against him, especially Boru's vindictive former wife and her son by another marriage. (If the notion of an ex-wife seems anachronistic, remember that the high Irish divorce rate was one of the reasons cited about 150 years later by Pope Adrian when he gave Henry II of England permission to invade the island.) Readers should note the portrait of the Viking named Brodir (Brodar). When he appears in the excerpt following this one, in an account commissioned by descendants of Brian Boru, he will be described as "blue, stark naked," and wielding a two-headed ax.

AS SOON AS THEY GOT A FAIR wind they put out to sea [from Iceland]. They had a long passage and hard weather. Then they quite lost their reckoning. It happened once that three great seas broke over their ship, one after the other. Then Flosi said they must be near some land, and that this was a groundswell. A great mist was on them, but the wind rose so that a great gust overtook them. They scarce knew where they were before they were dashed on shore at dead of night, and there the men were saved, but the ship was dashed all to pieces, and they could not save their goods.

Then they had to look for shelter and warmth for themselves. The day after they went up on a height. The weather was then good. Flosi asked if any man knew this land, and there were two men of their crew who had fared thither before, and said they were quite sure they knew it, and, say they, "We are come to Hrossey in the Orkneys." "Then we might have made a better landfall," said Flosi, "for Grim and Helgi, Njal's sons, whom I slew, were in earl Sigurd Hlodver's son's body-guard." Then they sought for a hiding-place, and spread moss over themselves, and so lay for a while, but not for long, ere Flosi spoke, and said, "We will not lie here so any longer until the landsmen are aware of us."

Then they arose and took counsel. Then Flosi said to his men, "We will go all of us and give ourselves up to the earl; for there is naught else to do, and the earl has our lives at his pleasure if he chooses to seek for them." Then they all went away thence. Flosi said that they must tell no man any tidings of their voyage or doings before he told them to the earl. Then they walked on until they met men who showed them to the home-stead. Then they went in before the earl, and Flosi and all the others hailed him. The earl asked what men they might be, and Flosi told his name, and said out of what part of Iceland he was. The earl had already heard of the Burning, and so he knew the men at once.

Then the earl asked Flosi, "What hast thou to tell me about Helgi Njal's son, my henchman." "This," said Flosi, "that I hewed off his head." "Take them all," said the earl. Then that was done. Just then in came Thorstein, son of Hall of the Side. Flosi had to wife Steinvora, Thorstein's sister. Thorstein was one of earl Sigurd's body-guard. But when he saw Flosi seized and held, he went in before the earl, and offered for Flosi all the goods he had. The earl was very wrath a long time, but at last the end of it was, by the prayer of good men and true, joined to those of Thorstein, for he was well backed by friends, and many threw in their word with his, that the earl took an atonement from them and gave Flosi and all the rest of them peace. The earl held to that custom of mighty men that Flosi took that place in his service which Helgi Njal's son had filled. So Flosi was made earl Sigurd's henchman, and he soon won his way to great love with the earl.

Those messmates Kari [Njal's son-in-law] and Kolbein the black put out to sea from Eyrar [in Iceland] half a month later than Flosi and his com-panions from Hornfirth. They got a fine fair wind, and were but a short time out. The first land they made was the Fair isle, it lies between

Shetland and the Orkneys. There that man whose name was David the white took Kari into his house; he tells him all that he had heard for certain about the doings of the Burners. He was one of Kari's greatest friends, and Kari stayed with him for the winter. Then they heard tidings from the west out of the Orkneys of all that was done there. Earl Sigurd bade to his feast at Yule earl Gilli, his brother-in-law, out of the Southern Isles; he had to wife Swanlauga, earl Sigurd's sister. Then too came to see earl Sigurd that king from Ireland whose name was Sigtrygg [Sitric, king of Dublin]. He was a son of Olaf, but his mother's name was Kormlada. She was the fairest of all women, and best gifted in everything that was not in her own power, but it was the talk of men that she did all things ill over which she had any power. [That is, she had the best natural gifts, but what she did out of her own will was bad.]

Brian [Boru] was the name of the king who first had her to wife, but they were then parted. He was the best natured of all kings. He had his seat in Ireland at Kincora. His brother's name was Wolf the quarrelsome, the greatest champion and warrior; Brian's foster-child's name was Kerthialfad. He was the son of king Kylfi, who had many wars with king Brian, and fled away out of the land before him, and became a hermit. But when king Brian went south on a pilgrimage, then he met king Kylfi, and they were atoned. Then king Brian took his son Kerthialfad to him, and loved him more than his own sons. He was then full grown when these things happened, and was the boldest of all men. Duncan was the name of the first of king Brian's sons; the second was Margad; the third, Takt, whom we call Tann, he was the youngest of them; but the elder sons of king Brian were full grown, and the briskest of men. Kormlada was not the mother of king Brian's children, and so grim had she got against king Brian after their parting, that she would gladly have him dead. King Brian thrice forgave all his outlaws the same fault but if they misbehaved themselves oftener, then he let them be judged by the law; and from this one may mark what a king he must have been.

Kormlada egged on her son Sigtrygg very much to kill king Brian. She now sent him to earl Sigurd to beg for help. King Sigtrygg came before Yule to the Orkneys, and there, too, came earl Gilli, as was written before. Men were so placed that king Sigtrygg sat on a high seat in the middle, but on either side of the king sat one of the earls. The men of king Sigtrygg and earl Gilli sat on the inner side away from him, but on the outer side away from earl Sigurd, sat Flosi and Thorstein, son of Hall of the Side, and the whole hall was full. Now king Sigtrygg and earl Gilli wished to hear of those tidings which had happened at the Burning, and so, also, what had befallen since. Then Gunnar Lambi's son was got to tell the tale, and a stool was set for him to sit upon.

Just at that very time Kari and Kolbein and David the white came to Hrossey unawares to all men. They went straightway up on land, but a few men watched the ship. Kari and his fellows went straight to the earl's homestead, and came to the hall about drinking time. It so happened that just then Gunnar was telling the story of the Burning, but they were listening to him meanwhile outside. This was on Yule-day itself. Now king Sigtrygg asked, "How did Skarphedinn [Njal's eldest son]] bear the burning?" "Well at first for a long time," said Gunnar, "but still the end of it was that he wept." And he went on giving an unfair leaning through all the story, but every now and then he lied outright. Kari could not stand this. Then he ran in with his sword drawn. . . .

So he ran in up the hall, and smote Gunnar Lambi's son on the neck with such a sharp blow, that his head spun off on to the board before the king and the earls, and the board was all one gore of blood, and the earl's clothing too.

Earl Sigurd knew the man that had done the deed, and called out, "Seize Kari and kill him." Kari had been one of earl Sigurd's body-guard, and he was of all men most beloved by his friends; and no man stood up a whit more for the earl's speech. "Many would say, Lord," said Kari, "that I have done this deed on your behalf, to avenge your henchman." Then Flosi said, "Kari hath not done this without a cause; he is in no atonement with us, and he only did what he had a right to do." So Kari walked away, and there was no hue and cry after him. Kari fared to his ship, and his fellows with him. The weather was then good, and they sailed at once south to Caithness, and went on shore at Thraswick to the house of a worthy man whose name was Skeggi, and with him they stayed a very long while.

Those behind in the Orkneys cleansed the board, and bore out the dead man. The earl was told that they had set sail south for Scotland. King Sigtrygg said, "This was a mighty bold fellow, who dealt his stroke so stoutly, and never thought twice about it!" Then earl Sigurd answered, "There is no man like Kari for dash and daring." Now Flosi undertook to tell the story of the Burning and he was fair to all; and therefore what he said was believed.

Then king Sigtrygg stirred in his business with earl Sigurd, and egged him on to go to the war with him against king Brian. The earl was long steadfast, but the end of it was that he said it might come about. He said he must have his mother's hand for his help, and be king in Ireland, if they slew Brian. But all his men besought earl Sigurd not to go into the war, but it was all no good. So they parted on the understanding that earl

Sigurd gave his word to go; but king Sigtrygg promised him his mother and the kingdom. It was so settled that earl Sigurd was to come with all his host to Dublin by Palm Sunday.

Then king Sigtrygg fared south to Ireland, and told his mother Kormlada that the earl had undertaken to come, and also what he had pledged himself to grant him. She shewed herself well pleased at that, but said they must gather greater force still. Sigtrygg asked whence this was to be looked for? She said there were two vikings lying off the west of [the Isle of] Man; and they had thirty ships, and "they are men of such hardihood that nothing can withstand them. The one's name is Ospak, and the other's Brodir. Thou shalt fare to find them, and spare nothing to get them into thy quarrel, whatever price they ask." Now king Sigtrygg fares and seeks the vikings, and found them lying outside off Man; king Sigtrygg brings forward his errand at once, but Brodir shrank from helping him until he, king Sigtrygg, promised him the kingdom and his mother, and they were to keep this such a secret that earl Sigurd should know nothing about it; Brodir too was to come to Dublin on Palm Sunday.

King Sigtrygg fared home to his mother, and told her how things stood. After that those brothers, Ospak and Brodir, talked together, and then Brodir told Ospak all that he and Sigtrygg had spoken of, and bade him fare to battle with him against king Brian, and said he set much store on his going. Ospak said he would not fight against so good a king. Then they were both wrath, and sundered their band at once. Ospak had ten ships and Brodir twenty. Ospak was a heathen, and the wisest of all men. He laid his ships inside in a sound, but Brodir lay outside him. Brodir had been a Christian man and a mass-deacon by consecration, but he had thrown off his faith and become God's dastard, and now worshipped heathen fiends, and he was of all men most skilled in sorcery. He had that coat of mail on which no steel would bite. He was both tall and strong, and had such long locks that he tucked them under his belt. His hair was black.

It so happened one night that a great din passed over Brodir and his men, so that they all woke, and sprang up and put on their clothes. Along with that came a shower of boiling blood. Then they covered themselves with their shields, but for all that many were scalded. This wonder lasted all till day, and a man had died on board every ship. Then they slept during the day. The second night there was again a din, and again they all sprang up. Then swords leapt out of their sheaths, and axes and spears flew about in the air and fought. The weapons pressed them so hard that they had to shield themselves, but still many were wounded, and again a man died out of every ship. This wonder lasted all till day. Then they slept again the day after. The third night there was a din of the same kind. Then ravens flew at them, and it seemed to them as though their beaks and claws were of iron. The ravens pressed them so hard that they had to keep them off with their swords, and covered themselves with their shields. This went on again till day, and then another man had died in every ship.

Then they went to sleep first of all, but when Brodir woke up, he drew his breath painfully, and bade them put off the boat. "For," he said, "I will go to see Ospak." Then he got into the boat and some men with him. But when he found Ospak he told him of the wonders which had befallen them, and bade him say what he thought they boded. Ospak would not tell him before he pledged him peace, and Brodir promised him peace but Ospak still shrank from telling him till night fell "for Brodir never slew a man by night." Then Ospak spoke and said—"When blood rained on you, therefore shall ye shed many men's blood, both of your own and others. But when ye heard a great din, then ye must have been shewn the crack of doom, and ye shall all die speedily. But when weapons fought against you, that must forbode a battle; but when ravens pressed you, that marks the devils which ye put faith in, and who will drag you all down to the pains of hell." Then Brodir was so wroth that he could answer never a word. But he went at once to his men, and made them lay his ships in a line across the sound, and moor them by bearing cables on shore, and meant to slay them all next morning.

Ospak saw all their plan. Then he vowed to take the true faith and to go to king Brian, and follow him till his death-day. Then he took that counsel to lay his ships in a line, and punt them along the shore with poles, and cut the cables of Brodir's ships. Then the ships of Brodir's men began to fall aboard of one another. But they were all fast asleep; and then Ospak and his men got out of the firth, and so west to Ireland, and came to Kincora. Then Ospak told king Brian all that he had learnt, and took baptism, and gave himself over into the king's hand. After that king Brian made them gather force over all his realm, and the whole host was to come to Dublin in the week before Palm Sunday.

Earl Sigurd Hlodver's son busked him from the Orkneys, and Flosi offered to go with him. The earl would not have that, since he had his pilgrimage [to Rome] to fulfil. Flosi offered fifteen men of his band to go on the voyage, and the earl accepted them . . .

The earl came with all his host on Palm Sunday to Dublin, and there too was come Brodir with all his host. Brodir tried by sorcery how the fight would go. But the answer ran thus, that if the fight were on Good Friday king Brian would fall but win the day; but if they fought before, they would all fall who were against him. Then Brodir said that they must not fight before the Friday. Then on the fifth day of the week a man rode up to Kormlada and her company on an apple-grey horse, and in his hand he held a halberd; he talked long with them.

King Brian came with all his host to the burg [Dublin], and on the Friday the host fared out of the burg, and both armies were drawn up in array. Brodir was on one wing of the battle, but king Sigtrygg on the other. Earl Sigurd was in the mid-battle. Now it must be told of king Brian that he would not fight on the fast-day, and so a shieldburg [a ring of men holding their shields locked together] was thrown round him, and his host was drawn up in array in front of it. Wolf the quarrelsome was on that wing of the battle against which Brodir stood. But on the other wing, where Sigtrygg stood against them, were Ospak and his sons. But in mid-battle was Kerthialfad, and before him the banners were borne. Now the wings fall on one another, and there was a very hard fight.

Brodir went through the host of the foe, and felled all the foremost that stood there, but no steel would bite on him. Wolf the quarrelsome turned then to meet him, and thrust at him twice so hard that Brodir fell before him at each thrust, and was well-nigh not getting on his feet again. But as soon as ever he found his feet, he fled away into the wood at once. Earl Sigurd had a hard battle against Kerthialfad, and Kerthialfad came on so fast that he laid low all who were in the front rank, and he broke the array of earl Sigurd right up to his banner, and slew the banner-bearer. Then he got another man to bear the banner, and there was again a hard fight. Kerthialfad smote this man too his death blow at once, and so on one after the other all who stood near him. Then earl Sigurd called on Thorstein, the son of Hall of the Side, to bear the banner, but then Amundi the white said, "Don't bear the banner! for all they who bear it get their death." "Hrafn the red!" called out earl Sigurd, "Bear thou the banner." "Bear thine own devil thyself," answered Hrafn. Then the earl said "'Tis fittest that the beggar should bear the bag"; and with that he took the banner from the staff and put it under his cloak. A little after Amundi the white was slain, and then the earl was pierced through with a spear. Ospak had gone through all the battle on his wing, he had been sore wounded, and lost both his sons ere king Sigtrygg fled before him.

Then flight broke out throughout all the host. Thorstein Hall of the Side's son stood still while all the others fled, and tied his shoestring. Then Kerthialfad asked why he ran not as the others. "Because," said Thorstein, "I can't get home to-night, since I am at home out in Iceland." Kerthialfad gave him peace. Hrafn the red was chased out into a certain river; he thought he saw there the pains of hell down below him and he thought the devils wanted to drag him to them. Then Hrafn said, "Thy dog, Apostle Peter! hath run twice to Rome, and he would run a third time if thou gavest him leave." [Meaning that he would go a third time on a pilgrimage to Rome if St. Peter helped him out of this strait.] Then the devils let him loose, and Hrafn got across the river.

Now Brodir saw that king Brian's men were chasing the fleers, and that there were few men by the shieldburg. Then he rushed out of the wood, and broke through the shieldburg, and hewed at the king. The lad Takt threw his arm in the way, and the stroke took it off and the king's head too, but the king's blood came on the lad's stump, and the stump was healed by it on the spot. Then Brodir called out with a loud voice, "Now man can tell man that Brodir felled Brian."

Then men ran after those who were chasing the fleers, and they were told that king Brian had fallen, and then they turned back straightway, both Wolf the quarrelsome and Kerthialfad. Then they threw a ring round Brodir and his men, and threw branches of trees upon them, and so Brodir was taken alive. Wolf the quarrelsome cut open his belly, and led him round and round the trunk of a tree, and so wound all his entrails out of him, and he did not die before they were all drawn out of him. Brodir's men were slain to a man. After that they took king Brian's body and laid it out. The king's head had [miraculously been reattached to his body]. Fifteen men of the Burners fell in Brian's battle, and there too fell Halldor the son of Gudmund the powerful, and Erling of Straumey.

THE WAR OF THE
GAEDHIL WITH THE GAILL
AN IRISH ACCOUNT

The War of the Gaedhil with the Gaill *could have been translated* Wars of the Irish with the Gauls. *The Gaedhil were the Irish descendants of Noah, which is to say the purest Irish of all, while the Irish word for the Gauls of France had come to mean any stranger from across the sea. In actual practice,* Gaill *meant "Viking." This account of the centuries-long struggle between the Dal Cais clan and the Norse intruders (ending with the triumph—and death—of Brian Boru at Clontarf) was once thought to have been written immediately after the battle by mac Liag, a member of Boru's court described in* The Annals of Clonmacnoise *as "the arch poet of Ireland and one that was in wonderful favor with king Bryan." Actually, although it may be based on earlier accounts, this seems to have been written several generations later as a work of family propaganda commissioned by Brian's descendants.*

As such, it is addressed to a lay audience (even though it was probably written by monks) with historical and religious references that include the Old Testament, Greek mythology, the ancient gods and goddesses of Ireland (who are still very active indeed), and orthodox Christianity. The battle descriptions are vivid and somewhat romanticized, especially when it comes to describing uniforms and clothing, and it should be remembered that Irish warriors of this period rarely used bows and—unlike the Vikings—never wore armor.

BRIAN BORU AND THE BATTLE OF CLONTARF

Brian was then on the plain of Ath Cliath [Dublin], in council with the nobles of the Dál Cais, and with Maelsechlainn [Malachy], and with Murchadh [Brian's son], and with Conaing, and with Tadhg, son of Cathal, and with the nobles of Conacht together, and with the men of Mumhain and the men of Midhe [Meath]; but it happened that the men of Midhe and Maelsechlainn were not of one mind with the rest.

Brian looked out behind him and beheld the battle phalanx, compact, huge, disciplined, moving in silence, mutely, bravely, haughtily, unitedly, with one mind, traversing the plain towards them; and three score and ten banners over them, of red, and of yellow, and of green, and of all kinds of colours; together with the everlasting, variegated, lucky, fortunate banner, that had gained the victory in every battle and in every conflict, and in every combat; by which seven battles had been gained before that time, namely, the gold-spangled banner of Fergal Ua Ruairc, chief king of the territory of Brefni and Conmaicni; and Fergal himself was there, and Domhnall, son of Ragallach, and Gilla-na-naemh, son of Domhnall, grandson of Fergal, and the nobles of the territory of Brefni and Conmaicni in like manner. And they came near the tent, and stopped there; and Fergal and the nobles advanced to where Brian was, to meet him, and Brian gave them a hearty friendly welcome; and Murchadh rose up to him, and seated him in his place. And Brian asked him the news, and he told him that Aedh, son of Ualgairg Ua Ciardha, king of Cairbri [parts of Counties Leitrim and Cavan], refused to accompany him to that battle in defence of Brian. And therefore Brian cursed Ua Ciardha, and the Cairbri, and gave a blessing to Fergal and to the men of Brefni also.

Some, indeed, have said that the pay of the pirates was spent the night before that battle, and that they had gone *homewards* as far as Benn Edair [Howth], when they saw the conflagration and devastation of the country; for they had offered Brian the night before, that if he would delay the burning until the morrow's sunrise, they would raise their sail-masts, and never return again; for they dreaded the valour of Murchadh, and of the Dál Cais in general.

But now the fleet returned, and came to one place; both the foreigners of Ath Cliath and the Laighin, and they formed seven great strong battalions. And then ensued a conflict, wrestling, wounding, noisy, bloody, crimsoned, terrible, fierce, quarrelsome: that conflict of the Dál Cais and the men of Munster, and of Conacht, and of the men of Brefni, and of the foreigners, and of the Laighin.

THE ENEMY FORCES

Now on the one side of that battle were the shouting, hateful, powerful, wrestling, valiant, active, fierce-moving, dangerous, nimble, violent, furious, unscrupulous, untamable, inexorable, unsteady, cruel, barbarous, frightful, sharp, ready, huge, prepared, cunning, warlike, poisonous, murderous, hostile Danars [Danes]; bold, hard-hearted Danmarkians, surly, piratical foreigners, blue-green, pagan; without reverence, without veneration, without honour, without mercy, for God or for man. These had for the purposes of battle and combat, and for their defence, sharp, swift, bloody, crimsoned, bounding, barbed, keen, bitter, wounding, terrible, piercing, fatal, murderous, poisoned arrows, which had been anointed and browned in the blood of dragons and toads, and water-snakes of hell, and of scorpions and otters, and wonderful venomous snakes of all kinds, to be cast and shot at active and warlike, and valiant chieftains. They had with them hideous, barbarous, quivers; and polished, yellow-shining bows; and strong, broad green, sharp, rough, dark spears, in the stout, bold, hard hands of freebooters. They had also with them polished, pliable, triple-plated, heavy, stout, corslets of double refined iron, and of cool uncorroding brass, for the protection of their bodies, and skin, and skulls, from sharp terrible arms, and from all sorts of fearful weapons. They had also with them valorous, heroic, heavy, hard-striking, strong, powerful, stout swords.

BRIAN'S TROOPS DESCRIBED

But on the other side of that battle were brave, valiant champions; soldierly, active, nimble, bold, full of courage, quick, doing great deeds, pompous, beautiful, aggressive, hot, strong, swelling, bright, fresh, never-weary, terrible, valiant, victorious heroes and chieftains, and champions, and brave soldiers, the men of high deeds, and honour, and renown of Erinn; namely, the heavy weight that broke down every stronghold, and cleft every way, and sprang over every obstacle, and flayed every stout head, that is to say, the descendants of Lugaidh, son of Oenghus Tirech, who are called the Dal Cais of Borumha, and the stainless intelligent heroes of the Gaidhil along with them. . . .

And these had for the purposes of battle and combat, above their heads, spears glittering, well riveted, empoisoned, with well-shaped, heroic, beautiful handles of white hazle; terrible sharp darts with variegated silken strings; thick set with bright, dazzling, shining nails, to be violently cast at the heroes of valour and bravery. They had on them also, long, glossy, convenient, handsome, white, neat, well-adjusted, graceful shirts. They had on them also, beautiful, many-coloured, well-fitting, handsome, well-shaped, well-adjusted, enfolding tunics, over comfortable long vests. They had with them also, great warlike, bright, beautiful, variegated shields, with bosses of brass, and elegant chains of bronze, at the sides of their noble, accomplished, sweet, courteous, eloquent clansmen. They had on them also, crested golden helmets, set with sparkling transparent brilliant gems and precious stones, on the heads of chiefs and royal knights.

They had with them also, shining, powerful, strong, graceful, sharp, glaring, bright, broad, well-set Lochlann axes, in the hands of chiefs and leaders, and heroes, and brave knights, for cutting and maiming the close well-fastened coats of mail. They had with them, steel, strong, piercing, graceful, ornamental, smooth, sharp-pointed, bright-sided, keen, clean, azure, glittering, flashing, brilliant, handsome, straight, well-tempered, quick, sharp swords, in the beautiful white hands of chiefs and royal knights, for hewing and for hacking, for maiming and mutilating skins, and bodies, and skulls.

Woe unto all who shunned not this people, who did not yield unto them. Woe to those who aroused their anger, if it was possible to escape from it. Woe to those who attacked them, if they could have avoided attacking them; for it was swimming against a stream; it was pummelling an oak with fists; it was a hedge against the swelling of a spring-tide; it was a string upon sand or a sun-beam; it was the fist against a sun-beam, to attempt to give them battle or combat; for it is not easy to conceive any horror equal to that of arousing the fierce battle and hard conflict of these warriors.

BOTH SIDES LINE UP FOR BATTLE

So these battalions were arranged and disposed in the following manner. The foreigners and the Laighen placed in the front the murderous foreign Danars, under Brodar, earl of Caer Ebroc, chieftain of the Danars; with Conmael, his mother's son, and with Siucaid, son of Lotar, earl of the Ore Islands, and with Plait, the bravest knight of all the foreigners, and with Anrath, son of Elbric, son of the king of Lochlann, and Carlus, and Torbenn the black, and Sunin, and Suanin, and the nobles of the foreigners of western Europe, from Lochlann westwards, along with them. A line of one very great strong battalion was formed of all the foreigners of Ath Cliath, and it was placed after the above, that is after the Danmarkians.

At their head were Dubhgall, son of Amlaf, and Gilla Ciarain, son of Glun-iaraind, son of Amlaf, and Donchad, grandson of Erulf, and Amlaf, Lagmund, son of Goffraidh, the four crown princes of the foreigners. At their head also, were Ottir the black, and Grisin, and Lummin, and Snadgair, four petty kings of the foreigners, and four chieftains of ships, and the nobles of the foreigners of Erinn along with them. A battalion was also formed of the Laighin and of the Ui Cennselaigh, and it was placed behind the above. And at the head of them were Maelmordha [brother of Brian's former wife Gormfhlaich], son of Murchadh, king of Laighin, and

Boetan, son of Dunlang, king of western Laighin, and Dunlang, son of Tuathal, king of Liphi, and Brogorban, son of Conchobhar, king of Ui Failghi, and Domhnall, son of Fergal, king of the Forthuagha of Laighin, and the nobles of Laighin likewise.

The front of Brian's battalion and of the nobles of Erinn with him, was given to the aforesaid impetuous, irresistible, troops, to the fine, intelligent, valiant, brave, active, lively heroes, viz., to the heroic, victorious Dal Cais, and to the Clann Luighdeach likewise. At the head of these was the matchless, ever victorious, Hector, of the many-nationed heroic children of Adam, namely, Murchadh, son of Brian, the yew of Ross, of the princes of Erinn; the head of the valour and bravery, and chivalry, munificence and liberality, and beauty, of the men of the world in his time, and in his career; for the historians of the Gaedhil do not relate that there was any man of the sons of Adam in his time who could hold a shield in mutual interchange of blows with him. Along with him were also, Tordhelbach, his son, the best crown prince of his time in Erinn, and Conaing, son of Doncuan, one of the three men most valued by Brian, that were then in Erunn; and Niall Ua Cuinn, and Eochaidh, son of Dunadach, and Cudulligh, son of Cennetigh, the three rear guards of Brian; and Domhnall, son of Diarmaid, king of Corcabhaiscinn, and the greater part of the men of bravery and valour of the Dal Cais along with them. One very strong and great battalion was also formed of the chosen hosts of all Mumhain, and was stationed in the rear of the former. At the head of these was Mothla, son of Domhnall, son of Faelan, king of the Desii, and Mangnus, son of Anmchadh, king of Ui Liathain, and the brave and heroic of all Mumhain along with them.

The battalion of Conacht also, was led by Maelruanaidh Ua-n-Eidhin, and by Tadhg Ua Cellaigh, king of Ui Mani, and by Maelruanaidh, son of Murghius, king of Muintir Maelruanaidh; and by Domhnall, grandson of Cuceninn, king of Ui nDiarmada; and with Ualgarg, son of Cerin, and with the nobles of all Conacht along with him.

The ten great stewards of Brian were drawn up, with their foreign auxiliaries, on one side of the army. Fergal Ua Ruairc, and the Ui Briuin, and the Conmaicne, were ordered to the left wing of the army.

Maelsechlainn [Malachy] also, son of Domhnall, king of Temhair, and the battalion of the men of Midhe, with him, were next; but he consented not to be placed along with the rest; because the counsel of the foreigners on the preceding night was that he should put a ditch between him and the foreigners; and that if he would not attack the foreigners, the foreigners would not attack him; and so it was done, for the evil understanding was between them.

BRIAN'S SON PREPARES FOR BATTLE

Some of the historians of Mumhain, however, say that Murchadh, son of Brian, was placed, mixed with the battalion of Desmumhain, along with his company, namely, seven score sons of kings that were in attendance upon him; for there was not a king of any one tribe in Erinn, who had not his son or his brother in Murchadh's household; for he was the lord of the volunteers of Erinn, and of her sons, next to Aedh Ua Neill. They say that the two battalions were side by side, namely, the battalion of Desmumhain, and the battalion of Tuadhmumhain, and it is clear that this is true; for when they were arranging the battalion, Murchadh went forward beyond the rest a hand's cast to attack the foreigners. Then Brian sent Domhnall, son of Emin, to tell Murchadh to fall back until he should be on a line with the Dalcais. Domhnall, son of Emin, went and told this to Murchadh. Murchadh answered that his counsel was timid and cowardly; for . . . he would not retreat one step backwards . . . in presence of the Gaill and Gaedhil. . . . Domhnall, son of Emin, said to Murchadh, "thy countenance is bad, O royal champion, although thy courage is great." Murchadh answered that he had cause for that, because many a false hero would leave his share of the battle to him at the end of the day. The son of Emin said that he would not leave his share. And he said truly; for he fulfilled his promise.

The battalions were placed side by side after that. Then Murchadh looked to one side and beheld approaching him, on his right side, alone, the heroical, courageous, championlike, active, beautiful, strong, bounding, graceful, erect, impetuous, young hero, Dunlang O'Hartugan; and he recognised him and made three springs to meet him, and he kissed him, and welcomed him; and "O youth," said he, "it is long until thou camest unto us; and great must be the love and attachment of some woman to thee, which has induced thee to abandon me; and to abandon Brian, and Conaing, and Donnchadh; and the nobles of Dal Cais in like manner, and the delights of Erinn until this day." "Alas, O king," said Dunlang, "the delight that I have abandoned for thee is greater, if thou didst but know it [he had been having a secret love affair with the goddess Aibhell], namely, life without death, without cold, without thirst, without hunger, without decay; beyond any delight of the delights of the earth to me, until the judgment; and heaven after the judgment; and if I had not pledged my word to thee, I would not have come here; and moreover it is fated for me to die on the day thou shalt die."

"Shall I receive death this day, then?" said Murchadh. "Thou shalt receive it, indeed," said Dunlang, "and Brian, and Conaing, shall receive it, and almost all the nobles of Erinn, and Toirdhelbhach thy son." "This is not good encouragement to fight," said Murchadh, "and if we had such news we would not have told it to thee; but, however," said Murchadh, "often was I offered, in hills and in fairy mansions, this world and these gifts; but I never abandoned for one night my country nor my inheritance for them." "What man," said Dunlang, "wouldst thou choose to be kept off thee this day." "There are yonder," said Murchadh, "sixteen men who are captains of fleets, and every one of them is a man to combat a hundred, on sea and on land; besides Brotor, and Cornabbliteoc, and Maelmordha, and the Laighin also." "Leave to me, then," said Dunlang, "Cornabbliteoc; and if I can do more, thou shalt have my further aid." "That is a severe service, indeed," said Murchadh, "O Dunlang, if thou didst but know it."

BATTLE BEGINS WITH A SINGLE COMBAT

The battalions were now arranged and drawn up on both sides, in such order and in such manner, that a four-horsed chariot could run from one end to the other of the line, on both sides [on the heads of the soldiers standing in line]; and the battalions then made a stout, furious, barbarous, smashing onset on each other. But, alas! these were the faces of foes in battle-field, and not the faces of friends at a feast. And each party of them remembered their ancient animosities towards each other, and each party of them attacked the other. And it will be one of the wonders of the day of judgment to relate the description of this tremendous onset. And there arose a wild, impetuous, precipitate, furious, dark, frightful, voracious, merciless, combative, contentious, vulture, screaming and fluttering over their heads. And there arose also the satyrs, and the idiots, and the maniacs of the valleys, and the witches, and the goblins, and the ancient birds, and the destroying demons of the air and of the firmament, and the feeble demoniac phantom host; and they were screaming and comparing the valour and combat of both parties.

First then were drawn up there, Domhnall, son of Eimin, high steward of Alban, on Brian's side, and Plait, son of the king of Lochlainn, brave champion of the foreigners; because of Plait having said the night before, that there was not a man in Erinn who was able to fight him, Domhnall, the son of Eimhin, immediately took him up, and each of them remembered this in the morning. Then Plait came forth from the battalion of the men in armour, and said three times, "*Faras Domhnall*," that is, "where is Domhnall?" Domhnall answered and said, "Here, thou reptile," said he. They fought then, and each of them endeavoured to slaughter the other; and they fell by each other, and the way that they fell was, with the sword of each through the heart of the other; and the hair of each in the clinched hand of the other. And the combat of that pair was the first [of the battle].

The person who was on the flank of the battalion of the pirates, was Dunnall, son of Tuathal, king of Liphe, with ten hundred men armed for battle. There met him on the flank of Brian's forces, against these, their equal in numbers and in might, namely, Ferghail Ua Ruairc, and Domhnall, son of Raghallach; and Gilla-na-Noemh, son of Domhnall O'Ferghail, and the nobles of the Ui Briuin and Conmaicni also. But now these attacked each other, and they detached themselves from the great body of the army, until there was the distance of a bow shot between them, on the north side of the great body; and they began to stab and hew each other. But these parties were equally matched in arms, in vesture, and in appearance. And none of them paid any attention to any evil that was done at Cluain-Tarbh on that day, excepting the evil and contention which they mutually occasioned against each other.

But they very nearly killed each other altogether; and historians do not relate that there survived of the Ui Briuin and Conmaicni, more than one hundred, with Ferghal Ua Ruairc; and the entire of the Ui Cendselaigh were routed there; and they were afterwards pursued to the battalion of the mail-clad men; for there was a wood of shelter near them, and they were in order of battle with their backs towards them; and it was then that nine of the household of Ferghal overtook Dunlang, the son of Tuathal, and killed him; and Mac an Trin, who was the captain of Ferghal's household, beheaded him, and he brought the head to Ferghal to congratulate him on it. And they went then, the few of them that were left, into Brian's battalion, and behind Murchadh's standard; and they had Ferghal's standard floating there, after the fall of all their other standards, and the killing of their chiefs, namely, ten standards and three score.

THE VIKINGS ATTACK

Then the fearful, murderous, hard-hearted, terrific, vehement, impetuous, battalion of the Danmarkians, and the vehement, irresistible, unanswerable phalanx; and the fine, intelligent, acute, fierce, valorous, mighty, royal, gifted, renowned, champions of the Dal Cais, and all the descendants of Oilioll Olum met in one place; and there was fought between them a battle, furious, bloody, repulsive, crimson, gory, boisterous, manly, rough, fierce, unmerciful, hostile, on both sides; and they began to hew and cleave, and stab, and cut, to slaughter, to mutilate each other; and they maimed, and they cut comely, graceful, mailed bodies of noble, pleasant, courteous, affable, accomplished men on both sides there. That was the clashing of two bodies of equal hardness, and of two bodies moving in contrary directions, in one place. And it is not easy to imagine what to liken it to; but to nothing small could be likened the firm, stern, sudden, thunder-motion; and the stout, valiant, haughty billow-roll of these people on both sides.

I could compare it only to the variegated, boundless, wonderful firmament, that had cast a heavy sparkling shower of flaming stars over the surface of the earth; or to the startling fire-darting roar of the clouds and the heavenly orbs, confounded and crashed by all the winds, in contention, against each other. Or to the summit of heaven, or to the rapid, awfully great sea, and the fierce, contentious roaring of the four transparent, pure, harsh, directly opposing winds, in the act of breaking loose from the order of their respective positions. Or to the stern terrific judgment–day that had come, to confound, and break down the unity of the four surrounding elements, to crush and finally shiver the compact world, and to take vengeance on it.

To all these could I compare the smashing, powerful, strong, barbarous, shield-shining, target-bossed, red, sparkling, starry onset of the Clann Ludech, under the stout bright axes of the stern, murderous Danars, mutilating, and crushing them; and the gleaming, bright, glassy, hard, straight swords of the Dal Cais, in hard, powerful clashing against the free, sparkling, thrice-riveted, stout, powerful, protective armour of the piratical Danmarkians, smashing with them the bones of their bodies and their skulls, so that the sound of them, and the uproar of them, and the echo of them were reverberated from the caverns, and from the cliffs, and from the woods in the neighbourhood; and it became a work of great difficulty to the battalions on both sides to defend their clear sparkling eyes, and their flushed bright cheeks from the heavy showers of fiery sparks which were sent forth by the royal champions of the Clann Lughdech from the sharp fearful points of their bright gleaming swords, in hacking and cutting the firmly hooked mail-coats off them; and it was attested by the foreigners and foreign women who were watching from the battlements of Ath Cliath, as they beheld, that they used to see flashes of fire from them in the expanse of air on all sides.

MALACHY'S ACCOUNT OF THE BATTLE

Another attestation of this is the description which Maelsechlainn gave of that crush, when the Clann Colmain asked him for an account of the battle. It was then he said, "I never saw a battle like it, nor have I heard of its equal; and even if an angel of God attempted its description, I doubt if he could give it. But there was one circumstance that attracted my notice there, when the forces first came into contact, each began to pierce the other. There was a field, and a ditch, between us and them, and the sharp wind of the spring coming over them towards us; and it was not longer than the time that a cow could be milked, or two cows, that we continued there, when not one person of the two hosts could recognise another, though it might be his son or his brother that was nearest him, unless he should know his voice, and that he preciously knew the spot in which he was; we were so covered, as well our heads as our faces, and our clothes, with the drops of gory blood, carried by the force of the sharp cold wind which passed over them to us.

And even if we attempted to perform any deed of valour we were unable to do it, because our spears over our heads had become clogged and bound with long locks of hair, which the wind forced upon us, when cut away by well-aimed swords, and gleaming axes; so that it was half occupation to us to endeavour to disentangle, and cast them off. And it is one of the problems of Erinn, whether the valour of those who sustained that crushing assault was greater than ours who bore the sight of it without running distracted before the winds or fainting."

INDIVIDUAL COMBATS

We must now speak of Dunlang. He rushed on the host of the pirates, and spared not one of them, because he had no friendship at all for the foreigners. And he approached Cornabliteoc, and each of them made a rough, fierce, unmerciful assault on the other. Then came three of the people of Cornabliteoc in front of him, and they made three simultaneous thrusts at Dunlang. But, it was not on them Dunlang's desire and attention were fixed, but on Cornabliteoc; for he gave him a rough, fierce, rapid blow of a spear, by which his ardour was excited, and his spirit roused, and his active mind occupied; for its rough point passed through him, both body, and body-armour. When this was perceived by Cornabliteoc's people, they formed a firm, compact, hard-hearted circle around him; and the thrice fifty of them that were there, turned themselves at the same time against Dunlang.

However, it is certain, that their defence procured neither respect nor mercy for their chief, for by Dunlang fell every one of them who waited to be wounded and beaten, until there remained no interposition between them; and they dealt ardent thrusts and fearful blows at each other. And this was one of the three hardest combats that took place at Cluain Tarbh, besides what Murchadh performed, of bone-breaking of heads and bodies. For his was the fierce rushing of a bull, and the scorching path of a royal champion. But to return, these brave champions nearly fell by each other; Dunlang, however, beheaded him.

We must next speak of Conaing. He faced Maelmordha, son of Murhcadh, king of Laghin, and sixteen men of the people were killed, each man of them, in front of his lord, before they themselves met, and fell by each other, viz., Conaing, king of Des-mhumha, and Maelmordha, king of Laghin.

THE MEN OF CONACHT FIGHT THE VIKINGS OF DUBLIN

We speak next of the men of Conacht. They advanced to the foreigners of Ath Cliath, and they attacked each other. And that was the decisive defeat that took place on the plain; for they were [almost] all killed, on both sides, there, for there escaped alive from it of the men of Conacht, one hundred only; and there escaped of the foreigners of Ath Cliath, but twenty, and it was at Dubhgall's Bridge the last man of these was killed, viz., Arnaill Scot, and those who killed him were the household troops of Tadhg Ua Cellaigh. The full events of that battle, however, and its deeds, God alone knows; because everyone besides who could have had knowledge of it fell there on either side; and every man had sufficient to do to know his own adventures, from the greatness of his distress.

PRAISE FOR BRIAN'S SON

To return to Murchadh, son of Brian, the royal champion. He grasped his two valiant strong swords, viz., a sword in his right, and a sword in his left hand, for he was the last man in Erinn who had equal dexterity in striking with his right and with his left hand. He was the last man that had true valour in Erinn. It was he that pledged the word of a true champion, that he would not retreat one foot before the whole of the human race, for any reason whatsoever but this alone, that he might die of his wounds. He was the last man in Erinn who was a match for a hundred. He was the last man who killed a hundred in one day. . . .

He was the metaphorical Hector of all-victorious Erinn, in religion, and in valour, and in championship, in generosity, and in munificence. He was the pleasant, affable, intelligent, accomplished Samson of the Hebrews, for promoting the prosperity and freedom of his fatherland and of his race, during his own career and time. He was the second powerful Hercules, who destroyed and exterminated serpents and monsters out of Erinn; who searched the lakes, and pools, and caverns, of noble-landed Fodhla [embodiment of the warrior as part of Ireland], whom no fortress or fastness in the world could resist. He was the Lugh Lamha-fada [Lug, the sun god who turned the tide at the second battle of Mag Tured], who, like him, sprang over every obstacle, laid bare every brave head, and exterminated and expelled the foreigners and pirates out of Erinn. He was the gate of battle, and the hurdle of conflict, and the sheltering tree, and the impregnable tower, against the enemies of his fatherland and of his race during his time and during his career.

When this very great, very valiant, royal champion, and brave power-ful hero saw the crushing and the repulse which the Danars and the pirat-ical Danmarkians gave to the Dal Cais, it operated on him like death, or a permanent blemish, to see the conflict of the foreigners with them; and he was seized with a boiling, terrible anger, and an excessive elevation, and greatness of spirit and mind. A bird of valour and championship arose in him, and fluttered over his head, and on his breath. And he made an active, brave, vigorous, sudden rush at the battalion of the Danmarkians, like a violent, impetuous, furious ox, that is difficult to catch; or like a fierce, tearing, swift, all-powerful lioness, that has been roused and robbed of her whelps; or like the fierce roll of an impetuous, deluging tor-rent, which shatters and smashes every thing that opposes it; and he made a hero's breach, and a soldier's field, through the battalion of the Danmarkians.

It is testified by his enemies after him, viz., the historians of the for-eigners, and of the Laighin, that there fell fifty by his right hand, and fifty by his left, in that onset; and he never repeated a blow to any one, but only the one blow, and neither shield nor mail-coat was proof to resist any of those blows, or prevent its cutting the body, the skull, or the bone of every one of them. Thrice, now, passed he through the battalion in that manner. He was followed, too, by the great, impetuous, irresistible, matchless, phalanx of the Clann Luighdech, and the fine, lively, valiant, brave, fierce champions, of his own household, namely, seven score sons of kings that were in his household; and the man of smallest patrimony amongst them was lord of a townland. These followed him sharply, quickly, and lightly, so that they touched each other foot to foot, and head to head, and body to body, behind him in every place that they came to. And it appeared to the people of Ath Cliath, who were watching them from their battlements, that not more numerous would be the sheaves floating over a great company reaping a field of oats; even though two or three battalions were working at it, than the hair flying with the wind from them, cut away by heavy gleaming axes, and by bright flaming swords. Whereupon the son of Amhlaibh, who was on the battlements of his watch tower, watching them, said, "Well do the foreigners reap the field," said he, "many is the sheaf they let go from them." "It will be at the end of the day that will be seen," said Brian's daughter, namely, the wife of [the son of] Amhlaibh.

THE BATTLE CONTINUES AS THE TIDE RISES AND FALLS

However, now, they continued in battle array, and fighting from sunrise to evening. This is the same length of time as that which the tide takes to go, and to flood, and to fill. For it was at the full tide the foreigners came out to fight the battle in the morning, and the tide had come to the same place again at the close of the day, when the foreigners were defeated; and the tide had carried away their ships from them, so that they had not at the last any place to fly to, but into the sea; after the mail-coated foreigners had been all killed by the Dál Cais. An awful rout was made of the foreigners, and of the Laighin, so that they fled simultaneously; and they shouted their cries for mercy, and whoops of rout, and retreat, and running; but they could only fly to the sea, because they had no other place to retreat to, seeing they were cut off between it and the head of Dubhgall's Bridge; and they were cut off between it and the wood on the other side. They retreated therefore to the sea, like a herd of cows in heat, from sun, and from gadflies, and from insects; and they were pursued closely, rapidly, and lightly; and the foreigners were drowned in great numbers in the sea, and they lay in heaps and in hundreds, confounded, after parting with their bodily senses and understandings, under the powerful, stout, belabouring; and under the tremendous, hard-hearted pressure, with which the Dal Cais, and the men of Conacht, and as many as were also there of the nobles of Erinn, pursued them.

It was then that Tordhelbhach, the son of Murchadh, son of Brian, went after the foreigners into the sea, when the rushing tide wave struck him a blow against the weir of Cluain-Tarbh [Clontarf] and so was he drowned, with a foreigner under him, and a foreigner in his right hand, and a foreigner in his left, and a stake of the weir through him. There was not of his age a person of greater generosity or munificence than he in Erinn; and there was not a more promising heir of the kingdom. For he inherited the munificence of his father, and the royal dignity of his grandfather; and he had not completed more than fifteen years at that time. He was also one of the three men who had killed most on that day.

Then it was that Brian's daughter, namely, the wife of Amhlaibh's son said, "It appears to me," said she, "that the foreigners have gained their inheritance." "What meanest thou, O woman?" said Amhlaibh's son. "The foreigners are going into the sea, their natural inheritance," said she; "I wonder is it heat that is upon them; but they tarry not to be milked, if it is." The son of Amhlaibh became angered and he gave her a blow.

THE DEATH OF MURCHADH

To return, however, to Murchadh, son of Brian. When he had passed through the battalions of the foreigners, accompanied by the champions of the Dál Cais, as we have said before, there was a party of soldiers of the foreigners still before him, who had not rushed into the sea as yet, who retained their senses and their memories, and who preferred enduring any amount of suffering rather than be drowned. It was then that Murchadh perceived Siucraid [Earl of Orkney], son of Lotar, Earl of Insi Orc, in the midst of the battalion of the Dál Cais, slaughtering and mutilating them; and his fury among them was that of a robber upon a plain; and neither pointed nor any kind of edged weapon could harm him; and there was no strength that yielded not, nor thickness that became not thin. Then Murchadh made a violent rush at him, and dealt him a fierce, powerful, crushing blow from the valiant, death-dealing, active right hand, in the direction of his neck, and the fastenings of the foreign hateful helmet that was on his head, so that he cut the buttons, and the fastenings, and the clasps, and the buckles that were fastening the helmet; and he brought the sword of the graceful left hand to hew and maim him after the helmet had fallen backwards from him; and he cut his neck, and felled that brave hero with two tremendous, well-aimed blows, in that manner.

Then came the heroic, valiant, noble, renowned warrior, the son of Ebric, son of the king of Lochlann, into the bosom and centre of the Dál Cais, and it was the clear stage of a warrior, and the breach of a hero was opened for him wherever he went; and he trampled to a litter one end of the battalion, dealing in all directions fierce, barbarous strokes, and victorious irresistible blows. Murchadh perceived this, and it was a heart-ache to him, and he turned obliquely upon the battalions of the mailed-men, and killed fifteen foreigners on his right, and fifteen on his left, who were mail-clad, until he reached [the son of] Elbric [Ebric], the son of the king of Lochlainn [Lochlann], for he was the head of valour and bravery of the army of Lochlainn, and of all the foreigners also. And they fought a stout, furious, bloody, crimson combat, and a fierce, vehement, rough, boister-ous, implacable battle. And the sword of Murchadh at that time was inlaid with ornament, and the inlaying that was in it melted with the excessive heat of the striking, and the burning sword cleft his hand, tear-ing the fork of his fist. He perceived that, and cast the sword from him, and he laid hold of the top of the foreigner's head, and pulled his coat of mail over his head forward, and they then fought a wrestling combat.

Then Murchadh put the foreigner down under him, by the force of wrestling, and then he caught the foreigner's own sword and thrust it into the ribs of the foreigner's breast, until it reached the ground through him, three times. The foreigner then drew his knife, and with it gave Murchadh such a cut, that the whole of his entrails were cut out, and they fell to the ground before him. Then did shiverings and faintings descend on Murchadh, and he had not power to move, so that they fell by each other there, the foreigner and Murchadh. But at the same time Murchadh cut off the foreigner's head. And Murchadh did not die that night, nor until sunrise the next day; until he had received absolution, and communion, and penance, and until he had taken the Body of Christ, and until he had made his confession and his will.

BRIAN PRAYS AND SINGS THE PSALMS

Let us speak now of the adventures of Brian, son of Cenneidigh, during this time. When the forces met in combat, his cushion was spread under him, and he opened his psalter; and he began to clasp his hands and to pray after the battle had commenced; and there was no one with him but his own attendant, whose name was Latean. Brian said to the attendant, watch thou the battles and the combats, whilst I sing the psalms. He sang fifty psalms, and fifty prayers, and fifty paternosters, and he asked the attendant after that what the condition of the battalions was. The atten-dant answered and said, "Mixed and closely confounded are the battal-ions, and each of them has come within the grasp of the other; and not louder in my ears would be the echoes of blows from Tomar's Wood, if seven battalions were cutting it down, than are the resounding blows upon heads, and bones, and skulls, on both sides." Then he asked what was the condition of Murchadh's standard; and the attendant said—"It is standing, and many of the banners of the Dál Cais are around it; and many heads are falling around it, and a multitude of trophies, and spoils, with heads of the foreigners are along with it." That is good news, indeed, said Brian.

His cushion was readjusted under him, and he sang the psalms, and the prayers, and the paters, in the same manner as before. And he asked of the attendant, again, what the condition of the battalions was; and the attendant answered and said—"There is not living on earth one who could distinguish one of them from the other. For, the greater part of the hosts at either side are fallen, and those who are alive are so covered with spatterings of the crimson blood, head, body, and vesture, that a father could not know his son from any other of them, so confounded are they."

He then asked what was the condition of Murchadh's standard. The attendant said that it was far from him, and that it passed through the battalions, westwards, and was still standing. Brian said, "The men of Erinn shall be well while that standard remains standing, because their courage and valour shall remain in them all, as long as they can see that standard."

His cushion was readjusted under Brian, and he sang fifty psalms, and fifty prayers, and fifty paters; and the fighting continued all that time. He asked then of the attendant, in what state were the forces? The attendant answered—"They appear to me the same as if Tomar's Wood was on fire, and the seven battalions had been cutting away its underwood [and its young shoots], for a month, leaving its stately trees and its immense oaks standing. In such manner are the armies on either side, after the greater part of them have fallen, leaving a few brave men and gallant heroes only standing. Their further condition is, they are wounded, and pierced through, and dismembered; and they are disorganized all round like the grindings of a mill turning the wrong way, and the foreigners are now defeated, and Murchadh's standard has fallen."

"That is sad news," said Brian; "on my word," said he, "the honour and valour of Erinn fell when that standard fell; and Erinn has fallen now, indeed; and never shall there appear henceforth a champion comparable to or like to that champion. And what avails it me to survive this, or that I should obtain the sovereignty of the world, after the fall of Murchadh, and Conaing, and the other nobles of the Dál Cais, in like manner." "Woe is me," said the attendant, "if thou wouldst take my advice, thou wouldst mount thy horse, and we would go the camp, and remain there amongst the servants; and every one who escapes this battle will come unto us, and around us will they all rally. Besides, the battalions are now mixed together in confusion; and a party of the foreigners have rejected the idea of retreating to the sea; and we know not who may approach us where we now are."

"Oh God! thou boy," said Brian, "retreat becomes us not, and I myself know that I shall not leave this place alive; and what would it profit me if I did. For, Aibhell, of Craig Liath [goddess who was Brian's protector], came to me last night," said he, "and she told me that I should be killed this day; and she said to me that the first of my sons I should see this day would be he who should succeed me in the sovereignty; and that is Donnchadh [his youngest son, who was fighting in Leinster], and go thou, Laidean," said he, "and take these steeds with thee, and receive my blessing; and carry out my will after me, viz., my body and my soul to God and to Saint Patrick, and that I am to be carried to Ard-macha,; and my blessing to Donnchadh, for discharging my last bequests after me, viz., twelve score cows to be given to the Comharba of Patrick, and the Society of Ard-macha; and its own proper dues to Cill da Lua, and the churches of Mumhain; and he knows that I have not wealth of gold or silver, but he is to pay them in return for my blessing, and for his succeeding me. Go this night to Sord, and desire them to come to-morrow, early, for my body, and to convey it from thence to Damhliag, of Cianan; and then let them carry it to Lughmhagh; and let Maelmuire Mac Eochadha, the Comharba of Patrick, and the Society of Ard-macha come to meet me at Lughmhagh."

BRIAN UNSHEATHES HIS SWORD

While they were engaged in this conversation the attendant perceived a party of the foreigners approaching them. The Earl Brodar was there, and two warriors along with him. "There are people coming towards us here," said the attendant. "Woe is me, what manner of people are they?" said Brian. "A blue stark naked people," said the attendant. "Alas!" said Brian, "they are the foreigners of the armour, and it is not to do good to thee they come." While he was saying this, he arose and stepped off the cushion, and unsheathed his sword. Brodar passed him by and noticed him not. One of the three who were there, and who had been in Brian's service, said—"Cing, Cing," said he, "this is the king." "No, no, but Priest, Priest," said Brodar, "it is not he," says he, "but a noble priest." "By no means," said the soldier, "that is the great king, Brian." Brodar then turned round, and appeared with a bright, gleaming, trusty battle-axe in his hand, with the handle set in the middle of it. When Brian saw him he gazed at him, and gave him a stroke with his sword, and cut off his left leg at the knee, and his right leg at the foot. The foreigner dealt Brian a stroke which cleft his head utterly; and Brian killed the second man that was with Brodar, and they fell both mutually by each other. . . .

However, that illustrious, all-victorious king, fell by the foreigners, in the eighty-eighth year of his age, and in the thirty-eighth year of his reign, in Mumhain; and in his twelfth year in the chief sovereignty of Erinn. In short, Erinn fell by the death of Brian; and the predictions came to pass, and the prophecies were fulfilled to Erinn, according to the saints and the righteous ones, as Berchan said—

> The noble and the plebeian fell
> > Foot to foot.
> > The Gaill and the Gaedhil will be the worse of it;
> > Blood-red shall be their conflicts.
> Evil shall be to Erinn from it.
> > Blood-red shall be their conflicts;
> > Thence to the judgment day;
> > Worse shall they be every day.
> There shall not be a pure church or city;
> > There shall not be a fortress or royal Rath;
> > A green wood, nor plain, nor good,
> > But all shall degenerate into lawlessness.

Two-thirds of the dignity and valour of the champions of Erinn fled on hearing this news. Two-thirds of the purity and devotion of the clerics of Erinn vanished at that news. Their modesty and chastity departed from the women of Erinn at the same news, as Bec Mac De said:

> The cows of the world shall be without the bull,
> > Modesty shall be wanting to young women;
> > Every territory shall be without mansions, for a time.
> > No king shall receive his tribute.

Two-thirds of their milk also departed from quadrupeds at that news.

THE DEATH TOLL

Moreover, there were killed in that battle together the greater part of the men of valour of the Gaill and the Gaedhil, of all the west of Europe. There was killed there, Brodar, son of Osli, Earl of Caer Ebroc, and along with him were killed a thousand plundering Danars, both Saxons and

Lochlanns. There was killed there Sitriuc, the son of Ladar, Earl of Innsi Orc. There were killed there two thousand of the foreigners of Ath Cliath, with Dubhghall, son of Amhlaibh, and with Gilla Ciarain, son of Gluniarann, and with Donnchadh O'hEruilbh, and with Amhlaibh, son of Laghman, and with Ernal Scot.

There were killed there, too, Oitir the black, and Grisin, and Luiminin, and Siogradh, the four leaders of the foreigners, and the four commanders of fleets. There fell there, too, Carlus, and Ciarlus, the two sons of the king of Lochlainn, and Goistilin Gall, and Amond, son of Duibhghin, the two kings of Port Lairge, and Simond, son of Turgeis, and Sefraid, son of Suinin, and Bernard, son of Suainin; and Eoin, the Baron, and Rickard, the two sons of the Inghen Ruaidh; and Oisill, and Raghnall, the two sons of Imhar, grandson of Imhar. It was the natural right of Brian that these should fall with him, for it was by Mathgamhain, and by Brian, in defence of their country and inheritance, that all the fathers of these were slain.

The son of Amhlaibh himself, king of Ath Cliath, went not into the battle on that day, and that was the reason why he was not killed, for no foreigner of any rank appeared in it who left it alive; and Ath Cliath would have been attacked on that day also, were it not for the son of Amhlaibh and the party he had with him. There fell there also Maelmordha, son of Murchadh, king of Laighin, and Brogarban, son of Conchobhar, king of Ui-Failghe and Domhnall, son of Ferghal, king of Fortuaith Laighen; and Dunlaing, son of Tuathal, king of Lifé, received a wound of which he died, and two thousand of the Lagenians along with them, and eleven hundred of the Ui-Ceinnselaigh. In a word, six hundred and three score hundreds was the total loss of the enemy's side in this battle. . . .

There fell there Murhcadh, son of Brian, and Toirrdhelbhach, his son. There fell there Conaing, son of Donnchuan, son of Cenneidigh, the son of Brian's brother, the wealthiest royal heir of Erinn. There fell there Eochaidh, son of Dunadhach, and Cuduiligh, son of Cenneidigh, and Niall O'Cuinn, the three rear-guards of Brian, and the greater part of the Dal Cais along with them. There fell there Domhnall, son of Diarmaid, king of Corco-Bhaiscinn; and Mothla, son of Faelan, king of the Desii; and the son of Anmchaidh, king of Ua Liathain; and Gebennach, son of Dubhagan, king of Fera-Muighe; and Dubhdabhorrenn, son of Domhnall, and Loingsech, son of Dunlaing, and Scannlan, son of Cathal, king of the Eoghanacht of Loch Lein; and Baedan, son of Muirchertach, king of Ciarraighe Luachra; and Maelruanaidh Ua hEidhin, king of Aidhne; and Tadhg Ua Cellaigh, king of Ui Maine; and Domhnall, son of Eimhin, and sixteen hundred of the nobles of Erinn along with them.

DUBLIN CAPTURED

When all these nobles were killed on both sides, and after the foreigners were defeated, all the men of Mumhain collected to one place; and they stationed themselves and encamped on the Green of Ath Cliath. And each sought for his friends and his acquaintances; and they remained two days and nights awaiting the return of Donnchadh, son of Brian; and he arrived with a great prey at the hour of vespers on the night of Easter Sunday; for it was on the Friday before Easter the battle was fought, viz., the ninth of the kalends of May; and little Easter was in the summer of that year.

Brian was met, as he had directed; and he was taken to Ard-Macha, and Murchadh along with him; and Donnchadh paid in full their bequests, and fulfilled Brian's will after him as he had himself directed.

Donnchadh brought with him a spoil of eight-and-twenty *oxen*, and they were all slaughtered on the Green of Ath Cliath; and the foreigners who were in Ath Cliath threatened to come out to give battle to Donnchadh and to such of the Dal Cais as were alive there, because it was great pain to them to have their cows killed in their presence. And a message came out from the son of Amhlaibh telling them to take an ox for every twenty, and to leave all the oxen behind except that number. Donnchadh said, "We have not been hitherto in the pay of the son of Imar, nor shall we be so in future; for it appears to us that our hostility to each other is now greater than ever;" and such of the oxen as were yet alive were then slaughtered in the sight of the foreigners of Ath Cliath; but the foreigners declined the battle from fear of Donnchadh and the Dal Cais.

On the next day they went to the field of battle and buried every one of their people that they were able to recognise, there; and they made sledges and biers for those of them who were alive although wounded; and they carried thirty of the nobles who were killed there to their territorial churches, wherever they were situated all over Erinn.

V.

THE

NORMAN

INVASION

INTRODUCTION

IN 1155, NEARLY A CENTURY after his great-grandfather William "conquered" England, Henry II was given permission by the pope to invade Ireland. Pope Adrian IV, the only Englishman ever to wear the ring of St. Peter (a fact that has not gone uncommented upon down the centuries), decried the sad moral state that the island and the local church had fallen into since the days of glory after St. Patrick converted the pagans to Christianity in the fifth century. Henry, preoccupied by wars in France and unrest at home, chose not to get involved in any new conflicts. So Ireland—in effect—came to him in the person of Dermot MacMurrough (or Diarmait Mac Murchada), the deposed king of Leinster.

There are several versions of the story of how Dermot lost his throne. The romantic one—favored by those who like to find parallels between the conquest of Ireland and the Trojan War—says that his troubles began when he abducted the beautiful wife of Tiernan O'Rourke (or Tigernan Ua Ruaric), the king of Breifne. The more prosaic version simply has him running afoul of the powerful high king, Rory O'Connor (or Ruaidri Ua Conchobair). In any case, he fled Ireland in 1166 to ask Henry to help him win back his crown. The king refused but gave him permission to raise, or hire, mercenaries. Dermot headed for south Wales, where he promised his kingdom and his daughter to the earl of Pembroke (Richard de Clare, often called Strongbow), who eventually began to organize the local Welsh-Normans—the FitzStephens, the FitzGeralds, the FitzHenrys, the de Barrys, all blood relations of Rhys ap Tewdwr, of the royal house that would become the Tudors—into an invasion army. With their large warhorses and heavy armor, they probably looked a good deal like their Norman ancestors who defeated King Harold at Hastings in 1066.

Dermot slipped back into Ireland, and after a long wait the first invasion forces led by Robert FitzStephen landed on the coast between Waterford and Wexford in May 1169. Strongbow himself arrived a year later, and his marriage to Dermot's daughter was said to have taken place on a battlefield so fresh that the hem of the bride's gown became stained with blood. The invaders soon held the land from Waterford to Dublin, and when Dermot died in 1171, Strongbow proclaimed himself king of Leinster.

All this may have been more than what Henry had in mind when he gave Dermot permission to hire mercenaries, although some historians have argued that the king's show of displeasure was an act since his Welshmen had succeeded in winning Ireland without tapping into the royal treasury. In any case, Henry himself arrived in Cork with his army in October 1172 to reprimand those who had exceeded their authority and to accept both their fealty and the fealty of the defeated Irish kings. Only Rory O'Connor refused to join with the other kings in bowing before Henry, but he later made a separate peace, one that still recognized him as high king of all the lands in Ireland outside the English-controlled areas in Dublin, Leinster, and Munster.

Meeting between Dermot MacMurrough and Henry II, c. 1172.

THE NORMANS ARRIVE, 1169

BY GERALD OF WALES

⚜

The Welsh-Norman known as Gerald of Wales (or Geraldus Cambrensis, 1146–1223) failed in his efforts to become bishop of St. David's in south Wales, but he did use his impressive family connections to produce a series of books—probably written to promote his candidacy for bishop—that form just about the best portrait we have of Ireland in the twelfth century. It is a highly prejudiced portrait (he doesn't seem to have liked much about the place except its music and— sometimes—its landscape), but out of his extended visits to the island, he wrote The Typography of Ireland *(1188) and soon after, perhaps the more important,* Conquest of Ireland [Expugnetio Hibernica]. *As a member of the de Barry family and a great-grandson of Rhys ap Tewdwr, he seems to have been either the cousin or nephew of just about all the major Norman figures in the invasion, Strongbow excepted. Although not an eyewitness to the invasion (his first visit to Ireland was in 1183), he clearly used family memories in writing his history.*

A good example of Gerald's low opinion of the Irish is his treatment of Dermot. Although the king had enough good sense, in Gerald's eyes, to seek help from England, he remained a barbarian, which accounts for the bizarre scene of Dermot frolicking with the severed heads of the enemy. And always it is the members of Gerald's own family who are given the highest and most unabashed praise. "Even if I had 'a hundred tongues, a hundred mouths and a voice of iron,'" he writes, "I could not relate all their deeds as they deserve. What a breed, what a noble stock."

HERE BEGINS THE BOOK OF Prophetic History compiled by Gerald of Wales concerning the successful conquest of Ireland

Diarmait Mac Murchada, prince of Leinster and ruler of that fifth part of Ireland, held in our time the eastern seaboard of the island adjacent to Great Britain, with only the sea separating the two. From his earliest youth and his first taking on the kingship he oppressed his nobles, and raged against the chief men of his kingdom with a tyranny grievous and impossible to bear. There was another unfortunate factor. On an occasion when Ua Ruairc king of Meath had gone off on an expedition to far distant parts, his wife, Ua Máelechlainn's daughter, whom he had left on an island in Meath, was abducted by the aforesaid Diarmait, who had long been burning with love for her and took advantage of her husband's absence. No doubt she was abducted because she wanted to be and, since "woman is always a fickle and inconstant creature," she herself arranged that she should become the kidnapper's prize.

Almost all the world's most notable catastrophes have been caused by women, witness Mark Antony and Troy. King Ua Ruairc was stirred to extreme anger on two counts, of which however the disgrace, rather than the loss of his wife, grieved him more deeply, and he vented all the venom of his fury with a view to revenge. And so he called together and mustered his own forces and those of neighbouring peoples, and roused to the same purpose Ruaidrí, prince of Connacht and at that time supreme ruler of all Ireland. The men of Leinster, seeing that their prince was now in a difficult position and surrounded on all sides by his enemies' forces, sought to pay him back, and recalled to mind injustices which they had long concealed and stored deep in their hearts. They made common cause with his enemies, and the men of rank among this people deserted Mac Murchada along with his good fortune. . . .

Mac Murchada, then, pursued Fortune, that ever elusive goddess, and put his faith in the changeableness of her wheel. His ship ploughed the waves, the wind was favourable, and he came to Henry II, king of England, intending to make an urgent plea for his help. Although Henry was across the seas in the remote region of Aquitaine, occupied with business in the way that princes are, yet withal he received Diarmait kindly and affectionately, and with the courtesy characteristic of his innate nobility and kindly nature. Accordingly, when he had duly heard the reason for his exile and arrival at the court, and had received from him the bond of submission and the oath of fealty, he granted him letters patent in the following terms: ". . . if any person from within our wide dominions wishes to help in restoring him, as having done us fealty and homage, let him know that he has our goodwill and permission to do this."

Diarmait returned by way of Great Britain and, although very much honoured and weighed down by gifts, the evidence of the king's generosity, he was much more elated by expectations aroused than by any concrete result. He travelled to the noble town of Bristol and spent some time there, supported in fitting style at the public expense, in expectation of the chance visit of ships which, coming from Ireland, had often in the past berthed in that port. For he was eager to learn from these the state of affairs in his country and among his own people. And when he had often caused the king's letter to be read in the hearing of many there, and had made many promises of money and lands to many people, all to no purpose, at last earl Richard lord of Strigoil, son of earl Gilbert, came to speak with him. On that occasion they got so far in their conversation as to give firm undertakings, the earl that he would help in restoring Diarmait the following spring, and Diarmait that he would give his eldest daughter to the earl in marriage, together with the succession to his kingdom.

When these agreements had been concluded fully and in due order as described, Diarmait, much fired by a desire to see his native land, and ever more feeling the pull of that sweet longing which draws all men to their native soil, hastened without delay to southern Wales and the region of St. David's. This land is separated from Leinster only by the sea which, in the course of a crossing lasting only one day, does not at any time deprive one of the sight of land. At that time Rhys ap Gruffydd was prince in that region under the suzerainty of the king, and David II was bishop of St. David's [where he met Robert FitzStephen and Maurice FitzGerald] . . . A firm agreement was made between them that Diarmait should confer upon Robert and Maurice under grant the city of Wexford with the two adjoining cantreds, and that they should promise their help in restoring him with the arrival of the west winds and the first swallows.

THE ARRIVAL OF FITZSTEPHEN AND THE TAKING OF WEXFORD

Robert FitzStephen did not forget his promise nor value lightly the pledge he had given. Having made his preparations, he put in at Bannow in three ships about the kalends of May [May 1, 1169], with thirty knights from among his nearest relations and dependants, and also a further sixty men wearing mail, and about three hundred foot-archers from among the military élite of Wales. At that time the celebrated prophecy of Merlin Silvester was clearly fulfilled: "A knight, sprung of two different races, will be the first to break through the defences of Ireland by force of arms." If you wish to understand the prophet's riddle, then look back to the original forbears of FitzStephen.

In the same company came Hervey of Montmorency, another fugitive from Fortune, unarmed and destitute, a spy sent in the interest of earl Richard, whose uncle he was, rather than a would-be conqueror of Ireland. When they had disembarked and drawn up their ships on the island of Bannow, a place ill-protected from all sides, they sent messengers to Diarmait. As is usually the way, rumour spread the news of their arrival, and some of those who lived by the coast, who had previously left Diarmait's side as soon as good fortune deserted him, immediately came flocking back to him again now that that same good fortune was returning. For as the poet says: "Loyalty stands and falls with Fortune." When Mac Murchada heard of their arrival, he immediately came to them in triumph with about five hundred men. However he sent his natural son Domnall on ahead of him. He was, although illegitimate, a man of great influence among his people. They renewed their agreements, and oaths were given many times over on both sides to ensure the safety of each party. They then joined forces and, with a common purpose and complete agreement uniting the two different races, directed both their gaze and their battle line towards the city of Wexford, which is about twelve miles distant from Bannow. When they heard this, the people of the city came out, about two thousand strong, hitherto unvanquished and with great faith in their long-standing good fortune. They decided to meet the enemy not far from their camp and engage in a trial of strength there. But when they saw the lines of troops drawn up in an unfamiliar manner, and the squadron of knights resplendent with breastplates, swords and helmets all gleaming, they adopted new tactics in the face of changed circumstances, burned the entire suburbs, and immediately turned back and withdrew inside the walls. FitzStephen and his men eagerly made preparations for the assault. They filled the town ditches with armed men, while the archers watched the ramparts from a distance. With a great rush forward and a mighty shout they all with one accord attacked the walls. But the citizens, very quick to defend themselves, straightway hurled down heavy pieces of wood and stones and drove them back some little distance, inflicting severe wounds on many.

Among these invaders a knight, Robert de Barry, exuberant with youthful hot-headedness and bravely scorning the risk of death, had crept up to the walls in front of everyone else, when he was struck by a stone on his helmeted head. He fell from a height into the bottom of the steep ditch, and in the end just managed to escape by being pulled out by his fellow soldiers. After an interval of sixteen years his molar teeth fell out as the result of the impact of this blow and, what was even more amazing, new ones immediately grew in their place.

Withdrawing from the walls and rushing eagerly to the shore nearby, they immediately set fire to all the ships they found there. But there was one ship lying at anchor in the harbour, which had come from Britain to trade, and was laden with wheat and wine. The greater part of the crack fighting men had bravely seized this, rowing out to it in boats. But now the anchor ropes were deliberately cut by the sailors, and as there was a following north wind, which drove the ship out into the open sea and greatly endangered their safety, it was only with difficulty that they reached land again with the aid of small skiffs and oars. So once again Fortune, unvarying only in her inconstancy, had almost deserted Mac Murchada and FitzStephen.

But on the next day, after the whole army had heard Mass solemnly celebrated, they proceeded to the assault better equipped and with their tactics more carefully thought out, supported by their skill as well as by their military strength, and relying on stratagem no less than on straightforward fighting. When they had come up to the walls, the citizens, mistrusting their capacity to defend themselves, and considering that they were acting wrongly in resisting their king, set about discussing peace after messengers were sent to them. So peace was restored through the mediation of two bishops who were in the city at that time, and other men of goodwill acting as peacemakers. The citizens surrendered themselves to Diarmait's authority and handed over four chosen hostages for their future loyalty to him. He for his part, being eager to encourage his followers, decided to reward the principal among them on the occasion of his first success. He therefore immediately assigned the city with all its lands to FitzStephen and Maurice according to the obligation incurred in the former agreement. To Hervey of Montmorency he assigned under grant the two cantreds which border on the sea and lie between the two cities of Wexford and Waterford.

THE SUBJUGATION OF THE MEN OF OSRAIGE

When all these matters had been settled as they wished, they added the citizens of Wexford to their forces and with an army of about three thousand men turned to attack Osraige [Osory]. Among all those who had rebelled against Diarmait, Domnall prince of Osraige had always been the most hostile. He had actually blinded Diarmait's oldest son, whom he had long held a prisoner, out of jealous hatred. This crowning injustice was the most severe of all Diarmait's misfortunes. To begin with they did not penetrate far into Osraige, but even at the very fringe of the area, in places that were restricted, and impassable because of woods and bogs, they found that the men of Osraige were no weaklings in defence of their homeland. They, relying on previous successes, pursued the invaders to a great distance, right out on to the plain. But FitzStephen's mounted knights turned back on them, and immediately launching a fierce attack, wounded them with their lances as they scattered over the plain, and threw them into confusion, causing considerable slaughter. Groups of Irish foot soldiers immediately beheaded with their large axes those who had been thrown to the ground by the horsemen. In this way the victory was won, and about two hundred heads of his enemies were laid at Diarmait's feet. When he had turned each one over and recognized it, out of an excess of joy he jumped three times in the air with arms clasped over his head, and joyfully gave thanks to the Supreme Creator as he loudly revelled in his triumph. He lifted up to his mouth the head of one he particularly loathed, and taking it by the ears and hair, gnawed at the nose and cheeks—a cruel and most inhuman act. But after that they several times penetrated to the more remote and innermost parts of the region, vigorously pursuing a policy of slaughter, plunder and burning. At last the prince of Osraige, on the advice of his own supporters, giving hostages and swearing oaths under the terms of a peace treaty which was nevertheless feigned and a pretence on both sides rather than genuine, apparently returned to his loyal obedience to Diarmait.

In these engagements, as in all others, Meiler and Robert de Barry were conspicuous among all the rest by reason of their praiseworthy valour. Now these two young men were both FitzStephen's nephews, the one his brother's son, the other his sister's. Their characters and dispositions were quite different. Only in valour did they nearly resemble each other. For Meiler loved praise and glory, and related all his actions to that end. Whatever could enlarge his reputation, that he was eager to accomplish by every possible means, and he was far more anxious to appear brave than actually to be brave. But the other, whose innate valour brought him great renown, did not demand praise, or pursue popular esteem. He preferred to be the best among those of the first rank rather than merely seeming to be so. Nature had so shaped his disposition that he was a man of maiden-like modesty, neither boastful nor a wordy braggart. He had no desire either to publicize his outstanding achievements or have them praised by others. The result was that, the less he sought fame, so all the more did he win it. For renown follows good qualities like a shadow and, deserting those who seek it, seeks out those who despise it. Indeed many please all the more from the very fact that they scorn to please, and in a wondrous way they win fame while avoiding it.

On one occasion the army was spending the night encamped in and around an old fortification in Osraige, and these two were sleeping beside each other as was their usual custom. Suddenly there were, as it seemed, countless thousands of troops rushing upon them from all sides and engulfing all before them in the ferocity of their attack. This was accompanied by no small din of arms and clashing of axes, and a fearsome shouting which filled the heavens. Apparitions of this sort used to occur frequently in Ireland around military expeditions. At this terrifying spectacle the greater part of the army took to flight and hid, some in the woods, others in the bogs. Only these two immediately rushed to arm themselves and bravely made for FitzStephen's tent, vigorously calling back their scattered companions to defend him and giving them new courage. In the midst of a general panic of such an order and such vehemence, Robert de Barry was anxiously looking after a sparrow-hawk, so that this bird, which he had with him there as a pet, and which aroused the admiration and envy of many, should not be lost. For among the various indications of his valour, this in particular is often said of him, that no violent attack, even if unexpected, no unforeseen occurrence or sudden event has ever found him despairing and fearful, ignominiously turning tail in flight, or overwhelmed with terror. He has always been found to be self-possessed, quick in defence and ready to take up arms. Assuredly that man is the bravest "who is ready to endure the terrifying if it should threaten him at close quarters, and powerfully to repel it." In this conquest of Ireland he was the first knight to receive a blow and to be wounded in martial conflict. He was also the first knight in this island to hunt the daughter of Nisus with a tame domesticated sparrow-hawk. . . .

THE PREPARATION OF EARL RICHARD DE CLARE

Mac Murchada now raised his sights to higher things and, now that he had recovered his entire inheritance, he aspired to his ancestral and long standing rights, and determined, by the use of his armed might, to bring under his control Connacht, together with the kingship of all Ireland. And so he met FitzStephen and Maurice secretly to discuss this, and revealed to them in full what was in his mind. They replied that this could easily be accomplished, if he took steps to surround himself with greater numbers of English troops. He then begged them in every way he knew to bring men of their own race and kin into the island in greater numbers, and to set about putting his plan into execution. Finally, the better to persuade them to do this, he offered each of them in turn his first-born daughter with the right of succession to his kingdom. But since at that time both of them had lawful wives, after a great deal of discussion they agreed that as soon as possible he should send messengers to earl Richard [de Clare], whom we mentioned above, and to whom, when he was in Bristol some time before, he had promised to give this same daughter in marriage. They were to carry with them a letter couched in the following terms: "Diarmait Mac Murchada prince of Leinster, greets earl Richard lord of Strigoil, son of earl Gilbert. 'If you were to reckon aright the days which we in our need are counting, then you would realize that our complaint does not come before its time.' We have watched the storks and the swallows. The summer migrants have come and, having come, have now returned with the west wind. But neither the east wind nor the west has brought us your presence, which we have so long awaited and desired. So make good your delay by successfully performing what you have promised and, by showing us deeds, ensure that your word appears 'false only in point of time.' Already the whole of Leinster has returned to our allegiance. If you come in good time and with strong military support, the other four parts of Ireland will easily be added to the fifth. So your arrival will be welcome, if it is expeditious; it will bring you renown, if it is swift; it will be felicitous, if it is speedy. A renewed display of affection draws a protecting scab over a friendship that has been wounded in some part by neglect. For a friendship is quickly healed by a kindness rendered, and a service graciously performed makes it grow even stronger and more perfect." . . .

THE ARRIVAL OF RAYMOND AND THE DEFEAT OF THE MEN OF WATERFORD AT DUNDUNNOLF

So having obtained from Henry permission of a sort—for it was given ironically rather than in earnest—after the end of the winter, about the kalends of May [1170], he sent on into Ireland in advance of himself a young man of his own retinue, by name Raymond [leGros], with ten knights and seventy archers. He was a vigorous and sturdy youth, well trained in the use of arms, nephew to both FitzStephen and Maurice by their oldest brother. Putting in to a rock which is called Dundunnolf, about four miles from Waterford and to the south of Wexford, they constructed a somewhat flimsy fortification of branches and sods. But when rumour immediately spread the news of their arrival, the citizens of Waterford, and Máelsechlainn Ua Fáeláin with them, viewed with mistrust the presence of foreigners close by. On taking council together they considered that they must oppose this venture right at the start, and with one accord decided to take up arms against them. So they crossed the river Suir, which divides Desmond from Leinster close by the city walls on the east side, and bravely approached the ditches of the English camp, about three thousand men drawn up in three companies for the assault.

But since it is virtually impossible for valour to be covered up and concealed, for the fires of courage to be quenched, or the spark of virtue to be suppressed and confined, Raymond with his men—conspicuous for their gallantry, though few in number—went out to meet them and engaged them in a most unequal contest. But because such a small force, though an excellent one, could not withstand such large numbers on level ground, they turned back to their camp. In their haste to enter it, they allowed the enemy, who were pursuing them from behind, inside the doors, which had not been completely hung up on their hinges. But when Raymond saw that he and his men were in a difficult position, or rather in the direst straits, he turned bravely to face the enemy, and in the very doorway transfixed with his sword the first to enter. With a loud shout, with this one blow and valiant rally he called his own men back to resume the defence and excited a fearful panic among the enemy. So, since the fortunes of war are always uncertain, those who had seemed to be vanquished suddenly became the victors and pursued the enemy, who had turned back in flight and were now scattered all over the plains, with such a massive slaughter that they killed five hundred and more there and then. And when they stayed their hands that were worn out by striking, countless others were hurled over the high cliffs into the sea. In this action a knight, William Ferrand, distinguished himself by his amazing bravery. He was physically in poor shape, but very stout hearted, for he wished, so it seems, to anticipate by an untimely but glorious death the malign disease of leprosy with which he was threatened.

It was here that the pride of Waterford took a tumble. Here the whole power of the city faded away. This event began the overthrow of a noble city. From it the English derived hope and comfort, their enemies fear and despair. For hitherto it had been unheard of in those parts for such a small force to cause such immense slaughter. But the victors, acting on bad advice, misused their good fortune by displaying deplorable and inhuman brutality. For when their victory was complete, they held seventy of the more important and influential citizens as prisoners in fetters within their camp. They could have received the city itself or a vast sum of money as ransom for these men. However . . . the citizens were condemned to die, their limbs were broken, and they were consigned to the cliff overlooking the sea.

THE ARRIVAL OF THE EARL AND THE TAKING OF BOTH WATERFORD AND DUBLIN

Meanwhile, having made the necessary preparations for such an important venture, earl Richard passed through the coastal regions of south Wales on his way to St. David's, and collected together the pick of the fighting men

The seal of Richard FitzGilbert de Clare, alias Strongbow.

in those parts. When everything needful for a naval expedition on such a scale had been procured and made ready, he embarked at Milford Haven, a following wind filled his sails, and he put in at Waterford with two hundred knights and about a thousand others around the kalends of September, in fact on St, Bartholomew's eve [actually August 23, 1170].

Then was fulfilled the saying of Merlin of Celidon: "A torch will precede the fiery pyre, and just as the spark calls forth the torch, so will the torch call forth the pyre." Likewise too the prophecy of Moling of Ireland: "A great one will come, forerunner of one yet greater. He will trample on the heads of both Desmond and Leinster, and, with forces excellently well-armed, will widen the paths that have already been prepared for him."

On the following day, when rumour had spread the news of this event, Raymond, greatly rejoicing, went to meet the earl with forty knights. On the morning after the feast, a Tuesday, they joined forces to carry forward to the assault of the city those battle standards which were already menacing its walls. They were twice vigorously repulsed by the citizens and the survivors of the slaughter at Dundunnolf. Then Raymond, who with general assent had now been made leader and commander of the whole army, and put in charge of military operations, noticed a small building which hung down from the town wall on the outside by a beam. He eagerly urged all his men to attack on all sides, and quickly sent in armed men to cut down the aforesaid beam. When it had been cut down, the building immediately collapsed, and with it a considerable part of the wall. The invaders eagerly effected an entry, rushed into the city and won a most bloody victory, large numbers of the citizens being slaughtered in the streets. The two Sitrics were taken in Raghnall's tower and put to the sword. Raghnall and MáelSechlainn Ua Fáeláin were likewise captured there, but their lives were spared through the intervention of Diarmait, who at that juncture had arrived with Maurice and FitzStephen. A garrison was assigned to the city, and there too Diarmait's daughter Eva was lawfully wed to the earl. Her father bestowed her on him, and also confirmed the treaty between them. Then all joined forces and turned their standards towards Dublin.

THE TAKING OF THE CITY OF DUBLIN

Now Diarmait knew that the citizens of Dublin had called almost all the inhabitants of Ireland to help in its defence and had blocked with armed men all the approach routes round the city, which were wooded and narrow of access. Consequently, being not unmindful of his father's downfall, he avoided the well wooded terrain and, coming by way of the flanking slopes of the hills of Glendalough, he brought his army intact right up to the city walls. He hated the citizens of Dublin more than all the other inhabitants of Ireland, not without good reason. For in the middle of a large building, where it was their custom to sit as if before the *rostra* in the *forum*, they had buried his father, whom they had killed, along with a dog, thus adding insult to injury. Envoys were despatched and there was, first of all, a discussion of peace terms. This was mainly the result of mediation by Laurence of blessed memory, who was at that time the archbishop of Dublin. But while this was taking place, Raymond from one side and from the other that courageous knight Miles de Cogan, together with the young men who were eager for battle and plunder, made an enthusiastic assault on the walls, were immediately victorious, and valiantly overran the city, with considerable slaughter of the inhabitants. But the greater part of them, led by Askulv, went on board ship, taking their most precious belongings, and sailed off to the northern isles. . . .

The earl spent some days making arrangements about the government of the city and left Miles de Cogan there as governor. Then at the urging of Mac Murchada who, in a spirit of revenge, called to mind ancient feuds, they overran and devastated the territories of Ua Ruairc king of Meath. When the whole of Meath had been ravaged by frequent raids, slaughter and burnings, Ruaidrí king of Connacht, seeing that it was very much his affair "when a neighbour's wall is ablaze," sent messages to Diarmait couched in the following terms: "Contrary to the conditions of our treaty you have invited into this island a large number of foreigners. Yet we put up with this with a good grace while you confined yourself within your province of Leinster. But now, since you are unmindful of your oath and without feelings of pity for the hostage you have given, and have arrogantly trespassed beyond the stipulated limits and your ancestral boundaries, you must either restrain the forays of your foreign troops for the future, or else we will send you without fail the severed head of your son." Diarmait gave a haughty response to this, and added besides that he would not be deflected from his purpose until he had brought under his control Connacht, which belonged to him by ancestral right, together with the kingship of all Ireland. Ruaidrí thereupon became enraged and condemned to death the son whom Diarmait had given him as a hostage.

THE COUNCIL OF ARMAGH

After all these events had taken place, the clergy of the whole of Ireland was called together at Armagh, and there was a lengthy debate concerning the arrival of the foreigners in the island. In the end the general consensus of opinion settled upon this as the reason: that because of the sins of their own people, and in particular because it had formerly been their habit to purchase Englishmen indiscriminately from merchants as well as from robbers and pirates, and to make slaves of them, this disaster had befallen them by the stern judgement of the divine vengeance, to the end that they in turn should now be enslaved by that same race. For the English, in the days when the government of England remained fully in their hands, used to put their children up for sale—a vicious practice in which the whole race had a part—and would sell their own sons and relations into Ireland rather than endure any want or hunger. So there are good grounds for believing that, just as formerly those who sold the slaves, so now also those who bought them, have, by committing such a monstrous crime, deserved the yoke of slavery. The aforesaid council therefore decided and publicly decreed by common consent that throughout the island Englishmen should be freed from the bonds of slavery and restored to their former freedom. . . .

EARL RICHARD SENT TO IRELAND AS GOVERNOR, AND RAYMOND REINSTATED AS COMMANDER OF THE GARRISON: A BATTLE AT SEA

. . . [Commanded by Raymond, the earl's troops] began to build up their resources again by taking vast quantities of booty, and to re-equip themselves most handsomely with arms and horses. From there they advanced on Lismore. Having plundered and ravaged the city and the territory belonging to it, they brought immense quantities of booty back to Waterford by the coastal route. With this they loaded thirteen ships, some of which had come with them from Waterford, while others they had found in the harbour of Lismore. When they had been waiting there for a west wind for some time, suddenly from the direction of Cork, which lies sixteen miles to the West, thirty-two ships packed with warriors sailed up to attack them.

So a naval battle began, with one side attacking fiercely with stones and axes, while the others put up a vigorous resistance with arrows and metal bolts, of which they had a plentiful supply. At last the men of Cork were beaten, and their leader Gilbert MacTurger was killed by a sturdy youth, by name Philip of Wales. Then Adam of Hereford, who in that place and on that occasion was in command of the picked force of fighting men, added to the number of his ships and sailed victorious to Waterford with his cargo of arms and plunder. Raymond, who chanced to have heard of this encounter, hastened to the area by the coast road, having with him twenty knights and sixty archers. He immediately dislodged Diarmait prince of Desmond from Lismore, where he had gone with a large army to support the men of Cork, and brought back to Waterford with him four thousand head of cattle.

[About this same time, the Irish of those parts made off with booty from the plain of Waterford and went a little way into the woods, and there, at the very edge of the woods, lay concealed in an ambush. The alarm was raised in the city and the garrison sallied out. Meiler was in the forefront, hasty and courageous as ever, and pursued the robbers right into the woodland thickets, with only one mounted companion. But when Meiler himself was about to turn back, the impetuous youth spurring his horse rushed forward, and penetrated right into the interior of the wood. Immediately the said youth was struck down by many blows and hacked to pieces by axes before Meiler's very eyes. While Meiler was trying in vain to come to his aid—one man against a thousand—and was making an onslaught on the enemy, he was hemmed in by them and seized by the arms on all sides. However this courageous man drew his sword and opened up a way of escape for himself by force of arms, vigorously lopping off here a hand, there an arm, and robbing yet another of his head and shoulders. Although he had three Irish axes stuck in his horse, and two in his shield, he nevertheless returned to the plain unharmed, and rejoined his men.] . . .

THE NOBLE TAKING OF LIMERICK

Meanwhile Domnall prince of Limerick began to conduct himself too arrogantly and, displaying a lack of respect as well as treachery, went back on the oath of loyalty which he had taken to the king. Raymond therefore collected together a force of sturdy fighting men, and with a hundred and twenty knight, three hundred archers, and four hundred foot archers, made a bold assault on Limerick around the kalends of October. When they reached the river Shannon, which encircles that noble city and winds its way round it, they found that the river was swift flowing and deep, and formed an intervening obstacle which they could not cross. Consequently the soldiery, who were eager to take booty and win renown, being as it were poised at the waters of Tantalus, could not endure this barrier, so close to their prize, without experiencing a great deal of frustration.

There was present there a sturdy, newly fledged knight, as yet untried in battle, Raymond's nephew David "the Welshman"—this was his surname rather than a family name, for he was Welsh by race rather than through any family connection—an excellent youth, handsome and tall. He was more impatient of the delay than all the others and, scorning the fearful danger of death in his eagerness for renown, he hurled himself headlong into the swiftly flowing river with its rough and rocky bed. So, working his way on a slanting course against the current, and keeping a watchful eye on the rest of the rippling waves, he was carried safely to the opposite bank on his noble steed, and shouted to his comrades that he had discovered a ford. But he found no one ready to follow him, except for a single knight, by name Geoffrey Judas. So he returned by the same route, but failed to bring that knight safely back with him; for on the way back he was snatched to the bottom and overwhelmed by the violent force of the torrent.

When Meiler, who had come there with Raymond, saw this, he begrudged David the boldness displayed by such a brave deed and the honour he had won by an action so noble and so daring. So mounted on his strong horse, he entered the river with a shout. Fired as he was with a desire to imitate David's achievement, and in no way held back by the horrifying warning of the knight who had just been drowned, he immediately succeeded in crossing to the other bank, not nervously or timidly, but in a spirit of boldness and daring.

In their efforts to repel, or rather to overpower him, the citizens met him with a hail of stones and missiles, both on the river bank and aiming from the city walls which overhung the bank. But this noble warrior, seeing on one side the fury of the enemy and on the other the raging torrent, warded off the blows with his helmet and shield and bravely held his ground, caught between these two perils and safe from neither. A great noise arose from each side. Thereupon Raymond, who as leader of the army and commander of the troops had stationed himself in the rear detachment, and knew nothing at all of all this, immediately rushed through the middle of the ranks and came to the water's edge.

When he looked across from the opposite bank and saw that his nephew was in a difficult position and, unaided, was exposed to attack by the enemy's troops, he was filled with anxiety and shouted out sharply to his men: "Men, we know that you have in your make-up a sturdy natural valour. We have tested your courage in so many difficult situations. Advance now, my men. We have been shown the way, and thanks to the courage of our comrades a stretch of water which hitherto seemed impassable has in fact turned out to be fordable. Let us then follow the man who has shown the way. Let us aid a brave youth who is being overwhelmed by the enemy. Under no circumstances must we allow one who has undertaken this feat to further our common cause to be within an ace of death for want of support, while we look on." Having spoken, Raymond was the first to plunge into the river, and with the whole army eagerly following him, entrusted himself and his men to fate. So they crossed over without loss, except for two archers and a single knight called Guido, who were drowned. The enemy were driven into the city and Raymond's men immediately overran the walls, inflicting great slaughter on the townspeople. Victory brought with it possession of the city, and greatly enriched by the booty and gold they had captured, they made up for the dangers they had endured by winning renown and fresh riches.

You must yourself, dear reader, decide which of these men were the most courageous; whether it was he who without any precedent was the first to make the crossing and showed everyone else the way; or he who, following on his example and the fearful warning of a man's death, succeeded in crossing and, alone, exposed himself to a vast number of the enemy; or he who, following in the wake of both these men, so bravely exposed himself with his whole army to such danger. At this point it seems worth noting that Limerick was taken on the day of Mars (Tuesday), that that same city was relieved on the day of Mars, that Waterford, Wexford and Dublin were all taken on the same day of Mars, and that this did not happen intentionally, but purely by chance. Yet it is neither wonderful nor unreasonable if the business of war is best concluded on the day dedicated to Mars.

THE SONG OF DERMOT AND THE EARL

ANOTHER VERSION OF THE INVASION

The Song of Dermot and the Earl (*or Le Chansun de Dermot et li Quenis*), *written in Old French, may have been the work of Morice Regan, an Irish poet and scribe in Dermot's court. He was traditionally credited with writing it within three years of the invasion, but more recent scholarship seems to suggest that the long poem was written perhaps as late as 1225 by a Norman, probably a monk, who had spent some time in Ireland and may have had access to an older rhymed account. Whoever the author, the poem remains, after Gerald of Wales's* Conquest, *our most important glimpse of the arrival of the Normans.*

At a time when history tended to deal only with highborn men, Le Chansun *contains at least one brief portrait of a lowborn woman. Alice of Abervenny, a Welsh widow or camp follower, performs an especially grisly task, probably because the Normans thought that to die at the hands of a female executioner would be especially insulting to the Irish.*

Another notable point is Strongbow's surprising willingness to swear allegiance to the Irish high king, Rory O'Connor, under the proper conditions. Late in the story—after Robert FitzStephen's capture by the Irish—Strongbow sends the archbishop of Dublin, the future saint Laurence O'Toole (or Lorcan Ua Tuathail), to the high king offering a deal, but Rory turns him down.

LANDING OF RAYMOND LE GROS

I wish to tell of King Dermot
How he delivered Wexford
To a noble baron,
The son of Stephen, Robert the baron [Robert FitzStephen].
And Maurice the son of Gerald [Maurice FitzGerald]
Fortified himself at Carrick,
By the permission and by the desire
Of Dermot, the potent king.

Then soon afterwards
Earl Richard [de Clare, i.e. Strongbow] sent over
Some of his men to Ireland,
With nine or ten of his barons.
The first was Raymond le Gros,
A bold and daring knight.
At Dundonuil they landed
Where they then constructed a fort
By the permission of the rich king
Dermot, who was so courteous.
There Raymond le Gros remained
With his knights and barons.
Then he plundered the territory,
Took and killed the cows.
But the men of Waterford
And of Ossory likewise
Assembled their hosts;
Against Dundonuil they resolved to go
In order to attack the fort.
They think surely to shame the English.
Donnell O'Phelan of the Decies,
And O'Ryan of Odrone,
And all the Irish of the country
Surrounded the fort.
By estimation the Irish were
As many as three or four thousand;
Raymond and his men
Were not more than a hundred.
They drove the cows into the fort
By the counsel of Raymond.
The men of Waterford
Came very fiercely
To demolish the fort;
They think to disgrace the English.

THE FIGHT AT DUN DONUL

Raymond speaks to his men:—
"Sir barons, hearken to me.
You see your enemies coming

Who have resolved to attack you.
It is more honourable for you here
Than within to be killed or taken.
Come now, do you all arm yourselves,
Knights, sergeants, and archers;
Thus shall we place ourselves in open field
In the name of the Almighty Father."

By the advice of Raymond le Gros,
Resolved to sally from the gates
In order to charge the Irish.
The cows were scared
At the men who were armed;
And owing to the tumult that they made
The cows all in front
By force and by strength
Sallied forth at the gate.
This was the first company
That sallied from the fort, I trow.
Upon the Irish they rushed
In a short space, in a few moments.
The Irish could not stand against them:
They were forced to separate;
And Raymond with his English
Threw himself amid the Irish.
Wherefore they were divided,
The Irish were discomfited,
So that the last company
Fled away through this fright.
There they were discomfited
All the Irish of this district.
On the field a thousand were left
Vanquished, killed, wounded, or taken,
By the force and by the strength
That the good Jesus created against them
And through dread and through fear
They were enfeebled that day.
Of the Irish there were taken
Quite as many as seventy.
But the noble knights
Had them beheaded.

To a wench they gave
An axe of tempered steel,
And she beheaded them all
And then threw their bodies over the cliff,
Because she had that day
Lost her lover in the combat.
Alice of Abervenny was her name
Who served the Irish thus.
In order to disgrace the Irish
The knights did this.
And the Irish of the district
Were discomfited in this way.
To their country they returned
Outdone and discomfited:
To their country they returned
Discomfited and outdone. . . .

LANDING OF EARL RICHARD DE CLARE

According to the statement of the old people,
Very soon afterwards Earl Richard [Strongbow]
Landed at Waterford.
Full fifteen hundred men he brought with him.
On the eve of St. Bartholomew
Did the earl land.
The most powerful persons in the city
Were called Ragnald and Sidroc.
On St. Bartholomew's day,
Earl Richard, the prudent,
Took by assault and won
The city of Waterford.
But there were many killed there
Of the citizens of Waterford
Before that it was won
Or taken by assault against them.

When the earl by his power
Had taken the city,
The earl immediately sent word
To King Dermot by messenger
That he had come to Waterford
And had won the city,
That the rich king should come to him
And should bring his English.
King Dermot speedily
Came there, be sure, right royally.
The king in his company
Brought there many of his barons,
And his daughter he brought there;
To the noble earl he gave her.
The earl honourably
Wedded her in the presence of the people.
King Dermot then gave
To the earl, who was so renowned—
Leinster he gave to him
With his daughter, whom he so much loved,
Provided only that he should have the lordship
Of Leinster during his life.
And the earl granted
To the king all his desire.
Then they turned aside
The king and Earl Richard.
Raymond le Gros joined them,
A bold and daring knight,
And Maurice de Prendergast
Likewise, as I hear;
For with the earl, of a truth,
He had returned, as people say.
By the advice of the earl
The warrior had returned.
At this council in sooth
Was Meiler the son of Henry,
And many a brave knight
Whose names I cannot mention.
There all the brave knights

Proceeded to advise
That they should go straight to Dublin
And should assault the city.
Then the king departed
Towards Ferns with his English.
He caused his men to be summoned
Everywhere and in great force.
When they were all assembled,
Towards Waterford they set out directly.
Earl Richard then gave
The city in charge of his men:
In Waterford he then left
A portion of his followers.
Then they turned towards Dublin
The king and the renowned earl.

THE IRISH AT CLONDALKIN

Now all the pride of Ireland
Was at Clondalkin in a moor [in Wicklow],
And the king of Connaught
Was at Clondalkin at this time.
In order to attack the English
He divided his troops.
They plashed the passes everywhere
In order to obstruct the English,
So that in fact they should not come
To Dublin without hostility.
And King Dermot was warned
By a scout whom he had sent
That the Irish were in front
About 30,000 strong.
King Dermot sent to ask
The earl to come to parley with him.
The earl speedily
Came promptly to the king.
"Sir Earl," thus spake the king,
"Hearken to me at this time:

Figure 1. Sometimes called the Tanderagee Idol for the bog near Newry where it was supposedly found, this Iron Age stone figure is now displayed in the Protestant cathedral in Armagh, not far from what was traditionally thought to be the grave of Brian Boru. Because of the curious way the figure holds his arm, some think he may represent Nuadu, king of the mythical De Dannan, who lost an arm in battle and replaced it with a magical silver one. Courtesy Fran Monson.

Figure 2. Dun Aengus, set high on a cliff on Inishmore in the Aran Islands, off the Galway coast, was hailed by nineteenth-century Irish antiquarians as "the most magnificent barbaric monument now extant in Europe." The huge stone structure, dating back to the Iron Age, was traditionally thought to have been built by the mythical Fir Bolgs after their defeat at the First Battle of Moirura, fought near Sligo. Long assumed to be a fort (*dún*), some archaeologists now suspect that because of its location (what's it defending?) and lack of drinking water, its purpose may have been more ceremonial than military. Courtesy the Irish Tourist Board.

Figure 3. In a scene similar to this, the young son of the king of Cooley killed a neighbor's dog. Conscience-stricken, the boy began calling himself Cuchulain, a variation of the animal's name. Thereafter, throughout his violent life, he was frequently and sometimes affectionately called "Little Hound." This early twentieth-century illustration by Arthur Rackham, although not specifically depicting Cuchulain, is from James Stephens' *Irish Fairy Tales*.

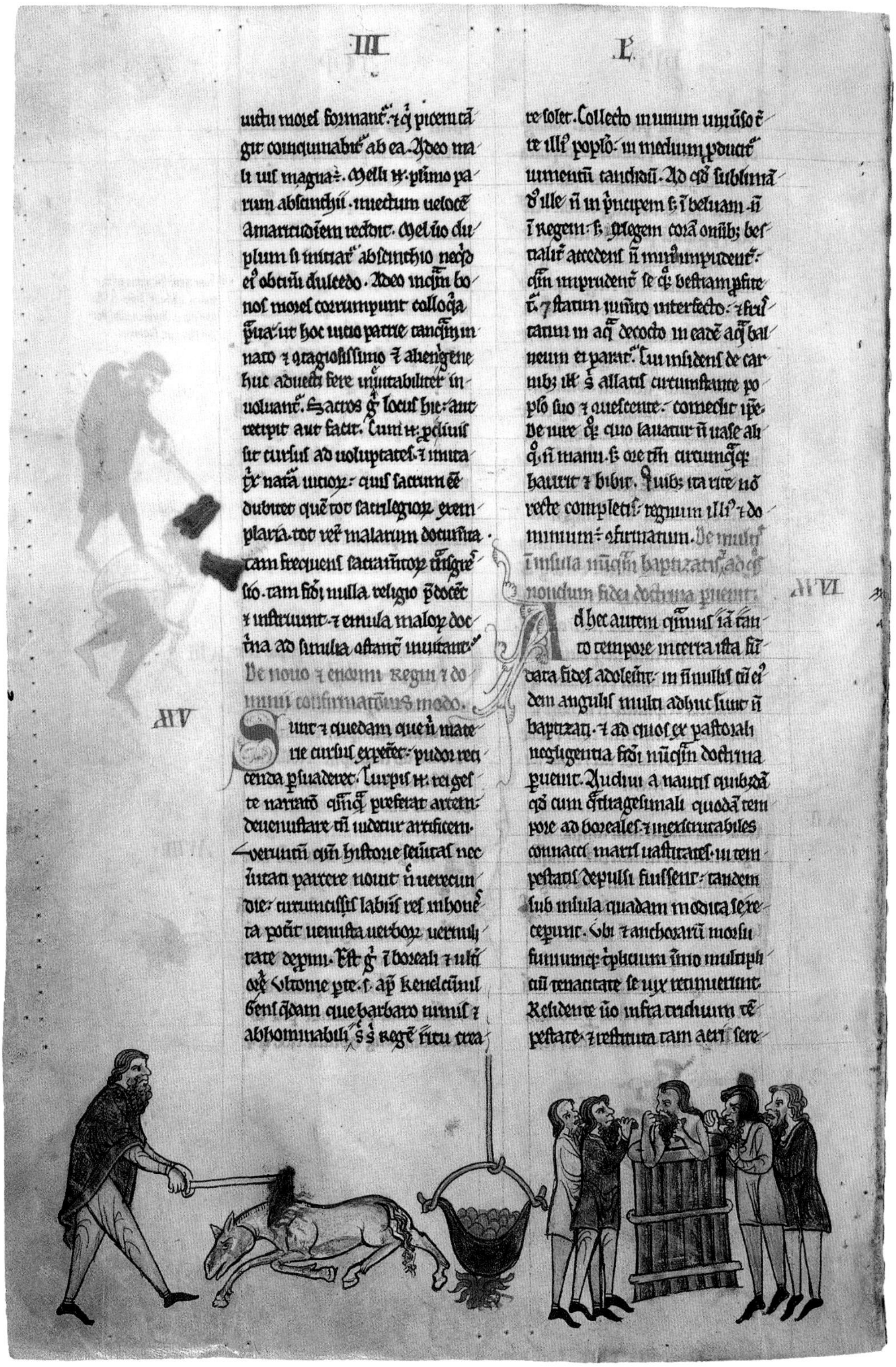

Figure 4. A coronation in Tyconnell (Donegal). This page, from a thirteenth-century manuscript copy of Gerald of Wales's twelfth-century *Typography of Ireland*, shows, on the left, a white mare slaughtered before being boiled in a pot. On the right, the new king (in a bath) and his court devour the sacrifice. Courtesy the National Library of Ireland.

Figure 9. Norse graffiti: A picture of a man high in the rigging of a Viking ship, scratched onto a plank unearthed at Wood Quay, the site of Dublin's earliest Viking settlement.

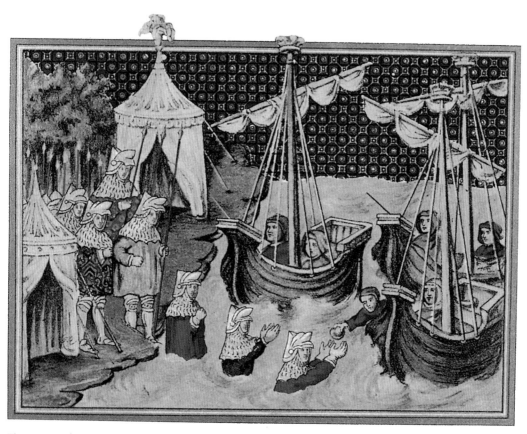

Figure 10. Ships in Dublin's harbor replenishing supplies for the English army in 1393. Artist unknown.

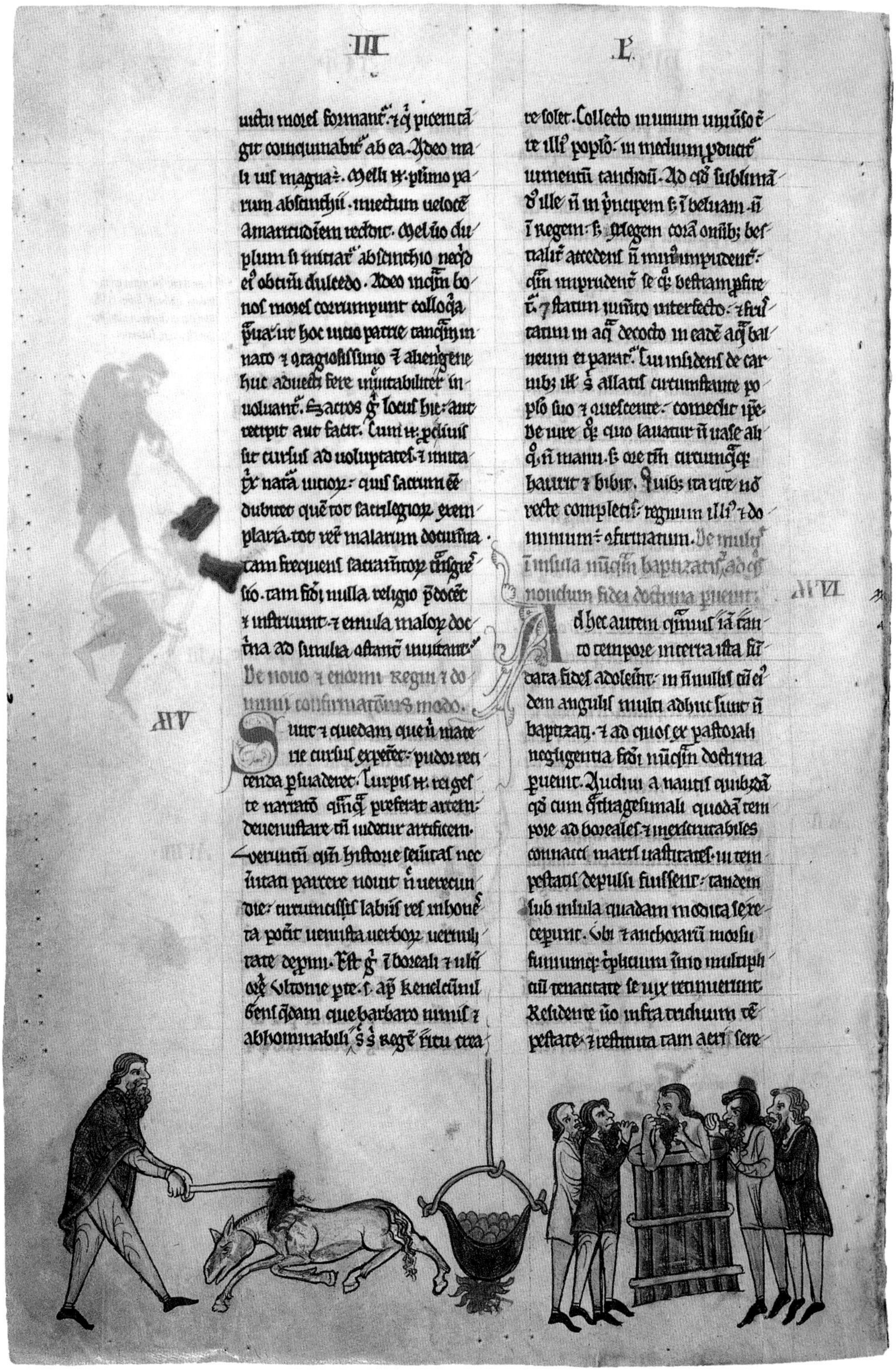

Figure 4. A coronation in Tyconnell (Donegal). This page, from a thirteenth-century manuscript copy of Gerald of Wales's twelfth-century *Typography of Ireland*, shows, on the left, a white mare slaughtered before being boiled in a pot. On the right, the new king (in a bath) and his court devour the sacrifice. Courtesy the National Library of Ireland.

Figure 5. The Hill of Tara in County Meath, where the high king (*ard ri*) was traditionally proclaimed, is composed of two small ring forts (*raths*) surrounded by a much larger ring called the royal enclosure. Also included on the hilltop, which has archaeological remains dating back to the second millennium B.C., are a burial mound (in the foreground) and indications of a banqueting hall resembling the one that appears in "The Second Battle of Moytura." The *rath* to the left is often regarded—without a great deal of supporting evidence—as being the coronation site.

Figure 6. Viking ships in Irish waters came first alone to pillage, then in fleets to conquer and to establish trading posts that grew into Norse city-states with names such as Dublin and Limerick. Artist unknown.

Figure 7. A re-creation of a Viking settlement in the Irish National Heritage Park.

Figure 8. The Rock of Cashel in the ancient kingdom of Munster bears the ruins of a twelfth- and thirteenth-century cathedral and a round tower. Tucked into the southern (left-hand) corner of the building is Cormac's Chapel, the oldest Romanesque church in Ireland. As an act of defiance against the O'Neills and the North, Brian Boru had himself crowned high king at Cashel rather than at Tara. Courtesy the Irish Tourist Board.

Figure 9. Norse graffiti: A picture of a man high in the rigging of a Viking ship, scratched onto a plank unearthed at Wood Quay, the site of Dublin's earliest Viking settlement.

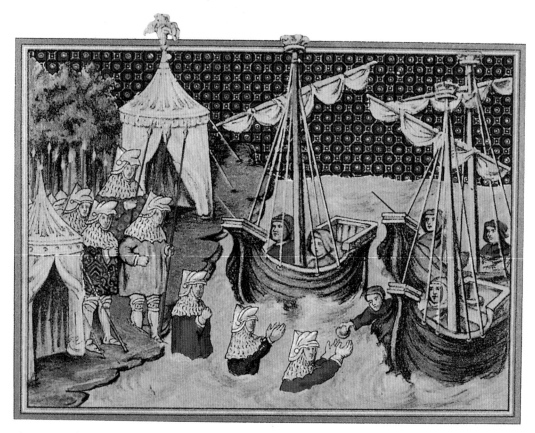

Figure 10. Ships in Dublin's harbor replenishing supplies for the English army in 1393. Artist unknown.

H. Corbould, del.   E. Finden, sculp.

Death of Brian Boru in his Tent.

Figure 11. The death of Brian Boru while praying in his tent at the battle of Clontarf in 1014, as imagined by the early nineteenth-century engraver Edward Finden. Brian, high king of Ireland, was battling a combined army of Vikings, Dublin-based Norsemen, and Irish rivals from the Kingdom of Leinster. Courtesy the Bridgeman Art Library.

Figure 12. The silver Gundestrup Cauldron was Viking booty probably seized in Ireland in the ninth century and taken back to Denmark, where it was later discovered. Recently some scholars have suggested that its detailed design may represent a cattle raid (*tain*), such as the legendary one at Cooley, and that it may show scenes from the life of Cuchulain, the mythical hero of *The Cattle Raid of Cooley* (*The Tain*), the story of that raid. Courtesy Erich Lessing/Art Resource.

Draw up your men in ranks
And marshal your sergeants.
We shall now go by the mountain
On the hard field and on the open ground;
For the woods are plashed
And the roads trenched across,
And all our enemies of Ireland
Are before us in a moor."

The earl then summoned
All the brave knights.
Miles came to him, first of all,
A noble and brave warrior:
Miles had the name de Cogan
And his body was bold and burly.
He was at the head in front
With seven hundred English soldiers;
And Donnell Kavanagh likewise
Remained with these men.
And then afterwards Raymond le Gros
With about eight hundred companions.
In the third company the rich king
With about a thousand Irish.
And Richard, the courteous earl,
Had with him three thousand English.
In this company there were about
Four thousand vassals, I trow.
In the rear-guard the king
Had the Irish drawn up in ranks.
They were all well armed,
The renowned English barons.
By the mountain did the king
Guide the English host that day.
Without a battle and without a contest
They arrived at the city.
Moreover the city was that day
Taken beyond gainsaying:
The day of St. Matthew the Apostle
The city of Dublin was burning.

City of Dublin coat of arms

DUBLIN IN FLAMES

When the Irish saw this
That King Dermot was come
And the earl also
With all his English troops,
And that the illustrious liege barons
Had surrounded the city,
The king of Connaught [Rory O'Connor, high king]
    went away
Without a word at this time,
And the Irish from this district
To their country departed.
Hasculf MacTorkil, the deceiver [Viking king of Dublin],
Remained in the city that day,
In order to defend the city
Of which he was acknowledged
Sire, lord, and defender,
Through all the country.
Outside the walls of the city
Was the king encamped;
While Richard, the good earl,
Who was lord of the English,
Remained with his English
And with King Dermot himself.
Nearest to the city
Was Miles encamped,
The good Miles de Cogan
Who was afterwards lord of Mount Brandon [in Dingle],
Which is the wildest spot,
Mountain or plain, in the world.

Now Dermot, the noble king,
Despatched Morice Regan,
And by Morice proclaimed
To the citizens of the city
That without delay, without any respite,
They should surrender without gainsaying:
Without any further gainsaying
They should surrender themselves to their lord.
Thirty hostages demanded
King Dermot of the city.
But those within, i' faith,
Could not separate among themselves
The hostages of the city
Who should be delivered to the king.
Hasculf accordingly made answer
To Dermot, the renowned king,
That on the morrow speedily
He would perform all his command.

THE CAPTURE OF DUBLIN

It greatly vexed the baron,
The good Miles de Cogan,
That the parley lasted so long
Between the king and all his people.
Miles shouted all at once:
"Barons, knights, A Cogan!"
Without the king's command
And without the earl's either,
He attacked the city.
The baron Miles with his followers
With audacity and with great fury
Then set upon the city.
The baron Miles, the renowned,
By main force took the city.
Before that Dermot knew it that day
Or Richard the good earl,
Had Miles, the strong-limbed baron,
Actually entered into Dublin,
Had already conquered the city,

And put MacTorkil to flight.
And the men of Dublin
Fled away by the sea;
But many remained there
Who were killed in the city.
Much renown acquired that day
Miles who was of such worth;
And the renowned barons
Found much wealth:
In the city they found
Much treasure and other wealth.
Thereupon there came
The king and the earl riding quickly:
To the city they came
The king and the earl together.
And Miles, the renowned baron,
To the earl gave up the city:
The city Miles gave up,
And the earl thereupon received it.
Much provision they found
And good victuals in great plenty.
The earl then abode
While he pleased in the city;
And the king returned
To Ferns in his own country [Leinster].
But on the festival of St. Remy,
When August was over,
Soon after Michaelmas,
Richard, the noble earl,
To Miles delivered, you must know,
The wardship of the city.
To Waterford he set out
The earl and his ample suite.
There the earl abode
So long as it pleased him.
At Ferns then tarried
King Dermot during this winter.
The king, who was so noble,
Lies buried at Ferns.
King Dermot is dead. May God have mercy on his soul!

RISING AGAINST THE EARL

All the Irish of the country
Revolted against the earl.
Of the Irish at this time
There remained with him only three:
Donnell Kavanagh, in the first place,
Who was brother to his wife,
O'Reilly of Tirbrun,
And thirdly Auliffe O'Garvy;
While the Irish of Hy Kinsellagh,
Who were with King Murtough [Dermot's nephew],
They then stirred up a great war
Against the earl of Leinster.
And the rich king of Connaught [Rory O'Connor]
Summoned to him
The Irish of all Ireland
In order to lay seige to Dublin.
They came on the day
That their lord had appointed for them.
When they were assembled
They were sixty thousand strong.
At Castleknock, at this time,
Was the rich king of Connaught;
And MacDunlevy of Ulster
Planted his standard at Clontarf;
And O'Brien of Munster
Was at Kilmainham with his brave men;
And Murtough, as I hear,
Was near Dalkey with his men.

The earl, you must know, at this time
Was within the city, of a truth.
The son of Stephen promptly sent
Some of his men to the earl:
In order to aid and succour him
He sent men to him at this crisis.

THE CAPTURE OF FITZSTEPHEN

When Robert had sent
About thirty-six of his men
To aid the earl Richard,
Who was [the subject of such anxiety],
The traitors without any delay
Fell upon Robert.
In the town of Wexford
They wrongfully slew his men:
His men they utterly betrayed,
Killed, cut to pieces, and brought to shame.
Within a castle on the Slaney,
According to what the geste here tells,
The traitors took Robert
And put him in prison at Begerin [an island in Wexford
    harbor]:
Five knights, in short,
They imprisoned in Begerin.
And there came Donnell Kavanagh
And the Irish of Hy Kinsellagh:
To Dublin he came
To the noble earl at this juncture.
With him came O'Reilly,
And Auliffe also.
To the earl they told all,
How Robert was imprisoned,
And how his men were slain,
Discomfited, and treacherously killed.
The earl thereupon replies:—
"Donnell, let it not appear,
Let it not appear, my friend,
That our men are brought to shame."

The earl then summoned
All the lord councillors
To come to him at once to advise
Speedily, without delaying. . . .

THE EARL'S PROPOSAL TO
HIGH KING RORY O'CONNOR

Knights barons as many as twenty:
All the barons of great worth
Came to their lord.
When the renowned barons
Were assembled in council,
The earl sought counsel
Of all his kinsfolk and friends.

"My lords," thus spake the valiant earl,
"May God of Heaven protect us!
You see, my lords, your enemies
Who have now besieged you here.
We shall have hardly anything to eat
Before the fortnight is out:
(For the measure of corn
Was sold for a silver mark,
And for a measure of barley
One got at that time half a mark:)
Wherefore, Sir Knights,
Let us send a message to the [high] king."
Then the renowned earl
Sent a message to the king
That he would become his man
And would hold Leinster of him.

"Come now, free-born lords,
To the king of Connaught two vassals
By your counsel we shall despatch,
And we shall send the archbishop,
That I shall be willing to do fealty to him,
And will hold Leinster of him."
An archbishop they sent,
Who was afterwards called St. Laurence [O'Toole].

The archbishop they then sent
And Maurice de Prendergast with him.
To the king they accordingly announced
The message of the earl.

Thereupon the king said to them
Without taking time or respite:
He answered to the messenger
That he would by no means do this;
No more than Waterford
Dublin and Wexford alone
Would he leave to Earl Richard
Of all Ireland as his share;
Not a whit more would he give
To the earl or to his followers.
The messengers turned back
To the city of Dublin:
The messengers returned
Speedily without delaying.
Aloud they tell their message
In the hearing of all the barons:
To the earl they told completely
The reply of the haughty king:—
That he would not give him more land
In the whole of Leinster,
Except only the three cities
Which I have already named to you;
And if this did not meet his pleasure
They would attack the city;
If he would not accept this offer
The king would hear no more,
For on the morrow, so said the king,
The English would be attacked.

PREPARING FOR THE SORTIE

When the earl had heard
What the archbishop related,
Then the earl caused to be summoned
Miles de Cogan the light of limb:

"Make all your men arm, barons,
Sally forth in the foremost van;
In the name of the Almighty Father
In the foremost van sally forth."
About forty horsemen
Are with Miles before in the front,
Sixty archers and one hundred sergeants
Had Miles under his orders.
And then next, Raymond le Gros
With forty companions,
And he had one hundred fighting-men
And three-score archers.
And then next, the good earl
With forty fighting-men
With one hundred hardy sergeants
And three-score archers.
Very well armed they were
Horsemen, sergeants, and hired soldiers.
When the earl had sallied forth
With his friends and his comrades,
Miles placed himself at the head in the van
With two hundred fighting vassals;
And then next Raymond le Gros
With about two hundred companions;
In the third company the noble earl
With two hundred hardy vassals.
Donnell Kavanagh, of a truth,
Auliffe O'Garvy likewise,
And O'Reilly of Tirbrun,
Of whom you have already heard,
Were in the van with Miles,
As the Song tells us.
But the Irish of the district
Knew nought of this affair:
Of the barons thus armed,
And equipped for battle.

Miles de Cogan very quickly
By the direct road towards Finglas
Towards their stockades thereupon
Set out at a rapid pace.

When Miles had drawn near
To where the Irish were encamped,
"A Cogan!" he shouted aloud,
"Strike, in the name of the Cross!
Strike, barons, nor delay at all,
In the name of Jesus the son of Mary!
Strike, noble knights,
At your mortal enemies!"
The renowned liege barons
At their huts and cabins
Attacked the Irish
And fell upon their tents;
And the Irish unarmed
Fled through the moors:
Throughout the country they fled away
Like scattered cattle.

Raymond le Gros also
Oft invoked St. David [patron saint of Wales].
And went pursuing the Irish
To work his will upon them;
And Richard the good earl
Did so well that day,
So well did the earl do,
That all were astonished;
And Meiler the son of Henry,
Who was of such renown,
Bore himself so bravely
That men wondered.
A hundred and more were slain
While bathing where they were beset,
And more than one thousand five hundred
Of these men were slain,
While of the English there was wounded
Only one foot-sergeant.
The field remained that day
With Richard, the good earl,
And the Irish departed
Discomfited and outdone:
As God willed, at that time,
The field remained with our English

So much provision did they find,
Corn, meal, and bacon,
That for a year in the city
They had victuals in abundance.
To the city with his men
The earl went very joyfully.

TO THE RESCUE OF FITZSTEPHEN

Earl Richard, light of limb,
Makes preparations for his journey.
To Wexford he resolved to go
To set free the baron [Robert FitzStephen].
The baron the son of Stephen
The traitors hold in prison:
The traitors of Wexford hold him, in short,
Imprisoned in Begerin.
The wardship of Dublin he gave
To the good Miles the warrior.
Then the earl proceeded
Towards Wexford night and day.
So much did the earl accomplish
By his day's marches, and so far go,
For so many nights and so many days
That he came to Odrone.
Now the Irish of the district
Were assembled at the pass:
To meet the earl Richard
At one side they were assembled:
To attack the English
Were the Irish assembled.
The earl Richard with his men
Through the midst of the pass in safety
Thought surely to advance,
When an obstacle met him.

The rebel king of Odrone,
O'Ryan was his name,
Shouted out loudly:
"To your destruction, Englishmen, have you come!"

He rallied his men to him,
And attacked the English sharply;
And the English, of a truth,
Manfully defended themselves.
But Meiler, the son of Henry
Carried the prize that day:
In the battle, know in sooth,
There was no better than the son of Henry.
And much renowned that day
Was Nichol, a cowled monk;
For with an arrow he slew that day
The lord of Odrone:
By an arrow, as I tell you,
Was O'Ryan slain that day.
And Meiler, the strong-limbed baron,
Was stunned by a blow
Of a stone in this fight,
So that he reeled to the ground.
But when O'Ryan was slain
The Irish separated.
This wood was afterwards named
And called the earl's pass,
Because the earl was attacked there
By his enemies.

Thence the earl turned
Toward Wexford city
To liberate the imprisoned Robert,
Of whom I have before told you.
But the perfidious traitors
Would not deliver him up to the earl.
To Begerin [Island] they fled
And Wexford they set on fire.
For the sea ran entirely
All around Begerin;
Werefore the noble earl,
Could not, i' faith, get at them.

KING HENRY SUMMONS THE EARL

Then the English king [Henry II] sent
To the earl to announce
That, without delay, without gainsaying,
Without taking time or respite,
The earl should come speedily
To speak to him at once.
And the earl at this juncture
To Miles gave the custody of Dublin:
A city much renowned,
Which was formerly called Ath-Cliath.
And the custody of the city of Waterford,
Which was called Port-Lairge,
The noble Earl Richard gave
To Gilbert de Boisrohard.
The earl then got ready,
He resolved to cross over to England;
The noble earl resolved to cross over
To speak to King Henry:
To King Henry Curt-Mantel,
Who was his rightful lord.
His ships he then equipped
To traverse the waves.
He resolved to cross the high seas,
He will go to speak to the English king.
So much did the earl hasten
That he soon crossed the sea.
In Wales he landed,
The earl who was so much dreaded.

Earl Richard at this time
At Pembroke found the rich king.
The noble earl of great worth
Into the presence of his lord,
With his friends and his comrades
Into the presence of his lord came.

The noble earl saluted him
In the name of the Son of the King of Majesty
And the king graciously
Made answer to Earl Richard.
The king thereupon replied:
"May God Almighty bless you!"

HENRY II COMES TO IRELAND
BY GERALD OF WALES

Gerald continues the story of the invasion by giving a slightly different version of FitzStephen's capture by the Irish (or the "traitors," as he calls them) and Strongbow's summons to Henry's court in England. He goes on to recount Henry's triumphal entry into Ireland and the homage paid the king both by the Irish kings and clergy.

There are also passages that reveal Henry (and Gerald's) enthusiasm for falconry and descriptions of some foul Irish weather that kept the king on the island longer than he intended.

BUT MEANWHILE, SINCE FORTUNE rings the changes and continually mixes up prosperity with adversity, to the end that she may prove a trusty companion to no man and that there can be no such thing in this world as reliable and perfect happiness, the men of Wexford, along with those of Uí Chennselaig, about three thousand strong, heedless of the bond of their oath and pledge of loyalty, were subjecting FitzStephen to ceaseless attacks. He had been quite unprepared, had not feared an attack of this kind, and was surrounded, with only five knights and a few archers. But the Irish realized that they would get nowhere by the use of force, for these men, although very few in number, were nevertheless very alert in defending themselves, and in particular a knight, a certain William surnamed Not, who in this defence far outshone all the others in courage. And so they had recourse to their usual weapons of falsehood and lying deceit. They led up to the castle ditch two bishops, of Wexford and Kildare, and others whose habit proclaimed them to be churchmen. They brought along relics also, and then all joined in taking an oath, giving their persons as surety, and asserted under oath that Dublin had been taken, that the earl, Maurice and Raymond, together with all the English, were now dead, and that the united armies of Connacht and Leinster were at that moment hurrying towards Wexford. They claimed, moreover, that they had done all this for FitzStephen's own good, in order that they could convey him safely to Wales with his followers before the arrival of a large force of men hostile to him. For, they said, he had shown himself a merciful and generous prince towards them. In the end FitzStephen believed their assertion and entrusted himself and his men to their pledged word. They immediately killed a number of his men, inflicted severe wounds on some and blows on others, put them in chains and incarcerated them. Almost immediately rumour, flying with swift wings, made known the true facts of the defeat at Dublin and the approach of the earl. At once the traitors themselves set fire to the whole city and sailed across to the island of Begeri, which lies at the mouth of the [Wexford] harbour, and which is also called Holy Island, taking with them all their possessions and all the prisoners. . . .

Meanwhile, as the earl was making his way to Wexford, the army of the men of Leinster advanced to engage him in the pass of Uí Dróna. The natural situation of this place made it narrow and impassable, but it had in addition been very much strengthened by artificial means, using felled trees. There a heavy engagement was fought, and at last, after a great number of the enemy had been killed, the earl escaped safely out on to the plains with all his men, excepting one youth who was killed. On this occasion Meiler, with his usual courage, outshone all the others. . . .

THE MEETING BETWEEN THE EARL AND THE KING OF ENGLAND

Immediately after this, while they [the earl's men] were coming down into the territory of Wexford, they were met by messengers, who told them what had happened to FitzStephen, how affairs stood, and how the city had been burned. Speaking for the traitors, they roundly asserted that if they should dare to approach, they would immediately send them the severed heads of all their people. When they heard this news, which filled them with great mental anguish, they wheeled their horses to the right and quickly made for Waterford. There they found Hervey, who had by now returned from the king of England, whither he had gone, and who by his letters and his words was urging the earl to make the same journey to England. So with the help of wind and sail he immediately crossed the sea, and at Newnham in Gloucestershire met the king, who was by now ready to cross to Ireland with a considerable force. There, after many arguments of varying outcome, and thanks to Hervey's mediation and adroit tactics, the king's anger towards the earl at last subsided. The result was that his bond of obedience was renewed, and he surrendered to the king the chief town of the kingdom, Dublin, along with the adjacent cantreds, and also the coastal cities and all castles. As for the rest of the land he had conquered, he and his heirs were to acknowledge that it was held of the king and his heirs. When matters had been settled in these terms, the king quickly took the coastal route towards St. David's. He came into Pembroke and within a short time assembled a splendid fleet in the harbour of Milford Haven.

THE DEFEAT OF UA RUAIRC AT DUBLIN

But in the meantime Ua Ruairc, the one-eyed king of Meath, seized the opportunity of the absence of the earl and of Raymond, who had continued in Waterford, and came to Dublin with a large force about the kalends of September. And when he found that there were very few men in the city—but they *were* men—with a great onslaught and much shouting his men made a fierce attack on the walls and ditches. But since valour cannot be confined, and fire when it is compressed bursts into flame, Miles de Cogan and his men suddenly sallied forth and immediately began pursuing the enemy, inflicting such massive casualties that they routed them and killed Ua Ruairc's son, an excellent young man, and countless others with him on that same occasion.

Meanwhile the English king began to storm at the magnates of south Wales and Pembroke with the direst threats because they had allowed earl Richard to cross to Ireland by that route. But in the end, on royal governors being assigned to their castles, this stormy bout of temper subsided into calm and his loud thunderings were not followed by the deadly blow of the thunderbolt.

At that time the king wished to amuse himself by flying birds in that locality. When he chanced to notice a fine falcon perched on a crag, he approached it by coming round at one side, and launched against it a Norwegian hawk which he was carrying on his left hand, a large bird of noble pedigree. But although the falcon was slower to begin with, nevertheless, having climbed with some difficulty high up in the sky, it turned the tables and, filled with anger and a desire for revenge, from being the prey it became the predator. It plunged violently down to earth from aloft, dealing out retaliation with the powerful impact of its breast squared to meet the shock and the superior armament of its talons, and, transfixing the hawk, laid it at the king's feet. So from that time on, each year about nesting time the king used to send for the falcons of that area, which are hatched on those sea cliffs. And in all his realm he found none more noble or more excellent than these. . . .

After this the king stayed for some considerable time at St. David's, making the preparations necessary for an enterprise so noble and on such a large scale, and repaired to the shrine of St. David, honouring the saint with devout prayer. He then took advantage of a suitable moment and favouring winds and weather, and entrusted himself to wind and sail. This courageous monarch crossed the intervening sea and put in at Waterford around the kalends of November, on St. Luke's day (18th October) [1172], with about five hundred knights and many mounted and foot archers. . . .

FITZSTEPHEN BROUGHT BEFORE THE KING IN CHAINS

While the king was staying for a few days at Waterford, the citizens of Wexford brought FitzStephen into his presence, a captive and in chains. They did this under the pretext of rendering obedient service to Henry, on the grounds that FitzStephen was the first to enter Ireland without Henry's consent, and presented others with an opportunity for wrong-doing. The king first of all reproached him severely for undertaking something so grandiose and so rash as the conquest of Ireland, displaying extreme rage and making many threats. At last he consigned him to Raghnall's tower for safe keeping, firmly fettered and chained to another man. Just after this, king Diarmait of Cork arrived. He was drawn forthwith into a firm alliance with Henry by the bond of homage, the oath of fealty, and the giving of hostages; an annual tribute was assessed on his kingdom and he voluntarily submitted to the authority of the king of England. The king moved his army from there and went first of all to Lismore, where he stayed for two days, and from there continued to Cashel. There, on the next day, Domnall king of Limerick met him by the river Suir. He obtained the privilege of the king's peace, tribute was assessed on his kingdom in the same way as on Diarmait's, and he too displayed his loyalty to the king by entering into the very strongest bonds of submission.

FITZSTEPHEN RECONCILED TO THE KING

So royal governors and officials were put in charge of Cork and Limerick. All the princes of southern Ireland made a voluntary submission, both those mentioned above, and also two others, who, although they were not of such cardinal importance, were nevertheless influential and had real authority among their people, namely Domnall of Osraige and

Maelsechnaill Ua Faeláin. Each of them returned to their own territory with honour, taking with them the presents given them by the king. He then returned to Waterford by way of Tibberaghny. There FitzStephen was led into his presence for a second time. When the king saw before him a man who had so often and to such a degree been exposed to the hazards of Fortune, his heart was moved to pity, and the hardships suffered by a man of such heroic stature aroused his compassion. When, moreover, certain influential men interceded for FitzStephen, he allowed all his former feelings of anger to abate, and fully restored to him his former freedom, only depriving him of Wexford and the adjacent territory. . . .

THE COUNCIL OF CASHEL

In the year of Our Lord's Incarnation 1172, in the first year in which the illustrious king of the English and conqueror of the Irish gained possession of that island, Christian bishop of Lismore and legate of the apostolic see, Donat archbishop of Cashel, Laurence archbishop of Dublin, and Catholicus archbishop of Tuam, with their suffragans and fellow bishops, abbots, archdeacons, priors and deans, and many other prelates of the Irish church, met in the city of Cashel at that same conqueror's command and held a council there, which was concerned with measures beneficial to the church and with the amelioration of the existing condition of that church. . . .

Thus in all parts of the Irish church all matters relating to religion are to be conducted hereafter on the pattern of Holy Church, and in line with the observances of the English church. For it is proper and most fitting that, just as by God's grace Ireland has received her lord and king from England, so too she should receive a better pattern of living from that same quarter. . . .

STORMS

Then Aeolus burst asunder the bars of his prison and the heaving billows of the sea were churned up. The storms raged so unceasingly and with such persistence that throughout that whole winter scarcely a single ship had succeeded in making the crossing to the island, and no one could get any news whatsoever from other lands. So severe were they that all men thought that they were being collectively threatened by God's wrath because of their sins. At that same time, due to the unusual force of the gale, the sandy shores of south Wales were laid bare of sand down as far as the subsoil, and the surface of a land that had been covered many centuries earlier appeared, and also the trunks of trees standing upright which reached down (the shore) into the sea itself. These had everywhere been felled, and the marks of the axes were visible as if they had been made only yesterday. The soil was very black and the wood of the tree trunks was like ebony. By an amazing transformation in the natural order of things, a shipping lane now became impassable to ships, and the shore no longer appeared as a shore but as a forest, which—either from the time of the flood, or perhaps from a much later period, but at any rate a period in the distant past—had been cut down and gradually engulfed and absorbed by the violent motions of the sea, which is continually flooding and eroding the land to an ever greater extent.

VI.

JOHN DE COURCY
AND THE
CONQUEST OF ULSTER

INTRODUCTION

T HE WORDS THAT USUALLY FOLLOW the name John de Courcy (died c. 1219) are "conqueror of Ulster." Gerald of Wales describes him this way:

> John was fair-haired and tall, with bony and sinewy limbs. His frame was lanky, and he had a very strong physique, immense bodily strength and an extraordinarily bold temperament. . . . He was so eager for battle and so headstrong that, whenever he was put in command of troops, he often abandoned the self-control required of a leader, laying aside the role as commander and assuming that of an ordinary soldier, so that when his troops were wavering he would rush impetuously among the leading ranks, and one got the impression that he had thrown away the chance of victory in his eagerness to win. . . .
>
> He took as his lawful wife the daughter of Guthred king of [the Isle of] Man, . . . and fortified all parts of Ulaid [Counties Down and Antrim] with castles built in suitable places, not without a great deal of toil, short rations and endurance of many dangers, settled it and established conditions of the utmost peace and stability.

De Courcy landed at Wexford in 1176. After the conquest, he moved north with the troops to Dublin, where, according to most reports, he was so disgusted by the corrupt practices of the occupation government that he picked out a small but elite force and headed north into Ulaid, where he defeated the last of the ancient Ulster kings, Mac Duinn Suibne. As conqueror, he had the reputation of being far more interested in the native culture than most of the invaders. He was especially fascinated by the local saints, St. Patrick in particular, and Gerald of Wales even reports that John carried with him a book of prophecies written in Irish that he seemed to be able to read.

Often using the title *princeps* (prince), he ruled Ulster as a semi-independent state until 1244, enjoying more support from the Irish than was usual for an Englishman. And when he was overthrown, it was not by the Irish but by a rival Norman, a member of the de Lacy family, who coveted his lands.

In the entry from *The Book of Howth* that follows, readers may find English being used in a most unfamiliar way. The grammar may seem strange, and the spelling of proper names is inconsistent even within paragraphs. But the account has the raw power of folk art with sentences such as: "Both through the battle of Irishmen he went and returned again and again, making lanes through them so many that his few men that he had might easily pass through and through."

THE BOOK OF HOWTH
THE NORTHERN CONQUEST BEGINS, 1177

The Book of Howth *was written in the middle of the sixteenth century
as a history of the lords of Howth, the port city on the north edge of
Dublin Bay, not far from the site of Brian Boru's Battle of Clontarf. In
its account of the victories of John de Courcy, there is a brief aside saying it contains stories not found in Gerald of Wales's history of the
Normans.*

*It begins with John and his small army abandoning a corrupt
Dublin that is commanded by a Norman named William Aldelme, who
is described: "Today he would thee worship; tomorrow he would thee
unworship. The meek and sober he would undo; the strong and mighty
he pleased; soft with the wild men, hard with the peace men . . . full of
treason, and envious, drunken, lewd, and lecherous."*

*In no time at all, after a few battles and against amazing odds, John
defeated the last of a dynasty that traced its roots back to the age of
Cuchulain and the fortress at Emain Macha.*

JOHN DE COURCY . . . took with him of the men of Dublin a few, but they
were good and manfully, hardy through all thing[s], so that he had two
and twenty knights, fifty squires, and footmen as might be three hundred,
and went into Ulester, where no Englishman went before him that was
ever seen. Then was fulfilled a prophecy of Marlen, that thus he said: "A
white knight sitting on a white horse, bearing fowls in his shield, shall
foremost assay Ulester." This John was a man white, and rode then upon
a white horse, and bare in his shield i-painted three herons. He went
through Mithth and Eriell in three days going, and the fourth day came
early to Doune [Down] without any let of any of his foemen, unknown to
any man but his own. The King [of Ulster] was sore afraid, notwithstanding, sped him out of the town; and his men they were misfeysed, and
very hungry; where they had at their coming meat and drink enough, and

spoil of gold and silver, and clothes, wherewith they were well arrayed, and their hearts well comforted.

Into the town was there come a Legate of Rome, [called] Vivien, and was come out of Scotland. This Legate was about peace to make between O'Donyll the King and John. Much he spake, and much he proferred to him, and promised him to bear every year a certain [reward] to the Englishmen, if they had left the land and turn again. But yet he [John] would not; till he had lost his life, he would not have left the land. Although the Legate spake as much as he could of fair speech, yet he could not speed. The King sent anon after his people. Within eight days he gathered together a host of 10,000 fighting men, and manfully came on towards the city of Doune, where Sir John was. The northern men [being] sturdier and stronger to fight than others.

Sir John saw the hosts coming to Doune. He was but 700 men; nevertheless they were full hardy and manfully of kind. He chose sooner to assay the adventure of battle in the field, rather than he would be kept in a cave within, like a bird in a cage. He came out of the town, and did put his men in good order, and divided them in three companies. He put his brother Sir Amorey de Sancto Laurensino with the horsemen, which was 140, and every horseman had a bowman behind him. Those was set on the left hand the battle. Roger de Power was put with a certain of footmen on the right hand, where as then a marsh ground was. Sir John led the third and last company, though they was but few in number.

The King, perceiving the horsemen but a few, thought to end with them ere that he would join his main battle. The ground was but narrow, where they should encounter, toward a great ditch and hedge, where no horseman could come within. Sir Amorey caused his footmen to be put within that hedge or ditch, and as the King did charge upon Sir Hamore, the shot of arrows came on so fast that their horses were so galled that the horses began to shrink back. Sir Amorey, with his few horsemen, did so fiercely set on that they never suffered the King's horsemen once to look back for their fellows, as their main battle of footmen, till the King was droven beyond a narrow pass.

Then Sir Amorey called to his few footmen that then was with him, and willed them so to keep the pass that no horsemen should return till they had finished the battle, and retired back, and sent to Sir John, and bade that he should come on and set on the King's footmen that stood in a great trench waiting the coming of their horsemen which was chased beyond the pass. Sir John did as his brother willed him.

There began such a cry on both sides that no instrument of the wars could be heard of neither side, with the wounded horses that galled was with spears and arrows, the wounded and pale-faced soldiers, which there was grovelling on the ground gaping with their mouths open for want of wind, which were galled and hurt with arrows and spears. The noise of weapon[s] upon helmets was as a hundreds of forges with their smiths and others with hammers and sledges beating upon anvils of steel. And also there was lighting of fire, spears brust [points], and arrows flying in the air. That noise and fight was like heaven and earth were at a combat together.

Who had seen these worthy knights and soldiers in that battle, strange it was to behold. Who had seen Sir John Curcy his brother and Roger Pouer, that was a great man in Ossery, must have said and report[ed] that in all the world there could be none better than they three found. There was none that day that Sir John strack but died with that stroke, beside others that was wounded, but like a wolf amongst a herd of lambs, so did he use himself. Both through the battle of Irishmen he went and returned again and again, making lanes through them so many that his few men that he had might easily pass through and through.

Roger Pouer on the right side with his company so well did that there was none that could pass on his side to take succour of the marsh ground that was nigh the battle on his side but died; that between him and the main battle there was no way but upon dead corpses, or harness, legs and heads, that lay on the ground, or such weapons that they had that was slain, for no man could tread on the ground or grass by reason of the premises, for the King's footmen, I mean the Irish, always they looked for the King and the aid of their horsemen, amongst whom were all their gentlemen [officers], in whom the footmen had all their trust. And perceiving the furious and terrible onset of the English, that so stalworthy did use themselves in their first charge on them, and no succour maintenance they could find, they as long as they might fought more out of order than it became such that so great a charge had to enterprise, always looking more for the comfort and aid of their leaders, captains, and gentlemen than they were willing to do that of themselves. And they perceiving all their fastness[es], as the moor, was taken from them, and that could be no succour for them by reason of the great slaughter that Roger Pouer did on that side, they with so much power as they had left made to the plain where as Sir Amore was with a few horsemen, thinking that the English soldiers was so tired with the great fight and sad harness [heavy armor], they [the Irish] being naked, was not able to travail nor follow them in the plain, being lighter and lustier than they in travail and footmanship.

As they came ahead in the plain, Sir Amore met them, running without order, and set upon them with his horsemen that few stop or could save himself, but he that was able to overrun a horse by speed. There was of this number a two hundred or thereabouts of the Irish, with their leader Rory A'Hanlane, that always kept together, and was like to take the plain. Sir Amore called to his banner or standard bearer, called Geffrey Moungomrey, and said, "It is not time for thee to stay back for this small company that so well hath done all this day, and if we should suffer those to escape it would be said that that goodness that we hath done were lost. I pray thee, Mongomry, let us give the setting on." "Nay," said Mongomry, "we are but forty horsemen able to fight; the rest are tired and wounded, and you will never give over your stout stomach till you win more dispraise than ever you won of commendation." "Well," said Sir Amore, "I never heard out of thee so uncourteous an answer. Is it dishonour to die manfully in battle? Can we win ever more commendation? Give me my standard in mine own hand, for we will end that that we hath well began." "Nay," said Mongomry, "with this standard I hath won my living, and with this standard I will end my life. Now come on, in the name of God and Saint Patrick."

Great work there was this time with these few horsemen, for Sir Amore was put twice on foot, and was helpen up to horse again, till the third time, being beyond a ford as the foremost passed through, was unhorsed, and his horse slain. But, as God would, three of his men lighted a-foot by him, which took four spears which they took of dead men that there was, and kept that ford upon the footmen till Sir John Coursey came to that rescusse, for his horsemen knew not where he be gone. Who that might behold that battle, first and last, would a-counted Sir Amorey worthy of high praise and commendation, were it not that he had been at the first onset upon these footmen wounded above the forehead, and the blood disturbed him much. His praise would have been as much as might be given to any knight or horsemen then alive.

During this sport few or none escaped; at which time this hundred men, that was left to keep the pass, was inforced to cut [down the trees in] the pass, and [lay] it over with wood, for the horsemen often charged upon them, thinking to come to rescue their fellows that was in the battle, where as in that pass was slain Lyonell Saint Larans, Sir Amore's nephew, and two gentlemen more, which over all other there did best; and if those horsemen and the King had not by such fortune be separate from the footmen, it had not be like the fortune of battle to turn on Sir John Coursey's side. They were of the Irish side ten thousand; of the English, seven hundred horsemen and footmen. You may see that policy helpeth good fortune, for this field was won by the help of God, to Sir John's great honour and worthy commendation.

This story, and divers other of the thrice noble and worthy conqueror, that none his peer was in all Europe for the manliness and stalworthness with his own hand, I mean Sir John de Coursy, Earl of Ulster, was left out of the book written by Geraldus Cameranse [Gerald of Wales], Archdeacon of Landaffe in England, and yet he was sent by the King with his son John to Ireland for the declaration of the truth.

It fortuned that A'Hanlone [O'Hanlon] and those of Yryell, finding a ship at Torsse Head in Euryell full of victual and other things else coming to Sir John Course to the north was by tempest of weather driven within a creek or haven, which was devoured by them [O'Hanlon], and the mariners slain, and other of Sir John's servants; the said Sir John, coming toward the Nuery [Newry] to revenge this shame, did understand that those Irishmen was gathered together with all their power to defend their cause . . . on the north side of Dondoygen. Sir John came, not thinking they were so many as they were indeed till they came within a mile and a half of the Irish camp, for then was the men of that quarters of the country all gathered at the same water side in camp.

Sir John called his brother Sir Amore, and Roger Pouer, and asked what was best to be done. Roger Pouer stood by, a valiant knight, and said, "Let us take fortune; the longer we do behold them, the worse our soldiers will think of them, for the sight of man is the marring and making of man, it giveth both courage and discourage to man." "What?" said Sir Amorey; "We cannot be so hasty in setting on, their number of men is greater than we have been accustomed to meet in so great a plain with so few a number of men as we are, for in battle three things are requisite, first the quarrel, the second the number of soldiers, and the third the place. In speaking these words I would not discourage no valiant heart. First, it is to be understand that we be come of noble parentage, which cannot be denied, and we are upon our peril to crave, win, and look for that we want, and that is a living in our old age, and then to be quiet. For this we asked of our Prince, and this same hath given to us our winnings and conquest for the reward of our perilous and painful service, for it is our necessity we look to relieve.

"To the second part, we are far less in number than our enemies, wherefore it were very requisite that a closer ground were our best advantage, which at this time we lack. Therefore, if you follow my advice, let us send a beggar or friar to the camp, and not to go ahead without reason, and cause him to say that Sir Hue de Lassy is come yesterday to Trodathe, for we must use policy [trickery] where force doth want; and that also he shall say that he saw coming out of the West, about a two mile off, a number of horsemen and footmen, supposing to him it was Sir Hue de Lasy and his English soldiers that came by night from Trodathe. And in the mean time we shall put our lackeys upon our bearing horses, with my son Nicholas and twenty good horsemen with him, that way that the friar shall say he saw that number of people, with a sign between him and me what he shall do; and I will with our horsemen ride toward them upon our chief horses, and I shall see by their moving and stirring what they mean to do. And if they shall turn their faces to us to fight, we shall without great losses return to Dondalke, for their footmen shall never overtake our footmen, and as for their horsemen we shall use them to their dishonour."

The which sayings Sir John liked well, and so did all the rest, saving they feared his son Nicholas to be over willing to battle, "which might turn all this device to all our undoings," saith they. "Well then," said Sir Amore, "prepare your footmen in a readiness." Sir John appointed Roger Pouer with certain in the rearward, and Sir John himself in the forebattle, as he that first should give the charge, and also if they were enforced to give back, that he would himself be in the rearward, for it was most danger, which was his only desire in all fight.

Sir John mustered his men upon a hill, as large and far off as with honesty he might, so that his enemies did not perceive his policy. The Irish, after they heard the friar's tale, and saw as they thought the number of horsemen coming out of the West, and saw the horsemen coming with Sir Amorey very nigh at hand, then said they plainly that the friar's tale was true, and that Sir Amorey would not be so bold in coming so nigh, but for that there was more succour at hand than Sir John Coursey's own men.

In the mean time there went a bold horsemen of A'Hanlon's to view and scout over-see the English horsemen, whose name was Dermot Karraghe; then being also afore Sir Amore, a bow shot, a base son of Sir Amorey's, called the Bastard Berefott, and encountered with that Irish horseman, and overthrew him, for he struck him through; at which time seeing now O'Hanlon said it was but the first token of their evil fortune; "therefore," saith he, "let us go over the water, for the sea is coming in apace, and once we be beyond this river we are safe, and may go where we will, for none can come at us."

Sir Amorey, seeing them going over the river, nigh half-endell of them, made signs to Sir John Coursey and to Nicholas his son to come on apace, and so incontinent did give the charge upon them, and by reason the water divided the Irish host or army a-two, and the further half, being beyond the water, could not come to succour their fellows being on the other side, they were slain and drowned nigh all.

After that done, Sir John and his men followed the rest through a ford that the friar learned them, and Sir Amorey with the horsemen did overtake the Irish footmen at the great water be-south the Lorgone [Larne] a mile, and skirmished with them a while till Sir John Coursey with the footmen did overtake them. The sea water came so speedily in that there they could not pass over, and also they were disturbed by the horsemen that run before, that very necessity constrained the Irish to fight, being then above the number of six thousand, and Sir John Coursey not then fully the number of one thousand.

The gentlemen and captains of the Irish, seeing that, did gather them in one place together which gave the charge upon Roger Pouer, then being in the woward, and did with very force constrain him and his to retire to Sir John and his band. The fight was so great, fought of necessity by the Irish, that Sir John was left alone amongst his enemies like a lion among a herd of sheep, for his men gave back. With that, young Nicholas came to his father Sir Amorey, riding apace, he then chasing the Irish horsemen, which then was broken upon, told that their footmen would not stand, and Sir John was left, and all was like to be lost. With that he came to the footmen, crying on them, and willed them to return, and that they should have good help. They promised that they would, so that he had lighted a-foot amongst them; for Sir John then they missed.

With that Sir Amorey called his son Nicholas, and spake these words: "My dear son, take the charge of these good horsemen, and do with them this day, for it shall then sound thy honour." And with that Sir Amorey light in the forefront of the footmen, and drew his sword, and thrust his horse through, and bade the footmen come on stoutly, and so did, with such a cry and force that they constrained the Irish to give back. At which first charge all the captains and gentlemen were slain of the Irish together in one heap, as sheaves of corn laid upon a ridge. After that they fled every man.

Who that had seen Sir John that day, being not in fear nor danger, might say he was [another Hercules]. He fought that day with a two-hand sword more like a lion than a lamb; his blows were so weighty and so to be wondered at that very strange it was to behold, for there was never blow he strack but slew a man or two, for no harness could bear out his force. For similitude he was like a mower in a field of thistles, for God gave him in this battle force, victory, and good fortune. And after this Sir John returned to Ullestere again, where as he made many castles and strong houses.

VII.

THE

SCOTS

INTRODUCTION

I N APRIL 1315, EDWARD BRUCE, younger brother of Robert Bruce, king of the Scots, landed at Larne in Ulster and soon after declared himself king of Ireland. It had been a year since the Bruces had soundly defeated the English at Bannockburn in Scotland. Several reasons have been given for the Irish adventure. One is that it was simply a diversionary tactic to keep England from trying to regain its hold on Scotland. The other is that it was the next step of a planned Celtic revolt in the British Isles, with Wales to follow.

Bruce had some Irish allies, the most important being Donal O'Neill (Donnall Ua Neill), who sent to Pope John XXII his "Remonstrance of the Irish Princes" defending his alliance with Edward ("sprung from our noblest ancestors"), and asking for the pope's blessing. O'Neill wrote, "In order to shake off the harsh and insupportable yoke of servitude to them [the English] and to recover our native freedom, which for the time being we have lost through them, we are compelled to enter a deadly war."

At first Edward had nothing but success, defeating the English and their Irish allies at Dundalk, Connor, Trim (where he gained the support of de Lacys), then skirting around Dublin to the west and back again. His brother Robert joined him for a while, but they never did try to take Dublin, although the Dubliners were so afraid of their arrival that they themselves burned down the suburbs outside the city walls to keep them from sheltering the Scots.

But the Irish as a whole never shared the opinion of Donal O'Neill and joined forces with Edward. The destruction of the countryside was widespread, and in *The Annals of Clonmacnoise* both sides are described in almost the same words. The English "spared neither spirituall nor Temporall land in every place they wen," while the Scots marched on "spoyling and Destroying all places where they came. Not sparing church or chapel, in so much as they did not leave neither field of corn undestroyed nor towne unransacked."

Edward was killed at the Battle of Faughart, north of Dublin, in 1318. The Scottish invasion was over, although not all the Scots returned home. By then, the famine that had been ravaging Europe had reached Ireland. With all the early talk of freedom, one of the annalists summed up the years of the invasion by writing: "Theft, famine and the destruction of men occurred throughout Ireland for the space of three years and a half, and people used actually to eat one another throughout Ireland."

Robert Bruce encouraging his troops before the Battle of Bannockburn (June 23, 1314). Edward II was routed in this battle. Courtesy Corbis/Bettmann.

EDWARD BRUCE
INVADES IRELAND

BY JOHN BARBOUR

John Barbour (c. 1316–95), archdeacon of Aberdeen, wrote the epic poem The Bruce *around 1375. Its high point is an account of Robert Bruce's defeat of the English at the Battle of Bannockburn (1314), with a section beginning "A! Fredome [Freedom] is a noble thing!" that has long been a favorite of Scottish nationalists. The 13,645-line poem also contains a lengthy detour to Ireland to follow Edward Bruce's adventures as invader and self-styled king. It's far from an uncritical portrait— he is even blamed for endangering his brother's life when Robert comes to Ireland to help out. The Reverend Barbour is also distrustful of the Irish. Even Bruce's allies are presented as treacherous and unreliable.*

Barbour, however, clearly enjoyed tactical trickery, and his Scots are adept in the use of disguises and ruses that fool the enemy. Using historical sources, he is at times accurate (the Battle of Connor in Antrim, for instance), and at times fanciful (Robert Bruce's journey to Limerick, oddly described as the southernmost city in Ireland). And he is aware of the unorthodox Irish fighting style. One of Edward's allies says, "Our tactics are [those] of this land, to follow and to fight while fleeing, and not to stand in open encounter until one side is defeated." Another example of complex interconnections of families in Ireland is that Richard de Burgh, earl of Ulster, whom Edward defeated at Connor, was Robert Bruce's father-in-law.

For a sense of the style and Scottish dialect of The Bruce, *compare these opening lines of Edward's arrival in Ireland with the prose translation that follows.*

> The erle off Carrik Schyr Edwar
> That stoutar wes rhan a lipard
> And had na will to be in pees
> Thocht that Scotland to litill wes
> Till his brother and him alsua,
> Tharfor to purpos gan he ta
> That he off Irland wald be king

SIR EDWARD, EARL OF CARRICK, who was stronger than a leopard and had no desire to live in peace, felt that Scotland was too small for both him and his brother; therefore he formed a purpose that he would become king of Ireland. To that end he sent and negotiated with the Irishry of Ireland who, in good faith, undertook to make him king of all Ireland, provided that he could overcome by hard fighting the Englishmen who dwelt in the land then, while they would help with all their might. He, hearing them make this promise, was very pleased in his heart, and, with the king's consent, assembled to himself men of great courage; then he took ship at Ayr in the following month of May, [and] took his way straight to Ireland. He had in his company there Earl Thomas, who was a fine [man], good Sir Philip Mowbray who was staunch under great pressure, Sir John Soules a good knight, and Sir John Stewart, a brave [one]; also Ramsay of Auchterhouse, who was brave and chivalrous, Sir Fergus Ardrossan and many another knight.

They arrived safely in Larne Lough without opposition or attack, and sent home all their ships. They have undertaken a great project when with so few as they were there—six thousand men, no more—they prepared to conquer all Ireland, where they would see many thousands come armed to fight against them. But although few, they were brave, and without fear or dread took the way in two divisions, towards Carrickfergus, to see it.

But the lords of that country, Mandeville, Bisset and Logan, assembled every one of their men—the Savages were there too—and when they were all gathered, they numbered almost twenty thousand. When they learned that such a company had arrived in their country, with all the folk that they had there, they went towards them in great haste. As soon as Sir Edward knew for a fact that they were coming close to him, he had his men arm themselves well. Earl Thomas had the vanguard and Sir Edward was in the rear. Their enemies approached to fight and they met them without flinching. There you could see a great mellee for Earl Thomas and his company laid into their foes so doughtily that in a short time men could see lying a hundred who were all bloody, for hobbies [small horses] who were stabbed there reared and thrashed and made a lot of space, throwing those riding on them. Sir Edward's company then attacked so hardily that they drove back all their foes. Anyone who chanced to fall in that fight was in danger of [not] rising. The Scotsmen in that fighting bore themselves so boldly and well that their foes were driven back [until] they took entirely to flight. . . .

Next they went to Carrickfergus and took lodging in the town. The castle was then well [and] recently provisioned with victuals and [garrisoned] with men; they set siege to it at once. Many a sally was made very boldly while the siege lay there, until eventually they made a truce, when the folk of Ulster had come entirely to his peace, because Sir Edward meant to undertake to ride forth further into the country.

There came to him and made fealty some of the kings of that country, a good ten or twelve, as I heard say; but they kept their faith to him only a short time. . . .

At Kilnasaggart Sir Edward lay, and very soon heard tell there that a gathering of lords of that country had been made at Dundalk. They were assembled in a host there. There was first Sir Richard Clare, who was Lieutenant of the king of England in all Ireland. The earl of Desmond was also there, the earl of Kildare, de Birmingham and de Verdon, who were lords of great reputation. Butler was also there, and Sir Maurice FitzThomas. These came with their men and were indeed a really mighty host.

When Sir Edward knew for a fact that such a chivalry was there, he had his host armed in haste and took the way towards [the enemy], taking lodging near the town. But because he knew for a certainty that there were a lot of men in the town, he armed his divisions then and stood arrayed in division, to hold them if they should attack. When Sir Richard Clare and other lords who were there learned that the Scotsmen with their divisions had come so near, they consulted [and decided] that they would not fight that night, because it was late, but that on the morrow, in the morning very soon after sunrise, all who were there would issue forth; for that reason they did no more that night but both sides made camp. That night the Scottish company were very well guarded, in good order, and on the morrow, when [the] day was light, they drew themselves up in two divisions; they stood with banners all displayed, fully ready for battle. Those who were inside the town when the sun had risen, shining brightly, sent fifty of those who were within [the town] to see the demeanour of the Scotsmen and their arrival. They rode forth and soon saw them, then returned without delay. When they had dismounted together, they told their lords who were there that the Scotsmen appeared to be worthy and of great valour, "but without doubt they are not half a dinner [compared] to us here." At this news the lords rejoiced and took great comfort, causing men to proclaim through the city that all should arm themselves quickly.

When they were armed and equipped and all drawn up for the fight, they went forth in good order; soon they engaged with their enemy, who resisted them right strongly. The fight began there fiercely, for each side put all their might into defeating their foes in the struggle, and laid into the others forcibly. The hard-fought engagement lasted a long time, so that men could not make out or see who most had the upper hand. From soon after sun-rise until after mid-morning the fighting continued in this uncertainty; but then Sir Edward, who was bold, with all those of his company, attacked them so fiercely that they couldn't withstand the fighting any more. All in a rush they took to flight and [the Scots] followed swiftly; into the town all together they entered, both intermixed. There you could see dreadful slaughter, for the right noble Earl Thomas, who followed the chase with his force, made such a slaughter in the town, such a dreadfull killing, that the streets were all bloody with slain men lying there; the lords had got quite away!

When the town had been taken as I tell you, by dint of much fighting, and all their enemies had fled or been killed, they all lodged themselves in the town where there was such profusion of food and so great an abundance of wine the good earl had a great fear that [some] of their men would get drunk and in their drunken state start brawling. So he made an issue of wine to each man so that he would be content, and they all had enough, *perfay*. That night they were very relaxed and much cheered by the great honour that accrued to them through their valour. After this fight they stayed there in Dundalk for no more than three days; then took their way southwards. Earl Thomas was always to the fore. As they rode through the country it was remarkable that they could see so many men upon the hills. When the earl would boldly ride up to them with his banner, they would one and all take to flight so that not one remained to fight. [The Scots] rode on their way southwards until they came to a great forest which was called Kilross as I heard tell, and they all made camp there.

All this time Richard Clare, who was the king's Lieutenant, had assembled a great host of all the baronage of Ireland. They were [in] five divisions, great and broad, seeking Sir Edward and his men [who] had come very near to him then. He soon got knowledge that they were coming against him and were so near. . . . The Scots were all on foot then, [the enemy] well equipped on horses, some [men] all protected in iron and steel. But Scotsmen pierced their armour with spears at the encounter, impaled horses and struck men down. It was a tough battle then, there. I can't tell [of] all their smiting, nor who struck down which other in the fight, but in a short while, I assure you, those of Ireland had been so resisted that they did not dare to stay there any longer, but fled, scattered, every one of them, leaving on the battlefield a great many of their good men dead. The field was wholly covered by weapons, arms and dead men. That great army had been forcibly driven off, but Sir Edward allowed no man to give chase, but they went back with the prisoners they had taken to the wood where their armour had been left. That night they made merry

[with] good cheer and praised God for his grace. This good knight, who was so worthy, could well be compared to Judas Maccabeus who in a fight avoided no host of men as long as he had one against ten. . . .

Then they rode towards O'Dempsy, an Irish king who had made an oath of fealty to Sir Edward, for before that he had begged him to see his land and [there] would be no lack of food or anything else that could help him. Sir Edward trusted in his promise and rode straight there with his force. [O'Dempsy] had them pass [by] a great river and in a very fair place which was down by a burn he had them make their camp, and said that he would go to have men bring victuals to them. He went off without staying any longer, because he meant to betray them. He had brought them to such a place where all the cattle were withdrawn [from them] by a good two days' [travel] or more, so that they could get nothing worth eating in that land. He meant to enfeeble them with hunger and then bring their enemies against them. This false traitor had caused his men to dam up the outlet of a lough a little above where he had lodged Sir Edward and his men, and let it out in the night. The water then came down on Sir Edward's men with such force that they were in danger of drowning, for before they knew it, they were afloat. They got away with great difficulty and by God's grace kept their lives, but [some] of their armour was lost. He made no great feast for them, *perfay*, but nonetheless they had their fill, for although they got no food, I can tell you they were good and wet.

They were placed in great distress because they so lacked meat, for they were placed between two rivers and could cross neither of them. The Bann, which is an arm of the sea [and] which can't be crossed on horseback, was between them and Ulster. They would have been in great danger there but for a sea-pirate who was called Thomas Dun, [who] heard that the army was placed in such straits and [who] sailed up the Bann till he came very close to where they lay. They knew him well and were greatly cheered. Then with four ships that he had captured he set them all across the Bann. When they came to populated land they found enough victuals and meat, and made camp in a wood. No-one of the land knew where they were; they relaxed and made good cheer.

At that time, close beside them, Sir Richard Clare and other great [men] of Ireland were camped with a great host in a forest side. Each day they had men ride [out] to bring them victuals of various kinds from the town of Connor which was good ten miles from them. Each day as they came and went, they came so near the Scots' host that there were only two miles between them. When Earl Thomas perceived them coming and going, he got him a goodly company of three hundred on horse, bold and brave. There was Sir Philip Mowbray, also Sir John Stewart with Sir Alan

Stewart, Sir Robert Boyd and others. They rode to meet the victuallers who were coming from Connor with their victuals, holding the way to their host. They assaulted them so suddenly that they were all dismayed so that they dropped all their weapons and piteously cried for mercy. [The Scots] took them into their mercy and so thoroughly cleaned them up that not one of them escaped. The earl got information about them, that [some] of their host would come out of the wood-side in the evening and ride [to meet] their victuals.

He thought then of an exploit, causing all his followers deck themselves in the prisoners' clothing, take their pennons with them too, wait till the night was near and then ride toward the host. Some of the [enemy's] great host saw them coming, and thought that these were indeed their victuallers, so they rode towards them dispersed, because they had no fear that these were their foes, and also they were very hungry, so they came higgledy-piggledy. When they were near, the earl and all that were with him in great speed assaulted them with unsheathed weapons, shouting aloud their rallying cries; then they, seeing their foes so suddenly attack them were so fearful that they had no heart to encourage them but went to the host, [while the Scots] gave chase and killed many [so] that all the fields were strewn [with corpses]; more than a thousand dead lay there. They chased them right up to their host, then took their way back. . . .

THE BATTLE OF CONNOR
SEPTEMBER 1315

[The Scots] took counsel then altogether that they would ride to the city [Connor] that very night, so that they should be with all their force between the town and those who were to come [from] outside. They did just as they had planned; they soon came before the town and only half a mile on the road from the city they halted. When the day dawned light, fifty nimble men on hobbies came to a little hill which was only a short distance from the town, and saw Sir Edward's camp; they were astonished at the sight, that so few dared at all undertake such a great enterprise as to come so boldly against all the great chivalry of Ireland to await battle. And so it was, without doubt, for there were gathered against them there, with Richard Clare the Warden, the Butler, with the two earls of Desmond and Kildare, Birmingham, Verdon, and Fitz-Warin, Sir Pascal Florentine who was a knight of Lombardy and was full of chivalry. The Mandevilles were there also, Bissets, Logans and various others; Savages too, and there was also a man called Sir Nicholas Kilkenny. With these lords, there were so many then that for each of the Scotsmen I believe they were five or more. When their scouts had seen the Scottish host like that, they went in haste and told their lords fully how they had come near to [the enemy]; there was no need to seek them afar. When Earl Thomas saw that those men had been on the hill, he took with him a good company on horse, perhaps a hundred in number, and they took their way to the hill. They lay in ambush in a declivity, and in a short time they saw coming riding from the city a company intending to reconnoitre to the hill. [The Scots] were pleased at that, and kept still until [the enemy] came near to them, then in a rush all who were there burst upon them boldly. Seeing those folk come on so suddenly, they were dismayed. Although some of them stayed there to fight stoutly, others took to their heels. In a very short time those who stayed behind were so defeated that they fled altogether on their way. [The Scots] chased them right to the gate, killing a great part of them, then returned to their host.

When those within [the city] saw their men killed like that, and driven home again, they were cast down and in great haste shouted aloud, "To arms!" Then all of them armed themselves and made ready for the battle. They came out, all well equipped, to the battle, banner displayed, prepared to the best of their ability to attack their foes in tough fighting. When Sir Philip Mowbray saw them come out in such good order, he went to Sir Edward Bruce and said, "Sir, it would be a good idea to prepare some deception which will do something to help us in this battle. Our men are few, but they are willing to do more than they can achieve. Therefore I suggest that our carts, without any man or boy, should be drawn up by themselves, so that they look like far more than we [are]. Let us stand our banners before them; yon folk coming out of Connor, when they can see our banners there, will believe for a certainty that we are there, and will ride thither in great haste. Let us come on them from the flank, and we shall have the advantage, for, when they have come to our carriage, they will be impeded and we can lay into them with all our might and do everything we can."

They did exactly what he had ordered. The [men] who came out of Connor addressed themselves towards the banners, quickly striking their horses with spurs, rushing suddenly among [the banners]. The barrels that were there soon impeded them [as they] were riding. Then the earl with his force rode up and attacked closely, [while] Sir Edward, a little nearby, fought so very boldly that many a doomed man fell underfoot; the field soon grew wet with blood. They fought there with such great fierceness, and struck such blows on each other with stick, with stone and with [blow] returned, as each side could land on the other, that it was dreadful to see. They kept up that great engagement, so knight-like on both sides, giving and taking violent blows, that it was past prime before men could see who might have the upper hand. But soon after prime was past the Scotsmen attacked so hard and assaulted them impetuously, as [if] each man was a champion, [so] that all their foes took to flight. None of them was so brave that he dared wait for his fellow, but each fled in their different ways.

The majority fled to the town. Earl Thomas and his force pursued so fiercely with drawn swords, that [they] were all mixed among them and came into the town all together. Then the slaughter was so ghastly that all the streets ran with blood. Those that they overtook [were] all done to death so that there were almost as many dead as on the battlefield. . . .

On the morrow, without delaying, Sir Edward had men go to survey all the victuals of that city. They found such a profusion there of corn, flour, wax and wine, that they were astonished at it; Sir Edward had it all carried to Carrickfergus. Then he and his men went there, pressing the siege very stalwardly until Palm Sunday had passed. Then both sides took a truce until the Tuesday in Easter week, so that they could spend that holy time in penance and prayer. But on the eve of Easter right to the castle, during the night, came fifteen ships from Dublin, fully laden with armed men—I'm pretty sure they numbered four thousand; they entered the castle. Old Sir Thomas Mandeville was captain of that company. They went into the castle secretly for they had managed to spy that many of Sir Edward's men were then scattered in the country. For that reason they meant to sally out in the morning, without delaying longer, and to surprise [the Scots] suddenly, for they believed that they would lie trusting in the truce that they had taken. But I know that dishonesty will always have a bad and unpleasant conclusion.

Sir Edward knew nothing of [all] this, having no thought of betrayal, but despite the truce he did not fail to set watches on the castle; each night he had men watch it carefully, and Neil Fleming watched that night with sixty worthy and bold men. As soon as day grew clear those who were in the castle armed themselves, got ready, then lowered the drawbridge and sallied forth in large numbers. When Neil Fleming saw them, he hastily sent a man to the king and said to those near him, "Now I promise you, men will see who dares to die for the sake of his lord. Now carry yourselves well, for assuredly I will fight against their whole company. By fighting we shall hold them until our master is armed." With those words, they fought; they were far too few, *perfay*, to fight with such a large force. But nonetheless with all their might they laid into [their foes] so boldly that all the enemy were greatly astonished that [the Scots] were all of such courage as if they had no fear of death. But their ruthless enemies attacked so that no valour could prevail. Then they were slain, one and all, so completely that no one escaped. The man who went to the king to warn him about their sally, warned him with great speed.

Sir Edward was commonly called the king of Ireland. When he heard that such a thing was happening, he got his gear in very great haste; there were twelve brave men in his chamber who armed themselves with speed, then went through the middle of the town with his banner. His enemies, who had divided their men into three, were coming very close. Mandeville, with a great company, held his way down right through the town, the rest kept on either side of the town to meet those who were fleeing; they thought that all that they found there would die without ransom, every one. But the game went quite otherwise, for Sir Edward with his banner and his twelve men that I mentioned before, attacked all that force so strongly that it was extraordinary.

For Gib Harper [a minstrel, who will appear again] went in front of him, who was the doughtiest in his deeds then living in his position, made such way with an axe that he felled the first to the ground, and a moment afterwards recognised Mandeville among three by his armour, and struck him such a blow that he fell to the earth at once.

Sir Edward who was nearby him turned him over, and in that very place took his life with a knife. With that Fergus Ardrossan, who was a very courageous knight, attacked with sixty or more men. They pressed their foes so, that they, having seen their lord killed, lost heart and wanted to be back [in the castle]. All the time, as the Scotsmen could be armed, they came to the encounter and laid into their foes so, that they all turned tail, and [the Scots] chased them to the gate. It was a hard fight and bitter struggle there. Sir Edward killed by his own hand there a knight who was called the best and most generous in all Ireland; by surname he was called Mandeville, [but] I can't say what his first name was. His men were pressed so hard that those in the donjon dared neither open the gate nor let down the drawbridge. Sir Edward, I promise, pursued those fleeing to safety there so hard that, *perfay*, of all those who sallied against him that day, not one escaped, [for] they were either taken or slain. For Macnacill then came to the fight with two hundred spear-men, killing all that they could overtake. This Macnacill won four or five of their ships by a trap and killed all the men [on them]. When this fighting came to an end Neil Fleming was still alive. Sir Edward went to see him; his dead followers lay around him all in a heap, on both sides, and he, in mortal pain, [was] about to die. Sir Edward was moved by his [fate] and mourned him deeply, lamenting his great courage and his valour in doughty deeds. He mourned so much that they were astonished, for in the usual way he was not accustomed to lament anything, nor would he listen to men making lamentations. He stood by there until [Neil] had died, then he took him to a holy place and had him buried with ceremony [and] great solemnity. That's how Mandeville sallied forth, but for sure deceit and guile will always come to an ill conclusion, as was obvious from this sally. They came out in time of truce, and in such a [holy] time as Easter day, when God rose to save mankind from the stain of old Adam's sin. For that, great misfortune befell them, that each, as you heard me say, was killed or taken there and those who were in the castle were so alarmed at that time, being unable to see where help could [come from] to relieve them, that they negotiated and shortly thereafter surrendered the castle freely to [Sir Edward], to save their life and limb, and he kept his word to them as was right. He took the castle into his hands, provisioned it well and appointed a good warden to guard it, and he rested there for a time.

We shall speak no more about him now, but we'll go to King Robert, whom we have left long unspoken of. . . .

ROBERT BRUCE JOINS HIS BROTHER IN IRELAND

[Robert Bruce, king of Scotland] took his way to the sea, taking ship at Loch Ryan in Galloway with his whole following; he soon arrived at Carrickfergus. Sir Edward was pleased by his coming, went down to meet him at once, welcoming him with warmth, as he did to all who were with [the king], especially Earl Thomas of Moray, who was his nephew. Then they went to the castle there and had a big feast and festivities. They stayed there for three days enjoying themselves.

King Robert arrived in Ireland in this way, and when he had stayed in Carrickfergus for three days, they consulted [and decided] that with all their men they would hold their way through all Ireland, from one end to the other. Then Sir Edward, the king's brother, rode ahead in the vanguard; the king himself took up the rear, having in his company the worthy Earl Thomas. They took their way southward, soon passing Innermallan. This was in the month of May, when birds sing on each branch, mixing their notes with harmonious sound, because of the softness of that sweet season; leaves sprout on branches, blooms grow brightly beside them and fields are decked with fine-scented flowers of many colours; everything becomes happy and joyful.

When this good king took his way to ride southward, as I said before, the warden at that time, Richard Clare, knew that the king had arrived thus, and knew that he planned to take his way to the south country. He assembled from all Ireland burgesses and chivalry, hobelars and peasantry, until he had nearly forty thousand men. But he still wouldn't undertake to fight in the field with his foes, instead thinking up a stratagem whereby he with all his great company, would lie in ambush in a wood quite secretly beside the road by which their enemies would pass; [he would] allow the van to pass far by and then attack boldly upon the rear with all their men. . . .

Sir Edward rode well ahead with those who were of his company, paying no heed to the rear. When Sir Edward had passed by, Sir Richard Clare in haste sent light yeomen, who could shoot well, to harrass the rear on foot. Two of those who had been sent harrassed them at the side of the wood there shooting among the Scotsmen. The king, who had a good five thousand brave and hardy men with him then, saw those two shooting among them so recklessly and coming so close. He knew very well, without [any] doubt, that they had support close at hand, so he issued an order that no man should be so bold as to gallop to them, but [should] always ride in close order ready for battle, to defend themselves if men sought to attack. "For I'm sure," he said, "that very soon we shall have to cope with more."

But Sir Colin Campbell, who was nearby where those two yeomen were shooting boldly among them, galloped against them at full speed, soon overtaking one of them, [whom] he quickly killed with his spear. The other turned and shot again, killing his horse with one shot. With that the king came hastily, and in his annoyance gave Sir Colin such a bash with a truncheon in his fist, that he slumped on his saddle-bow. The king ordered him to be smartly pulled down, but other lords who were near him, calmed the king somewhat. He said, "The breaking of orders can lead to defeat. Do you think that yon wretches would dare attack so near us in our formation, unless they had support nearby? I know very well, without [any] doubt, that we shall have [much] to do very soon; so let each man look to being prepared."

At that a good thirty and more archers came and so harrassed that they hurt [some] of the king's men. The king then had his archers shoot to drive them back. With that they entered open ground and saw standing, drawn up against them in four divisions, forty thousand. The king said, "Now lords, show who is to be valiant in this fight. On them, without more delay."

They rode so stoutly against them, and attacked so fiercely, that a great part of their foes lay [slain] on the ground at the encounter. There was such a breaking of spears as each [side] rode against the other, that it made a truly great crashing [noise]. Horses came charging there, head to head, so that many fell dead to the ground. As each [man] ran against another many a bold and worthy man was struck down dead to the ground; red blood gushed out of many a wound in such great profusion that the streams ran red with blood. Those who were wrathful and angry struck others so hardily with drawn and sharp weapons, that many a brave man died there. For those who were hardy and brave, fighting face-to-face with their enemies, pushed to be foremost [in the fight]. You could see fierce fighting and a cruel struggle there. I'm sure that such hard fighting was not seen in the whole Irish war; although Sir Edward doubtless had nineteen great victories in less than three years, and in various of those battles he defeated twenty thousand men and more, [their] horse with trappings right to the feet. But at all times he was still [only] one to five when he was least [in numbers]. But in this engagement the king always had eight of his enemies to one, but he bore himself so [well] then that his good deeds and generosity so encouraged all his followers [and] the shakiest was bold. For where he saw the thickest press he rode so hardily against them that he always made space around him.

Earl Thomas the worthy was always close to him, fighting as though he were in a fury, so that, by their great valour, their men took such courage that they would avoid no danger, but exposed themselves [to danger] so stoutly, assaulting them so hardily, that all their foes were terrified. And [the Scots] who perceived well from the bearing [of the Irish] that they were avoiding the fight somewhat, then pushed on with all their might and pressed them, striking so hard that eventually they turned [to flee].

[The Scots], seeing them take to flight, pressed them then with all their might, and slew many as they were fleeing. The king's men gave such chase that every one of them was scattered. Richard of Clare took the way to Dublin in a mighty hurry, with other lords who fled with him. . . .

The king who was so estimable, saw right many slain on the field. He saw one of those who was taken [prisoner] there and was decked out splendidly crying with great tenderness, and asked him why he made such a face. He said to [the king], "Sir, it's not surprising that I'm crying. I see many here [who've] lost their life-blood, the flower of all northern Ireland, [men] who were stoutest of heart and deed, and most feared in a tight corner." The king said, "You're wrong, *perfay*; you've more reason to laugh, because you've escaped death."

When bold Edward Bruce heard that the king had fought like that against so many men, and in his absence, you couldn't see an angrier man. But the good king said then to him that it was his own folly, for he rode so carelessly so far in advance, with no vanguard made to the men behind; for, he said, anyone who wants to ride in the van in war, should never press far out of sight from his rearward, because great danger could arise therefrom. We shall speak no more about this battle.

The king and all those with him rode forwards in better order and closer together than they had done previously. They rode openly through all the land, finding that no-one stood in their way. They even rode before Drogheda and then before Dublin also, but they found no-one to give battle. Then they went southward in the land holding their way right to Limerick, which is the southernmost town to be found in Ireland. They lay there for two or three days, then prepared to travel again. And when they were all ready, the king heard a woman cry. He quickly asked what that was. "It's a laundry-woman, Sir," someone said, "who is taken in childbirth now, and will have to remain behind us here, so she's making that awful noise." The king said, "It would indeed be a pity to leave her at that crisis; for there is no man, I'm sure, who won't have pity on a woman then." He halted the whole army then, and soon had a tent pitched; [he] had her go in hastily and other women to be with her, [and] waited until she had been delivered, then rode forth on his way; and before ever he set forth, he gave orders how she was to be transported. It was a very great kindness that such a king, so mighty, had his men wait in this way, for a mere poor laundry-woman. They took their way northwards again, and thus passed through all Ireland, through Connaught right to Dublin, through all Meath, then Uriel, and Munster and Leinster then wholly through Ulster to Carrickfergus, without a battle, for there was no-one who dared attack them.

Then all the kings of the Irishry came to Sir Edward and did their homage to him, except for one or two. They came to Carrickfergus again—on all that way there was no battle unless there were any skirmishes not to be spoken of here. Then every one of the Irish kings went home to their own parts, undertaking to be obedient in all things to the bidding of Sir Edward, whom they called their king. He was well set now, [and] in a good way, to conquer the land altogether, for he had on his side the Irish and Ulster, and was so far on with his war that he had passed through all Ireland from end to end, by his own strength.

If he could have controlled himself by discretion, and not been too self-indulgent but governed his actions with moderation, it was doubtless very probable that he could have conquered the whole land of Ireland, every bit. But his excessive arrogance and stubbornness, which was more than hardy, distorted his resolve, *perfay*, as I shall tell you afterwards. . . .

THE BATTLE OF FAUGHART
OCTOBER 14, 1318

But [Edward], always irritated by inaction, always wanting to be busy, a day before the arrival of those who had been sent him by the king, took his way to go southwards, despite all those who were with him. For he had in that land no more than two thousand men, I believe, apart from the kings of the Irish who rode with him in great contingents. He took the way toward Dundalk, and when Richard Clare heard news that he was coming with so small a following, he gathered all the armed men from all Ireland that he could, so that he had there with him then twenty thousand horse with trappings, apart from those [men] who were on foot, and held northwards on his way. When Sir Edward heard tell that they had come near to him, he sent scouts to see him—they were Soulis, the Steward and also Sir Philip Mowbray. When they had seen them coming they went back to make their report, saying that they were indeed very numerous.

Quickly Sir Edward answered them saying that he would fight that day, [even] though they were treble or quadruple [the number]. Sir John Stewart said, "Now, I advise you, don't fight in such a hurry. Men say my brother is coming nearby with fifteen thousand men; if they were combined with you, you could stay to fight more confidently." Sir Edward glowered angrily and said swiftly to Soulis, "What do you say?" "Sir," he said, "*perfay*, I agree with what my companion said." Then he spoke to Sir Philip. "Sir," said he, "as God sees me, I think it no folly to wait for your men, hurrying to ride [to us]. For we are few and our foes are many; God may deal our fates very well, but it would be remarkable if our force could overcome so many in battle." Then with great anger, "Alas," [Edward] said, "I never thought to hear that from you! Now let whoever wants to, help, but rest assured [that] I will fight, today, without more delay. Let no man say while I'm alive that superior numbers would make me flee! God forbid that anyone should blame us for defending our noble name." "Well, let it be so," said they. "We shall take whatever God sends."

When the kings of the Irish heard it said, and knew for a fact, that their king meant to fight with so few against a force of such great power, they came to him very quickly and advised him gently to wait for his men, [while] they would keep their enemies busy all that day, and one the morrow also, with the raids they would make. But their advice had no effect; whatever came, he would have battle. When they saw he was so determined to fight, they said, "You may well go to fight with yon great company; but we discharge ourselves completely—none of us will stand to fight. So don't rely on our strength, for our tactics are [those] of this land, to follow and to fight while fleeing, and not to stand in open encounter until one side is defeated." He said, "Since that is your custom, I ask no more of you than this, that is, that you and your followers should be arrayed all together, standing a distance away, without leaving, and see our fight to the end." They said that they would indeed do so, and then went toward their men who numbered nearly forty thousand.

Edward, with those who were with him, who weren't fully two thousand, drew themselves up to stand stalwartly against forty thousand and more. That day Sir Edward would not wear his coat of arms; but Gib Harper, whom men held also [to be] without an equal in his position, on that day wore all Sir Edward's apparel. They waited for the fight in this way, their enemies came in great haste all ready to engage [them] and they met them boldly.

To tell the truth they were so few that they were pushed back by their enemies, [while] those who struggled most to stand [firm] were killed dead, and the remainder fled to the Irish for help. Sir Edward, [a man] of such courage, was dead, as were John Stewart and John Soules too, and others also of their company. They were so quickly defeated that few were killed in the field, for the rest took their ways to the Irish kings, who were there and hovering in one whole force. John Thomasson who was leader of [the men] of Carrick who were there when he saw the defeat, withdrew to an Irish king of his acquaintance, who received him in fidelity. When John had come to that king, he saw led from the fighting the brave Sir Philip Mowbray, who had been knocked senseless in the fight. He was led by the arms by two men, upon the causeway that was between them and the town, [and] stretched in a long straight line.

They held their way toward the town, and when they were half-way along the causeway, Sir Philip recovered from his dizziness and saw that he had been taken and was led by the two like that. He soon threw one away from himself, and then swiftly the other; then he drew his sword swiftly and took his way to the fight along the causeway, which was then filled in great numbers with men going to the town. On meeting them, he made them such payment where he went, that he caused a good hundred men [to] leave the causeway, despite their [companions]. As John Thomasson, who saw all his achievement, said truthfully, he went straight towards the battle.

John Thomasson, who well raised that they had been completely defeated, shouted to him as quickly as possible, and said, "Come here, none of them is alive, for they are all dead." Then [Mowbray] stood still for a while and saw that they had all been deprived of life, then went close toward [Thomasson]. This John then behaved so sensibly that all those who then fled thither, although they lost [some] of their gear, came sound and safe to Carrickfergus. Those who were at the fighting looked for Sir Edward to get his head among the folk who lay there dead, and found Gib Harper in his gear; because his arms were so noble, they struck off his head, then had it salted in a box and sent it to England as a present to

King Edward. They believed that it was Sir Edward's but they were deceived about the head by the armour, which was splendid, although Sir Edward died there.

This is how these noble men were lost there through stubbornness, a sin and a great sorrow.

IRELAND DURING THE BRUCE INVASION

FROM HOLINSHED'S CHRONICLES OF IRELAND

Raphael Holinshed (died c. 1580) was more of an English publisher and book packager than an author. He is best remembered not for the Chronicles of England, Scotland, and Ireland that bear his name, but for one of his readers. Shakespeare, it is commonly thought, mined and adapted the plots of many of his historical plays from Holinshed.

Most of his Irish chronicles were simply a translation of various monastery annals, although passages in the first edition offended members of Queen Elizabeth's court and the book was withdrawn and reissued in a censored version. The pages dealing with Edward Bruce do not present a tidy, linear record of what happened. Their focus is often eccentric, as in the curious incident on the aftermath of the disastrous battle outside Athenry. (A knight named O'Kelly tries to lure away the squire of an enemy.) But as a panorama the book does present a memorable portrait of a land gripped by chaos. The Bruces are described much like the Vikings of the past, while rival lords in the west take advantage of the confusion to war against each other. And all the while the land is being gripped by a famine (a great "dearth" in the words of the chronicler) that had spread across Europe and made its way to the island. There is even a report of cannibalism in which some starving soldiers are said to be reduced to "eating leather and eight Scots."

IN THE NINTH YEARE OF KING EDWARDS reigne [Edward II of England], Edward Bruce, brother to Robert Bruce king of Scots, entered the north part of Ireland with six thousand men. There were with him diverse capteins of high renowne among the Scotish nation of whome the chiefe were these: the earles of Murrie and Mentith, the lord John Steward, the lord John Campbell, the lord Thomas Randolfe, Fergus de Andressan, John Wood, and John Bisset. They landed near to Cragfergus in Ulster the five & twentieth of May, and joining with the Irish, conquered the earledome of Ulster, and gave the English there diverse great overthrowes,

213

tooke the towne of Dundalke, spoiled & burnt it, with a great part of Urgile: they burnt churches & abbeies, with the people whom they found in the same, sparing neither man, woman nor child. Then was the lord Edmund Butler chosen lord justice, who made the earle of Ulster and the Giraldines friends, and reconciled himselfe with sir John Mandevill, thus seeking to preserve the residue of the realme which Edward Bruce meant wholie to conquer, having caused himselfe to be crowned king of Ireland. The lord justice assembled a great power out of Mounster, and Leinster, and other parts thereabouts, and the earle of Ulster with another armie came unto him near unto Dundalke, where they consulted togither how to deale in defending the countrie against the enimies: but hearing the Scots were withdrawne backe, the earle of Ulster folowed them, and fighting with them at Coiners, he lost the field.

There were manie slaine on both parts, and William de Burgh the earls brother, sir John Mandevill, and sir Alane Fitzalane were taken prisoners. Herewith the Irish of Connagh and Meth began foorthwith to rebell against the Englishmen, and burnt the castell of Athlon and Randon. And the Bruce comming forward burnt Kenlis in Meth, and Granard, also Finnagh, and Newcastell, and kept his Christmas at Loghsudie, From thense he went through the countrie unto Rathimegan and Kildare, and to the parties about Tristeldermot and Athie, then to Raban, Sketlier, & near to Ardskoll in Leinster: where the lord justice Butler, the lord John Fitzthomas, the lord Arnold Powre, and other lords and gentlemen of Leinster and Mounster came to incounter the Bruce: but through discord that rose among them, they left the field unto the enimies, sir William Pendergast knight, and Heimond le Grace a right valiant esquier were slaine there. And on the Scotish side sir Fergus Andressan and sir Walter Murreie, with diverse other that were buried in the church of the friers preachers at Athie.

After this the Bruce in his returne towards Meth burnt the castell of Leie, and so passed foorth till hee came to Kenlis in Meth. In which meane time Roger lord Mortimer, trusting to win himselfe fame if he might overthrow the enimies, called forth fifteene thousand men, and understanding that the Scots were come to Kenlis, made thitherwards, and there incountering with them, was put to the woorse, his men (as was supposed) wilfullie shrinking from him, as those that bare him hollow hearts. With the newes of this overthrow, upstart Irish of Mounster, with fire and sword wasted all from Arclow to Leix. With them coped the lord justice, and made of them a great slaughter, fourescore of their heads were sent to the castell of Dublin.

In time of these troubles and wars in Ireland by the invasion thus of the Scots, certeine Irish lords, faith-full men and true subjects to the king of England, did not onelie promise to continue in the loyal obeisance towards him, being their sovereigne prince; but also for more assurance delivered hostages to be kept within the castell of Dublin. The names of which lords that were so contented to assure their allegiance were these, John Fitzthomas lord of Offalie, Richard de Clare, Morice Fitzthomas, Thomas Fitzjohn le Power baron of Donoille, Arnold le Power, Morice de Rochford, David de la Roch, and Miles de la Roch. These and diverse other resisted with all their might

The Battle of Athenry in 1316 is commemorated in this town seal. The severed heads are thought to represent the vanquished chieftains of the Connacht.

and maine the injurious attempts of the Scots, although the Scots had drawne to their side the most part of the wild Irish, and no small number also of the English Irish, as well lords, as others of meaner calling: so that the countrie was miserablie afflicted, what by the Scots on the one part, and the Irish rebels on the other, which rebels notwithstanding were over-throwne in diverse particular conflicts.

But yet to the further scattering of the English forces in Ireland, there rose four princes of Connagh, but the Burghes and Birminghams discom-fited them, and slew eleven thousand of them beside Athenrie. Amongst other were slaine in this battell Fedelmicus, Oconhur king of Connagh, Okellie, and diverse other great lords and capteins of Connagh and Meth. The lord Richard Birmingham had an esquier that belonged to him called John Husseie, who by the commandement of his maister went foorth to take view of the dead bodies and to bring him word whether Okellie his mortall foe were slaine among the residue. Husseie comming into the field with one man to turne up and survey the dead carcases, was streight espied by Okellie, that lay lurking in a brake bush thereby, who having had good proof of Husseie's valor before that time, longed sore to train him from his capteine, and presuming now upon his good oportunitie, dis-closed himselfe, not doubting, but either to win him with courteous per-suasions, or by force to work his will of him, and so comming to him said: "Husseie, thou seest that I am at all points armed, & have my esquire here likewise furnished with armour & weapon readie at mine elbow; thou art naked [unarmed] with thy page, a yoongling, & not to be accounted of:

so that if I loved thee not, and meant to spare thee for thine own sake, I might now doo with thee what I would, and slay thee for thy master's sake. But come & serve me upon this request here made to thee, and I promise thee by St. Patrick's staff to make thee a lord in Connagh, of more possessions than thy master hath in Ireland." When these words might were said, his own man (a great stout lubber) began to reprove him of folie, for not consenting to so large an offer, which was assured with an oath.

Now had Husseie three enimies, and first therefore turning to his knave, he dispatched him. Next he raught unto Okellies esquier such a knock under the pit of the ear, that down he came to the ground and there he lay. Thirdly, he laid so about him, that before any help could be looked for, he had also slain Okellie, and perceiving the esquire to be but astonied he recovered him, and holpe him up again, and after he was somewhat come to himself, he forced him upon a trunchion, to bear his lords head into the high towne before him, who did so; and Husseie presented it to Birmingham, who after the circumstances declared, he dubbed Husseie knight, advancing him to many preferments. The successors of that familie afterwards were barons of Galtrim.

Sir Thomas Mandevill and others in this meane while made oftentimes enterprises against the Scots, and slew diverse of them in sundrie conflicts. But howsoever it chanced, we find recorded by Henrie Marlburrow, that either the said sir Thomas Mandevill (that thus valiantlie behaved himselfe against the Scots) or some other bearing the same name, and his brother also called John Mandevill were both slain shortlie after at Downe, upon their comming foorth of England, by the Scots that were readie there to assaile them.

Thus may we see, that those lords and knights, which had given pledges for their loyaltie to the king of England, sought by all ways and meanes how to beat back the enimies: which they might have done with more ease if the Irish had not assisted the Scots, and presuming of their aid, rebelled in sundrie parts of the countrie; who neverthelesse were oftentimes well chastised for their disloyal dealings, as partlie we have touched; although we omit diverse small overthrowes and other particular matters, since otherwise we should increase this booke further than our first purposed intent would permit.

Whilest the Scots were thus holden up in Ireland, that they could not in all things work their wiles, Robert le Bruce king of Scots came over himselfe, landed at Cragfergus to the aid of his brother, whose souldiors most wickedlie entered into churches, spoiling and defacing the same of all such toomes, monuments, plate, cones, & other ornaments which they found and might lay hands upon.

The castell of Cragfergus, after it had been strictly besieged a long time, was surrendred to the Scots, by them that had kept it, till they for want of other vittels were driven to eat leather and eight Scots (as some write) which they had taken prisoners. . . .

The fourteenth of September, Conhor Mac Kele, & five hundred Irishmen were slain by the lord Wiliam de Burgh, and lord Richard Birmingham in Connagh. Also on the Monday after the feast of All saints, John Loggan and sir Hugh Bisset slew a great number of Scots, among the which were one hundred with double armors, and two hundred with single armors: so that of their men of armes there died three hundred beside footemen.

The fifteenth of November chanced a great tempest of wind and rain; which threw down manie houses, with the steeple of the Trinitie church in Dublin, and did much other hurt both by land and water. On the fifth of December, sir Alane Steward that had been taken prisoner in Ulster by John Loggan, and sir John Sandale, was brought to the castell of Dublin. After Canlemas, the Lacies came to Dublin, & procured an inquest to be impanelled to inquire of their demeanor, for that they were accused to have procured the Scots to come into Ireland: but by that inquest they were discharged, and therewith took an oath to keep the kings peace, and to destroy the Scots to the uttermost of their power. In the beginning of Lent, the Scots came in secret unto Slane, with twentie thousand armed men: and with them came the armie of Ulster, destroieng all the countrie before them. Moreover, on Monday before the feat of S. Matthias the apostle, the earle of Ulster living in the abbeie of S. Marie, near to Dublin, Robert Notingham maior of that citie, with the communaltie of the same went thither, took the earle, and put him in prison within the castell of Dublin, slew seven of his men, and spoiled the abbeie.

The same week, Edward Bruce marched towards Dublin, but herewith, turning to the castell of Knoke, he entred the same, and took Hugh Tirrell the lord thereof, togither with his wife, and ransomed them for a sum of monie. The citizens of Dublin burnt all their suburbs for fear of a siege, and made the best purveyance they could to defend their citie, if the Bruce had come to have besieged them: but he turning another way, went unto the town of Naas, and was guided thither by the Lacies, contrary to their oath. From thense he passed unto Tristeldermot, and so to Baliganam, and to Callan, at length he came to Limerike, and there remained till after Easter. They of Ulster sent to the lord justice lamentable informations of such crueltie as the enimies practised in those parts, beseeching him to take some order for their relief in that their so miserable estate. The lord justice delivered to them the kings power with his standard, wherewith under pretense to expell the Scots, they got up in armor, and ranging through the countrie, did more vexe and molest the subjects than did the strangers. The Scots proceeded and spoiled Cashels, & wheresoever they lighted upon the Butlers lands, they burnt and spoiled them unmercifully.

In this meanwhile had the lord justice and Thomas Fitzjohn earle of Kildare, Richard de Clare, and Arnold le Powre baron of Donnoill levied an armie of thirty thousand men, readie to go against the enimies, and to give them battell, but no good was doone. For about the same time the lord Roger Mortimer was sent into Ireland as lord justice and landing at Yoghall, wrote his letters unto the lord Butler, & to the other capteins, willing them not to fight till he came with such power as he had brought over with him. Whereof the Bruce being warned, retired first towards Kildare. But yet after this he came within four miles of Trim, where he lay in a wood, and lost manie of his men through famine, and so at length about the beginning of May he returned into Ulster.

The lord Edmund Butler made great slaughter of the Irish near to Tristledermot, and likewise at Balithan he had a good hand of Omorch, and slew manie of his men. The lord Mortimer pacified the displeasure and variance betwixt Richard earle of Ulster, and the nobles that had put the said earle under safe keeping within the castell of Dublin, accusing him of certain riots committed to the prejudice and loss of the kings subjects, whereby the Scots increased in strength and courage, whose spoiling of the countrie caused such horrible scarsitie in Ulster, that the soldiors which the year before abused the kings authoritie, to provide themselves of over-fine diet, surfetted with flesh and *Aqua vitœ* all the Lent long, prolled and pilled insatiable wheresoever they came without need, and without regard of the poor people, whose only provision they devoured. These people now living in slaverie under the Bruce, starved for hunger, having first experienced manie lamentable shifts, even to the eating of dead carcasses. . . .

A great dearth this yeere afflicted the Irish people: for a measure of wheat called a chronecke was sold at four and twentie shillings, & a chronecke of oats at sixteene shillings, and all other vittels likewise were sold according to the same [high] rate; for all the whole countrie was sore wasted by the Scots and them of Ulster, insomuch that no small number of people perished through famine.

About the feast of Pentecost the lord justice Mortimer took his journey towards Drogheda, and sent to the Lacies, commanding them to come unto him, but they refused so to do. Whereupon he sent sir Hugh Crofts unto them, to talk with them about some agreement of peace: but they slew the messenger, for whom great lamentation was made, for that he was reputed & known to be a right woorthie knight. The lord justice sore offended herewith, gathereth an armie & goeth against the Lacies, whom he chased out of Connagh, so that Hugh Lacie withdrew to Ulster, & there joined himself with Edward Bruce. Whereupon, on the Thursday next before the feast of saint Margaret, the said Hugh Lacie and also Walter Lacie were proclamed traitors. This year passed very troublesome unto the whole realm of Ireland, as well through slaughter betwixt the enimies one to another, as by dearth and other misfortunes. Hugh Canon the kings justice of his bench was slain by Andrew Birmingham betwixt the town of Naas and castell Marten. Also in the feast of the purification, the popes bulles were published, whereby Alexander Bignor was consecrated archbishop of Dublin. About the same time was great slaughter made of Irishmen, through a quarrell betwixt two great lords in Connagh: so that there died in fight to the number of four thousand men on both parties. . . .

Richard de Clare with four knights . . . and others (to the number of four score persons) were slain by Obren and Mac Arthie. It was said that the enimies in despite caused the lord Richards bodie to be cut in pieces, so to satisfie their malicious stomachs; but the same pieces were yet afterwards buried in the church of the friers minors at Limerike. Also before the lord Mortimers returne into England, John Lacie was carried to Trim, where he was arreigned and adjudged to be pressed to death, and so he died in prison.

Immediatlie upon his arrival, the lord John Birmingham being generall of the field, and having with him diverse capteins of worthie fame . . . led forth the kings power, to the number of one thousand three hundred foure and twentie able men against Edward Bruce, who being accompanied with the lord Philip Mowbraie, the lord Walter de Soules, the lord Alaine Steward, with his three brethren, sir Walter, and sir Hugh, sir Robert, and sir Aimerie Lacies, and others, was incamped not past two miles from Dundalke with three thousand men, there abiding the Englishmen, to fight with them if they came forward: which they did with all convenient speed, being as desirous to give battell as the Scots were to receive it.

The primat of Armagh personallie accompanieng the English power, & blessing their enterprise, gave them such comfortable exhortation, as he thought served the time before they began to incounter. And herewith [at Faughart] buckling togither, at length the Scots fullie and wholie were vanquished, and two thousand of them slain, togither with their capteine Edward Bruce. Maupas that pressed into the throng to incounter with Bruce hand to hand, was found in the search dead aloft upon the slaine bodie of Bruce. The victorie thus obteined upon saint Calixtus day, made an end of the Scotish kingdom in Ireland, & lord Birmingham sending the head of Bruce into England, or as Marlburrow hath, being the messenger himselfe, presented it to king Edward, who in recompense gave to him and his heires male the earledome of Louth, and the baronie of Ardich and Athenrie to him and his heirs generall for ever. Shortlie after sir Richard de Clare with four other knights of name, and manie other men of war were slaine in Thomond.

VIII.

WARFARE

IN THE KINGDOM

OF THOMOND

INTRODUCTION

A S WE SAW IN *HOLINSHED'S CHRONICLES*, the Bruce invasion provided cover for a number of small local wars that had little or nothing to do with the Scots. One of the most decisive broke out in Brian Boru's old kingdom of Thomond in 1318.

For generations two factions of the O'Brien family had been battling each other over the crown. In 1318, the king of Thomond was Murtough, a descendant of Thurlough O'Brien, and his challenger was Mahon, from the Brian O'Brien side of the family, who had a powerful ally in Richard de Clare. De Clare, himself a descendant of the invader Strongbow, ruled—at least in theory—most of the west of Ireland from Limerick or his castle at Bunratty. In practice, however, the English respected the sovereignty of Thomond and remained outside its borders. De Clare's alliance with Mahon O'Brien, however, gave him an excuse to invade the kingdom. The two sides—Murtough's Irish and de Clare's "pale Englishmen," as they are frequently called in the text—met in battle in May 1318, at Dysert O'Dea near the present town of Ennis in County Clare.

Although horses are mentioned in accounts of the battle, it was a battle fought on foot that began with the Irish typically setting up an ambush that, this time, turned into a pitched battle. A curious thing about this particular fight is that some of the Irish seem to have worn armor and in its final moments—when fresh Irish troops arrived to save the day for Murtough—they looked so much like de Clare's men that there was some confusion as to what side they were on.

Another distinctive aspect of this battle is that the Irish clearly won it. Almost six hundred years later, writing about the 1916 Easter Week uprising then in progress, James Stephens, a Dubliner with no love for the English, noted that for the Irish fighting well was more important than winning. He quotes, "'They went forth always to the battle; and they always fell.'" And he adds, "Indeed, the history of the Irish race is in that phrase." But Dysert O'Dea was an undisputed win for the Irish, and for centuries to come the English left Thomond alone as a place for the O'Briens to rule and squabble over. Not until the early years of Hugh O'Neill's rebellion at the end of the sixteenth century would there be another such clear-cut victory. Ironically, by then most of the O'Briens would become allies of the English against their fellow Irishmen.

THE TRIUMPHS OF THURLOUGH
THE BATTLE OF DYSERT O'DEA

The Triumphs of Thurlough (Catthreim Thoirdhealbhaigh) *was written late in the fourteen century, probably by John mac Rory MacGrath, and it contains the only detailed account of the Battle of Dysert O'Dea. It was, of course, a propaganda piece, promoting the cause of the Thurlough faction of the O'Briens, but it is full of such exact bits of information (such as how an ambush is set up) that it is probably based on earlier documents. It says something about the early rise of Irish nationalism that the fiercest verbal attacks are not on rival O'Briens but on the English, who, in a passage that precedes the account of the battle, are called an "abominable, perverse English gang, cruel and insatiable, over-bearing, surly, sullen, fully of spite malevolence and ill design." Never, except by "bravery" and "war" will the Irish achieve "freedom or truce, peace or goodfellowship."*

Besides battlefield tactics and diplomatic maneuvers, this excerpt includes one of the best prophesying hags in early Irish literature. Readers should also watch for how cattle are used. The account begins with Murtough O'Brien's men capturing all of Mahon's livestock in an effort to drive him out of Thomond, while cattle later become useful in luring an enemy into a trap. In keeping track of who is on which side, remember that Mahon O'Brien (both names are always used), his sons, and Robert de Clare are called the English, Galls, or foreigners. Murtough (usually called simply O'Brien or Thomond), Mac Conmara, and the O'Deas are the Irish or the Gaels.

SINCE APPARENTLY WAR THEY must have, they [the men of Murtough O'Brien] would harry and banish Mahon O'Brien so that he should not be in their midst, and de Clare on their outer side, to vex them with hostilities. For to elude their enemies and to provide against them on one hand alone, seemed easier than it would be with some of them in their own bosom.

At early morn and in the one day, rigorously, unsparingly, with all circumstance of hostile fury and resentment, from the Leap to S. Mac

Duach's church they made the intended creachs [raids]. So efficiently and skilfully they congregated flocks and herds, that whether of single horses or of whole studs, of kine by the head or kine in frightened droves, of swine, of small cattle few or many, of sheep, of plough-teams, of wolfdogs or of hounds in packs, of "agriculture" [implements and produce], of gear and goods of value, of raiment and of arms, they left not a jot but speedily and completely they swept clean and forcibly brought away. . . .

It came to pass now, that within the city of Limerick Ireland's principal barons appointed a general meeting, having for its purpose a composition of some sort between O'Brien and the gentlemen of Thomond of the one part, de Clare and Mahon O'Brien of the other. All concerned, both Gall and Gael, answered the tryst; Murtough O'Brien and Mac Conmara, with many others of degree, coming (under protection of the chief Butler and of sir Maurice, joined with Thomas and sir William Oge Burke) with proposals of redress to de Clare and Mahon, in the matter of preyings done on the latter.

They propounded their terms, with guarantee of the barons that they should have effect; but de Clare refused the security and insisted rather that they should submit themselves to his honour, that is to say: their tender of reparation to be duly carried out at maturity, or [failing that] themselves to lie [in his hands] as pledges of fulfilment. The other side, as well knowing what measure of grace would be theirs if they gave in to de Clare, repelled such settlement. . . .

Of the barons under whose protection they were, Thomond now prayed that they would convoy them safe [out of de Clare's immediate grasp]. They did so, coming with them as far as the head of Thomond-bridge, where the barons told them that injustice was done them, and added: "it just happens well for you that at this departing on your journey both tide and moon at the full await you." The Butler went on: "I beseech you injure not this night aught that is de Clare's, but suffer him to use [this present favourable] opportunity of the sea to gain Bunratty; for he himself says that, at all times when it may be his chance personally to oppose you, no whit he cares for your war. Wherefore be ye not again cozened in the same quarter; so shall ye fare well." They took leave one of the other, and O'Brien's party sought the place in which their horses their riding-gear and horseboys expected them.

With spirits bent on action, yet prudently contained, roundly they coasted along the Cratalachs' ["Cratloes"] thick-sheltering fruitful-branched mast-abounding woods; entered into Hy-Amrid of the high hills with pleasant levels, clear good horse-paths and salmon-yielding rivers; past hazel-woody Ballymulcashel towards the much-resorted hard-flagged strath of Cullane, with its tracks among the rocks and eminences of pleasant prospect; on to *Tulach na nespoc* ["hill of bishops"] sanctified by bell and precious Mass, by relics gold-enshrined, by rare piety and notable miracles. In shelter of which famous church that night they lay, and on the irachts enjoined to keep good watch and ward in their "gaps of danger" [at their vulnerable points], at the common border-fords, and to guard the ways; to be alert and vigilant, ready to meet all alarms assaults and sudden war. On the extreme verge of demarcation [between de Clare and him] O'Brien pitched a standing camp to hold that position. With a strong body of horse Mac Conmara penetrated to Bunratty of the wide roads, oared galleys and safe harbour, where past and close to the town's outskirts he drove a trifling stealth of cattle, sheep and horses; and de Clare pursued, because he thought that Mac Conmara would be found following close in the wake of the prey, whereby opportunity might be had to detain him; and that day he had it too, had his own numbers but been sufficient.

Concerning Mahon O'Brien's two sons: out of Connacht by night they came with a troop of horsemen and rode through Thomond to Bunratty, to speak with de Clare. . . .

Concerning O'Brien and the men of Thomond: the aforesaid night was the same during which they set themselves in motion to execute a creach on de Clare, who [so soon as he was advised that they stirred] determined himself to go in pursuit and to effect their detention.

The cows and the families that tended them [the entire contemplated prey in fact] lay in Maethal, where precisely Mahon O'Brien's sons had left their horses and horseboys; and there it was that O'Brien appointed his men to lie low: along the very way by which he supposed that de Clare would come [on his avenging progress, and so walk fair] in among the ambushed parties. In the morning he covered Maethal with squads of marauders [apparently] rashly daring, and ostentatious with flying colours, who to the baron's contumely, by main force yet without a blow stricken, pillaged and gutted the place of its horses, its stock of all other kinds, its plenishing and wealth.

When de Clare beheld these preys boldly before his face lumped together and, without zig-zag or twist or wavering without offer to evade, without let or hindrance driven straight along the road; in his heart he understood that it was on behalf of Thomond's main host and Murtough O'Brien the chief that this overweening attack so was pushed home on him. For which reason he suffered not a man of his own pursuing force to press or follow the raiders, nor with the children of Cas to content for this ample haul that they had made.

O'Brien marking that de Clare persevered not in the quest he made his men to rise out of the lurking watch that they had kept; and when the baron saw the ranks start up out of their hiding places, the conduct that he had observed pleased him vastly. Well for him who had shunned those young men's weaponed vigour, and refrained from meddling with them!

As from the English aforesaid they had had neither fight nor other hardship, jovianly and prosperously they followed the preys, droves and herds, into Echtge's woody deep-valleyed white-rocked lofty-hilled pap-peaked fastnesses, and there divided their creachs and other booty. A good thing and an opportune too they judged it that they had hold of Mahon O'Brien's sons' horsemen: horsemen of them that came for de Clare to go and meet their enemies' flittings, for ever meddling and making to their mischief, and fomenting constant war upon them.

De Clare now despatched messengers to sir William Oge Burke to bid him protect Mahon O'Brien and Kineldunal with their irachts and flittings [baggage], and convey them to Kilnasula's causeway, whither he with his full numbers would repair to meet them. [On arrival of the envoy] Mac William mustered heavily, and on that day [of his start] came as far as Ardrahen; de Clare in the same day marching to the venerable fane of Quin. That night he abode in S. Finian's church, and on the morrow's morn early advanced into grassy apple-fruitful *fiadh uachtarach*; thence up to the glittering river and rushing water of Curra-Neill, not fairly practicable for horses. But as they were for crossing the cool broad pools, boiling eddies, swelling volume and clear calm backwaters of huge-fish-containing Fergus, there they saw await them a horrific beldam [hag], that in the current washed and with huge exertion dipped old armours, satin vestments, goldthreaded jacks of price, smooth finetextured silken shirts, handsome oversea-fashioned wares, with other garments and strippings of a host; so that of all the river below her was made a broo of blood and water, while from above the sunlighted glaucous spoutings, in gurgling torrent of pure water, over smooth sand rolled down to her.

From the frightful being's fists [as she wrang those fabrics], violently the red blood squirted and fell, dyeing the river over. De Clare with his cavalry and the rest took heed to her fashion and behaviour, to the work she had in hand and to the change of the fair proud river's hue; then to the gentlemen of the Gael that for the nonce were with him, he signified that, in a tongue by vehicle of which she might [be made to] comprehend, this strange and hideous creature they should question as to whose gear and armour was that which she washed. [This being done] she answered them, and to this effect:—

"Armour, raiment and other strippings of de Clare with this sons, chief barons, knights, and young lads of gentle birth, with his squires of high degree, his oversea-men and his noble Gael, are these which now I wash. Blood and gore of their hurts and wounds and bodies are these crimson rills which thou [that speakest with me] seest carried away with this rushing stream. Haughty as ye go on this your errand, your immolation all together (some few excepted) is very near to you."

He that conversed with her asked her what was her name, her business and original habitation, and she said: "I am 'the Water-doleful,' that in this land's hill-dwellings often sojourn, but in my origin I am of Hell's tuatha; and to invite you all I am come now, for but a little while and we [you and I] shall be denizens of one country."

At this point de Clare enquired: "what is yon weird thing's message?" and her fellow in the dialogue replied: "in melancholy grumbling wise, and with discordant voice, she makes for us ill-omened presage and evil prophecy on this course we run. But for the very reason that she is fallen in our way, the rather should we infer that all good luck attends us; inasmuch as we may tell that 'tis as a wellwisher to clan-Turlough-More she comes to frustrate us of this expedition."

"It is not she that has it in her," said de Clare, "neither can that she utters work us harm, because a witch cannot be truthful; and she shall not prevail to hinder us but that this time we overrun all Thomond and make her tributary to us. For Murtough O'Brien has not means to encounter even ourselves; whereas the Burkes' host is on the way to act with us and for ever to hunt Murtough away out of the country." With that they pass on; but of that colloquy with the hag it resulted that for the night they needs must halt in the open ground of Ruane's grassgrown hollow cahers.

Concerning the judicious Conor O'Dea: his scouts and sentinels come in with intelligence of de Clare's being on his way towards him. To O'Hechir (Lochlainn) therefore, and to O'Conor (Felim), hastily he sends to show them the baron's journey and to pray them come with their irachts in full force, and without delay, to meet the same; to the end that of de Clare (if to such pass it came) they collectively should have terms of peace all the more favourable for the fact that the individual means of each would be found ranked on the same side [so that he could not hope to use them one against the other as his wont was]. Moreover, to de Clare he commissioned O'Grifa (Thomas mac Urhilly) to offer him conditions and tribute.

De Clare's answer was that, at this time of asking, nor peace nor satisfaction whatsoever would he grant, whether to him [O'Dea] or to any other whom he held to live in inveterate enmity to him, as always they had been with his friends before him.

Which bad news having reached O'Dea (Conor), out of all quarters he calls in his people, discloses to them de Clare's reply; hurriedly they debate of this quandary, and that which they hit off and agreed upon was: to ambush the great bulk of their good men well to the rear, out of sight of de Clare's army; the remnant to hold the "fighting ford" [that which was to be the pivot of the battle] and to protect their preys until Felim O'Conor's and Lochlainn O'Hechir's advent to relieve them. To accelerate those captains, again he sends them despatches bearing de Clare's answer to his overtures.

Let us return to the English leader: as morning broke, he wondered at the stillness of the country round about, just as though every one had been at peace with him. He made of his force three divisions to waste the land in all directions, to kill their women and their "silly [little] boys": one he detailed to pass by Tulach-O'Dea and westwards on to Rath; another to follow the Fergus through Kinelcualachta down to Magowna; while as straight as might be, he with the notables of his host held a due-west course for Disert, where at that time O'Dea's residence was, to sack it. When they were come thither, they saw a well ordered detachment of horse and foot that diligently conveyed a heavy prey across the stream westwards; whereupon universally that dense mass of de Clare's follows them, and by the English a good share of the rearmost chase are killed before they could win over the ford. Withal, boldly O'Dea turns to hold the ford against the enemy, so that, ere long, it had been hard to count them that on either side were slain.

When de Clare made out that it was by that small number the ford so stiffly was held against him, in furious temper he urging on his troops put himself at their head. At sight of the baron in person advancing on them, O'Dea's handful began "to fight and back" [fight on the retreat] towards the ford at which, and close to hand, the ambush lay. The English continue to follow them hard and massacre them, so that along with de Clare a large body of his men impetuously cross the ford westwards.

Now for the ambush: smartly and boldly they stand up; and while one party of them independently goes to help hold the ford against the heavy shock of the enemy's main corps [which as yet was not come over], the lesser section joins the chase in lashing and smiting de Clare and company insomuch that, before the overwhelming strength of his reserves could succour him, the O'Deas killed both himself and every man that he had with him. Howbeit, those Gael (so many of them as lived) were forced to refuge in a neighbouring wood; and there their assailants "make of themselves a battle-hedge" to surround them.

But over the hill of Scule, out of the west, here comes red-sworded Felim O'Conor; in whom as in his merry men all, when they were certified of the many slain, their spirit was magnified and without roundabout or digression he presses on until he is in the thick of it. For the O'Deas, he hacked and rent out a passage, a high road, by which to come out of the wood to join him; and they now, all being of a side, fell to lacerating of their eternal enemies and to fending for themselves, de Clare's forces all the time {after abandoning of their preys and enormous plunder, marching up compact and crowded and coming on the field). Both parties, Gall and Gael, mowed down and mishandled each other: some diving into and rigidly keeping up the fray and "setting foot to fulcrum"; others indeed scared, and even terrified into flight from off the ground: so that of either set many gentles and fine warriors were destroyed.

That in which the Gael were now, was a sad plight indeed, the greater part of their men having perished, and before their faces lying piled in death, they were driven to form themselves into a fast impenetrable phalanx that their enemies should not break though them; and he among them that had the least on his hands, him four of his fierce foes beset at once. Besides and beyond all which, O'Conor (Felim) and de Clare's arrogant hot-headed son (that after his father's death was fair gone wud [mad], rushing at all and sundry) came together. Equally rapid as were their well-meant blows, yet not long their combat retained this equilibrium; for Felim wounds and rewounds and triple-wounds the Englishman and, in all his gentlemen's despite, converted him upon the spot into a disfigured corpse.

Again now we take up O'Brien and the men of Thomond: after having at the goad's point driven Mahon O'Brien's prey, in Echtge's leafy borders they rested when certain of their own near friends and favourers that were in de Clare's host hurried off to the chief advice of the baron's vigorous enterprise, and the motive of his journey. To Murtough O'Brien it was as a violent mortal sickness that ever his faithful natural friends should come to lie under merciless oppression of those English; therefore on the instant his gentlemen and irachts all (horse and foot) assemble and, before clearing and full shining of the day, across the grasslands of the open plain strike westwards, past the pleasant hill of Uarchoill [Spancelhill], westwards still to the Fergus, ever as hard as they could go. Broad Fergus being crossed, in all directions they see the land aflame, hear it resound as with one mighty outcry. Soon they descry headlong folk (hard to stay), and swiftly flying groups that head towards them; insomuch that they found it a main effort to check the fugitives in their mad career. Dejectedly then, and they scarce able to contain themselves, these narrate the deaths and losses [of which we have heard].

As for O'Brien's gentlemen and men, as one they intensify their travail to relieve their friends in common danger: some abandon their mantles and "rampart-arms" [missile weapons]; others leave behind them their horses and all superfluous weight; for they (so many as thus divested themselves of armour) thought that on foot they would make better play over the rough intricate paths. When at last they neared the spot in which the tug of war went on (which they did without halt for formation, without consideration or respect shewed by loon to lord, by man-at-arms to high commander), O'Conor seeing them at a distance [and not knowing them] said, angrily despairing: "a pity 'tis; for we this poor remainder of the Gael stand in need of succour more than does our foe. Still, now that out of this pinch there is no way for us (since to fly beseems us not), on our bitter enemies avenge we ourselves handsomely, and in such guise that after us they shall not muster strong enough to offer battle to our friends!"

With the lionlike chief's exhortation their valour blazed and their strength expanded, in such measure that right through the pale English they made for themselves "a warrior's gap" and common path, to go [as they thought] to this fresh enemy's encounter. But when they knew their fellows, loudly they emitted three cries: one of joy and welcome; one of triumph and exultation for the deeds that they had done, the slaughter they had made; lastly, a groanful cry of lamentation for their own hurts and losses. Here [at last] the wounded fell to the rear of the others as they fought; from their respective directions both parties [O'Conor and the O'Deas on the one hand, O'Brien and Clancullen on the other] charge each towards each, in form so grim that neither may one count nor [consequently] recite all that fell of them [friend and foe] while the thing lasted, so imperious was their desire to reach their comrades and to join their forces. So dour the hand-to-hand work was, that nor noble nor commander of them [the English] left the ground, but the far greater part fell where they stood. Nor was Lochlainn O'Hechir with his iracht who came on the scene a little before O'Brien, idle in the tight-jammed press.

There remains but to say that the gentles of the pale English being extinguished utterly: both knecht and battle-baron, both knight and aspirant, the common herd (so many as survived) took to shift for themselves. Which when the Gael perceived they followed them hard and close; seeking to get round them [head them off] so that not a soul of them should pull through, for they esteemed that now, de Clare and his son and Mahon O'Brien's two sons with the gentlemen of his iracht and people being fallen, there was an end of the cleavage among them [the Dalcassians] all. Nevertheless, by main fighting strength Brian Bane mac Donall mac Brian Rua came off; but he never cried halt until he had crossed Shannon eastwards [into Duharra], where for his race he (with Murtough O'Brien's goodwill) effected a settlement.

As for O'Brien and his people: with cutting down and expeditious slaying of their perpetual enemies, earnestly they follow the rout right into Bunratty of the spacious roads; and (a thing which never had happened) the manner in which he found the town before him was: deserted, empty, wrapped in fire. For upon his wife's and household's receiving of the tidings that de Clare was killed, with one consent they betake them to their fast galleys and shove off on Shannon, taking with them the choicest of the town's wealth and valuable effects, and having at all points set it on fire. From which time to this, never a one of their breed has come back to look after it.

IX.

THE BATTLE

OF

AXE HILL

INTRODUCTION

ERALD FITZGERALD, known as Gerrold Mor or Gerald the Great, the eighth earl of Kildare (1456–1513), was the most powerful man in Ireland for over thirty years. A descendant of one of the original twelfth-century Norman invaders, he called himself an Englishman, married the cousin of an English king, and was rewarded for his services to the crown with that most English of orders, Knight of the Garter. Although he spent part of the year 1495 imprisoned in the Tower of London as a traitor, this had more to do with his support of the House of York during the War of the Roses than with anything Irish. A year later he was reinstated as the king's deputy (governor) of Ireland. It was a post he would hold until his death in 1513 from a gunshot wound, making him one of the first—if not *the* first—major Irish political figure to end a career that way.

The earl was first appointed deputy in 1478 by Richard III. It was a sign of his importance—and usefulness—that he was reappointed by Henry VII, the first Tudor king, who had killed Richard at Bosworth Field to win the crown. Henry is quoted in the sixteenth-century *Book of Howth* as saying of Gerald, "He is meet to rule all Ireland, seeing all Ireland cannot rule him."

A dramatic example of Kildare's power at work was the Battle of Knockdoe (Axe Hill) in 1504, when Gerald mobilized half of Ireland to defeat his son-in-law, Ulrick de Burgh (or Burke). A domestic reason given for the confrontation was that Ulrick had been abusing Gerald's daughter, but it is more likely that the king's deputy's call to battle was triggered by Ulrick's seizure of the city of Galway and some of its surrounding castles. At first glance, it looks as though it was a fight between the east and the west: Kildare's forces from what was called the English Pale versus Connacht. But it was also a north-south clash, with the earl of Kildare's support coming from the northern families and Burke's from the southern.

The gathering was huge for an Irish battle, with probably more than ten thousand men involved. Both sides used Scottish mercenaries called gallowglass. On August 19, they met at Knockdoe, a low hill just northeast of Galway. This is the first Irish battle in which firearms are mentioned, although there is no mention of a gun being fired. (Spears and darts were the Irish weapons of choice, the Scots favored battle-axes, while the English preferred arrows and swords.) A soldier from Dublin is simply described as using two hands to bash an enemy over the head with one.

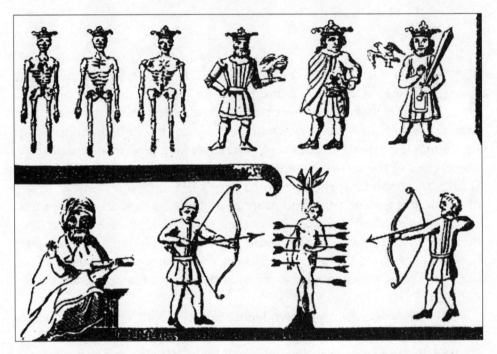

A mural in Abbey Knock Moy, located on the edge of the Knockdoe battlefield.

THE BOOK OF HOWTH
BATTLE OF KNOCKDOE

The Book of Howth, *which was probably written in 1544 and after, retells the history of the St. Laurence family, the lords of Howth. St. Laurences are not given a major role in this battle, but the lord of Howth is the soul of reason in the parlay of Kildare allies that precedes the fight.*

Two interesting points are understated in the account. One is that although both the de Burghs and the FitzGeralds were old Norman families, the western de Burghs—who now call themselves Burkes— are considered Irish, while the FitzGeralds—from the Pale—are outspokenly English. Another is that when the baron of Delwin promises to be the first to cast a spear at the Irish, he is making a daring statement. In 1498, the Irish Parliament had passed a law requiring that troops from the Pale must use "English" weapons such as crossbows and swords and not "Irish" spears and darts. (Other laws from the same time prohibited traditional Irish battle cries in favor of calling out the names of St. George or the current king of England and outlawed the wearing of Irish-style clothing.) Perhaps the baron was feeling unusually Irish or wanted to taunt the enemy. Or maybe he simply thought a spear was a more effective weapon.

AFTER THIS THE EARL [Gerald FitzGerald, Earl of Kildare] married another daughter of his to a great man in Connoght [Ulrick de Burgh, or Burke, and she] was not so used as the Earl could be pleased with; and said he would be revenged upon this Irishman, who stood at a defiance with the Earl and all his partakers. The Earl sent to all the Irish lords that then was his friends, as O'Neyll [O'Neill], O'Rely [O'Reilly], O'Conner of Afaley, and all the power of the English Pale so many as he could possibl[y] make, for the Earl understood that all the Irish in Ireland were divided between him and his adversaries. They was a great number, whereof he had good experience. Therefore he made the better provision of all things, and best men in all the English Pale, both spiritual and temporal; and being a twenty mile east of Cnocke-two [Knockdoe], called the noblemen to Council. Amongst all were certain bishops and men of law.

When O'Neyll saw them he said, "My Lord of Kyldare [Kildare], command the bishops to go home and pray, for bishops' counsels ought not to be taken in matters of war, for their perfection is to pray, to preach, and to make fair weather, and not to be privy to manslaughter nor blood shedding, but in preaching and teaching the Word of God; and I assure you it is a presumption for any proud prelate to come where as such matters is to be done, for it is contrary to his religion."

And so A'Conore asked the Earl what he would do with the judges and men of law in his company. "We have no matters of pleading, no matters of arguments, no matters to debate, nor to be discussed by pen and ink, but by the bow, spear, and sword, and the valiant hearts of gentlemen and men of war by their fierce and lusty doings, and not by the simple, sorry, and weak and doubtful stomachs of learned men; for I never saw those that was learned ever give good counsel in matters of war, for they were always doubting, staying, and persuading more in frivolous and uncertain words, more than Ector or Launselot's [Hector or Launcelot's] doings. Away with them! They are overbold to press amongst this company; for our matter is to be discussed by valiant and stout stomachs of prudent and wise men of war, practised in this same faculty, and not matters of law nor matters of religion."

The Baron of Delven, called Richard, said his learning was not such that with a glorious tale he could utter his stomach; "but I promise to God and to the Prince I shall be the first that shall throw the first spear amongst the Irish in this battle; say now on whos[o] will, for I have done."

The Lord of Gormanstoune said that it was good to be advised what is to be done, for after a good advisement there shall come a good end, for a hasty man never lacked woe. "Let us understand the matter ere we take this weighty matter in hand, for many perils may fall unless we take the better keep [head] thereof. Let us understand the quarrel again, and debate the matter whether we shall proceed or no, ere we begin; and let the King be privy to this weighty and uncertain enterprise, for we may put the whole realm in hazard if we speed not well, for I understand that they are many against us; and this is so much as I at this time mean to say."

This Council was at three of the clock afternoon before the day of battle. Then, within a few miles from the field appointed, Sir Nicholas [St. Laurence], Lord of Houthe, said, "The sayings of A'Neyll and A'Conore is not to be disallowed; let it be as they have said. And my Lord of Gormanstoune's opinion is good, so it had been spoken before our com-

ing to the field; and for that, here is my opinion, seeing the time is short."
For at this time appeared upon a hill two miles from the English camp
above two hundred horsemen; whereunto Gerot, the Earl's son, would
have been at them, and asked of the Council to go to them. But the Lords
of the Council said that none should go till they had gone all, and so
stayed this lusty and stalworth gentleman; of which young Gerot was very
sorry, as though he should never have his fill in fighting.

"Well," said the Lord of Houth to answer the Lord of Gormanstoune,
"this matter was determined before we came hither deliberately by the
Council, and if it were not, the time is not now to argue the cause, our
enemies being in sight. And for the displeasure of our Prince, if we win
this battle, as I am [as]sured we shall, tho' the King [of England] frown a
little with his countenance, his heart will rejoice. And admit he will be
offended upon losing this field, he that shall live let him bear the blame or
burden, and as for my part I am assured to win this battle or to lose my
life, and then all the world is gone with me. . . . But to the matter; let us
send away our sons and heirs, to revenge our quarrel if need so require,
and prescribe our battles in perfect order this night, that every man shall
know to-morrow his charge, for it is not when we shall go to fight that we
should trouble us with discussing that matter."

"Well," said the Earl, "my dear cousin, you hath well spoken; be it as
you hath said." "No!" said young Gerott, the Earl's son; "by God's blood,
I will not go home and leave so many of my friends in battle, for I mean
to live and die amongst you all." "Well," said the Lord of Houth; "boy,
thou speakest natural, for ever thy kind is such one from thy first generation and first coming into Ireland, for thou art to be borne withall, thou
worthy gentleman and lion's heart."

The Lords of Kyllen and Tremlestone thought the number of Irishmen
very great, as they were credibly informed by certain spials which brought
them word, and that the number of younglings were not the sixth man to
a man; and said in plain terms, that a good giving back [retreat] were better than a[n] evil standing, and in further time better provision might be
made to serve such a turn. "It is well spoken," said the Baron of Slane and
the Lord of Donesany.

"O good God!" said the Lord of Houthe; "by our blessed Lady, that
bliste [blessed us] in the north church of Houth, you four might have spoken these words in some other ground than this is, and our enemies now
being in sight and the night at hand."

"Well," said the Earl; "call to me the captain of the galoglas, for he
and his shall begin this game. . . ."

"I am glad" said the captain; "you can do me no more honour, by

God's blood!" and took his axe in his hand, and began to flourish.

"No," said the Lord of Houth, "I will be the beginner of this dance, and my kinsmen and friends, for we will not hazard our English good[s] upon the Irish blood; howbeit it is well spoken by the captain of the galoglas, nor they shall not be mixed among us."

Then all things was according to the matter prepared; the bowmen put in two wings, which the Lord of Gormanstoune and Kyllen had the charge, being good men that day; the billmen in the main battle, which the Lord of Houthe was leader, and in the woward himself; the galoglas and the Irish in another quarter; the horsemen on the left side the battle under the guiding of the worthy Baron of Delven, by reason there was a little wall of two foot height on the other side the battle, which would somewhat have troubled the horsemen.

After all things put in order, they went to supper, and after to their lodging to rest the residue of the night. The ground was appointed, and all such things as was necessary for such a purpose. At midnight a horseman came from the Irish camp to the Earl, and willed him to get away and save his life, and said it was but folly to fight, for this man was afore this time a horse boy with the Earl, and gave him first horses. The Earl came incontinent to the Lord of Houth, being in a sound sleep, to tell it him, and a long while he was ere he could wake him, for he called upon him divers times, which the Earl marvelled, for he could not awake him by his voice he slept so sad; and at length awoke by stirring of him, and blamed him, who answered that all things was before determined in his mind, and so nothing else in his mind to trouble him, but sleep; "for it must be ours or theirs," said the Lord of Howthe; "therefore my mind is settled, but before this I could not rest well," [et]c.

"Well," said the Earl, "here is the business; this man is come to me as a trusty friend"; and so told the whole matter as he told the Earl before. "Well," said the Lord of Houth, "suffer him to pass, and I pray you tell this tale to no more, for it would sooner do harm than good"; and with that he arose and incontinent after the day appeared.

And so they went, and prepared themselves in good order of battle, and did appoint young Gerot, a valiant young gentleman, with a chosen company for relief, fearing so great a number of enemies would enclose them about, being far less in number than they.

The [enemy] Irish, as O'Kelly, McWilliam, O'Brens, and the rest, all that night was watching, drinking, and playing at cards, who should have this prisoner and that prisoner; and thus they passed the night over, and at morrow they prepared to battle in such order as their custom was. They set forward their galoglasse and footmen in one main battle, and all their horsemen on their left side, and so came on.

The Earl of Kyldare, after his battle set, willed that they should stand within that little walls of two foot high that was made afore by those that dwelled there for sa[fe]guard of their corns, and rode upon a black horse, and made his oration, "My friends and kinsmen, I say to you that there is against us a great number of people without weapon, for a great number of them hath but one spear and a knife. Without wisdom or good order, they march to battle, as drunken as swine to a trough, which make[s] them more rash and foolish than wise and valiant. Remember all that we have doth rest upon this day's service, and also the honour of our Prince; and remember how we are in a country unknown to the most number of us, and far from our towns and castles."

The Earl did not well finish those words, when they heard three great cries that disturbed his oration.

A company of stalworthy gentlemen being in the forefront of the English battle, amongst all was Holywod of Tartaine, which seldom heard the like. "What meaneth this cry?" said he; "do they think that we are crows, that we will flee with crying?" and sware, "By the holy Saint Nicholas, that blisse in Tertayne, they shall find us men ere we depart."

With that the Irish galoglas came on, to whom the English archers sent them such a shower of arrows that their weapon and their hands were put fast together. MackSwine, captain of the Irish galoglasse, came foremost, and asked where was Great Darsey? Darsey answered that he was at hand, which he should well understand. With that McSwine strack Darsey such a blow upon the helmet that he put Darsey upon his knees. With that Nangell, Baron of the Nowan, being a lusty gentleman that day, gave McSwine such payment that he was satisfied ever after.

They fought terrible and bold a while. The Irish fled; amongst whom there came a horseman running amongst the English, and asked who had the Earl of Kildare and the rest of the Lords of the English Pale prisoners? With that one Skquyvors, a soldier out of Dublin, strack him with a gun with both his hands, and so beat out his brains. The young Gerotte this time being left for relief, seeing the battle joining, could not stand still to wait his time as he was appointed by the Earl his father, but set on with the foremost in such sort that no man alive could do better with his own hands than he did that day, for manhood of a man; but by reason of his lustiness not tarrying in the place appointed, all the English carriages was taken away by the Irish horsemen, and a few of the English gentlemen take[n] prisoners. That was on that side of the battle.

When the battle was done, and a great number of the Irish slain, as it was reported nine thousand, the Lord of Gormanston said to the Earl,

"We have done one good work, and if we do the other we shall do well."
Being asked what he meant, said he "We hath for the most number killed
our enemies, and if we do the like with all the Irishmen that we have with
us, it were a good deed."

This battle was fought the 19 day of August 1504, at Knocke-twoe,
which is from Galwe five miles. The hill is not high, but a great plain. The
greatest of the Irish was Richard Bourke. . . . The Baron of Delven, a little before the joining of the battle, took his horse with the spurs, and
threw a small spear amongst the Irish, and slew by chance one of the
Bourkes, and turned. The Earl said to him that he kept promise well, and
well did and stalworthly, saving that after his throw he retired back. After
they went to Galway, where as the Irish gathered again, and said they
would give to the Earl another field, but they durst not fight a battle never
after with the English Pale. The Earl bestowed thirty tun of wine amongst
the army. . . .

The Earl of Kyldare was made Knight of the Garter after the field of
Cnocktwo.

X.

HUGH

O'NEILL

TRIUMPHANT

INTRODUCTION

Beginning in 1593, Hugh O'Neill (1550–1616), the earl of Tyrone, a man of whom it was said could speak Irish like an Irishman and English like a gentleman, led a long and sustained uprising that, for a time at least, had the English terrified. Called both the Nine Years War and Tyrone's rebellion, it began with O'Neill—who as a boy after his father's assassination during an O'Neill family squabble received what he later called his "education amongst the English"—pretending to be an English ally while secretly directing the uprising. (In Brian Friel's play about O'Neill, *Making History*, Hugh is depicted as having gone to England to be schooled, but the earl's comment probably meant that he received his education within the English Pale in Dublin.) His chief deputy was Hugh O'Donnell (1572–1602) of Donegal, whose family had been the traditional enemy of the O'Neills for centuries. The earl dropped all pretenses in 1595 with his open attack on a fort on the Blackwater River just north of Armagh and was promptly outlawed as a traitor by Queen Elizabeth's government.

O'Neill's rebellion proved to be the most complex military campaign in Ireland since the Bruces's invasion in the fourteenth century, and it remained successful for as long as it remained a guerrilla operation. On the Irish side were O'Neills, O'Donnells, and members of other northern families as well as a number of "redshank" mercenaries hired in Scotland. About a third of them had firearms, although they had almost no artillery, which made attacks on walled cities nearly impossible. Most of the English forces were seasoned troops who

Hugh O'Neill, earl of Tyrone.

had battle experience fighting on the continent.

For the first time, religion played an important role in an Irish war. When Queen Elizabeth's father, Henry VIII (who had named Hugh's grandfather Earl of Tyrone), broke with Rome, he made the struggle in Ireland not only a conflict between the Irish and the English but between Catholics and Protestants. Besides perfecting the art of the military ambush, O'Neill also honed the art of diplomacy, constantly dangling peace proposals before the English as a delaying tactic. He hoped, if he waited long enough, to win the support of the so-called Old English (long established English settlers who were Catholics) and to establish a military alliance with England's most powerful European enemy, Spain. As a Catholic prince, a descendant of the high kings of Ireland, O'Neill looked for help from His Most Catholic Majesty, King Philip III of Spain.

As with most Irish conflicts, the family connections were intertwined. Hugh O'Donnell was Hugh O'Neill's son-in-law (a long-established way of binding together two former adversaries), but O'Neill was also married to the sister of Sir Henry Bagenal, marshal of Ireland, the general Hugh's forces defeated—and killed—at the battle at Yellow Ford.

THE ANNALS OF
THE FOUR MASTERS

THE BATTLES OF CLONTIBRET
AND YELLOW FORD

✟

*The running ambush of the English relief column at Clontibret in 1595
and the rout three years later at Yellow Ford (probably named for the
color of the water of a marshy stream that ran into the Blackwater
River) are almost textbook examples of the advantages of a native
guerrilla army over a traditional occupying force. The former took
place between Monaghan and Newry, the latter—not far away—near
the present village of Blackwater, a few miles north of Armagh.*

*In this selection, the Four Masters provide a somewhat cryptic
account of the surrender of Sligo to the rebels, which gives some suggestion of the precarious balance maintained by the government army.
The officers may have been English, but many of the men were Irish
more in sympathy with their enemy than with their commanders.*

*There seems to be some disagreement over the size of the New Fort
(which the Irish called Fortmore or Fortuna) on the Blackwater. Fynes
Moryson, an Englishman, called it an "Eye-sore" which was "only a
deep trench or wall of earth to lodge some one hundred soldiers,"
while Cuegory O'Cleary, an Irishman, described it as a strong earthen
fort with "fighting towers" and loophole windows to fire through, garrisoned by three hundred men.*

*The Four Masters' account of the battle at Yellow Ford includes a
rare but brief glimpse of an ordinary soldier—unnamed, of course—
who discovers the dangers of gunpowder.*

THE AMBUSH OF CLONTIBRET AND THE CAPTURE OF SLIGO

For some time [in 1595] the English did not dare to bring any army into
Ulster, except one hosting which was made by Sir John Norris and his
brother, Sir Thomas Norris, the President of the two provinces of
Munster, with the forces of Munster and Meath, to proceed into Ulster.
They marched to Newry, and passed from thence towards Armagh. When
they had proceeded near halfway, they were met by the Irish, who pro-

249

ceeded to annoy, shoot, pierce, and spear them, so that they did not suffer them either to sleep or rest quietly for the space of twenty-four hours. They were not permitted to advance forward one foot further; and their chiefs were glad to escape with their lives to Newry, leaving behind them many men, horses, arms, and valuable things. The General, Sir John Norris, and his brother, Sir Thomas, were wounded on this occasion. It was no [ordinary] gap of danger for them to go into the province after this.

[Bingham, an English commander] returned to Sligo, after having plundered the monastery of the Blessed Virgin at Rath-Maelain, and the church of St. Columbkille on Torach; but God did not permit him to remain for a long time without revenging them upon him, for there was in his company a gentleman of the Burkes, who had twelve warriors along with him, namely, Ulick Burke [an Irish ally]. Upon one occasion he was offered insult and indignity by [Bingham] and the English in general, at which he felt hurt and angry; and he resolved in his mind to revenge the insult, if he could, and afterwards to get into the friendship of [Hugh] O'Donnell, for he felt certain of being secure with him. He afterwards got an advantage of the aforesaid [Bingham], one day as he was in an apartment with few attendants; he went up to him, and upbraided him with his lawlessness and injustice towards him, and as he did not receive a satisfactory answer, he drew his sword, and struck at him till he severed his head from his neck. He then took the castle, and sent messengers to Ballyshannon, where O'Donnell's people then were; and these dispatched messengers to Tyrone, where O'Donnell himself was. They relate the news to him, and he then went to the Earl O'Neill; and both were much rejoiced at that killing. On the following day O'Donnell bade the Earl farewell, and, setting out with his army, did not halt, except by night, until he arrived at Sligo. He was welcomed; and Ulick Burke delivered up the town to him, which made him very happy in his mind. This happened in the month of June. . . .

THE BATTLE OF YELLOW FORD

The New Fort [on the Blackwater River near Armagh] was defended during the time of peace and war by the Queen's people; but when the English and Irish did not make peace [as had been expected] in the beginning of summer, [Hugh] O'Neill laid siege to the fort, so that the warders were in want of provisions in the last month of summer [of 1598]. After this news arrived in Dublin, the Council resolved to assemble together the most loyal and best tried in war of the Queen's soldiers in Ireland, [who were those] in the neighbourhood of Dublin and Athlone; and when these [soldiers] were asembled together, four thousand foot and six hundred horse were selected from among them, and these were sent to convey provisions to the New Fort. A sufficient supply of meat and drink, beef, lead, powder, and all other necessaries, were sent with them. They marched to Drogheda, from thence to Dundalk, from thence to Newry, and from thence to Armagh, where they remained at night. Sir Henry Beging [Bagenal], Marshal of Newry, was their General.

When O'Neill had received intelligence that this great army was approaching him, he sent his messengers to [Hugh] O'Donnell, requesting of him to come to his assistance against this overwhelming force of foreigners who were coming to his country. O'Donnell proceeded immediately, with all his warriors, both infantry and cavalry, and a strong body of forces from Connaught, to assist his ally against those who were marching upon him. The Irish of all the province of Ulster also joined the same army, so that they were all prepared to meet the English before they arrived at Armagh. They then dug deep trenches against the English in the common road, by which they thought they [the English] would come to them.

As for the English, after remaining a night at Armagh, they rose next morning early; and the resolution they adopted was, to leave their victuals, drink, their women and young persons, their horses, baggage, servants, and rabble, in that town of Armagh. Orders were then given that every one able to bear arms, both horse and foot, should proceed wherever the Marshal and other officers of the army should order them to march against their enemies. They then formed into order and array, as well as they were able, and proceeded straightforward through each rood before them, in close and solid bodies, and in compact, impenetrable squadrons, till they came to the hill which overlooks the ford of Beal-an-atha-bhuidhe. After arriving there they perceived O'Neill and O'Donnell, the Ui Eathach Uladh, and the Oirghialla, having, together with the chieftains, warriors, heroes, and champions of the North, drawn up one terrible mass before them, placed and arranged on the particular passages where they thought the others would march on them.

When the chiefs of the North observed the very great danger that now threatened them, they began to harangue and incite their people to acts of valour, saying that unless the victory was their's on that day, no prospect remained for them after it but that of being [some] killed and slaughtered without mercy, and others cast into prisons and wrapped in chains, as the Irish had been often before, and that such as should escape from that battle would be expelled and banished into distant foreign countries: and they told them, moreover, that it was easier for them to defend their pat-rimony against this foreign people [now] than to take the patrimony of others by force, after having been expelled from their own native country. This exciting exhortation of the chiefs made [the desired] impression upon their people; and the soldiers declared that they were ready to suffer death sooner than submit to what they feared would happen to them.

As for the Marshal and his English [forces], when they saw the Irish awaiting them, they did not shew any symptom whatever of fear, but advanced vigorously forwards, until they sallied across the first broad [and] deep trench that lay in their way; and some of them were killed in crossing it. The Irish army then poured upon them vehemently and boldly, furiously and impetuously, shouting in the rear and in the van, and on either side of them. The van was obliged to await the onset, bide the brunt of the conflict, and withstand the firing, so that their close lines were thinned, their gentlemen gapped, and their heroes subdued. But, to sum up in brief, the [English] General, i.e. the Marshal of Newry, was slain; and as an army, deprived of its leader and adviser, does not usually main-tain the battle-field, the General's people were finally routed, by dint of conflict and fighting, across the earthen pits, and broad, deep trenches, over which they had [previously] passed. They were being slaughtered, mangled, mutilated, and cut to pieces by those who pursued them bravely and vigorously.

At this time God allowed, and the Lord permitted, that one of the Queen's soldiers, who had exhausted all the powder he had about him, by the great number of shots he had discharged, should go to the nearest bar-rel of powder to quickly replenish his measure and his pouch; and [when he began to fill it] a spark fell from his match into the powder in the bar-rel, which exploded aloft overhead into the air, as did every barrel near-est, and also a great gun which they had with them. A great number of the men who were around the powder were blown up in like manner. The sur-rounding hilly ground was enveloped in a dense, black, gloomy mass of smoke for a considerable part of the day afterwards. That part of the Queen's army which escaped from being slaughtered [by the Irish], or burned or destroyed [by the explosion], went back to Armagh, and were eagerly pursued [by the Irish, who] continued to subdue, surround, slay, and slaughter them, by pairs, threes, scores, and thirties, until they passed inside the walls of Armagh.

The Irish then proceeded to besiege the town, and surrounded it on every side; and they [of both parties] continued to shoot and fire at each other for three days and three nights, at the expiration of which time the English ceased, and sent messengers to the Irish to tell them that they would surrender the fort [at the Blackwater], if the warders who were [stationed] in it were suffered to come to them unmolested to Armagh, and [to add] that, on arriving there, they would leave Armagh itself, if they should be granted quarter and protection, and escorted in safety out of that country into a secure territory. When these messages were communicated to the Irish, their chiefs held a council, to consider what they should do respecting this treaty. Some of them said that the English should not be permitted to come out of their straitened position until they should all be killed or starved together; but they finally agreed to give them liberty to pass out of the places in which they were, on condition, however, that they should not carry out of the fort meat or drink, armour, arms, or ordnance, powder or lead [or, in fine, any thing], excepting only the captain's trunk and arms, which he was at liberty to take with him. They consented on both sides to abide by those conditions; and they sent some of their gentlemen of both sides to the fort, to converse with the warders; and when these were told how the case stood, they surrendered the fort to O'Neill, as they were ordered. The Captain and the warders came to Armagh, to join that part of his people who had survived. They were all then escorted from Armagh to Newry, and from thence to the English territory. After their departure from Tyrone, O'Neill gave orders to certain persons to reckon and bury the gentlemen and common people slain. After they had been reckoned, there were found to be two thousand five hundred slain, among whom was the General, with eighteen captains, and a great number of gentlemen whose names are not given.

The Queen's people were dispirited and depressed, and the Irish joyous and exulting, after this conflict. This battle of Athbuidhe [Yellow Ford] was fought on the 10th day of August. The chiefs of Ulster returned to their respective homes in joyous triumph and exultation, although they had lost many men. . . .

When it was told to the Queen of England and the Council that the Irish had risen up against her in the manner already described, and the vast numbers of her people who had been slain in this year, the resolution adopted by the Sovereign and the Council was, to send over Sir Richard Bingham with eight thousand soldiers, to sustain and carry on the war here, until the Earl of Essex should [be prepared] to come, who was then ordered to go to Ireland after the festival of St. Bridget with attire and expense, and an army, such as had not been attempted to be sent to Ireland, since the English had first undertaken to invade it, till that time.

O'NEILL'S VICTORIES

BY PHILIP O'SULLIVAN BEARE

‡

Philip O'Sullivan Beare (c. 1590–c. 1650) was born in the western part of County Cork during the reign of Queen Elizabeth, a member of a family that fought alongside O'Donnell and O'Neill, and when he writes of his countrymen he usually refers to them not as "Irish" but as "Catholics." This is important, for it is a sign of a new sense of identity in Ireland. O'Neill and O'Donnell's early victories are seen here as religious rather than nationalist triumphs.

O'Sullivan was a theologian, and even this work, which is a lively propaganda piece clearly intended for a popular audience, was written in Latin. It contains two surprising appearances: one is St. Patrick (died c. 461) helping the O'Neill cause by flying around the spire of his cathedral in Armagh, the other is the devil as a black man in a scene right out of Faust.

The "sow" mentioned during O'Sullivan's account of the English attack on Sligo Castle was a roofed-over siege device with roots going back to the Romans. In a contemporary account of a 1641 attack on Ballyally Castle, a sow is described as being thirty-five feet long, nine feet wide, riding on four wheels, and covered with cow hides and sheep skins "so no musket bullet or steel arrow could pierce it, while men worked under it to destroy the fortress walls."

THE ENGLISH GARRISON DRIVEN OUT OF PORTMORE AND BESIEGED IN THE CASTLE OF MONAGHAN.

These risings increased daily. There is in Ulster a river which the Irish call the Abhainn-mhor, and the English the Blackwater, either because it is more turbid than other Irish rivers, which are usually clear and pellucid, or because the English often met with defeat and disaster on its banks. On this river there was a fort, famous in many occasions in this war, as will appear later on, called by the English, the Blackwater fort, and by the Irish, Portmore, that is to say the great fort. It was situated three miles beyond Armagh, the seat of the Primate of Ireland, and seven miles south of Dungannon, Earl Tyrone's chief town. From this fort the Queen's English garrison and heretical minister were expelled by certain Irishmen. Moreover, some of the MacMahons besieged Monaghan castle, the capital of Oriel, unjustly taken from that family by the Viceroy's decree and fortified by an English garrison. The besiegers cutting off all supplies, it seemed as if the garrison must surrender from want. A quarrel having broken out in Armagh, as we have seen, between the Catholic priest in charge of the principal church and some English soldiers, a certain Irish nobleman, who at the time chanced to be there, cleared the town of all the Queen's garrison who were well punished, some severely wounded and some killed. For all these things the English laid the blame on [Hugh] O'Neill.

THE EQUIPMENT AND LEADERS OF BOTH PARTIES. EARL TYRONE INAUGURATED THE O'NEILL.

By these risings of the Catholics, commotions, and defeats, Elizabeth, Queen of England, was sorely worried, and strained every nerve to quiet Ireland and break down the Catholic forces. In the year 1594 she appointed William Russell viceroy instead of William Fitzwilliam, who had held that office but had resigned. She recalled from France the English veterans who were employed there against His Catholic Majesty, Philip II, and ordered a levy in England and Ireland. John Norris, an English knight, with 1,800 English veterans from France, speedily landed in Ireland. Such royalist troops as he found in Ireland—veterans and raw recruits alike—he summoned to his standard, and hastened into Ulster as if to relieve Monaghan castle which, as above mentioned, was surrounded by the MacMahons.

At this time died Turlough, who had been The O'Neill, and who was regarded as the impediment to the Earl of Tyrone's making war on the English. On his death Tyrone [Hugh O'Neill] was after the Irish fashion declared The O'Neill by the clansmen and by this title we shall henceforth call him. However, he wrote to Norris asking him not to take extreme measures and stating that he would prefer to preserve the Queen's friendship than to be her enemy; that he had never conspired against the Queen's crown; and that he had been unjustly accused by envious persons. He sent a similar letter to the Queen. But Bagnal, the Governor of Ulster, and O'Neill's bitterest enemy intercepted and suppressed both letters. O'Neill when he saw that an answer to his letters was too long delayed and that the enemy was approaching, prepared to meet him and prevent him relieving Monaghan, which MacMahon's people with the slender

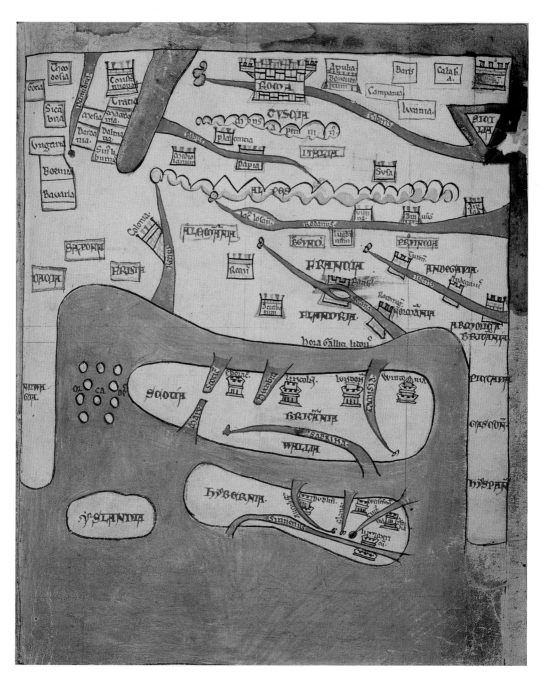

Figure 13. Europe, c. 1200. In this map from Gerald of Wales's *Typography of Ireland*, mainland Europe is at the top; England and Scotland are in the middle; and Iceland and Ireland are at the bottom. Irish cities on the map are Waterford, Wexford, and Limerick. The charted rivers are the Slane, the Suir, the Shannon (which is drawn to include the Erne), and the Liffey, called the Auenliffus. Courtesy the National Library of Ireland.

Figure 14. King Dermot MacMurrough of Leinster—losing a war with high king Rory O'Connor—asked Henry II to invade Ireland. Henry declined, but in 1169 the Normans living in southern Wales accepted. This illustration is from a thirteenth-century manuscript of *The Typography of Ireland* by Gerald of Wales, who, in his history of the English conquest of Ireland, depicts Dermot frolicking on the battlefield with the heads of his Irish enemies.

Figure 15. King John was declared Lord of Ireland by his father, Henry II, in 1177 when he was ten years old. In 1185, still a prince, he was dispatched to administer the English-held parts of the island in person, although he soon returned to London. Under his older brother, Richard I, he continued his lordship from afar and reigned as king from 1199 to 1216.

Figure 16. This illustration depicts an Irish officer or nobleman of the sixteenth century. Unlike Irish or English common soldiers, he is fully armored in a suit of plate-mail. Artist unknown.

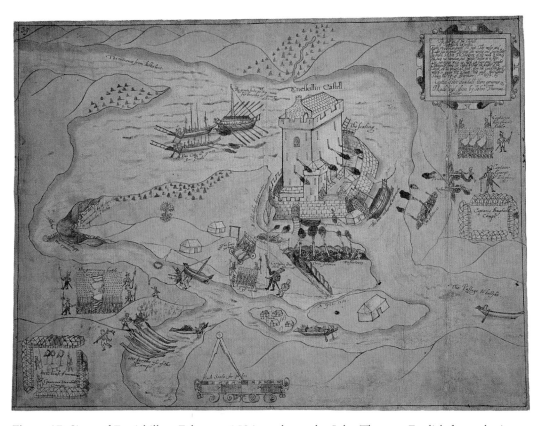

Figure 17. Siege of Enniskillen, February 1594, as drawn by John Thomas. English forces besiege a castle on the southern tip of Lough Erne held by Hugh Maguire, an ally of Hugh O'Neill and Hugh O'Donnell. The siege equipment is much the same as that used seven years later at Kinsale. Courtesy the British Library.

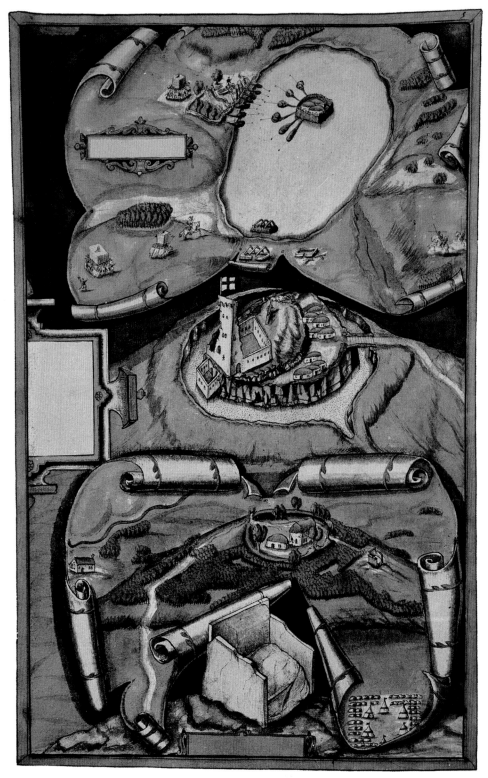

Figure 18. Ulster, 1600-1603. A three-part illustrated map by Richard Bartlett showing (top) an attack on a dwelling in a lake; (middle) the O'Neill castle at Dungannon; and (bottom) the O'Neill coronation chair at Tara. Courtesy the National Library of Ireland.

Figure 19. Art MacMurrough (with spear), an Irishman, confronts the Earl of Gloucester in an ambush during Richard II's journey to Ireland in 1399. The English appear in full armor while MacMurrough rides without a saddle. From Jean Creton's account of the expedition, illustrated by an unnamed Parisian painter between 1401 and 1405.

Figure 20. A knight—or perhaps a gallowglass—displaying the insignia of the De Burgo family from the west of Ireland. From the *De Burgo Genealogy* that dates from about 1583.

Figure 21. Although his helmet is not the pointed one usually associated with the gallowglass (mercenary soldiers from Scotland), the long-handled battleaxe and the chain-mail jerkin (as well as the fact that he is not barefooted) suggest that he is a Scot and not an Irish foot soldier, or *kern*. The figure is a detail from Queen Elizabeth's charter to the city of Dublin.

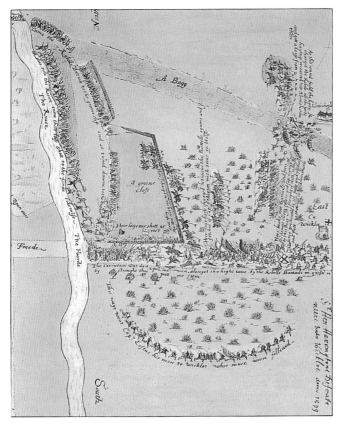

Figure 22. "The execution was don upon our men alongst this high waie by the rebells," reads a notation on this English map of a 1599 ambush by O'Neill's allies near a ford on a stream in Wicklow. Another note reads, "Heer broke our battaille and heer fell downe all our collors."

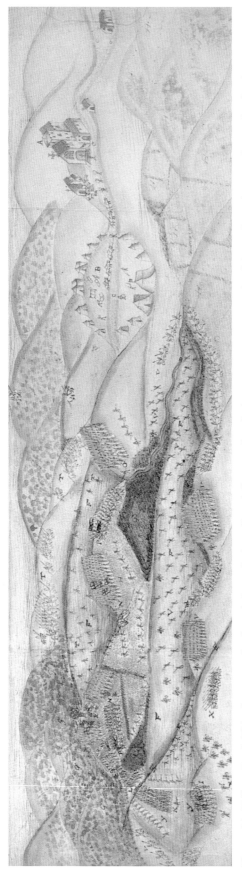

Figure 23. Yellow Ford. This short stretch of road through the rolling hills near the Blackwater River, just north of Armagh, is the site of one of Ireland's greatest psychological victories against the English. In 1598, the small forces of O'Neill and O'Donnell overwhelmed the English troops, killed their general, and sent shock waves through Elizabeth's court in London. Artist unknown.

force at their command, could not do. Maguire, a most redoubtable hero and Chief of Fermanagh, who was captain of the horse; O'Kane and other chiefs at the head of about 2,000 horse and foot, accompanied him. Norris is said to have increased his army to 4,000 horse and foot splendidly armed. Some were English veterans trained in France, some Anglo-Irish, others old Irish, especially O'Hanlon, Chief of Orior in Ulster, who by hereditary right was royal standard-bearer beyond the river Boyne. Bagnal, Governor of Ulster, was in attendance, and Norris himself, who had displayed the greatest courage and military skill in fighting the Spaniards during the French and Belgian wars, in which he had deservedly earned glory and fame, for in truth he was the greatest of the English generals of his time, although in this war fickle fortune or rather Divine Justice showed him little favour.

O'NEILL AND NORRIS ENCOUNTER FOR THE FIRST TIME AT CLONTIBRET, AND MONAGHAN IS SURRENDERED TO THE CATHOLICS.

The great General Norris, with his army, entered Oriel in MacMahon's country and came to a place not far from Monaghan which is called Clontibret (Cluoin Tiburuid), where he displayed his forces to the enemy. O'Neill, not less skilful as a general, but very inferior in strength, came against him. Here for the first time the two far-in-a-way most illustrious Generals of the two most warlike islands faced each other. The ground here was an open and level plain, but somewhat heavy with moisture. The waters flowing from the surrounding bog formed a ford over which the English might most conveniently cross. O'Neill blocked this ford; Norris tried to force it. O'Neill endeavoured to drive him back. A cavalry fight and musketry skirmish commenced simultaneously round the ford. The Royalist horse were better armed; the Irish troops were more nimble. The Irish sharpshooters were far better marksmen. This advantage was often common to both parties since there were generally more Irish than English in the Royalist army. The Queen's musketeers were twice worsted by the Catholics, and recalled by Norris, who was always the last to leave the fight, and had even a horse shot under him by a leaden bullet. All of both parties justly admitted the superiority of Maguire's cavalry. Norris being annoyed at his men having been twice repulsed and unable to hold their ground, James Sedgreve, an Irish Meath-man of great size and courage, thus addressed him and Bagnal—"Send a troop of cavalry with me and I promise you I will drag O'Neill from his saddle." O'Neill was stationed on the other side of the ford supported by forty horse and a few muske-teers surveying the battle thence and giving his orders. For the third time the cavalry and musketeers renewed the fight and Sedgreve accompanied by a troop of picked Irish and English horse charged the ford. In the ford itself a few horse fell under the fire of O'Neill's bodyguard, but Sedgreve rushed upon O'Neill and each splintered his lance on the corslet of the other. Sedgreve immediately seized O'Neill by the neck and threw him from his horse. O'Neill likewise dragged Sedgreve from his horse and both gripped each other in a desperate struggle. O'Neill was thrown under but such was his presence of mind, that prostrate as he was, he slew Sedgreve with a stab of his dagger under the corslet between the thighs and through the bladder. Eighteen illustrious cavaliers of the Royalists fell round Sedgreve and their colours were captured; the rest sought safety in flight. With them all the Queen's forces were likewise compelled to retreat, hav-ing lost seven hundred more or less, whilst the Catholics had only a few wounded, and no number of killed worth mentioning. On the following day as Norris retreated, being short of powder, he was followed and attacked by O'Neill at Bealach Finnuise, where O'Hanlon, Chief Standard Bearer of the Royalist Army, was wounded in the leg and others were shot down by leaden bullets. Hinch, an Englishman, who held the Castle of Monaghan with three companies of foot and a troop of horse, was obliged to surren-der it for want of provisions. He, himself, was let go scot free as agreed.

THE CATHOLICS FORTIFY TWO CASTLES TAKEN FROM THE ENGLISH IN CONNAUGHT.

While this campaign between O'Neill and Norris was in progress in that part of Ulster which adjoins Meath and faces England there was no lack of activity between [Hugh] O'Donnell and Richard Bingham in that other part of Ulster which adjoins Connaught and in Connaught itself.

In Connaught George Bingham Oge held Sligo Castle [for the English] with 200 foot, of whom some were Irish. Leaving this in charge of Ulick Burke, son of Raymond, an Irish chief, with some of the soldiers, Bingham himself with the rest sailed round to Ulster in two ships and raided Rathmullan, the chief town of MacSweeny Fanad who was then absent; dismantled the Carmelite Convent and forced the monks to fly to the cas-tle. Laden with booty, he returned to Sligo. Ulick thought that the Irish soldiers were defrauded in the division of the booty and took council with them as to how they should be revenged on Bingham and the English. He arranged to wrest the castle from them on a certain day, and when it came round the Irish attacked the English. Bingham was poniarded [stabbed] by Ulick and the others were either killed or seeking safety in flight, paid the penalty of their sacrilege in raiding the home of the holy Carmelites. The castle was surrendered to O'Donnell, who appointed Ulick commander of it. About this time Tomaltagh and Cathal MacDonough took Ballymote castle from George Bingham the Elder.

In the following autumn, about the time of Norris's defeat by O'Neill, Richard Bingham made an incursion to recover Sligo and take vengeance on Ulick for the slaughter of his kinsmen. He besieged Ulick locked up in Sligo castle. Ulick sallying out every day with the defenders fought before the walls. O'Donnell hastened with 1,600 troops to raise the siege. He pitched his tent at Duraran within view of the enemy. On the first two days the cavalry of both sides riding up to the river which flowed between them, skirmished with javelins. On the third day Roderic, brother of O'Donnell, with Felim MacDevit and another gentleman, having crossed the river, reconnoitred the camp. Against him came Martin, an Englishman, who was accounted the best horseman in Bingham's army, accompanied by his troop. Roderic giving reign to his horse fled to his own people. Martin followed and was the first of his troop to rush the ford when Felim turning round pierced him with a spear and knocked him dead from his horse, into the stream, while Roderic and Felim and their comrade got off safely. On the following day, the fourth of the siege, Bingham raising the blockade, returned home, O'Donnell following and harassing him with missiles.

RUSSELL, THE VICEROY AND NORRIS, WORSTED BY O'NEILL, BINGHAM VIGOROUSLY BUT FRUITLESSLY ATTACKS SLIGO CASTLE.

In the following year the English proclaimed O'Neill an enemy and traitor to his country, and now, thoroughly incensed against him, Russell the Viceroy and Norris, commander of the Queen's army took the field.

There is in Ulster a town called Newry, which the English always kept strongly garrisoned. Thence the royalists with all their forces sallied forth, fully determined to capture the city of Armagh, the seat of the [Catholic] Primate of Ireland. However, they had gone scarcely eight miles when at Kilcloney, O'Neill met them with half as numerous forces, and accompanied by Maguire, O'Kane, the sons of O'Hanlon and other noblemen. Here a battle commenced after midday, and the royalists having suffered severely, were forced to retreat to Newry. On this day the Catholics had 200 and the Royalists 600 killed.

Bingham on his side was by no means asleep. He summoned the Irish earls of Thomond and Clanrickarde, and made a levy in Connaught. He collected the garrisons and Anglo-Irish gentry of Meath, and with 24 standards attacked and blockaded Sligo. Ulick Burke and his garrison advancing outside the ramparts fought stoutly, but at last was shut up in the castle by the overwhelming numbers of the besiegers and kept off the enemy by hurling missiles from the towers, battlements, windows, and other fortifications. The Royalists advanced a sow under the walls of the castle and began to bore and undermine them. Ulick pounded the roof of the sow and the soldiers in it with a beam of great size fastened by ropes to the battlements and alternately raised and dropped. O'Donnell advanced to the rescue of the besieged, and Bingham fled. Six hundred Royalists perished in that siege. However the castle was so troublesome to defend that O'Donnell demolished it.

THE ROYALISTS TREAT FOR PEACE WITH THE CATHOLICS; OCCUPY ARMAGH; AND UNSUCCESSFULLY ASSAIL O'NEILL.

Since the Royalists were unsuccessful in the field, they made truces with O'Neill and O'Donnell and opened negotiations for peace. Henry Wallop, Treasurer of Ireland, and Robert Gardner, Chief Justice, came to them to ascertain with what terms they would be satisfied. O'Neill complained that the reward of his labours and merits had been intercepted by [Marshal of the Army] Bagnal, and that he had been falsely accused of crimes, and also complained bitterly of other wrongs. Amongst other terms he asked a full pardon for all offences and that he and his people should be allowed to profess the Roman Catholic faith, and that the Queen's judges and ministers should never enter his country. O'Donnell and others made the like demands, first complaining much of their wrongs.

Meantime 1000 English foot who were hired in Belgium by the Batavians against the Spaniards, were recalled and sent into Ireland. Russell the Viceroy and Norris quickly marched into Ulster these and the veteran English and Irish troops from France and Ireland, as well as the English recruits in Munster, Leinster and Meath, and so called Anglo-Irish:—a regular army three times the size of O'Neill's. Without any resistance they entered Armagh, the most celebrated and holiest metropolitan city of Ireland, expelled the monks, priests, and holy nuns, and other townspeople, the town being without natural protection and entirely defenceless. They entered and profaned the churches, turning them into stables and to profane uses. They fiercely destroyed images of the saints and in the height of their delight went on not doubting but that with so strong an army they would on this single expedition crush O'Neill and all the Catholics and cow their resolution. However, they had not gone more than a mile and a half from Armagh when O'Neill at the head of his slender forces met them, later than, perhaps, he would have wished, as he would have desired to keep them out of Armagh. At Beal antha Killotir [the battle at Yellow Ford] O'Neill blocked the road and vigorously attacking the English veterans from France and Belgium in the midst of their triumph, he threw them into confusion and drove them before him, and pursued them as with broken ranks they retreated to Armagh, killing and wounding many. The Catholics lost only forty, amongst them two noblemen, Farmodirrhy O'Hanlon and Patrick MacGuilly. The Royalists leaving 500 soldiers under Francis Stafford, knight, at Armagh, returned and halted not far from Dundalk, whence the Viceroy leaving the entire management of the war against O'Neill to Norris, returned to Dublin to look after affairs in Leinster and Connaught.

THE SPANISH AMBASSADORS PREVENT THE CONCLUSION OF PEACE. THE GARRISON OF ARMAGH STRANGELY CHASTISED BY SAINT PATRICK.

Negotiations for peace were again opened. The Queen offered fair and honourable terms to the Catholic clergy and laity. Hostages were given by O'Neill and O'Donnell and other Irishmen that they would agree to fair and honourable terms and not prosecute the rebellion any further. But before peace was concluded or arms laid down Cobos and other ambassadors of Philip II, King of Spain, reached O'Neill and O'Donnell, bidding the Irish in the King's name to be of good heart, that an army would be sent to their assistance by His Catholic Majesty without delay. The result of this embassy was to break off negotiations for peace, and the war was renewed on both sides. O'Hanlon, Magennis, and all Ulster except the Royalist garrison towns and the Anglo-Irish of Louth, joined the Confederation. The war spread in Leinster, and Connaught was very unsettled.

O'Neill was so sorely vexed at the holy city of Armagh being contaminated by heretics, that he determined to cut it off from provisions, not daring to assault it while so strongly garrisoned. St. Patrick, however, the Patron and Guardian of Ireland, and who was the first to consecrate this city to God, would not put off the punishment of the crime which impiously defiled the sacred town with heretics. It is believed that he was the Bishop who, clad in pontificals, frequently and plainly appeared to the English at night and threatened them; took away the iron tips of their spears; and extracted the bullets and powder from their guns. Rowley, an English captain, was so terrified by these portents, that he became almost insane; and Baker, an English adjutant, being carried by the Bishop to the pinnacle of the church, swore he would never again profane churches and dreading Divine vengeance, he abandoned the army, was converted to the Catholic faith, and began to do penance. Meditating on this incident, I cannot restrain my tears or refrain from deploring the state of things in these times and the perverse behaviour and madness of not merely the new, but even of many of the ancient Irish who, although they were Catholics, assisted the English heretics who had placed a garrison in the holy city of Armagh and defiled it, laying impious hands on the images of St. Patrick, the Patron of Ireland, and of other saints and expelling God himself as present in the Holy Sacrament of the Eucharist, trampling them under foot or hacking with their swords when pursued. Nor do I bewail so much the folly of laymen as the crass stupidity of our parochial guides and masters and other clergy who during this war yielded obedience and afforded assistance to the heretics. Baker, an English heretic soldier, swears to Saint Patrick that he will never again violate churches in Ireland, and, lest he be compelled to break his oath, he gives up the army, his pay, rank and glory, and (O shame!) the Anglo-Irish Catholic priest will not influence Irish Catholics against assisting the English heretics who have desecrated the Church of Saint Patrick and attacked its defenders.

O'NEILL INTERCEPTS THE SUPPLIES SENT TO ARMAGH AND BY STRATAGEM CUTS OFF MANY OF THE GARRISON. ARMAGH IS SURRENDERED TO HIM. HE VAINLY ATTACKS CARLINGFORD CASTLE.

To return to our subject. A great swarm of lice afflicted the garrison of Armagh and many perished of this plague. Famine soon followed. The Royalists, exercised by this circumstance, sent three companies of foot and one troop of horse with supplies. O'Neill with eight companies and some horse intercepted these at Mount Bued, routed them in a night attack, and captured the provisions. At dawn the next day he dressed some of his own cavalry and foot in the English uniform and ordered them to go towards the city carrying the captured standards and the provisions. He, himself, followed with the rest and commenced a feigned attack. The cavalry on both sides dexterously encounter and break their spears on one another's cuirasses: guns are briskly fired at the report and flash of which soldiers fall as if wounded. Stafford the Governor of

Armagh garrison, seeing this, sent half of the garrison to assist those conveying the supplies. There is a monastery within a gunshot of Armagh, having passed which the garrison were attacked in the rear by Con, son of O'Neill, who had been placed in ambush in the monastery with some foot, and in front O'Neill with all his men who had been engaged in the feigned fight bore down and destroyed them under Stafford's eyes. Not long after this Stafford was compelled by want of food to surrender Armagh to O'Neill, and as agreed, was sent to his own people.

Twenty-four miles from Armagh and eight from Newry is Carlingford castle, overhanging the river and fortified by nature and art. It was now held by half a company of English with whom were Thomas Kellody and eight other Irishmen. Thomas and the eight Irishmen, as arranged with O'Neill, suddenly attacked the English and killed six and drove the rest out of the castle. O'Neill had promised Thomas that he would be at the castle at cock-crow that night and Thomas waited for him in the castle until near dawn, but O'Neill delaying too long, Thomas left the castle and fled. At break of day O'Neill halted with his men before the castle, and fearing lest it was held by the English did not venture too close, until Thomas should give the signal. The English who had been expelled from the castle, seeing O'Neill halting and no signal given from the castle, guessed that it had been abandoned by Thomas, and themselves entered the empty fort and defended it. O'Neill disappointed in his expectations returned home.

NORRIS OCCUPIES ARMAGH A SECOND TIME: ERECTS MOUNTNORRIS; LOSES BOTH: AND UNSUCCESSFULLY ENCOUNTERS O'NEILL.

Again Norris with all his forces seeks Armagh deserted by O'Neill, and places there a garrison of four companies under Henry Davers, a knight. Thence he makes for Fortmore and occupies that place also; the fort having been dismantled and the buildings burned by O'Neill. He was prevented advancing further by O'Neill's appearance with his army, encamped on the road where he could not be attacked with advantage. Norris commenced to erect a fort which he called after himself Mountnorris. O'Neill endeavoured to obstruct him. Fighting went on for some days, some falling on both sides but the Royalists suffering most. At last Norris retired, leaving a garrison under Williams in the new fort. After his retirement O'Neill soon reduced this fort and Armagh into his possession by cutting off the garrisons from supplies. He sent the garrisons safely away as agreed. Norris again set out in force to recover

Armagh. At Mullaghbrack, in Orior, O'Neill ventured a battle and routed and scattered the enemy, who reorganised by Norris, renewed the fight. Again they were defeated by the skill and valour of O'Neill's gunmen and of Maguire, his master of the horse. For a second time reanimated by Norris they renew the combat, and for the third time are compelled to retire before the fierce attack of the Catholics, and to retreat, Norris himself receiving a bullet wound, according to many. The gentlemen of both parties justly conceded the honours of this day to Maguire.

NORRIS VAINLY TREATS WITH O'DONNELL FOR PEACE IN CONNAUGHT AND CARRIES ON AN UNSUCCESSFUL WAR.

I do not find that after this day Norris again faced O'Neill. Setting out for Connaught he halted at Athlone and assembled all his forces. Thither came the Earls of Thomond and Clanrickarde; Na-long; and other Irish chiefs of the English party; the Anglo-Irish; the levies of Munster, Leinster and Meath; Irish and English veterans; and the reinforcements recently sent from England. He is said to have had about 10,000 horse and foot. O'Donnell mustered his forces of 5,000 against him. At this time there accompanied O'Donnell out of Ulster, the three MacSweenys and O'Doherty, bound to him by ancient ties of fealty, and the ever valiant Maguire; out of Connaught came O'Rourke, MacWilliam, O'Kelly, MacDermott, O'Connor Roe, O'Dowd. With him came also Murrough MacSheehy, a Munster gentleman of birth, with 300 men, who had been for about two years lurking in the woods in Munster and there raiding the heretics as opportunity offered and going through many trials in harassing them. There were also some ecclesiastics, especially Raymond O'Gallagher, Bishop of Derry, and Vice-Primate of Ireland, who absolved from the ban of excommunication those who went over from the Royalist army to the Catholics. Norris advancing from Athlone with his great and well-ordered army came to the village of Ballinrobe in MacWilliam's country and halted there to the south of the river as O'Donnell was encamped on the other side thereof. On the first day and following night a brisk fire was kept up on both sides. On the following day Norris beat a parley, to which O'Donnell agreed. Out of the conference arose negotiations for peace. Every day under truces terms of peace were discussed, and the entire nights were spent in fighting, making attacks on one another's camps, capturing outposts and scouts and fighting hand-to-hand and at long range. It happened that on one night when Na-long was on sentry, three hundred Royalists were killed. Some fled from Norris to O'Donnell, especially

Thady O'Rourke, The O'Rourke's brother, who had lived with his kinsman the Earl of Ormond from his childhood. In treating for peace Norris offered O'Donnell, O'Rourke, MacWilliam and others, great advantages if they would return to the Queen's allegiance. The treaty was delayed by the arrival at this time in Donegal of a Spanish ship urging O'Neill, O'Donnell and the other Irish chiefs in the name of his Catholic Majesty not to abandon the course they had begun, and assuring them of Spanish aid. And so when the negotiations had wasted a whole month, Norris being about to return, shifted his camp. O'Donnell followed him and seriously harassing his rear ranks and outside wings with missiles. Norris, however, decided not to help his distressed followers until the Catholics who were attacking them crossed the nearest hedge, thinking, indeed, that those who should cross the hedge might easily be cut off by his men. O'Donnell also seeing this, and being mounted on a fleet horse, rode up to the hedge and recalled his men who were eager to cross it. Norris baulked in this plan, railed with terrible imprecations against the fate which condemned him to lose in Ireland, the smallest speck of the wide world, that fame which his great valour and military skill had earned for him in France and Belgium, and complained sorrowfully that the enemy's generals were not to be surpassed by him in military skill nor their troops to be excelled by his in stoutness and steadfastness. And fairly, indeed, might so great a general launch complaints against the fickleness of fortune. For in the opinion of all whom I have consulted in this matter, Norris was of all the English who flourished at this time, first alike in military skill and in valour, and in France and Belgium earned a great name by the success of his campaigns. Therefore I do not doubt but that it was Divinely ordained the Catholics should have most luck, but the Royalists, although stoutly and courageously fighting, should nevertheless be unfortunate. Nor is this strange, for I have no doubt but that the Irish Catholics in the Royalist army must have fought with a heavy conscience against the Catholic religion, and the English were not as strong and as suited for sustaining the burthens of war and battle as the Irish, and O'Neill studiously chose ground suitable for himself to meet Norris upon and where he fought at an advantage which seemed necessary to him, as he was inferior in point of numbers.

RELATES SOME EVENTS IN LEINSTER. THE EXTRAORDINARY DEATH OF NORRIS.

Now I must notice events in Leinster which, although provided with meagre resources, yet joined the Catholic confederation with great resolution and valour. After the removal by treachery of that resolute hero and relentless enemy of heretics, Fiagh O'Byrne, his sons Felim and Raymond took up their father's arms. While Raymond headed risings against the heretics, started in Leinster, Felim went into Ulster, to O'Neill, to ask help, and having got from O'Neill nearly 300 foot under command of Brian O'More, surnamed Reagh, a Leinster chief, most opportunely came to the assistance of his struggling brother and after some successful forays recovered his entire patrimony, at this time nearly altogether lost. Thence Brian harassed with sudden raids those English who inhabited Wexford, and the Irish of the English party. As he was driving off a prey, four English companies with 400 Irish auxiliaries overtook him in an open plain. Brian having drawn up his column of 400 Irish foot (he had no more), hazarded a battle and by the Divine assistance conquered. The English were slain to a man, and not a few of their Irish auxiliaries were missing. The rest sought safety in flight. The risings in Leinster swelled when Owny O'More came of age. He was the son of Roderic, of whom we have made mention above, and having been concealed and reared by Fiagh O'Byrne was, with his brother Edmund, sent by Fiagh's sons into Leix before he was of an age for war. Here, with the aid of some kinsmen and of some of his father's tenants in Leix, he endeavoured to recover the patrimony of his ancestors from the heretics. Wareham St. Leger, Governor of Leix, endeavouring to suppress his young efforts, was defeated with the loss of about 50 men.

I have detailed these out of many incidents of the time of Russell and Norris, who were deprived of their government for their unsuccessful management of the war, and a successor was appointed. The Presidency of Munster was left to Norris, and he filled this office for three years until he met a most extraordinary death. It is said that as he was amusing himself by night at Mallow, a person of black visage and garments suddenly entered the room, with whom Norris, leaving his game, retired into his bedroom, whence all witnesses were excluded except one boy, who concealed himself near the door and heard the conversation which is said to have been somewhat as follows: "It is time," said the black one, "for us to put the finishing touch to our plans." "I don't wish to do it," said Norris, "until we have wound up the Irish war." "On no account," said the other, "will I wait longer than the appointed day which is now come." Suddenly a great uproar was heard, attracted by which, those at play and the servants forced the door and burst into the room, when the Black one, who undoubtedly was the Devil, was nowhere to be found, but Norris was on his knees with his neck and shoulders so twisted that the top of his chest and his face were over his back. He was, however, still living and ordered the trumpeters and drummers to be called to sound his death-knell, and whilst they were clamouring, he died about midnight. His body was embalmed with aromatic and fragrant perfumes, and sent into England. A propos of this incident, I am amazed at the folly of the heretics in bestowing this great honor on the corpse of an impious man, while they scatter the relics of saintly martyrs. It may, however, be seen how much the Good God helped O'Neill in not only often defeating Norris, the most skilled of the English generals and superior in every warlike equipment, but even in conquering the Devil himself, who it is thought agreed to help Norris.

THE PAPERS OF
SIR JOHN HARINGTON
ESSEX AND ELIZABETH

One consequence of the panic in London after the English defeat at Yellow Ford was that Queen Elizabeth dispatched Robert Devereux, earl of Essex, to Ireland as lord lieutenant. Essex (1567–1601), who is usually referred to rather smirkingly as the queen's "favorite," landed in Ireland with an army of sixteen thousand men in April 1599. Rather than confronting the rebels at their strongholds in the north, he marched his huge army around in circles in the south. Eventually ordered north by the queen, he met O'Neill alone in a stream on the border of Counties Louth and Monaghan and, rather than fighting, claimed—later—to have made a cease-fire agreement. Essex's adventure was both a military and a personal disaster that ended with his recall to London, no longer a favorite. After a failed coup attempt in 1601, he was executed.

In the following exchange of letters, Essex describes his meeting with O'Neill to the queen, writing—like Julius Caesar in his Gallic War—*in the third person. In her blistering reply, the queen upbraids him for wasting his military advantage, for keeping secret what O'Neill actually said, and for falling for the rebel chief's now-familiar trick of stalling for time. It is also clear that in using phrases such as "you do but piece up a hollow peace," the queen writes with a fine Shakespearean flair.*

Sir John Harington (1561–1612), whose published papers contained these letters, was Elizabeth's godson, a poet, translator, and inventor. A flush toilet he designed was installed in one of the queen's palaces and was said to be the first such convenience in England. He accompanied Essex on his Irish adventure and is probably best known for an epigram that seems especially apt, considering his friendship with Essex: "Treason doth never prosper. What's the reason? For if it prosper, none dare call it treason."

THE JOURNAL OF THE LORD LIEUTENANT
KEPT FOR HER MAJESTY, THE QUEEN

. . . The L. Lieutenant marched with his army towards Ferny, and lodged the 2 of September [1599] betwixt Roberts Towne and Newcastel. The 3rd he went from thense to Ardoff, where he might see Tirone with his forces on a hill, a mile and a half from owre quarter, but a river and a wood betwixt him and us. The L. Lieutenant first imbattelled his army, and then lodged it uppon the hill by the burnt castel of Ardoff, and because theare was no wood for fyre nor cabines but in the valley towards Tirone's quarter, his Lo [Lord Lieutenant] commaunded a squadron of every compagny to goe fetch wood, and sent 500 foote and 2 compagnies of horsse for their garde. Tirone sent downe some horsse and foote to impeache them and offer skirmish, but after directed them not to passe the foorde, when he sawe owre men resolved to dispute it. Some skirmish theare was, from one side of the river to the other, but to little purpose; for as they offended us little, so we troubled owre selvs as little with them.

The next day the L. Lieutenant marched thorough the playne country to the mill of Louthe, and incamped beyond the river towards Ferny, and Tirone marched thorough the woodes, and lodged in the next wood to us, keeping his skowtes of horsse in sight of owre quarter. At this quarter the L. Lieutenant being driven to stay for a supply of victuall from Dredagh, consulted what was to be donn uppon Tirones armie, or how theire fastnesse might be entred. It was protested by all, that owre army being farr lesse in strength, was not to attempt trenches, and to fight uppon such infinit disadvauntage: but a strong garrison might be placed at Louthe, or some castel thereabouts, to offend the bordering rebells, and defend the whole coumpty of Lowthe; and that since we were theare, we should one day draw owte and offer battayle, with oure 2500 foote to theare 5000, and with oure 300 horsse to theire 700.

According to which resolution the L. Lieutenant first viewed Lowthe, and found it utterly unfitt, theare being no fewell to be gotten neere it, nor any strength to be made in short tyme; and the same day, being the 5th of September, he had a gentleman sent unto him from Tirone, one Henry Hagan, his constable of Dungannon and a man highly favored and trusted of him. This Hagan delivered his masters desire to parly with the L. Lieutenant, which his Lo refused; but told Hagan he would be the next morning on the hill, betwixt both theire camps, and if he would then call to speake with him, he would be found in the head of his troupes.

With this answer Hagan returned, and the next morning, being the 6th of September, the L. Lieutenant drew owte 2000 foote and 300 horsse, leaving a colonel with 500 foote and 20 horsse to garde owre quarter and baggage.

The L. Lieutenant first imbatteled his men uppon the first great hill he came to, in sight of Tirone; and then marched forward to an other hill, on which Tirones garde of horsse stoode, which they quitted, and theare owre army made good the place till it was neere 3 of the clocke in the afternoone. During which tyme Tirones foote never showed themselves out of the wood, and his horsemen were putt from all the hills which they came uppon betwixt us and the woode: by which occasion some skirmish was amongst the light horsse, in which a French gentleman of the Earl of Southamptons were all that were hurt of owre side.

After this skirmish, a horseman of Tirones called to owres, and delivered this message;—that Tirone would not fight, nor drawe forthe, but desired to speake with the L. Lieutenant, but not betwixt the 2 armies. Whereuppon the L. Lieutenant, towards 3 of the clocke in the afternoone, drew back agayne into his quarter, and after his returne thither, placed a garrison of 500 foote, and 50 horsse, at Niselerathie, half a mile from the mill of Lowthe, where theare is a square castel and a great bawne with a good dytche rounde abowte it, and many thatchd houses to lodge owre men in.

The commaundement of the garrison was given to Sir Christopher St. Laurence. The next morning, being the 7th of September, we dislodged and marched to Drumconrogh; but ere we had marched a mile, Hen. Hagan comes agayne to the L. Livetenant, and in the presens of the Earle of Southampton, Sir G. Bourgcher, Sir Waram St. Leger, and diverse other gentlemen, delivered this message:—that Tirone desired her Majesties mercy, and that the L. Livetenant would heare him; which if his Lo agreed to, he would gallop abowte and meete his Lo at the forde of Bellaclinche, which was on the right hand by the way which his Lo tooke to Drumconrogh. Uppon this message his Lo sent 2 gentlemen with H. Hagan to the foorde, to vew the place. They found Tirone theare, but the water so farr owte as they told him they thought it no fitt place to speake in.

Whereupon he grew very impatient, and sayed, "Then I shall despayre ever to speake with him; and at last, knowing the foorde, found a place, where he, standing up to the horsses belly, might be neere enough to be heard by the L. Lieutenant, though he kept the harde grownde; upon which notice the L. Lieutenant drew a troupe of horsse to the hill, above the foord, and seing Tirone theare alone, went doune alone: at whose comming Tirone saluted his Lo with a greate deale of reverence, and they talked neere half an houre, and after went ether of them up to their compagnies on the hills.

But within a while, Con O'Neale, Tyrone's base sonn, comes downe and desired from his father, that the L. Livetenant would lett him bring downe some of the principall men that were with him, and that his Lo would appoynte a number to come downe on ether side. Whereuppon his Lo willed him to bring downe 6, which he did: namely, his brother Cormock, McGennys, McGwire, Ever McCowle, Henry Ovington, and one Owen, that came from Spayne, but is an Irishe man by birthe. The L. Livetenant seing them at the foorde, went down, accompagnied with the Earle of Southampton, Sir G. Bourgcher, Sir Waram St. Leger, Sir Hen. Davers, Sir Edw. Wingfeild, and Sir Will. Constable. At this second meeting, Tirone and all his compagny, stood up allmost to theire horsses bellies in water, the L. Livetenant with his, uppon harde grounde. And Tirone spake a good while, bare headed, and saluted with a greate deale of respect all those which came downe with the L. Livetenant. After almost half an howres conference, it was concluded that theare should be a meeting of certayne commissioners the next morning, at a foord by Garret Flemings castel, and so they parted: the L. Livetenant marching with his armie to Drumconrogh; Tirone returning to his campe.

The next morning the L. Livetenant sent Sir Waram St. Leger, Sir William Constable, Sir William Warren, and his secretarie, Henry Wotton, with instructions, to the place of meeting. Tirone came himself to the parlie, and sent into Garret Flemings castel 4 principal gentlemen, as pledges for the safetie of our commissioners. In this parlie was concluded a cessation of armes for 6 weeks, and so to continue from 6 weeks to 6 weeks, till May day, or to be broken uppon 14 Days warning. . . .

This being concluded on the 8th of September, on the 9th the Lord Livetenant dispersed his army, and went himself to take phisicke at Dredagh; and Tirone retired with all his forces to the hart of his countrie.

THE QUEEN TO THE ERL OF ESSEX, IN ANSWER TO HIS LETTRE WITH HIS JOURNALL.

Right trustie and right welbeloved cousin and councellor, we greet you well. . . .

We never doubted but that Tyrone whensoever he sawe anie force approache, ether himselfe or anie of his principall partisans, wold instantly offer a parley, specially with our supreme Gouvernor of that kingdome, having often don it to those who had but subalterne authority, always seaking these cessations with like wordes, like protestations, and uppon such contingents, as we gather these will prove, by your advertisement of his purpose to goe consult with Odonnell.

Herein, we must confesse to you that we are doubtfull least the successe wilbe suteable with your owne opinion heretofore, when the same rebels heald like coorse with others that preceaded you. And therefore to come to some aunsweare for the present, it appeareth to us by your jornall, that you and the traitor spake togither halfe an howre alone, and without anie bodyes hearinge: wherein, though we that truste you with our kingdome are farre from mistrusting with a traitor; yet, both for comelines, example, and for your owne discharge, we mervaile you wolde cary it no better, especially when you have seemed in all thinges since your arrivall to be so precise to have good testimony for your actions; as, whensoever there was anie thinge to be don to which our commandement tyed you, it seamed sufficient warrant for you if your fellowe councellors allowed better of other wayes, though your owne reason caryed you to have pursued our directions against their opinions; to whose conduct if we had meant that Irlande (after all the calamities in which they have wrapped it) should still have been abandoned, (to whose coorses never any could take more exceptions then your selfe,) then was it very superfluous to have sent over such a personage as you are, who had decyphred so well the errors of their proceadings, being still at hand with us and of our secreatest councell, as it had been one good rule for you amongst others, in moste thinges to have varyed from their resolutions, especially when you had our opinion and your owne to boote.

Furthermore, we cannot but muse that you shoulde recite that circumstance of his beinge sometime uncouvered, as if that were much in a rebell, when our person is so represented, or that you can thinke that ever anie parlee (as you call it) was uppon lesse termes of inequallity then this, when you came to him and he kept the depth of the brooke between him and you; in which sorte he proceaded not with other of our ministers, for he came over to them. So as never coulde anie man observe greater forme of greatenes then he hath don, nor more to our dishonour, that a traitour must be so farre from submission, as he must have a cessation granted because he may have time to advise whether he shoulde goe further or no with us. And thus much for the forme.

For you have dealt so sparingly with us in the substance, by advertising us onely, at first, of the halfe howres conference alone, but not what passed on either side; by letting us also knowe you sent commissioners, without shewing what they had in charge; as we can not tell (but by divination) what to thinke may be the issue of this proceadinge. Onely this we are sure of, (for we see it in effect,) that you have prospered so ill for us by your warfare, as we can not but be very jealous least you shoulde be as well overtaken by the treatie:—For ether they did not ill that had the like meetinges before you, or you have don ill to keape them companie in their errors; for no actions can more resemble others, that have been before condemned, then these proceadinges of yours at this time with the rebels.

For you must consider that as we sent you into Irlande, an extraordinary person, with an army exceeding anie that ever was payde there by anie prince for so longe time out of this realme, and that you ever supposed that we were forced to all this by the weake proceadinges even in this point of the treaties and pacifications. So, if this parlee shall not produce such a conclusion, as this intollerable charge may receave present and large abatement, then hath the managinge of our forces not onely proved dishonorable and wastefull, but that which followeth is like to prove perilous and contemptible. Consider then what is like to be the end, and what wilbe fitte to builde on.

To truste this traytor uppon oath, is to truste a divill uppon his religion. To truste him uppon pledges is a meare illusorye, for what pietye is there among them that can tye them to rule of honestie for it selfe, who are onely bound to their owne sensualityes, and respect onely private utilitye. And therefore, whatsoever order you shall take with him of laying aside of armes, banishinge of strangers, recognition of superiority to us, or renouncinge of rule over our rights, promising restitution of spoyles, or anie other such like conditions, which were tolerable before he was in his overgrowen pride, by his owne successe against our power, which of former times was terrible to him: yet unlesse he yeald to have garrisons planted in his own countrye to master him, to deliver Oneales sonnes, (whereof the detayning is most dishonorable,) and to come over to us personally here, we shall doubte you doe but peece up a hollowe peace, and so the end prove worse then the beginninge. And therefore, as we well approve your owne voluntary profession, (wherein you assure us that you will conclude nothinge till you have advertised us, and heard our pleasure,) so doe we absolutely commande you to continew and performe that resolution.

Allowinge well that you heare him what he proffers, draw him as high as you can, and advertise us what conditions you wolde advise us to affoorde him, and what he is like to receave: yet not to passe your worde for his pardon, nor make anie absolute contract for his conditions, till you doe particularly advertise us by writinge, and receave our pleasure hereafter for your further warrant and authority in that behalfe. For whatsoever we doe, ought to be well weyed in such a time, when the worlde will suspect that we are glad of anie thinge out of weaknes, or apt to pardon him out of mistrust of our power to take due revenge on him: considering that all which now is yealded to on our parte, succeadeth his victoryes and our disastres. In our lettres of the fourteenth of this month to you and that councell, we have written those thinges that are fitte for them to aunsweare and understande: and therefore we will expect what they can say to all the partes of that lettre, with which our pleasure is that they be fully acquainted, aswell for your discharge an other time, if you vary from their opinions, (when we direct otherwise,) as also because we wold be glad to receave their answeare aswell as yours.

Given under our signett, at Nonsuch, the xvijth day of September, 1599, in the xljth yeare of our raigne.

XI.

THE BATTLE

OF

KINSALE

INTRODUCTION

I N THE FALL OF 1601, Hugh O'Neill finally got what he had been praying for: a Spanish army landed in Ireland to support his rebellion. It
turned out to be a classic example of the danger of answered prayers.
Although there had been rumors of a Spanish invasion for years, when it
came, it was as much a surprise to the rebels as it was to the English. They
put ashore not in the north—as O'Neill and O'Donnell had hoped—but
just outside the city of Cork, which was about as far south as they could
get. This meant that with little preparation—and delaying only to burn a
few villages near Dublin in a vain hope of diverting some English troops—
the rebels had to dash down the entire length of the island to meet up with
their new allies who had captured the walled village of Kinsale. It also
meant that the Irish had to give up the guerrilla tactics that had so frustrated the English. Until Kinsale, O'Neill had rarely attacked a fort or a
city. In this he resembled the fourth-century Goth general who explained
why he did not lay siege to a Roman town by saying, "I do not war
against walls." O'Neill's highly successful tactic—which he used at
Clontibret, Yellow Ford, and numerous other engagements—was to lure
an advancing enemy into a vulnerable position, then attack.

The English troops that had bottled up the invading Spaniards within
the walls of Kinsale were under the command of Charles Blount, Lord
Mountjoy (1563–1606), the new lord deputy who replaced the disgraced
Essex. Mountjoy reacted quickly to the invasion, arriving at Kinsale less
than a week after the Spanish put ashore, and before long there were over
7,000 of his men surrounding the town.

Only about 3,500 Spaniards were involved in the invasion, a little
more than half the number O'Neill had requested, and the decision to
land in the south was not—for them—misguided. If the occupation was
to be a long one, the fertile south was far better suited to feed an army
than the rocky north. And if the point of the invasion was really to establish a staging area for a future invasion of England, what better place was

there than the south coast? For as O'Neill was to learn, the Spanish were not there to support Irish—or Catholic—liberty but to confront an old enemy, England.

In the end, after a long siege through the beginnings of a dreadful Irish winter, there was a battle that lasted less than three hours. It would have been almost comic in its ineptness, if the results had not been so disastrous for the course of Irish history.

THE ANNALS OF
THE FOUR MASTERS

O'DONNELL AND O'NEILL
HEAD SOUTH TO KINSALE

The Four Masters compiled their annals at a Donegal monastery almost within the shadow of an O'Donnell family castle. Readers ever since have noticed a certain partisanship shown the local lords. In the following entry, the two Hughs—O'Neill and O'Donnell—rush south to Kinsale upon hearing of the Spanish landing, but the Masters are clearly much more interested in O'Donnell's passage through the west than O'Neill's through the east. Both men take time to inflict damage to the English (and pro-English Irish) along the way. O'Donnell even allows time for a bit of sightseeing (a side trip for some of the men to visit Clonmaurice) and escapes being trapped by the enemy near Cashel. In his diary, the Englishman Fynes Moryson writes that the escape was helped by an ice storm ("frost"), but the Masters take no note of the foul winter weather. Perhaps, as Donegal men, there was nothing noteworthy about it.

1601: A SPANISH FLEET ARRIVED in the south of Ireland. Don Juan de Aguila was the name of the chief who was general over them. The place at which they put in was the harbour of Kinsale, at the mouth of the green river of Bándon, on the confines of Courcy's country on the one side, and Kinalea, the country of Barry Oge, on the other. On their arrival at Kinsale they took to themselves the fortifications, shelter, defence, and maintenance of the town from the inhabitants who occupied them till then. They quartered their gentlemen, captains, and auxiliaries, throughout the habitations of wood and stone, which were in the town. They conveyed from their ships into the town their stores of viands and drink, [their] ordnance, powder, lead, and all the other necessaries which they had; and then they sent their ships back again to their [own] country. They planted their great guns, and their other projectile and defensive engines, at every point on which they thought the enemy would approach them. They also appointed guards and sentinels, who should be relieved at regular hours, as had been their constant custom before their arrival at that place, for they were very sure that the Lord Justice would come to attack them with the Queen's army, as soon as the news [of their arrival] should reach him.

There was another castle, on the east side of the harbour of Kinsale, called Rinn-Corrain, situate[d] in Kinelea, the territory of Barry Oge; in this town the Spaniards placed a garrison of some of their distinguished men, to guard it in like manner.

When the Lord Justice of Ireland [Mountjoy] heard these news, he did not delay until he arrived at Kinsale, with all the forces he was able to muster of those who were obedient to the Queen in Ireland. Thither arrived the President of the two provinces of Munster, with the forces of Munster along with him. The Earl of Clanrickard, and every head of a host and troop that was obedient to the command of the Lord Justice in Connaught, together with their forces, arrived at the same place. Thither in manner aforesaid came the Leinstermen and Meathmen, as they had been commanded by the Lord Justice.

After they had come together at one place, they pitched and arranged a camp before Kinsale, and from this they faced Rinn-Corrain; and they allowed them [the garrison there] neither quiet, rest, sleep, nor repose, for a long time; and they gave each other violent conflicts and manly onsets, until the warders, after all the hardships they encountered, were forced to come out unarmed, and surrender at the mercy of the Lord Justice, leaving their ordnance and their ammunition behind them. The Lord Justice billeted these throughout the towns of Munster, until he should see what would be the result of his contest with the other party who were at Kinsale. It was on this occasion that Carbry Oge, the son of Carbry Mac Egan, who was ensign to the son of the Earl of Ormond, was slain.

The Lord Justice, and his forces, and the Spaniards at Kinsale, continued to shoot and fire at each other during the first month of winter, until the Queen and Council advised the Earl of Thomond to go with many ships and vessels, with men, good arms, and stores, to relieve and succour the Sovereign's people in Ireland. On the Earl's arrival with the fleet in the harbour of Kinsale, they landed on that side of the harbour at which the Lord Justice's people were. Four thousand men was the number under the Earl of Thomond's command, of this army. Some say that, were it not for the great spirit and courage taken by the Lord Justice at the arrival of the Earl of Thomond and this force, he would have left the camp void and empty, and afterwards would have distributed the English [forces] among the great towns of Munster. The Earl of Thomond pitched a camp apart to himself, at that angle of the Lord Justice's camp which was nearest to Kinsale.

At this time the Spaniards made an assault by night upon a quarter of the Lord Justice's camp, and slew many men; and they thrust stones and wedges into a great gun of the Queen's ordnance, in order that they might prevent their enemies from firing on them out of it; and they would have slain more, were it not for the Earl of Clanrickard, for it was he and those around him that drove the Spaniards back to Kinsale. There was not one hour's cessation, by day or night, between these two camps, without blood being shed between them, from the first day on which the Lord Justice sat before Kinsale until they [ultimately] separated, as shall be related in the sequel.

When O'Neill, O'Donnell, and the Irish of Leath-Chuinn in general, heard the news of [the arrival of] this Spanish fleet, the resolution they came to, with one mind and one intention (although their chieftains and gentlemen did not assemble together to hold their consultation or conclude their counsel), was, that each lord of a territory among them should leave a guard and protection over his territory and fair land, and proceed, without dallying or delaying, to aid and assist the Spaniards, who had come at their call and instance; for it was distress of heart and disturbance of mind to them that they should be in such strait and jeopardy as they were placed in by their enemies, without relieving them, if they could.

O'Donnell was the first who prepared to go on this expedition. Having left guards over his creaghts [cattle herds] and all his people in the county of Sligo, he set out from Ballymote in the very beginning of winter. The following were some of the chiefs who were along with him: O'Rourke (Brian Oge, the son of Brian); the sons of John Burke; Mac Dermot of Moylurg; the sept of O'Conor Roe; O'Kelly; and the chiefs who had been banished from Munster, and were with him during the preceding part of this year, namely, Mac Maurice of Kerry (Thomas, the son of Patrickin); the Knight of Glin (Edmond, the son of Thomas); Teige Caech, the son of Turlough Mac Mahon; and Dermot Mael, the son of Donough Mac Carthy. These forces marched through the county of Roscommon, through the east of the county of Galway, and through Sil-Anmchadha, and to the Shannon. They were ferried over the Shannon at Ath-Croch; and they proceeded from thence into Delvin-Mac-Coghlan, into Fircall, as far as the upper part of Slieve-Bloom, and into Ikerrin.

O'Donnell remained near twenty days on the hill of Druim-Saileach, in Ikerrin, awaiting O'Neill, who was marching slowly after him; and, while stationed at that place, O'Donnell's people continued plundering, burning, and ravaging the country around them, so that there was no want of anything necessary for an army in his camp, for any period, short or long.

As soon as the Lord Justice of Ireland heard that O'Donnell was marching towards him, he sent the President of the two provinces of

Munster, namely, Sir George Carew, with four thousand soldiers, to meet him, in order to prevent him from making the journey on which his mind was bent, by blocking up the common road against him. When O'Donnell discovered that the President had arrived with his great host in the vicinity of Cashel, he proceeded with his forces from Ikerrin westwards, through the upper part of Ormond, by the monastery of Owny, through Clanwilliam, on the borders of the Shannon, to the gates of Limerick, and south-westwards, without halting or delaying by day or night, until he crossed the Maigue, into Hy-Connell-Gaura. As soon as the President perceived that O'Donnell had passed him by into the fastnesses of the country, and that his intention was frustrated, he returned back with his force to the Lord Justice. On this occasion Mac Maurice was permitted by O'Donnell to go with a part of the army to visit and see Clanmaurice. As they were traversing the country, they got an advantage of some of the castles of the territory, and took them. These were their names: Lixnaw, the Short-castle of Ardfert, and Ballykealy. In these they placed warders of their own. It was on the same occasion that O'Conor Kerry (John, the son of Conor) took his own castle, namely, Carraic-an-phuill, which had been upwards of a year before that time in the possession of the English, and that he himself, with the people of his castle, joined in alliance with O'Donnell.

O'Donnell remained nearly a week in these districts of Hy-Connell-Gaura, plundering, devastating, ravaging, and destroying the territories of every person in his neighbourhood who had any connexion or alliance with the English. After this O'Donnell proceeded over the upper part of Sliabh-Luachra, through Clann-Auliffe, through Muskerry, and to the Bandon in the Carberys. All the Irish of Munster came to him there, except Mac Carthy Reagh (Donnell, the son of Cormac-na-h-Aaoine) and Cormac, the son of Dermot, son of Teige, Lord of Muskerry. All these Irishmen promised to be in alliance and in unison with him from thenceforward.

As for O'Neill, i.e. Hugh, the son of Ferdorcha, son of Con Bacagh, he left Tyrone a week after Allhallowtide, to go to assist the aforesaid Spaniards. After he had crossed the Boyne he proceeded to plunder and burn the territories of Bregia and Meath. He afterwards marched through the west of Meath, and through the east of Munster, westwards across the Suir; but his adventures are not related until he arrived at the [River] Bandon, where O'Donnell was. John, son of Thomas Roe, son of the Earl [of Desmond], was along with O'Neill on this expedition.

When the Irish chiefs and their forces met together at one place, they encamped a short distance to the north of the camp of the Lord Justice at Bel-Guala, in Kinelea. Many a host and troop, and lord of a territory, and chief of a cantred, were along with O'Neill and O'Donnell at this place. Great were the spirit, courage, prowess, and valour, of the people who were there. There was not a spot or quarter in the five provinces of Ireland where these, or some party of them, had not impressed a horror and hatred, awe and dread of themselves among the English and Irish who were in opposition to them, till that time. Frequent and numerous had been their battles, their exploits, their depredations, their conflicts, their deeds, their achievements over enemies in other territories, up to this very hour. They met no mighty man whom they did not subdue, and no force over which they did not prevail, so long as the Lord and fortune favoured, that is, so long as they did the will of their Lord God, and kept his commandments and his will. Efficient for giving the onset, and gaining the battle over their enemies, were the tribes who were in this camp (although some of them did not assist one another), had God permitted them to fight stoutly with one mind and one accord, in defence of their religion and their patrimony, in the strait difficulty in which they had the enemy on this occasion.

AN ENGLISHMAN'S SIEGE
AND BATTLE DIARY

BY FYNES MORYSON

⚜

Fynes Moryson (1566–1630), Lord Mountjoy's private secretary and his official historian of the Nine Years War, was hardly unbiased about Ireland. A critic once said that Moryson could find nothing in Ireland to praise but the whiskey. But his day-by-day account of the tedium and discomfort of the wintertime siege of Spanish-held Kinsale becomes, in its own dogged way, downright harrowing: a long and painful build-up to a battle that lasted less than three hours. It's a siege in which the besiegers see themselves as being as badly off as the besieged.

OF THE BESIEGING OF THE Spaniards at Kinsale, with the delivery of the Towne to the Lord Deputy, and their returne into Spaine.

The 16 day of October, his Lordship [Mountjoy] with the Army rose from Corke, and encamped five miles short of Kinsale, at a place called Owny Buoy. The 17 the army rose, & marching towards Kinsale, encamped within half a mile of the towne under a hill called Knock Robin, where some few shot [from] the Spaniards offered to disturbe our sitting downe, but were soone beaten home. Wee had at that time scarce so much Powder as would serve for a good dayes fight, neither had wee any competent number of tooles, so as wee could not intrench our selves, for these provisions were not yet come from Dublin. . . .

The eighteenth: the Army lay still, and we viewed the fittest places to incampe neere the Towne: but our Artillerie being not come, we removed not. And that night the Spaniards made a salley, much greater then the former, to disturbe our Campe, but our men soone repelled them without any losse to us. The nineteenth: wee lay still, expecting provisions, and that day, our men sent to view the ground, had some slight skirmishes with the enemy, and Don Jean [de Aguila, the Spanish commander] after professed, that hee never saw any come more willingly to the sword, then our men did. . . .

The one and twentieth: Cormock Mac Dermot a [loyal] Irish man, chiefe of a Countrie called Muskerie, came with the rising out (or souldiers) of his Countrie, to shew them to the Lord Deputy, who to the end the Spaniards might see the meere Irish served on our side, commanded them at their returne to passe by the Spanish trenches, made without the Towne on the top of the hil, but lodged strong parties (out of the enemies sight) to second them. The Irish at first went on wel, and did beat the Spanish guards from their ground, but according to their custome, suddenly fell off, and so left one of the Lord Presidents horsemen ingaged, who had charged two Spaniards: but Sir William Godolphin commanding the Lord Deputies troope, when he saw him in danger, and unhorsed, did charge one way up on their grosse, and Captain Henry Barkley Cornet of the same troope, charged another way at the same instant, and drove their shot into the trenches, and so rescued the horseman with his horse, comming off with one man hurt, and onely one horse killed, from the great numbers of Spanish shot, whereof foure were left dead in the place, divers carried off dead into the Towne, and many hurt. . . .

The three & twentieth: the Dublyn shipping arrived at Corke, & were directed to come presently to Oyster Haven, where we might unlade the Artillery (which could not be brought by land), and other provisions for the present use of the Army.

The foure and twenty day it was resolved, we should rise and incampe close by the Towne, but the shipping being not come about with the artillery and other necessaries, that day was spent in dispatching for England. And by night Captaine Blany and Captaine Flower were sent out, to lie with five hundred foote, to intertaine the Spaniards which were drawne out of the Towne, but they came no further, and so our men returned.

A LETTER TO LONDON

This day his Lordship and the Counsell wrote to the Lords in England this following letter.

. . . We can assure your Lordships that we doe not thinke our selves much stronger (if any thing at all) in numbers then they are, whose army at their setting to sea, did beare the reputation of sixe thousand. . . . It must in reason be thought, that our Companies generally are weake in numbers, seeing they have had no supplies of a long time, and that we desire two thousand to reinforce them, besides that many are taken out of them for necessary wards, some are sicke, and many of the Northern Companies lie yet hurt, since the late great skirmishes against Tyrone, which they performed with good successe but a little before they were sent for to come hither. Wee doe assuredly expect, that many will joine with Tyrone, (if hee onely come up towards these parts), and almost all the Swordmen of this Kingdome, if we should not keepe the field, and the countenance of being Masters thereof, how ill provided soever wee doe find our selves. . . . And although (grieved with her Majesties huge expence) we are loth to propound for so many men as are conceived to be needefull and profitable for the present prosecution of this dangerous warre, yet wee are of opinion, that the more men her Majesty can presently spare, to be imployed in this Countrie, the more safe and sudden end it will make of her charge. And not without cause we are moved to solicite your Lordships to consider thereof, since wee now perceive that we have an Army of old and disciplined souldiers before us of foure thousand Spaniards (that assuredly expect a far greater supply), and much about twenty thousand fighting men, of a furious and warlike nation of the Irish, which wee may justly suspect will all declare themselves against us, if by our supplies and strength out of England, they doe not see us likely to prevaile. These Provincials (a few of Carbry only excepted, appertaining to Florence Mac Carty) do yet stand firme, but no better then neutralitie is to be expected from those which are best affected, nor is it possible to discover their affections, untill Tyrone with the Irish Forces doe enter into the Province, who (as the Councell at Dublin write) is providing to come hither. . . . Wherefore wee humbly beseech the sending of them away, which will not onely give us a speedie course to winne the Towne, but also assure the coasts for our supplies, and give an exceeding stay to the Countrie (the enemie fearing nothing more, and the subject desiring nothing so much as the arrivall of her Majesties Fleet). . . .

On the other side, Don Jean de l'Aguyla the Spanish Generall, hath used many arguments to move the Irish to defection, and among other (which is very forceable and fearefull unto their wavering spirits), he telles them, that this is the first great action that the King his Master hath undertaken, and assures them he hath protested, that he will not receive scorne in making good his enterprise, and that he will rather hazard the losse of his Kingdoms, then of his Honour in this enterprise. The Priests likewise (to terrifie the consciences) threaten hell and damnation to those of the Irish, that doe not assist them (having brought Bulles for that purpose), and send abroad Indulgences to those that take their parts. These and such like pollicies (as their offering of six shillings a day to every horseman that will serve them) doe so prevaile with this barbarous Nation, as it is a wonder unto us, that from present staggering they fall not to flat defection, as they will soone doe, if they once discover them of abilitie to give us one blow, before the comming of our supplies and meanes, which wee are most earnestly to solicite your Lordships to hasten. . . . Sir I will trouble you no longer, being desirous to doe somewhat worth the writing. God send us an Easterly winde, and unto you as much happines as I doe wish unto my owne soule. From the Campe by Kinsale this 24 of October 1601.

Yours Sir most assured for ever
to doe you service,
Mountjoy.

THE SIEGE CONTINUES WITH AN ATTACK ON CASTLE RINCORANE

The five and twenty: the Army was ready to rise, but the weather falling out very foule, direction was given not to dislodge. Foure naturall Spaniards came this day to us from the Enemy, who the next day were sent to Corke. This night Sir John Barkeley went out with some three hundred foot, having with him Captaine Flower, Captaine Morris, and Captaine Bostocke, and fell into the Spaniards trenches, and did beate them to the Towne, fell into the gate with them, and killed and hurt above twenty of the Spaniards, having but three hurt of our men. Hitherto we lodged in Cabbins, so as it rained upon us in our beds, and when we changed our shirts.

The sixe and twenty: the Army dislodged and incamped on an hill on the North-side before Kinsale, called the Spittle, somewhat more then musket shot from the Towne, and there intrenched strongly. When we sat downe, we discovered that the Spaniards had gotten a prey of two hundred or three hundred Cowes, and many sheepe, which were (in an Iland as it seemed) upon the South-east side of the Towne, beyond the water, which wee could not passe but by going eight or nine mile about, where there was a necke of land to goe into it. Captaine Taffe being sent with horse and foot, used such expedition in that businesse, as he attained the place before night, and by a hot skirmish recovered the prey, save onely some twenty Cowes that the Spaniards had killed, although they were under the guard of a Castle, called Castle Ny Parke, which the Spaniards had in possession. . . .

Now the Spaniards held the Castle of Rincorane from their first landing, and because it commanded the Harbour of Kinsale, so that our shipping could not safely land our provisions neere the Campe, it was thought fit to make the taking thereof our first worke. To which purpose Sir John Barkeley, Sir William Godolphin, and Captaine Josias Bodley Trench-

Master, were sent to chuse a fit place to plant our Artillerie against the Castle. The 28 day two Colverings which had not been long used, were made fit, and the next day they were mounted. The Spaniards were in the towne foure thousand strong, and wee had not many more in the Campe by Pole, though our Lyst were more. That night the Spaniards issued out of the Towne by water, to relieve the Castle, but Captain Buttons ship did beate them backe. The thirtieth day the two Culverings began to batter the Castle, but one of them brake in the eavening.

In the meane time the Spaniards gave an Alarum to our Campe, and drew a demy Canon out of the Towne, wherewith they plaied into the Camp, killed two with the first shot, neere the Lord Deputies tent, shot through the next tent of the pay-Master, (wherein we his Lordships Secretaries did lie) brake a barrell of the Pay-Masters money, with two barrels of the Lord Deputies beare in the next Cabin, and all the shot were made, fell in the Lord Deputies quarter, and neere his owne tent.

This night the Spaniards attempted againe to relieve the Castle, but Sir Richard Percy having the guard, with the Lord Presidents Regiment under his command, did repulse them. The one and thirtieth day the colvering battered the Castle, and that morning another culvering, & a canon, being planted, they plaied without intermission, which while we were busily attending, 500 of their principall Spaniards came out of Kinsale (with shew to go to relieve Rincorran by land) and drew toward a guard we kept betweene Rincorran and the Towne. . . . And seeing the Spaniards come up close with their Pikes to give a charge, he joyned with Captaine Roe, and incountring them, did beate them back to their seconds, making them to retire hastily, the Spaniards then playing upon our men with shot from every house in that part of the Towne. In this charge Sir Oliver Saint John received many pushes of the Pike on his Target, and with one of them was slightly hurt in the thigh, but hee killed a Leader and a common souldier with his owne hand. The Lord Audley coming up with his Regiment, was shot through the thigh. Sir Garret Harvy was hurt in the hand, and had his horse killed under him, Captaine Buttlers Lieutenant was slaine, and foure other of our part. Sir Arthur Savages Lieutenant was shot through the body, and fourteene other of our part were hurt. The ene-mie left ten dead in the place, besides their hurt men, which we apparantly saw to be many, and the next day heard to be seventie, by one who saw them brought to the house, where their hurt men lay, and who reported, that eight of them died that night. Likewise in this skirmish Juan Hortesse del Contreres was taken prisoner, who had been Serjeant Major of the Forces in Britany, and our men got from them divers good Rapiers, and very good Armes.

All this while our 3 pieces battered the Castle, till six of the clock at night, when those of the Castle did beate a Drumme, which the Lord President (whom the Lord Deputie had left there, when himselfe in the evening returned to take care of the Camp) admitted to come unto him. With the Drum came an Irish man borne at Corke, and these in the name of the rest, prayed that with their Armes, Bagge and Baggage, they might depart to Kinsayle. This the Lord President refused, and said hee would not conclude with any but the Commander of the Castle, neither had commission to accept any composition, but yeelding to her Majesties mercie. Presently they sent another Drumme, and a Serjeant with him, but the Lord President refused to speake with them. At their returne the Commander himselfe, being an Alfiero (or Ensigne) called Bartholomeo del Clarizo (for the Captaine had his legge broken) came unto the Lord President, but insisting on the condition to part with Armes, Bag and Baggage to Kinsale, his offer was refused. After he was put safe into the Castle, wee began afresh the battery, and they more hotly then ever before bestowed their vollies of shot on us. But the first of November at two of the clocke in the morning, when they found how the Castle was weakened by the fury of our battery, they did againe beate a Drumme for a parley, but we refusing it, many of them attempted to escape under the rocke close to the water side, which our men perceiving, drew close up to the Castle, and hindered their escape.

The first of November: . . . About one hower of the day the Alfiero sent word to the Lord President that he would quit all their Armes, and render the place, so as they might be suffered thus unarmed to goe into Kinsale, which being refused, hee intreated that himselfe alone might hold his Armes, and bee put into Kinsale, which being also refused, he resolutely resolved to burie himselfe in the Castle. His Company seeing him desperately bent not to yeeld, did threaten to cast him out of the breach, so as they might be received to mercy. So as at last he consented to yeeld, and that all his people should be disarmed in the Castle (which was committed to Captaine Roger Harvy then Captaine of the Guards, to see it done), that the Alfiero himself should weare his sword till hee came to the Lord President, to whom he should render it up. And this being done, they were all brought prisoners into the Campe, and immediatly sent from thence to Corke. The Spanish thus yeelded, were in number fourescore and sixe, and foure women (whose names I have, but omit them for brevitie), besides a great multitude of Irish Churles, Women and Children, but not any Swordmen; for those being skilfull in the waies, had all escaped. . . .

THE CAMP TO BE FORTIFIED AGAINST TYRONE

The fifth of November: foure barkes with munition and victuals that were sent from Dublin, arrived in Kinsale harbor, and upon certaine intelligence, that Tyrone was comming up with a great Army to joyne with the Spaniard, it was resolved by the Counsell of State, and the Colonels of Councell at warre, that the next day the Camp should be fortified against Tyrone, on the North side furthest from the towneward, and that the next day following, the Lord President with two Regiments of foote, consisting of two thousand one hundred men in Lyst, and with three hundred twentie five horse, should draw to the borders of the Province, to stop, or at least hinder Tyrones passage. To which purpose the Lord Barry, and the Lord Bourke, with the forces of the Countrie, had direction to attend the Lord President.

The sixth day the Campe was accordingly fortified, and the seventh in the morning, the Lord President with the said horse and foote left the Campe, at which time it was concluded by both Counsels, that wee could attempt nothing against the towne, untill either the Lord President returned, or the new Forces and provisions promised from England arrived, it being judged a great worke for us in the meane time, to continue our lying before the Towne, since the Spaniards in the Towne were more in number, then we who besieged them. . . .

The eight of November: certaine ships to the number of thirteene, were discried to passe by Kinsale to the Westward, but it was not knowne whether they were English or Spaniards. The tenth day we had newes that the Earl of Thomond was landed with one thousand foote, left to the Lord Deputies disposall, and with an hundred horse, appointed in England to be commanded by the said Earle; and these were the thirteene ships discovered to passe Westward.

By this time the Spaniards had gotten knowledge of the Lord Presidents departure from the Campe with good part of our forces, and thereupon supposing us to be much weakened, (as in deed we were, and inferiour in bodies of men to them in the Towne); they drew out this day about noone most part of their forces, and soon after sent some sixty shot and Pykes to the foot of the hill, close by our Campe, leaving their trenches very well lined for their seconds: some of ours were presently drawne out to entertaine skirmish with those that came up, and another strong party was sent out towards Ryncorran, who from the bushy hill plaied in flanckes upon their trenches, and did beate them from the same; so as they that were first sent out close to our Campe, being beaten backe by our shot, and thinking to find the seconds they left behind them, were disappointed by their

293

quitting of the Trenches, and by that meanes driven to follow the rest to the succour of the Towne. Our men following with much fury, hurt and killed divers, amongst whom they brought off the body of a Sergiant, and possessed the enemies trenches, the which the enemies (being reinforced) made many attempts to regaine, but were repulsed and beaten backe into the Towne. Wee heard by divers, that Don Jean committed the Sergiant Major, who commanded then in chiefe, presently after the fight, and threatned to take his head, commended highly the valour of our men, and cried shame upon the cowardise of his owne, who he said had beene the terrour of all Nations; but now had lost that reputation, and hee gave straight commandement upon paine of death, which hee caused to bee set up on the Towne gates, that from thenceforth no man should come off from any service, untill hee should be fetched off by his Officer, though his powder were spent or his Peece broken, but make good his place with his Sword. Captaine Soto one of their best Commanders, was that day slaine, (for whom they made very great mone), and some twenty more, besides those we hurt, which could not be but many. On our side, onely some ten were hurt, and three killed; among whom Master Hopton a Gentleman of the Lord Deputies band, was sore hurt, and in a few daies died thereof. If this skirmish had not beene readily & resolutely answered on our part, the Spaniards had then discovered the smalnes of our numbers, and would no doubt have so plied us with continuall sallies; as we should hardly have beene able to continue the siege.

The eleventh day: we had newes, that the one hundred horse and the thousand foot embarked at Bastable, (both which were left to the Lord Deputies disposall, the horse to be made new troopes, the foot to be dispersed for supplies, or to raise new Companies as his Lordship should thinke fit) were arrived at Waterford. . . .

The thirteenth day: our Fleet recovered the mouth of Kinsale Harbour, but could not get in, the wind being strong against them. The foureteenth day the Fleete with much difficulty warped in, and recovered the Harbour, whence the Admirall and Vice-Admirall came to the Lord Deputy at the Campe. This night and the next day the two thousand foot, sent under Captaines in the Queenes shippes, were landed, and came to the Campe. And the fifteenth day in the afternoone, the Lord Deputy went aboard the shippes, whence returning to the Campe, the Enemy discerned him riding in the head of a troop of horse, and made a shot out of the Town at him, which grazed so neere him, that it did beat the earth in his face. In these ships were sent unto us not onely artillery and munition, but also speciall Officers to attend the same, as five Canoneers, two Blacke-smiths, two Wheel-wrights, and two Carpenters. . . .

CASTLE NYPARKE BATTERED

The Queenes ships after they had saluted the Lord Deputy at his going aboard with thundering peales of Ordinance, had direction the next day to beat upon a Castle in the Iland, called Castle Nyparke, which the Lord Deputy was resolved to make his next worke, & to beat the Spaniards out of it, and so to invest the Towne on that side. This some of the ships performed, and brake the top of the Castle, but finding that they did it no greater hurt, and that the weather was extreame stormy, they ceased shooting. This day his Lordship gave direction, that the hundred horse & one thousand foot, which first landed at Castle Haven, and now were arrived from thence in the Harbour of Kinsale, should be conducted to Corke, to refresh themselves, for being beaten at Sea, and now landed in extreame weather, and in a Winter Campe, where they had no meanes to be refreshed, they beganne to die, and would have beene lost or made unserviceable, if this course had not beene taken to hearten them. This day and for many daies after, divers Spaniards ranne from the Towne to us, by whom we understood that in the tenth daies skirmish, the above named Captain Soto, a man of speciall accompt, was slaine.

The seventeenth day: the weather continued stormy, so as neither that day nor the next we could land our Ordinance, or doe any thing of moment, yet because this was the day of her Majesties Coronation, which his Lordship purposed to solemnize with some extraordinary attempt, if the weather would have suffered us to looke abroad, wee sent at night when the storme was somewhat appeased, the Serjant Major and Captaine Bodley with some foure hundred foot, to discover the ground about Castle Nyparke, and to see whether it might be carried with the Pickaxe, which was accordingly attempted; but the engine we had gotten to defend our men, while they were to worke, being not so strong as it should have beene, they within the Castle having store of very great stones on the top, tumbled them downe so fast, as they broke it, so that our men returned with the losse of two men, & proceeded no further in that course. . . .

The nineteenth day: a Demy Cannon was unshipped, assoone as it was calme, and placed on this side of the water, which plaied most part of the day upon the Castle Nyparke, being a great reliefe to the besieged, & brake many places, but made no breach that was assaultable. In the night they of the Towne attempted to releeve the Castle by boates, but were repelled by Captaine Tolkerne and Captaine Ward, who lay with their Pinnaces betweene the Iland and the Towne.

Hitherto nothing could possibly bee attempted against the Towne, more then had beene done. For considering that the numbers of the defendants not onely equalled, but by all report, exceeded the number of the besiegers, . . . and considering that if wee had undertaken the carrying of approaches, with a purpose to batter, the whole Army must either have been tired with watching night and day, without shelter, in tempestuous weather, or disgracefully have forsaken the worke, or (to say the best) incurred the hazard of fight in places of disadvantage, with an expert enemy. And considering that the Countrey stood upon such tickle tearmes, and so generally ill affected to our side, that almost the least blow, which in the doubtfull event of warre might have lighted upon us, would have driven them headlong into a generall revolt. And further, that our Army consisted for a third part (at the least) of Irish, who being not fit to make good an entrenched campe, & much lesse fit to give upon a breach, would without question, either presently have quitted us, or turned their weapons against us, if the Spaniards had had any hand over us; and considering that in al sound judgement, this little army, (which was to be the soule of that body that should oppose it selfe against these invaders and rebels), was by all possible meanes to bee preserved as much as might be, and not at all ventured, but with manifest assurance to prevaile. These things with other like circumstances considered, what could there be more done, during the time that we wanted our supplies and seconds. . . .

INTELLIGENCE OUT OF THE TOWNE

Six Irish Gentlemen horsemen came into the towne of Kinsale on Sunday the fifteenth of November, and one Owen Conde came the same day, and they are all readie to goe out againe, and Father Archer with them. Don Jean says privately, that the Lord Deputy was borne in a happy [hour], for he will have the Towne, unlesse they be relieved from the North. They have nothing but ruske and water. They have but foure pieces of Artillery, one small piece is at the Churchyard, one great and a small in James Meaghes Garden, and the other biggest of all is at the Watergate, to play upon the shipping, and all foure are mounted. The Spaniards were five thousand by report at their setting out from Spaine, they landed at Kinsale three thousand five hundred, they are yet 3000, there are two hundred sicke and hurt in the hospitals, they lost 100 at Rincorran, and 17 and a boy at Castle Nyparke. They had nine slaine when they offered to relieve the Castle, and five when Captaine Soto was slaine. . . .

They fill the old Abbey at the West gate with earth, that they may mount a great piece there, which they make account wil command the ground where the English battery is planted at the North Gate, where the Mount is raised, yet it is not likely they will mount any Ordinance there, but rather keep it as a hold. They have store of powder and munition, which lies at John Fitz Edmonds Castle, but they meane to remove it presently, and put it in a seller within the towne. Their treasure lies at the house where Captaine Bostock lay. They are much afraid the Lord Deputie will place some Ordinance at Castle Nyparke, or thereabouts, which will much annoy them; but most of all they feare the placing of it at a place neere the water side for which cause they raised their mount, but especially filled up the old Abbey, from whence it is best commanded. Don Jean lies at Phillip Roches. A shot made from the English on Friday at night, hit the house where Don Jean lay. The Townesmen will stay no longer there, for feare of the shot, and then the Spaniards will be in great distresse. One went from Don Jean to Tyrone about nine daies agoe to hasten his coming, the man was blind of one eye. . . .

The same two and twentieth day foure Pieces were planted by the Cannon and demy Cannon, which altogether played into the Towne, one of which shot killed foure men in the Market place, and strucke off a Captaines leg, called Don John de Saint John, who after died of that hurt, we likewise planted three Culverings in the Iland beyond the water, in which the foresaid Castle Nypark stands, and from whence we heard, that Don Jean feared annoiance.

The three and twentieth: these did beate upon the old Towne with good effect. And the same day our other six Pieces on the North-East side plaied upon the Towne, and so continued till night, in which time (in all mens judgments, and by report of the prisoners we tooke) they did great hurt to the Towne. This day while the Lord Deputie, the Marshall and Serjeant Major were viewing the ground where the approches were intended, a private souldier of Sir John Barkleys, in their sight, and in face of the Spanish guards, attempting to steale a Spanish sentenel (as hee had stolne divers before) this sentenel being seconded by foure, that he saw not, he fought with them all five, whereof one was the Serjeant Major, whom he had almost taken; and when he found he could doe no good upon them all, he came off without other hurt, then the cutting of his hand a little, with the breaking of a thrust, which one of them made at him, and he hurt the Serjeant Major.

The night following, we began certaine neere approches on the North-East side of the Towne on a hill, which by the naturall situation thereof, was free from sudden sallies, by reason of a valley betweene it and the Towne, so as it might bee speedily seconded from the Campe. There with much expedition was raised a Fort (and Artillery planted, to play into the Towne). . . . For making those approches, the Lord Deputy drew out one thousand foote, continuing the worke all night; and although the ground were extreme hard, by reason of the Frost, and the night very light, yet that night they brought the worke to very good perfection. The enemy played all the night upon them with great vollyes, but hurt onely three men, either in the trenches, or in divers sallyes they made (in the one whereof a squadron of our new men did beat them back to the Gates).

This day the Lord President advertised that O donnell [Hugh O'Donnell], by advantage of a Frost (so great as seldome had been seene in Ireland), had passed a Mountaine, and so had stolne by him into Mounster, whereupon he purposed to returne with the forces hee had, to strengthen the Campe. And in the evening Sir Richard Levison, by the Lord Deputies direction, drew the Admirall and Vice-Admirall in betweene the Iland and Kinsale, whence the foure and twentieth day they shot into the Towne.

The five and twentieth day: all the Artillery still played upon the Towne: but the shot from the ships doing little hurt, save onely upon the base Towne, the Lord Deputie gave direction to spend few shot more, except it were on the high Towne. This night direction was given to make a platforme for the Artillery upon the trenches, which was made the three and twentieth at night. Somewhat after midnight the Spaniards made a sudden salley, with purpose to force the trench, but were soon beaten backe by Sir Francis Barkeley, who commanded the watch that night in that place.

The sixe and twentieth: the Lord President with the two Regiments of foote, and with his horse he had led out against Odonnell, together with a Connaght Regiment under the Earle of Clanrickard, and a Regiment of the Pale under Sir Christopher Saint Laurence (which upon the way were commanded to joyne with the Lord President), came to the Campe; and these foure Regiments were that night quartered by themselves, upon the West-side of Kinsale, to invest the Towne more closely, and to keepe Odonnell and the Spaniards from joyning together. . . .

This day the three Culverings were brought from the Iland beyond the water on the East-side, and were planted on a hill, in a point of land neere the water on this side of the Haven, lying to the East of our Fort newly built there, to which hill the Towne lay neere and very open. In the meane time the Spaniards from the Towne, played upon our ships with a Demy-Cannon, and shot our Admirall twise, and our Vice-admirall once, while they rode (as aforesaid) close by the Towne, but our ships within few shot exchanged, did dismount their Demi-Cannon, so as they could make no more shot with it, and at the same shot hurt their chiefe Gunner. . . .

KINSALE SUMMONED

The foresaid eight and twenty: in the morning, we sent a Trumpet to summon Kinsale, who was not suffered to enter the Towne, but received his answere at the gate, that they held the Town first for Christ, and next for the King of Spaine, and so would defend it Contra tanti. Upon his returne with this answere, the Lord Deputy commanded to make battery with all our Artillery, (planted all on the East side of the Towne), which was presently performed, and continuing till towards night, brake downe great part of the East gate. In the meane time the Spaniards being retired in great numbers into their trenches on the West side, to escape the fury of our Ordinance on the East side, Sir Christopher S. Laurence was commanded to draw out from our new Campe, on the West side, and to give upon them in their trenches, which he performed, and did beat them out of the Trenches, following them to the very gate of the Towne, killing many, and hurting more of them, and so returned without losse of a man on our side, having onely some few hurt. The nine & twentieth all our Artillery plaied upon the Town, and brake downe most part of the Easterne gate, and some part of a new worke the Enemy had made before the gate. This day two Spaniards wrote from Kinsale to some of their friends prisoners in our Campe, whom they stiled poore Souldiers, when we knew them to be men of accompt, and withal sent them such money as they wanted, yet under the title of Almes, as if they had neither mony of their owne, nor were of credit to be trusted for any.

The last day of November: Sir Richard Wingfield the Marshall tooke some fifty shot, and went to the wall of the Towne, to view the fittest place for us to make a breach, the Spaniards made a light skirmish with them, and hurt some few. The Marshall when he had well viewed the wall, drew the shot off, and judging the wall, close to the Easterne gate on the right hand, to be fittest for the making of a breach, he gave present order that our artillery should beat upon that place, which was done without intermission, and therewith we brake downe before night a great part of the wall, which the Enemy in the night attempted to make up againe, but was beaten from it by our Guards, who plaied upon them with small shot most part of the night. In the evening a Spaniard ranne away from Kinsale to our campe, who reported to the Lord Deputy that our Artillery had killed divers Captaines and Officers in the Towne, besides many private souldiers.

The first of December: it was resolved . . . that some foote should bee drawne out of the campe, to give the Spaniard a bravado, and to view if the breach we had made were assaultable, and also to cause the Spaniards to shew themselves, that our Artillery might the better play upon them. To this purpose two thousand foot . . . and drawne neere the wals of the Towne, who entertained a very hot skirmish with the Spaniards, who were lodged in a trench close to the breach without the Towne. During this skirmish, our Artillery plaied upon those that shewed themselves, either in the breach or in the trench, and killed many of them, besides such as were killed and hurt by our small shot.

Among the rest one Captaine Moryson a Spaniard, (of whom . . . we shal have cause to speake hereafter) walked crosse the breach, animating his men, and though Sir Richard Wingfield our Marshall caused many both great and smal shot to be made at him, with promise of 20 pound to him that should hit him, or beat him off, (whereupon many great shot did beat the durt in his face, and stones about his eares); yet all the skirmish he continued walking in this brave manner, without receiving any hurt. Many thinke them best souldiers, who are often and dangerously hurt, but it is an errour: for wounds are badges of honour, yet may befall the coward assoone as the valiant man; and I have knowne most adventurous men who never received wound. Pardon this my digression, not warrantable in a journall, I will onely adde, that brave souldiers (for the starres have a kinde of power in our birth) are by some secret influence preserved, when others intruding themselves into that course of life, or driven to it by necessity of estate, fall at the first allarum. . . . After an howers fight, when we had taken full view of the breach, and found it not assaultable, our men were drawne off, with little or no dammage on our part, onely three of our men were hurt, and Captaine Guests Horse was killed under him, which Captaine first had killed two Spaniards with his owne hand.

The same day it was resolved in counsell, to plant a Fort on a Rath on the West side of the Towne, to lodge therein some foote, for seconds to the guard of our artillery, intended to be planted neere the same. And to this purpose, in the night following, the Marshall, the Sergiant Major, Captaine Edward Blany, and Captaine Josias Bodley Trenchmaster, (the Lord Deputy being almost all night present with them), drew out five and twenty of each company, and intrenching themselves on the said hill, not halfe Callivers shot from the Towne, beganne to cast up a small Fort. And though the Spaniards perceived not their purpose, yet many of them lying in a trench they possessed close to the West gate, did play very hotly all night on our men, guarding the Pyoners, and ours did no lesse on them, so that divers were hurt and killed on both sides. But the second day of December, about nine in the morning, when a great myst beganne to breake, and they discovered our worke a yard high, then from the said

Trenches, and more from the Castles, and high places in the Towne, they plied us all the day with small shot. Notwithstanding which annoyance, our men brought the work to very good perfection before the night. In the meane time, a Serjeant to Captaine Blany, drew out some seven or eight shot, and suddenly fell into a Trench which some Spaniards possessed, close by the Towne, of whom the Serjeant killed two, and each of the rest one, with their owne hands. But when not content therewith, they attempted another Trench, something distant from the first, the Serjeant in going on was shot through the body and two of his Company were hurt in bringing him off and so returned with this and no more losse.

This night the Trenches where the Cannon was planted on the East side of the Towne, were manned with the Lord Deputies guard. . . . Now within . . . two houres before the Moone rose, it being very darke and rainy, the Spaniard impatient off the Forts building, the day before so close to the Townes West gate, and resolving to attempt bravely on our Ordinance, planted on the East side, made a brave sally with some two thousand men, and first gave slightly towards the Trenches on the West side, but presently with a grosse and their chiefe strength fell upon the Trenches, in which the Artillery lay on the East side, continuing their resolution to force it . . . having brought with them Tooles of divers sorts, to pull downe the Gabbyons and the Trenches, as also spykes, to cloy the Ordinance. The allarum being taken in the campe, the Marchall and Serjeant Major . . . with some one hundred men fell directly towards the Port of the Towne next to the Campe, and the Lord Deputy sent out Sir Oliver Saint Johns with seconds. Upon the Marshals arrivall and charge, the enemy brake, and our men did execution upon them. Sir Benjamin Berry fell directly upon the enemies seconds, whom he charged and brake, killing many of them, and taking the Commander of that body, being an ancient Captaine, of great estimation with the enemy. At the same time the enemy gave upon our trenches and Fort built the day before on the West side, and continued the attempt long with great fury, till Captaine Flower in heate and without direction, sallying out of the Fort, to follow part of their forces discomfited, the enemie entered the Fort before he could returne, and possessed themselves of our trenches. Yet still our men continued the fight, and Sir William Godolphin gave many brave charges with his horse, to countenance our men, till the Earle of Clanrickard was sent to second them on this part. . . . Then his Lordship and the rest charged the enemies grosse, being without the Fort, and brake them, and did execution upon them falling towards the towne, and so returning thence, entered the West Fort again, with little resistance, for the enemie abandoned it. . . . In this salley in all the enemy left in the field above one hundred and twenty dead bodies, besides such as were killed neere the Towne, and could not next day bee discerned by us. And wee tooke thirteene prisoners . . . After we heard by some of the Towne, that they left dead above two hundred of their best men . . . and that more then two hundred of them were hurt. On our part Captaine Flower, Captaine Skipwith, and the Earle of Clanrickards Lieutenant were hurt, and Captaine Spencer, and Captaine Dillon, and Captaine Flowers Lieutenant, were killed in the West Fort, who staying in the Fort when Captaine Flower sallied, were there found dead in the place which they were commanded to make good, and with their faces to the enemie, in as honourable manner as could be expected from any souldier. . . . The trenches about the cannon were in some places filled with dead bodies; for in that particular attempt they left seventy two bodies dead in the place, and those of their best men, whereof some were found having spikes and hammers to cloy the cannon. And in generall among the dead bodies many were found to have spels, caracters, and hallowed meddals, which they woare as preservations against death, and most of them when they were stripped, were seene to have scarres of Venus warfare [venereal disease]. Wee tooke some fortie shovels, and as many mattocks, and much Armes, left in the field, which tooles were so massie, as they had great advantage of us therein, and the sight of them would have put her Majesties Ministers of the Ordinance to shame, who for private gaine sent sale ware to us, unfit to be used. . . .

Some hower before this skirmish, the Lord Deputie was advertised by one Donnogh O Driscoll, that sixe Spanish ships were put into Castle Haven, and that six more were sent with them from the Groyne, but in the way were scattered from these by tempest, and that since it was not knowne what became of them. That in these six ships arrived, were two thousand Spaniards, with great store of Ordinance and Munition, and that by their report twentie thousand more were comming presently after them. The third of December, by reason of rany weather, nothing could be done. . . .

A Drumme was sent to the Towne, to offer Don Jean liberty to bury his dead, which message he received with due respect, but prayed us to burie them, with promise to do the like for any of ours happening to fall in his power. And because our Drum, according to his direction, expostulated with Don Jean, that howsoever the Spanish prisoners were well used by us . . . one of our men taken in the last salley, after he was hurt, so long as he gave himselfe out to be an Irish man, was kept in the hospitall, but after being discovered to be an Englishman, was drawne out, and killed. For this cause Don Jean sent backe with him a Spanish Drum to the Lord Deputy, intreating buriall for his dead, with the foresaid promise to doe the like for ours. . . . His Lordship promised to doe, as a Christianlike act, though he knew the inequalitie of the offer, having so many of their bodies presently in his power. . . .

A CHALLENGE SENT BY DON JEAN

His Lordship also excepted to a kind of challenge sent by Don Jean, that the question betweene England and Spaine should be tried by combat betweene them two, this triall being in neither of their powers by commission, nor in Don Jeans will, though hee had the power, besides that the Councell of Trent forbad the Romanists to fight in Campo Steccato (or combat in the field) so as this message was rather quarrelsome then honourable, which otherwise his Lordship protested to bee most willing to accept, with thankes for the noble offer. Lastly, his Lordship remembred, that at our first setting downe, he sent a Drum to Don Jean, with this message; That whereas his Lordhsip understood certaine Ladies and women to bee in the Towne, he offered them before the playing of our Artillerie free leave to depart, or remaining there still, to command any provision for themselves which our campe afforded. And that Don Jean made an uncivill answere, That he would not be his Baud. To these exceptions hee answered with a Spanish shrug of the shouldier, as having no knowledge nor commission, to satisfie his Lordship therein. So his Lordship protested, that all the courtesie offered hitherto by him, proceeded out of that honourable respect which useth to passe betweene honourable enemies, and because he would ever be true to his owne Honour, whatsoever others were to theirs. But in case it were conceived to proceede of any respect of the greatnes or power of the Spanish Nation, or his owne feare, that he would hereafter shew how much he disdained such ill interpretations of courtesie. And so his Lordship dismissed the Drum.

This night the Spaniards attempted something by boats against our Sentinels, but were soone beaten backe againe. The fifth day Sir Richard Levison, though the wind hindered the going out of Kinsale Harbour, yet with towing, got out the Warspite, the Defiance, the Swiftsure, the Marline, one Merchant, and a Carvill, and with them went to seeke the Spanish Fleete newly arrived at Castlehaven. . . .

The sixth day: at ten in the morning, our Fleete arrived at Castle haven, and before foure in the after-noone one Spanish ship was sunke, the Spanish Admirall with nine foote water in hold drove to the shore upon the rocks, the Vice-admirall with two others drove likewise aground, most of the Spaniards quitting their ships. Our Fleete was forced to stay there the next day by contrary winds, and the Spaniards having landed some Ordinance, plaied upon our ships all the day, but the night following they warped out, and the day after returned to Kinsale.

The sixt day likewise, a Scottish Barke bringing soldiers from Spaine, and being one of the Fleet newly arived at Castlehaven, but severed from them at sea by storme, came into the Harbour of Kinsale, and put the Spaniards, being fourscore, into our hands, who were brought to the campe, and examined before the Lord Deputie. . . .

The Spaniards then examined on oath, said, That there is in the Fleete with Siriago not above one thousand, divers of them taken out of the Gaoles, and very poore and naked, whereof one whole Companie of Portingals was taken out of prison . . . that a Regiment of three thousand Italians was to come for Ireland. That the whole Fleete was bound for Kinsale, and they thought the Queenes Fleete was their ships of Spaine. That all the shipping was to be gathered together at Lisbone, against the Spring, and foure thousand Italians were comming for England.

O'DONNELL AND O'NEILL DRAWING TOWARDS KINSALE

This sixth day of December: we were advertised, that Odonnel was joyned with those Spaniards which landed lately at Castle-Haven, and that hee, together with Tyrone, assisted by all the Rebels force in Ireland, were drawing up towards Kinsale to relieve it, and were come within few miles of the campe. Of all these newes the Spaniards in Kinsale had knowledge, and thereupon tooke heart againe, when they were otherwise ready to yeeld upon reasonable composition. For this respect, it was thought enough for us to keepe the ground we held, against all these enemies, till wee should be further supplied out of England, since upon the least defeate or disaster befalling us, the whole Kingdome would have been hazarded (if not lost), by reason of the peoples inclination to a generall revolt.

We fortified the foresaid campe on the West (or South-West) side, where the Earle of Thomond lay with foure Regiments, and it was resolved, that two smal forts should be cast up, and manned, betweene that campe and the water side Southward (the said forts and campes, each one flancking the other), thereby so to invest the Towne, as all succour from the countrie might be cut off from it. Further it was resolved, that the ditches of the Lord Deputies campe should bee deepned, and the trenches highthned, and that the backe part furthest from the Towne, lying open hitherto should now bee closed, and made defensable against Tyrones forces, as the side towards the Towne was made against the

Spaniards, if they both at one time should give upon us. And that all the Forts should be barracadoed, and by all possible art all the accesses to the towne betweene our two campes be stopped.

The seventh day: the Lord Deputy advertised Master Secretary in England, of all these particulars, adding that we daily heard very hot Alarums of Tyrones purpose, to relieve the Towne, who strengthened with the above named forces, was now lodged in Woods, and in accessable strengths, very neere to our campe, so as hee hindered us from forage for our horse, and from the helpes wee formerly had out of the country, for sustentation of our Army. And that his neighbourhood on the one side, and the Spaniards in Kinsale on the other, kept us at a bay, from proceeding in our aproches and battery. Besides that our last supplies were in this short time incredibly wasted, the new men dying by dozens each night, through the hardnes of the winter siege, whereunto they were not inured. . . .

The eight day: . . . In the evening the Rebels Horse were discovered, about two miles off, and after supper all our men were drawne into Armes, upon notice given us by the scouts, that the Rebels drew nigh, but after a small time, all saving the watch were dismissed to rest. . . .

THE PRECARIOUS STATE OF THE ENGLISH CAMP

The thirteenth day we drew three peeces of Artillery from the Lord Deputies campe, and planted them on the West side neere the other campe, to play upon an Abby, which flancked that part where wee intended to make a new breach. The same day the . . . Lord Deputy and the Counsell wrote this following Letter to the Lords in England:

". . . Since the arrivall of the Queenes shippes, the forces, artillery, and other provisions out of England, we have so annoied this Towne with battery in all parts thereof, as the breach was almost assaultable, and the Houses in the Towne much beaten downe, to the great weakening of the defendants, in so much as we were not without hope to be offered it by composition, or within a little more time to have entered it by force, though that was held a course of much hazard and losse, in regard they within are very strong in bodies of men, which we know to be most certaine.

"The Spaniard finding how hardly he was laid to, importuned Tyrone and Odonnell with their forces to come to releeve him, they both are accordingly come, and encamped not farre from the Towne. And now one thousand more Spaniards are arrived at Castle Haven, with great store of munition & artillery, and report that a greater force is coming after, which doth so bewitch this people, as we make accompt all the Countrey will now goe out, as most of them have done already, as in our former letters we signified that we feared.

"Odonnels forces are said to be foure thousand, and to be joined with the Spaniards that landed at Castle Haven, and Tyrones (as we heare generally) to be as many more, and since his passage through the Countrey hither, Tyrrell with many other Lemster Rebels, (as it is said) are joined with him, and comming also hither. By these meanes wee are induced to leave our battery for a time, and to strengthen our Campes, that we may be able to indure all their fury, as wee hope we shall, and keepe the Towne still besieged, and so invested, as wee are not out of hope in the end to carry it, notwithstanding all that they can doe. Yet since it is now most apparent, that the King of Spaine meanes to make this place the seate of the Warre, not onely for the gaining of this Kingdome, but from time to time to push for England, if he should get this, (for so some that we have taken and examined, doe confesse), and that the whole strength of the Irish are drawne and drawing hither, to set up their rest, to get that liberty (as they call it) that they have so long fought for. . . .

"Notwithstanding the severe courses we have taken, by executing some for a terrour to the rest, by making Proclamations upon paine of death, that none should depart the campe without licence, by giving direction to the Port Townes that they should be staied and apprehended: and lastly, by sending speciall men to Corke, Yoghall, Waterford, and Wexford, to see the same duly put in execution, for which purpose they have commission for martiall law, all which is well knowne to every private man in the campe, and yet they steale away daily in such numbers, as besides those that by devises doe get passages, there are at this present taken betweene this and Waterford, at the least two hundred ready to be returned; though we confesse the misery they indure is such, as justly deserveth some compassion, for divers times some are found dead, standing centinell, or being upon their guard, that when they went thither were very well and lusty, so grievous is a Winters siege, in such a Countrey: For the sicke and hurt men we have taken the best course we can devise, for at Corke we have provided a guesthouse for them, where they are most carefully looked unto, and have their lendings delivered in money, to buy them what the market doth affoord, with an increase of what is held fit for them, allowed out of the surplusage of the entertainement for the Preachers and Cannoneers, (which we conceave your Lordships have heretofore heard of).

"And for those that are sicke or sickely at the campe, because we much desire to keepe them well (if it were possible), we take this course. First their owne meanes is allowed them very duly, Sir Robert Gardner being appointed a Commissioner for that purpose, that the souldier in all things may have his right, with proclamation that whosoever found him selfe in any want, should repaire to him; and secondly, out of a generall contribution from the Officers and Captaines of the Army, there is fifty pound a weeke collected for them, and bestowed in providing warme broth, meate, and lodging, so as a marvellous great number are thereby releeved. And yet all this doth not serve, but that a great many are still unserviceable which we have here noted at the greater length, that it might appeare unto your Lordships that it proceeds not from want of care or providence in us, but from keeping the field in such a season, where humane wit cannot prevent their decay.

"We must further earnestly intreat your Lordships, that the Fleete may remaine upon this Coast during the warre with the Spaniards, and to furnish us with victuals, munition and money, for Easterly winds are rare at this time of the yeere, and without every of these, this action cannot bee maintained, but that the Army will breake, and come to nothing. Neither will this Countrey now affoord us any thing, no not so much as meat for our Horses; and therefore wee must likewise bee humble suters, that two thousand quarters of Oates may speedily be sent us, without which undoubtedly our Horses will be starved. . . .

"Lastly, whereas the Enemies Fleet at Lysbone, under the conduct of Bretandona, is (by intelligence from Spaine) assuredly intended for these parts, to bring supplies to Kinsale within a moneth or six weekes: And whereas we find the great importance of this service depending on the countenance of her Majesties Fleet, to have the same with us as well to guard the Harbour and repell the enemies landing, as also to guard our Magazins of munition and victuals, which must be kept in ships, we having no other conveniency to keepe them: We have made humbly bold to stay the Fleet commanded by Sir Richard Levison, and doe in like sort beseech your Lordships to victuall them for three moneths longer, with all possible speed; for they are now victualled onely till the twentieth of January. And because so great a quantity of victuals as will serve them for that time, can hardly be soone provided; we humbly desire that this supply of their victuals may be sent unto them in parts, as it can be made ready: And because this Fleet, by the opinion of the best experienced in Sea services, (whom we for our parts doe beleeve), must necessarily be divided, and yet is too small to serve in two parts, we humbly pray that some such addition of ships, as in your wisdoms shal be thought meet, may be sent hither . . .

"By the same dispatch the Lord Deputy wrote this following letter to Master Secretary in England:

. . . We have taken above two hundred Spanish prisoners; there are (as wee are certainely enformed) above one thousand dead and killed of them in the Towne, the which we have now as throughly invested as may be: but on the other side the whole force of Tyrone and Odonnell, with all the strength of the Rebels of Ireland, do lie within six miles of us, and to their assistance they have the Spanish supplyes, and (that which is worst) their munition and provisions; the whole Province either is joyned with them, or stand neutrals; and what use soever the enemie maketh of them, I am sure wee receive by them no manner of assistance. Ending all this, I hope wee shall give a good account of the besieged; but wee have reason to proceede with great caution, having a desperate enemie before us, and so manie that are ingaged in the same fortune behind us. For Tyrone and O Donnell have quit their owne Countries, to recover them here, or else to loose all. . . . I beseech God to send mee the height of my ambition, which is, with the conscience of having done her Majestie the service I desire, to injoy a quiet, private life, and that her Majestie may never more have need of men of our profession."

The foureteenth day was so rainy, and so tempestious in winds, as wee could not stirre out, to proceede any thing in our businesses. The fifteenth our Artillerie, planted by the Campe on the West-side, did play upon the toppes of the Castles in the Towne, where the enemies shot were placed, that from thence they might annoy our men, working in the trenches, and in the platforme, and attending our Artillerie. Our pieces brake downe many of these Castles, and killed many of their shot lodged in them. Likewise in the night, while our men were making new approches, our Ordinance plaied upon the Towne, and many volleys of small shot were exchanged betweene us and the enemy.

The sixteenth day: the same Ordinance plaied in like sort upon the Castles in the Towne, and did much hurt to the men there lodged. The seventeenth day was very tempestious with raine, and especially wind, and so continued all night, for which cause our Artillery plaied but seldom upon the towne. And this night the Spaniards sallyed, and brake downe a platforme, which we had begun the day before, with purpose to plant our Artillery there; whereupon a slight skirmish fell betweene us and them, but with little or no hurt on either side. The eighteenth day our Artillerie continued to play upon the Towne.

And this day his Lordship intercepted the following letter, which he commanded me to translate out of Spanish into English.

DON JEAN DEL AGUYLA'S LETTER TO O NEALE AND O DONNELL

To the Prince O Neale, and Lord O Donnell:

. . . I beseech you now you will doe it, and come as speedily and well appointed as may bee. For I assure you, that the enemies are tired, and are very few, and they cannot guard the third part of their trenches, which shall not availe them, for resisting their first furie, all is ended. The manner of your comming, your Excellencies know better to take there, then I to give it here. . . .

Though you be not well fitted, I beseech your Excellencies to dislodge, and come toward the enemy, for expedition imports. It is needfull that we all be on horsebacke at once, and the greater haste the better.

Signed by Don Jean del Aguyla.

The night was stormy, with great lightning and terrible thunder, to the wonder of all, considering the season of the yeere, and this night came certaine intelligence, that Tyrone, drawne on by Don Jeans importunity, determined presently to set up his rest for the reliefe of the Towne, and that the next night he would lodge within a mile and halfe of our Campe.

The one and twentieth: our scouts confirmed the same, and towards night Tyrone shewed himselfe with all his horse and foote, upon a hill within a mile of us, in the way to Corke. Whereupon two Regiments of our foote, and most of our horse being drawne out of the Campe, made towards them: but when they saw our men resolutely come forward, they fell back to a Fastnesse of wood and water, where they encamped.

This night being light with continuall flashings of lightning, the Spaniards sallied againe, and gave upon a trench, newly made beneath our Canon, but were the sooner repelled, because we kept very strong Guards, and every man was ready to be in Armes, by reason of Tyrones being so neere unto us.

The two and twentieth: Tyrones horse and foote often shewed themselves from an Hill, beyond which they incamped in a Wood, yet our Artillery still plaied upon the Towne, breaking downe the Wall, and some Turrets, from whence the Spaniards shot annoyed our men. Many intelligences confirmed, that Tyrone on the one side, and the Spaniards on the other, had a purpose to force our Campe.

This night the Spaniards sallied, and gave upon a trench close to the West-side of the Towne, which the Serjeant that kept it did quit: but Sir Christopher Saint Laurence appointed to second him, came up with some foote, and did beat the Spaniards into the Towne, before they could doe any great hurt, save onely a little defacing it. Our Artillery still plaied upon the Towne, that they might see wee went on with our businesse, as if wee cared not for Tyrones comming, but it was withall carried on in such a fashion, as wee had no meaning to make a breach, because wee thought it not fit to offer to enter, and so put all to hazard, untill wee might better discover what Tyrone meant to doe, whose strength was assured to bee very great, and wee found by letters of Don Jeans, which wee had intercepted, that hee had advised Tyrone to set upon our Camps, telling him that it could not bee chosen, but our men were much decayed by the Winters siege, and so, that wee should hardly bee able to maintaine so much ground, as wee had taken when our strength was greater, if wee were well put to, on the one side by them, and on the other side by him, which hee would not faile for his part to doe resolutely. And it was most true, that our men dailie died by dozens, so as the sicke and runnawaies considered, wee were growne as weake as at our first setting downe, before our supplies of foure thousand foote. . . .

This evening [December 23] one of the chiefe Commanders in Tyrones Army, having some obligations to the Lord President, sent a messenger to him for a bottle of Usquebagh, and by a letter wished him, that the English army should that night bee well upon their guard, for Tyrone meant to give upon one Campe, and the Spaniards upon the other, meaning to spare no mans life but the Lord Deputies and his. Don Jean de l'Aguila after confessed to the Lord President, that notwithstanding our sentinels, he and Tyrone the night following, had three messengers the one from the other. All the night was cleare with lightning (as in the former nights were great lightnings with thunder) to the astonishment of many, in respect of the season of the yeere. And I have heard by many horsemen of good credit, that this night our horsemen set to watch, to their seeming did see Lampes burne at the points of their staves or speares in the middest of these lightning flashes.

Tyrones guides missed the way, so as hee came not up to our Campe by night, as the Spaniards ready in Armes howerly expected, but earely about the breake of the next day.

THE BATTLE BEGINS

The foure and twentieth of December: some halfe hower before day, the Lord Deputie in his house sitting at Counsell with the Lord President and Master Marshall, as thinking the intended enterprise of the enemie by some accident to bee broken, suddenly one of the Lord Presidents horsemen called him at the dore, and told him, that Tyrones Army was come up very neere to our Campe. And Sir Richard Greame, having the Scout that night, when hee discovered that Tyrone with his forces was on foote marching towards the Campe, presently advertised the Lord Deputy thereof, and his Lordship being alwaies in readinesse to intertaine them (seldome going to bed by night), and at this time setting in Counsell, when he heard that they were advanced within three quarters of a mile of our Campe, caused all our men to draw into Armes in our quarter, and himself with the Marshall attending him, advanced towards our scouts . . . to take view of the enemy, and hee brought him word that they were in the same place formerly advertised. Upon his returne, the Lord Deputie left for defence of the great Campe on the Northside. . . . This done, the Lord Deputie sent a Corporall of the field unto our lesser Campe . . . and directed how to set all the Companies in their severall guards. . . . By this time the Marshall . . . advanced with twenty score of the enemie, the ground rising so high betweene them and our men, as they could not see one the other.

It was now the breake of the day, whereas mid-night was appointed the time appointed for the Rebels to meete with Don Jeans forces, the Spaniard being to set upon our lesser Campe, and Tyrrell leading the Rebels Vantguard (in which were the Spaniards lately landed at Castle-Haven), and Tyrone leading their Battaile, and O Donnell their Reare, being all to set upon our chiefe Campe, conceiving themselves of sufficient strength to force both our Campes at one instant, and to make no great worke of it.

The Lord Deputy, with the Lord President in his company, being come up to our forces, led out against Tyrone, and resolving there to give him battaile, commanded Sir John Barkeley Serjeant Major to draw out of the Campe two Regiments. . . . Upon their comming up, the enemy finding us resolved to fight, retyred himselfe over a Ford, and the Marshall seeing them disordered in their retrait, sent word thereof . . . to the Lord Deputie, desiring leave to fight, and his Lordship . . . gave him leave to order that service according as hee in his discretion, should find the disposition of the enemie, and therewith sent backe Sir George Carew Lord President with three troopes of horse, to the great Campe, to command both Camps in chiefe, and to make head against the Spaniards, if they should sally out of the Towne.

But the Spaniards still expecting the comming up of the Rebels, according to their mutuall project, and never imagining that wee with our small forces, could draw out sufficient bands to meete and beate the Rebels, contained themselves within the towne walles, till (as by the sequell shall appeare) their sallies could little profit them.

After the said message sent to the Marshall, presently the Earl of

Clanrickard came up and exceedingly importuned the Marshall to fight. Whereupon the Marshall drew a Squadron of foote with their Drumme to the Ford, and willed Sir Richard Greames with his horse to march directly to the Ford. Then the enemy retired hastily with horse and foote over a boggy ground to firme land, hoping to keepe that boggie passage against us. Then the Marshall directed Sir Henry Davers (commanding the horse under him), with his horse, and Sir Henrie Power with his Regiment of foot to advance, who presently came over the foresaid Ford unto him. The Lord Deputy being upon the hill with two Regiments of foote, commanded the Serjeant Major.

So the Marshall having the Earl of Clanrickard, and Sir Henrie Davers with him, advanced with some hundred horse, and began with a hundred Harqubusiers (led by Lieutenant Cowel a valiant Gentleman marked by a red cap he wore, to be a special instrument in this fight) to give occasion of skirmish on the Bog side, which the rebels with some loose shot entertained, their three Battalions standing firme on the one side of the Bog, and our Fort on the other side. In this skirmish our foot were put up hard to our horse, which the Marshall perceiving, put forth more shot, which made the Rebels retire towards their Battaile. Then the Marshiall finding a way through a Ford, to the ground where the Rebels stood, he possessed the same with some foote, and presently he passed over with the Earle of Clanrickard, Sir Richard Greames . . . and their horse, and offered to charge one of the Rebels Battailes of one thousand eight hundred men: but finding them stand firme, our horse wheeled about.

Now Sir Henrie Davers with the rest of the horse, Sir William Godolphin with the Lord Deputies, and Captain Minshall with the Lord Presidents troopes (kept by the Lord Deputie to answere all accidents), and our Serjeant Major with two Regiments . . . came all up, whereupon the Marshall with the horse charged home upon the Reare of the Battaile, and the Irish not used to fight in plaine ground, and something amazed with the blowing up of a Gun-powder bagge . . . but most discouraged to see their horse flie (being all Chiefes . . . and Gentlemen, to the number of five or sixe hundred), were suddenly routed, and our men followed the execution. The other two Battailes that stood stil, now finding this routed, made haste to succour them. Whereupon the Lord Deputy sent instantly . . . Sir Oliver Saint Johns Regiment . . . to charge on the Flanck of the Vanguard, which presently retired disorderly, being followed by our foote and horse: but the Spaniards landed at Castle-Haven, marching there, and being not so good of foote as the Irish, drew out by themselves . . . soone broken, and most of them killed, the rest (with their chiefe Commander Don Alonzo Del Campo) being taken prisoners, namely, two Captaines, seven

Alfieroes, and forty souldiers, whereof some were of good qualitie.

In the meane time many of the light footed Irish of the Van escaped, as did likewise almost all the Rere, by advantage of this execution done upon the Spaniards and the maine Battaile, (of which body farre greater then either of the other, all were killed), but onely some sixty or there abouts.

Thus the Irish horse first leaving the foote, then two of the Battalions being routed, they all fell to flie for life, our men doing execution upon many in the place. On our part Sir Richard Greames Cornet was killed, Sir Henry Davers, Sir William Godolphin, Captaine Henry Crofts Scoutmaster were slightly hurt, onely six souldiers hurt, but many of our horses killed, and more hurt.

The Irish Rebels left one thousand two hundred bodies dead in the field, besides those that were killed in two miles chase: we tooke nine of their Ensignes, all their Drummes and Powder, and got more than two thousand Armes. And had not our men been greedy of the Spaniards spoile, being very rich, had not our foote been tired with continuall watchings long before, in this hard winters siege. Had not our horse especially been spent by ill keeping and want of all meate for many daies before, (by reason of Tryones neerenesse, so as the day before this battaile it had been resolved in Counsell to send the horse from the Campe for want of meanes to feede them, and if Tyrone had laine still, and not suffered himselfe to bee drawne to the plaine ground by the Spaniards importunitie, all our horse must needs have been sent away or starved.) Had not these impediments been, wee [could have] then cut the throates of all the rebels there assembled; for they [the Irish] never made head against them that followed the execution, nor scarce ever looked behind them, but every man shifted for himselfe, casting off his Armes, and running for life. In so much as Tyrone after confessed himselfe to be overthrowne by a sixth part of his number, which he ascribed (as wee must and doe) to Gods great worke, beyond mans capacitie, and withall acknowledged that he lost above one thousand in the field, besides some eight hundred hurt. This we understood by the faithfull report of one, who came from his some few daies after, and told the L. Deputy moreover, that he tormented himself exceedingly for this his overthrow.

THE SPANISH EMERGE

After the battell, the Lord Deputy in the middest of the dead bodies, caused thanks to be given to God for this victory, and there presently knighted the Earle of Clanrickard in the field, who had many faire escapes, his garments being often peirced with shot and other weapons, and with his owne hand killed above twenty Irish kerne [foot soldiers] and cried out to spare no Rebell. . . . So before noone his Lordship returned to the campe, where commanding vollies of shot for joy of the victory, the Spaniards perhaps mistaking the cause, and dreaming of the Rebels approach, presently sallied out [of Kinsale], but were soone beaten into the Towne, especially when they saw our triumph, and perceived our horsemen from the hill on the West side, to wave the Colours we had taken in the battell. . . .

The seven and twentieth: the Lord Deputy . . . wrote to Master Secretary [in London] the following letter: . . . "God hath given the Queene the greatest victory that ever was obtained in this Country. . . ."

The twenty-eighth day of December: the Lord Deputy was advertised that Syrriago, a principal Commander of the Spaniards, landed in the West parts, having received newes of Tyrones overthrow, was suddenly gone for Spaine without acquainting any of the Spaniards therewith, and that he carried with him on the same ship Hugh Odonnell. . . .

The nine and twentieth day: his Lordship had advertisements from diverse places that Tyrone in his flight out of Mounster, passing the Blackwater, lost many of his carriages, and had some one hundred and fortie of his men drowned, fear making them so hasty, as they could not attend the passing of their owne fellowes, much less the fall of the waters.

The last of December: Don Juan Generall of the Spaniards offerred a Parley, [saying] that having found the Lord Deputy (whom he tearmed Viceroy) though a sharpe and powerfull, yet an honourable enemy; and the Irish not onely weake and barbarous, but (as hee feared) perfidious friends, hee was so farre in his affection reconciled to the one, and distasted with the other, as he was thereby induced to make an overture of such a composition as might be safe & profitable for the state of England, with least prejudice to the Crown of Spaine, by delivering into the Viceroyes power the towne of Kinsale, with all other places held by the Spaniards in Ireland, so as they might depart upon honourable tearmes.

THE ANNALS OF
THE FOUR MASTERS
THE BATTLE OF KINSALE, AN IRISH VIEW

The Four Masters' account of the battle continues. The interesting point here is the disagreement between the two Hughs. O'Neill does not want to attack the English troops. Continuing to follow his unconventional tactical style, he wants to keep the English trapped between the Irish rebels and the Spanish-held city and starve them into submission. O'Donnell—his younger, more impetuous son-in-law—sees the trapped English being attacked from both sides as easy pickings. O'Donnell wins the day in the council of war, but as we know from Fynes Moryson's diary, the Spanish never realize a battle is going on until the English fire their cannon to celebrate victory.

WHEN THE IRISH CHIEFS AND their forces met together at one place, they encamped a short distance to the north of the camp of the Lord Justice at Bel-Guala, in Kinelea. Many a host and troop, and lord of a territory, and chief of a cantred, were along with O'Neill and O'Donnell at this place. . . .

The Irish reduced the English to great straits, for they did not permit hay, corn, or water, straw or fuel, to be taken into the Lord Justice's camp. They remained thus for some time watching each other, until Don Juan, the General of the Spaniards, sent a letter privately to the Irish, requesting them to attack a part of the Lord Justice's camp on a certain night, and [adding] that he himself would attack the other part of it on the same night; for they [the Spaniards] were reduced to great straits by the English, as the English were distressed by the Irish.

The chiefs of the Kinel-Connell and Kinel-Owen began to deliberate in council on this suggestion; and they were for some time dissentient on adopting this resolution, for it was O'Neill's advice not to attack them immediately by any means, but to keep them still in the strait in which they were, until they should perish of famine, and the want of all the necessaries of which they stood in need, as some of their men and horses had already perished. O'Donnell, however, was oppressed at heart and ashamed to hear the complaint and distress of the Spaniards without relieving them from the difficulty in which they were, even if his death or destruction, or the loss of his people, should result from it; so that the resolution they finally agreed to was, to attack the Lord Justice's camp, as they had been ordered.

When the particular night upon which it was agreed they should make this attack arrived, the Irish cheerfully and manfully put on their dresses of battle and conflict, and were prepared for marching. Their chiefs were at variance, each of them contending that he himself should go foremost in the night's attack; so that the manner in which they set out from the borders of their camp was in three strong battalions, three extensive and numerous hosts, shoulder to shoulder, and elbow to elbow. O'Neill, with the Kinel-Owen, and such of the people of Oriel and Iveagh-of-Uladh as adhered to him, were in a strong battalion apart; O'Donnell, with the Kinel-Connell, his sub-chieftains, and the Connaughtmen in general, formed the second battalion; [and] those gentlemen of Munster, Leinster, and Meath, with their forces, who had risen up in the confederacy of the Irish war, and who had been in banishment in Ulster during the preceding part of this year, were in the third battalion, [and marched] steadily and slowly, without mixing with any other host.

After they had marched outside their camp in this manner, the forces mistook their road and lost their way, in consequence of the great darkness of the night, so that their guides were not able to make their way to the appointed place, opposite the camp of the Lord Justice, until clear daylight next morning. Some assert that a certain Irishman had sent word and information to the Lord Justice, that the Irish and Spaniards were to attack him that night, and that, therefore, the Lord Justice and the Queen's army stationed themselves in the gaps of danger, and certain other passes, to defend the camp against their enemies. When the darkness of the night had disappeared, and the light of the day was clear to all in general, it happened that O'Neill's people, without being aware of it, had advanced near the Lord Justice's people; but, as they were not prepared, they turned aside from them to be drawn up in battle array and order, and to wait for O'Donnell and the other party, who had lost their way, as we have before stated.

As soon as the Lord Justice perceived this thing, he sent forth vehement and vigorous troops to engage them, so that they fell upon O'Neill's people, and proceeded to kill, slaughter, subdue, and thin them, until five or six ensigns were taken from them, and many of their men were slain.

O'Donnell advanced to the side of O'Neill's people after they were discomfitted, and proceeded to call out to those who were flying, to stand their ground, and to rouse his own people to battle [and so continued], until his voice and speech were strained by the vehemence and loudness of the language in which he addressed all in general, requesting his nobles to stand by him to fight their enemies. He said to them, that this unusual thing which they were about to do, was a shame and a guile, namely: to turn their backs to their enemies, as was not the wont of their race ever till then. But, however, all he did was of no avail to him, for, as the first battalion was defeated, so were the others also in succession. But, although they were routed, the number slain was not very great, on account of the fewness of the pursuers, in comparison with those [flying] before them.

Manifest was the displeasure of God, and misfortune to the Irish of fine Fodhla, on this occasion; for, previous to this day, a small number of them had more frequently routed many hundreds of the English, than they had fled from them, in the field of battle, in the gap of danger (in every place they had encountered), up to this day. Immense and countless was the loss in that place, although the number slain was trifling; for the prowess and valour, prosperity and affluence, nobleness and chivalry, dignity and renown, hospitality and generosity, bravery and protection, devotion and pure religion, of the Island, were lost in this engagement.

The Irish forces returned that night, with O'Neill and O'Donnell, to Inis-Eoghanain. Alas! the condition in which they were that night was not as they had expected to return from that expedition, for there prevailed much reproach on reproach, moaning and dejection, melancholy and anguish, in every quarter throughout the camp. They slept not soundly, and scarcely did they take any refreshment. When they met together their counsel was hasty, unsteady and precipitate, so that what they at length resolved upon was, that O'Neill and Rury, the brother of O'Donnell, with sub-chieftains, and the chiefs of Leath-Chuinn in general, should return back to their countries, to defend their territories and lands against foreign tribes; [and] that O'Donnell (Hugh Roe), Redmond, the son of John Burke, and Captain Hugh Mus, the son of Robert, should go to Spain to complain of their distresses and difficulties to the King of Spain. . . .

After this defeat of Kinsale had been given by the English, on the third day of the month of January, to the Irish and the few Spaniards of the King of Spain's people who happened to be along with them at that time, O'Donnell (Hugh Roe) was seized with great fury, rage, and anxiety of mind; so that he did not sleep or rest soundly for the space of three days and three nights afterwards; so that he despaired of getting succour in Ireland. At the expiration of that time, the resolution he came to (by the advice of O'Neill, who, however, gave him this advice with reluctance), was, to leave Ireland, and go to Spain to King Philip III, to request more forces and succour from him; for he thought that the King of Spain was the person who could render him most relief, and who was the most willing to assist those who always fought in defence of the Roman Catholic religion; and, moreover, on account of his [Philip's] attachment to the Gaels, from their having first come out of Spain to invade Ireland, as is manifest from the Book of Invasions.

AFTERWORD
THE FLIGHT OF THE EARLS

HUGH O'DONNELL FLEES TO SPAIN and with a tidy symmetry that seems unheard of in Irish history, the story has come to an end right back where it began, with the ancient *Lebor Gabala, (The Book of Invasions)*. In the terrible aftermath of Kinsale, O'Donnell rushed to the court of King Philip with a copy of the book under his arm. He no doubt showed the king and anyone who would listen the concluding chapters in which Myles, "The Soldier from Spain," conquers Ireland, and his followers, the Milesians, become the ancestors of the Irish. But Ireland no longer fit into Spain's plans for harassing the English. No more soldiers from Spain arrived. O'Donnell—"Red Hugh," the lord of Ticonnell—died a year later, still in Spain. Some said he was poisoned. Tyrone's rebellion dragged on, but everyone seemed to know it was lost after Kinsale.

O'Neill continued fighting and negotiating, still stalling for time until he finally gave up in 1603 and eventually made his way to Rome, where he died in 1616, ending his life as either a heroic exile or a pitiful drunk depending on who was telling the story. Some see his flight, and the flight abroad of the other rebellious earls, as the symbolic beginning of the great wave of Irish emigration.

The rebellion cost England a staggering two million pounds, more than all of Elizabeth's European campaigns combined. Some historians say O'Neill and O'Donnell with their guerrilla tactics could never have captured Dublin anyway, and no one can rule Ireland without holding the capital. But the defeat of the Irish at Kinsale certainly marked the end of the hope that the kings of Ireland would play a role in Ireland's future as anything more than something for the storybooks. From then on the cause of liberty that Donal O'Neill wrote to the pope about at the time of the Scottish invasion would have to be taken up by the kind of men and women who usually went unmentioned or unnamed in the annals of the kings.

GLOSSARY

OF COMMON IRISH WORDS
USED IN PLACE-NAMES

⚜

ARD	high place, or in the case of *ard ri*, high king
ATHA	ford
BALLA	wall
BALLE, BALLY	town
BEG	small
BEN	mountaintop
CATH	battle
CATHER	stone fort larger than a *cashel*
CARRICK, CARRIG	stone-walled enclosure
CASHEL	fort, usually with a stone wall
CLARE	bridge, usually level
CLON	meadow
CRANNOG	landfill, an artificial island often used for defensive purposes in battle
DERG, DEARG	red
DERRY	grove of trees
DOE	ax
DRUM	ridge
DUB	black
DUN	fort
ENNIS, INNIS	island
GLAN	valley, glen
GORT	field
INCH	island
KIL, KILL, CILL	originally a monastic place, later a holy play, still later simply a place
KNOCK	hill
LIN	a pool, a deep place in a stream
LIS	earthen fort or cattle pen
LOUGH	lake
MAG, MAIG, MOY	a plain

MOR, MORE	great, big
MUCK	pig
NOAMH	saint, also holy
OUGHTER	upper
OWEN	river
RATH	circular rampart, usually earthen
ROS, ROSS	promontory
SKELLIG	rocky pinnacle
SLIEVE	steep mountain or pass
TERMON	boundary cross
TOBAR, TOBER	well, originally a holy well
TULL, TULLY	small hill
TURLOUGH	vernal pond
TYR, TER	territory of (a prefix)

A GUIDE TO PRONUNCIATION

CONSONANTS

Consonants at the beginning of a word have the same sound as they do in English, except that C is always pronounced K.

Within words, consonants are pronounced as follows:

B = V
C = G or K
D = TH (as in *that*)
G = soft GH
M = V (in most cases)
S followed or preceded by an E or an I = SH
T = D.

VOWELS

Short vowels are pronounced as in English, while long vowels (which are marked by an accent when in the lower case, no accents in capital letters) are pronounced as follows:

A = awe
E = ay
I = ee
O = owe
U = ee
E at the end of a word is pronounced.

The pronunciation of vowel combinations is as follows:

AI = A in the first syllable; Ô elsewhere
IU = U
UI = I
EI = E.

FREQUENTLY USED NAMES AND
THEIR PRONUNCIATION

Ath	*Awth*
Aedh	*AA (as in* day*)*
Badb	*Bibe*
Bodb	*Bove*
Conchubar	*Conachboor*
Cuailgne	*Cooley*
Cuchulain	*C'hoolin*
Dun	*Doon*
Emain	*Avvan*
Eoghan	*Owen*
Laeg	*Loygh*
Lugh	*Loo*
Mag Tured	*Moy Tura*
Medb	*Mave*
Midhe	*Mee*
Niamh	*Neev*
Og	*Og*
Sidhe	*Shee*
Suibne	*Suivnee*
Tain	*Toin*

SOURCES

✤

I. MYTHICAL WARS AND WARRIORS

Gray, Elizabeth A., trans. *The Second Battle of Mag Tured*. London: Irish Texts Society, 1982. Reprinted with the permission of the Irish Texts Society.

Joyce, P. W., trans. *Old Celtic Romances*. Dublin: Roberts Wholesale Books, 1907.

Kinsella, Thomas, trans. "The Great Carnage on Muirtheimne Plain" from *The Tain*. New York: Oxford University Press, 1970. Reprinted with the permission of Thomas Kinsella.

O'Keeffe, J. G., trans. *Buile Suibne*. London: Irish Texts Society, 1910.

II. KINGS AND BATTLES

The Four Masters. *The Annals of the Kingdom of Ireland*. Trans. John O'Donovan. Dublin: Hodges and Smith, 1851.

O'Mahony, John A., trans. *Geoffrey Keating, Foras Feasa Ar Eirinn Foras Feasa Ar Eirinn*. New York: P. M. Haverty, 1857.

III. THE VIKINGS

Bugge, Alexander, trans. *Cathreim Cellachain Caisil*. Christiania (Norway): J. C. Gundersens, 1905.

Todd, John H., trans. *The War of the Gaedahl with the Gaill*. London: Public Record Office of Great Britain, Chronicles and Memorials, 1867.

IV. BRIAN BORU AND THE BATTLE OF CLONTARF

Dasent, G. W., trans. *Njal's Saga*. London: Public Record Office of Great Britain, Chronicles and Memorials, 1894.

Todd, John H., trans. *The War of the Gaedhil with the Gaill*. London: Public Record Office of Great Britain, Chronicles and Memorials, 1867.

V. THE NORMAN INVASION

Oppen, G. H., trans. *The Song of Dermot and the Earl*. Oxford: Clarendon Press, 1892.

Scott, A. B., and Martin, F. X., trans. Giraldus Cambrensis. *Expugnatio Hibernica*. From *A New History of Ireland*. Dublin: Royal Irish Academy, 1978. Reprinted with the permission of the Royal Irish Academy.

VI. JOHN DE COURCY AND THE CONQUEST OF ULSTER

"The Book of Howth." In *The Calendar of the Carew Manuscripts Preserved in the Archepiscopal Library at Lambeth*. 6 vols. London, 1867–73.

VII. THE SCOTS

Barbour, John. *The Bruce*. Trans. and editor A.A.M. Duncan. Reprinted by Permission of Canongate Books, 14 High Street, Edinburgh, Scotland EH1 1TE. Published as a Canongate Classic in 1997.

Holinshed, Raphael. *The Chronicles of Ireland*. London, 1808.

VIII. WARFARE IN THE KINGDOM OF THOMOND

MacGrath, John mac Rory, *The Triumphs of Turlough*. Trans. Standish H. O'Grady, London: the Irish Texts Society, 1929.

IX. THE BATTLE OF AXE HILL

"The Book of Howth." In *The Calendar of the Carew Manuscripts Preserved in the Archepiscopal Library at Lambeth*. 6 vols. London, 1867–73.

X. HUGH O'NEILL TRIUMPHANT

Beare, Philip O'Sullivan. *Ireland under Elizabeth*. Trans. Matthew J. Byrne. Dublin: Sealy, Bryers and Walter, 1903.

The Four Masters. *The Annals of the Kingdom of Ireland*. Trans. John O'Donovan. Dublin: Hodges and Smith, 1851.

Harington, Sir John. *Nugae Antique: The Papers of Sir John Harington*. Ed. Henry Harington and Thomas Park. London: J. Wright, 1804.

XI. THE BATTLE OF KINSALE

The Four Masters. *The Annals of the Kingdom of Ireland*. Trans. John O'Donovan. Dublin: Hodges and Smith, 1851.

Moryson, Fynes. *An Itinerary*. Glasgow: James MacLehose and Sons, 1908.

ADDITIONAL
BIBLIOGRAPHY

Bartlett, Thomas, and Keith, Jeffrey. *A Military History of Ireland*. New York: Cambridge University Press, 1996.

Byrne, Francis J. *Irish Kings and High Kings*. London: B. T. Batsford, 1973.

Connolly, S. F. *The Oxford Companion to Irish History*. New York: Oxford University Press, 1998.

Davies, John. *A History of Wales*. London: Allen Lane, 1993.

Dillon, Myles. *Early Irish Literature*. Chicago: University of Chicago Press, 1948.

Duffy, Sean. *Ireland in the Middle Ages*. New York: St. Martin's Press, 1997.

———. *The Macmillan Atlas of Irish History*. New York: Macmillan, 1997.

———. "Medieval Scotland and Ireland: Overcoming the Amnesia." *History of Ireland* 7, no. 3 (autumn 1999): 17-21.

Freeman, A. Martin. *Annala Connacht*. Dublin: Dublin Institute for Advanced Studies, 1996.

Gregory, Lady Augusta. *Cuchulain of Muirthemne*. New York: Charles Scribner, 1903.

———. *Gods and Fighting Men*. London: John Murray, 1904.

Hayes-McCoy, G. H. *Irish Battles*. London: Longmans, 1969.

Heath, Ian, and Sque, David. *The Irish Wars, 1485–1603*. London: Reed International Books, 1993.

Jones, Gwyn. *A History of the Vikings*. New York: Oxford University Press, 1984.

Kennedy, Conan. *Ancient Ireland*. Killala, Ireland: Morrigan Books, 1997.

Koch, John T. *The Celtic Heroic Age*. Andover, Mass.: Celtic Studies Publications, 1994.

MacKillop, James. *Dictionary of Celtic Mythology*. New York: Oxford University Press, 1998.

———. *Fionn Mac Cumhaill: Celtic Myth in English Literature*. Syracuse: Syracuse University Press, 1986.

Morgan, Hiram. *Tyrone's Rebellion*. Woodbridge, Suffock: Royal Historical Society/Boydell and Brewer, 1993.

Murphy, Denis, trans. *The Annals of Clonmacnoise*. Dublin: University Press, 1896.

Newman, Roger Chatterton. *Brian Boru, King of Ireland*. Dublin: Anvil Books, 1983.

Robinson, Tim. *The Stones of Aran: Labyrinth*. Dublin: Liliput Press, 1995.

———. *The Stones of Aran: Pilgrimage*. Dublin: Liliput Press, 1989.

Roche, Richard. *The Norman Invasion of Ireland*. Dublin: Anvil Books, 1995.

Schermann, Katharine. *The Flowering of Ireland*. Boston: Little, Brown, 1981.

Simms, Katharine. "Warfare in the Medieval Gaelic Lordships." *The Irish Sword 12* (winter 1975): 92-108.

Sjoestedt, Marie-Louise. *Gods and Heroes of the Celts*. Dublin: Four Courts Press, 1994.

Smyth, Daragh. *A Guide to Irish Mythology*. Dublin: Irish Academic Press, 1986.

Spenser, Edmund. *A View of the State of Ireland*. Ed. Andrew Hadfield and Willy Malley. Oxford: Blackwood, 1997.

Squire, Charles. *The Mythology of the British Isles*, London: Gresham, 1905.

Walsh, Micheline Kerney. *An Exile of Ireland: Hugh O'Neill, Prince of Ulster*. Dublin: Four Courts Press, 1997.

Wilde, Sir William R. W. "On the Battle of Moytura." *Proceedings of the Royal Irish Academy 9* (1866): 546-550.

INDEX

DAVID WILLIS McCULLOUGH's most recent book is a historical anthology, *Chronicles of the Barbarians: Firsthand Accounts of Pillage and Conquest from the Ancient World to the Fall of Constantinople*. His other anthologies include *American Childhoods* and *Great Detectives*. He is also the author of *Brooklyn . . . and How It Got That Way* (an informal social history), *People, Books and Book People* (interviews with authors), and the mystery novels *Think on Death* and *Point No-Point*.

McCullough and his wife, Frances, live in Hastings-on-Hudson, New York.